EDI DEVELOPMENT STUDIES

Preventing Bank Crises

Lessons from Recent Global Bank Failures

Proceedings of a conference co-sponsored by the

Federal Reserve Bank of Chicago
and the
Economic Development Institute
of the World Bank

Edited by

Gerard Caprio, Jr.
William C. Hunter
George G. Kaufman
Danny M. Leipziger

The World Bank
Washington, D.C.

Copyright ©1998
The International Bank for Reconstruction
and Development / THE WORLD BANK
1818 H Street, N.W.
Washington, D.C. 20433, U.S.A.

The Economic Development Institute (EDI) was established by the World Bank in 1955 to train officials concerned with development planning, policymaking, investment analysis, and project implementation in member developing countries. At present the substance of the EDI's work emphasizes macroeconomic and sectoral economic policy analysis. Through a variety of courses, seminars, and workshops, most of which are given overseas in cooperation with local institutions, the EDI seeks to sharpen analytical skills used in policy analysis and to broaden understanding of the experience of individual countries with economic development. Although the EDI's publications are designed to support its training activities, many are of interest to a much broader audience. EDI materials, including any findings, interpretations, and conclusions, are entirely those of the authors and should not be attributed in any manner to the World Bank, to its affiliated organizations, or to members of its Board of Executive Directors or the countries they represent.

The material in this publication is copyrighted. Requests for permission to reproduce portions of it should be sent to the Office of the Publisher at the address shown in the copyright notice above. The World Bank encourages dissemination of its work and will normally give permission promptly and, when the reproduction is for noncommercial purposes, without asking a fee. Permission to copy portions for classroom use is granted through the Copyright Clearance Center Inc., Suite 910, 222 Rosewood Drive, Danvers, Massachusetts 01923, U. S. A.

The backlist of publications by the World Bank is shown in the annual *Index of Publications*, which is available from the Office of the Publisher.

Library of Congress Cataloging-in-Publication Data

Preventing bank crises : lessons from recent global bank failures ;
    proceedings of a conference sponsored by the Federal Reserve Bank of
    Chicago and the Economic Development Institute of the World Bank /
    edited by Gerard Caprio, Jr. . . . [et al.].
        p.   cm.—(EDI development studies, ISSN 1020-105X)
    Includes bibliographical references and index.
    ISBN 0-8213-4202-9
    1. Bank failures—Congresses.   2. Bank failures—Case studies
—Congresses.   I. Caprio, Gerard.   II. Federal Reserve Bank of
Chicago.   III. Economic Development Institute (Washington, D.C.)
IV. Series.
HG1521.P74   1998
332.1—dc21
                                                    98-5911
                                                    CIP

Contents

Abbreviations and Acronyms

BIS	Bank for International Settlements
BNA	Banco de la Nación de Argentina
CCPC	Cooperative Credit Purchasing Company (Japan)
CEE	Central and Eastern Europe
CMEA	Council for Mutual Economic Assistance
DIC	Deposit Insurance Corporation (Japan)
DIS	Deposit insurance system
EU	European Union
FDICIA	Federal Deposit Insurance Corporation Improvement Act
FSA	Financial Supervisory Agency (Japan)
FSU	Former Soviet Union
G-7	Group of Seven
G-10	Group of Ten
GDP	Gross domestic product
IMF	International Monetary Fund
S&L	Savings and loan institution
SOCB	State-owned commercial bank
SOE	State-owned enterprise

Foreword

The papers in this volume were prepared for the conference "Preventing Bank Crises: Lessons from Recent Global Bank Failures," held in Chicago in June 1997. The conference was organized jointly by the Federal Reserve Bank of Chicago and the Economic Development Institute of the World Bank. Among the 120 participants from 36 countries were senior government officials from central banks and finance ministries, heads of bank supervision bodies, regulators, bank executives, academics, representatives of the financial press, and experts from the World Bank and the International Monetary Fund.

During the past 15 years, bank failures and insolvencies have emerged all over the globe, both in industrial and in developing countries. East Asian economies currently dominate the news as their financial sectors demonstrate severe weaknesses, and the International Monetary Fund, the World Bank, and governments intervene to provide financial support. Not only have the crises been widespread, but their costs have been extremely high, thereby creating an urgent need to encourage governments and bank regulators to establish and strictly enforce oversight measures and not to delay in redressing banking sector weaknesses.

The conference exposed participants to the underlying causes of bank failures as well as to the approaches for dealing with them effectively. This volume focuses on lessons learned internationally and on ways to avoid major banking crises. It therefore addresses one of the key issues currently facing international financial markets and sheds additional light on the topic.

Vinod Thomas, Director
Economic Development Institute

Acknowledgments

This volume was a joint effort of the Federal Reserve Bank of Chicago and the Economic Development Institute of the World Bank, and many people were involved in its preparation at both institutions. The authors thank Shirley Harris, who helped organize and coordinate both the conference and this volume, and Rita M. Molloy, who provided valuable editorial assistance. The authors also thank Mary Elizabeth Ward for coordinating the preparation of the manuscript. She was ably assisted by Chip Vance. John Didier provided oversight and guidance, and Belle Lamdany helped prepare the volume for publication. Alice S. Dowsett did a superb job of editing the entire volume.

Introduction

As the organizers of the conference on which this volume is based, we could not have predicted that the 1997 East Asian financial crisis would follow our conference within the space of weeks. What we did know, however, was that bankers and policymakers had not sufficiently internalized the lessons of past bank crises to reduce materially the chances of further crises.

The conference on "Preventing Bank Crises: Lessons from Recent Global Bank Failures" was a joint effort of the Economic Development Institute of the World Bank and the Federal Reserve Bank of Chicago. It took place near Chicago on June 11–13, 1997, and was noteworthy both because of the quality of the speakers and participants (see the conference agenda and the list of participants at the end of this volume) and because it brought together a broad range of experience from industrial, developing, and transition economies. Therefore this volume allows us to compare experiences as we search for common causes, evaluate resolution processes, and seek to prevent such crises in the future.

Surprisingly, a seminar at the World Bank in 1983 on the consequences of banking system failure in developing countries elicited a common reaction: interesting issues, but aside from a few countries in Latin America, why should this topic be of general concern to development experts? Many were quick to point out that losses were "merely" transfers from one group of society to another, and thus beneath the concern of any worthy macroeconomists. Now, 14 years and about 100 episodes later, those who shrug off banking system problems are in the minority, especially after the East Asian crises of 1997–98.

The last one-and-a-half decades have been unprecedented in financial history in the commonality of systemic banking problems, whether covert, in the form of financial distress in which net worth in the banking system is negative, or overt, in the form of runs on the banking system and usually on the country's currency as well. From the richest countries—Japan, the Scandinavian countries, the United States—to the poorest in Sub-Saharan Africa, from the fastest growing countries in East Asia to the new transition economies, few countries have been spared some form of banking crisis.

Beyond their sheer numbers, these events have been extraordinarily expensive in terms of their fiscal costs alone. When losses reach the point where the depositors fear for the safety of their funds, the functioning of the banking system is suspect, the payments system may be compromised, and the real sector ceases to find credit, governments step in. Although the U.S. savings and loan crisis of the 1980s received worldwide attention and cost U.S. taxpayers an estimated US$150 billion to US$180 billion, this event was small (3 percent) in relation to gross domestic product compared with many other crises. Indeed, according to official data, by this measure it would not make the top 25 U.S. crises, and perhaps not even the top 50 given available anecdotal information. Current crises in Japan, the Republic of Korea, Indonesia, and Thailand will probably produce losses several times the size of those of the United States.

Such large costs imply enormous transfers. Whereas the bill for crises can be readily spread out over time in industrial countries' capital markets, these markets are generally shallow in the developing world, implying a reliance on international markets that are notoriously fickle. Thus, when a large bill looms, government officials tend to delay its recognition, even though case after case—several of which are reviewed in this volume—has demonstrated that this supervisory forbearance allows the losses to increase as bankers continue their money losing operations and gamble for resurrection. When large fiscal bills have to be repaid, they can destabilize the best laid macroeconomic programs, and in extreme cases force authorities to pay by printing money. More tellingly, large-scale bank insolvency means that a significant misallocation of resources has occurred, often in the form of vacant or half-finished buildings in many crisis countries and white elephant investments in others. This misallocation leads to slower growth and poorer distribution.

As banking crises are clearly an important public policy issue, how to prevent them, or at least minimize their cost, is an important concern of officials, advisers, academics, and indeed, all those concerned with economic welfare. Although many reviews of banking crises have taken place in the last two years, this volume distinguishes itself by the breadth of cases covered and the mix of perspectives offered, namely, those of regulators, crisis managers, policymakers, and academics, some of whom held multiple roles in addition to trying merely to understand the nature of the problem. The cases covered here—in Japan, the United States, Eastern Europe, Latin America, and Scandinavia—are all reviewed by experienced experts from these regions.

Topics discussed in this volume include the following:

- Government guarantees of bank liabilities
- Market discipline to supplement regulatory discipline
- Accuracy and truth in accounting and reporting to make private markets more efficient and enhance the responsiveness and accountability of bankers and regulators
- Transparency and disclosure of bank and regulatory agency activities
- Independence of bank regulators from political influence and greater accountability to the public
- Adequacy of privately provided capital to absorb bank losses and adverse exogenous shocks
- Privatization of publicly owned banks
- Foreign ownership of banks to augment domestic private capital and intensify competition
- Legal systems, particularly with respect to bankruptcy laws
- Bank infrastructure, including the training of both bankers and bank regulators.

There appears to be a broad consensus that we know how to resolve most ongoing banking problems, but that there are serious political problems in implementing the necessary solutions, particularly when public agreement is required to use public (taxpayer) funds to resolve insolvencies and validate both explicit and implicit government guarantees to protect depositors from losses. Governments and regulators are under political pressure to delay taking actions that they know are correct, but would probably be painful and unpopular. By reducing the threat of runs on banks, the safety net permits regulators to forbear taking these actions. Evidence from around the world clearly demonstrates that many regulators have become poor and unfaithful agents for their principals (the taxpayers) and have, albeit unintentionally, exacerbated the frequency of banking crises. This agency problem has been as costly as the banks' moral hazard problem. Thus a failure to police reckless drivers puts other drivers at risk. Likewise, highway departments have learned that putting guardrails on mountain passes encourages some drivers to increase their speed and increase, rather than decrease, the likelihood and severity of accidents.

The issue of moral hazard is at the root of many of the recent financial crises in East Asia, as banks avoid due diligence in the belief that governments will cover their mistakes. Foreign lenders compound this problem by substituting implicit sovereign guarantees for their own financial due diligence and failing to discriminate among borrowers. Supervisory failures compound failures of corporate governance, and systematically weak segments of the financial sector—ranging from short-term finance companies in Thailand to merchant banks in the Republic of Korea—precipitate systemwide bank failures. Financial liberalization is unaccompanied by proper supervision and regulation. In a number of countries procedures for failure resolution are lacking, allowing one sphere of the financial sector's weaknesses to jeopardize the entire banking system.

These lessons are seen repeatedly in the cases presented in this volume. The disparity between enacting sound laws and regulations and implementing those regulations is also seen. Weak enforcement is at the root of almost all the crises examined. The need to move to best practice is therefore compelling.

Many of the episodes reviewed here followed episodes of financial reform, and saying that the reforms caused the crises is tempting. This would be the wrong conclusion. First, it assumes the absence of problems before the reform, which is clearly untrue. A more probable situation is that the prereform controls helped conceal the problem, and indeed, were responsible for the incentives that sowed the seeds of crisis. Second, and extremely important for authorities considering financial reforms, is the observation that a common element of many reform programs was the early implementation of "stroke of the pen" reforms, while difficult institutional development, such as creating sound financial supervision, was delayed. The cases examined highlight the importance of correct financial sector incentives, regulatory structures, and supervision infrastructure.

Although participants were reminded of the role that bankers' disaster myopia plays—the tendency of humans to assign unrealistically low probabilities to events that are more distant in time—this myopia also affects foreign investors, resident depositors, and taxpayers. Consequently, authorities need not only allow some participants to be exposed to risk, but need to educate and remind various groups of that fact. Good economic times erode not just lending standards, but the political will to pursue sound financial regulation. By highlighting the causes and consequences of crises and what it takes to prevent them, this volume should help keep these issues at the forefront of concern.

During the conference panels of renowned experts drawn from academia, banking, and regulatory agencies reviewed the causes of the crises and the lessons to be drawn, creating a mixture of individual cases with cross-country lessons. Officials in countries currently in the midst of a crisis or those fearing the commencement of one in their own economy will profit from the material presented here. Notwithstanding the diverse proximate causes and the particular ways in which crises play out in different financial circumstances, most feature not only troublesome macroeconomic environments, but also perverse incentive problems in banking. Thus beyond the standard plea for better economic management, the authors of this volume posit that achieving incentive-compatible financial regulation, that is, a system that induces participants to behave in a safe and sound manner, is a prime concern for governments, and ultimately for electorates.

This volume contains observations by knowledgeable observers of and actors in financial crises, as well as novel recommendations for improving banking sector resiliency and recuperative abilities. Given the events of 1997, these clearly warrant close examination.

Part I. Avoiding Banking Crises

1

Preventing Banking Crises

Jeffrey A. Frankel

As a member of the administration, I spend a great deal of time talking about the current exceptionally good economic performance of the United States: the economy is booming; the unemployment rate has declined to a level unseen since the 1973 oil shock, while inflation has remained tame; investment is high; exports are strong; consumers are confident; and we are well down the road to the first balanced federal budget since 1969.

Unfortunately, the United States' strong performance coincides with weakened economic performance by some of its international partners. This is particularly striking in Asia, where Japan is still recovering from a severe recession in the early 1990s. Even some other Asian economies whose breakneck pace was undisturbed by the Group of Seven recessions of the early 1990s, like the Republic of Korea, Singapore, and Thailand, slowed down in 1996, engendering an attack of economic angst. Thus since 1990 the United States appears to have traded places with East Asia. Then the Japanese and other Asian economies looked unstoppable, as if Asia had discovered some secret for investment, growth, and economic performance that the United States lacked. This led economists to examine the many structural differences across the Pacific and to focus on the benefits of the Asian system compared with the U.S. system. The comparison extended to banking and finance. Considering how and why views have changed since then is instructive.

Shifting Financial Models

Capitalism is broad enough to encompass competing models, including competing models of financial systems. The U.S. model—shared with the United Kingdom, and so sometimes referred to as the Anglo-Saxon model—emphasizes arms-length market relationships. For example, it relies heavily on securities markets. To be sure, banks play an important role, but even bank loans tend to be made on arms-length terms. Certainly the government has little to say about where bank credit is allocated. By contrast, the system that has developed in some Asian countries has followed more in the footsteps of the Japanese model. Without denying the important differences among these countries, the Asian systems traditionally seem to place greater reliance on bank loans than on securities markets, exhibit high debt-equity ratios, have closer relationships between banks and the companies that borrow from them, allow extensive corporate cross-shareholding, and feature greater guidance from the government in their credit allocation decisions. A common feature has been the imposition of compulsory financing of certain activities on banks, in combination with repression of the rest of the financial system through, for instance, taxes on securities transactions. This is in some sense the classical Asian financial model. It probably best characterizes Japan some 30 to 40 years ago, and is a more up-to-date characterization of some other Asian countries (for references see Frankel 1995).

Germany and other continental European countries have their own systems, but their emphasis on banking relationships versus securities markets resembles the Japanese model more closely than the Anglo-American model. Of course, this simple dual classification of the world's financial systems omits a lot. To take one example, Germany's universal banking system, which has spread to the rest of Europe and to Canada, could be viewed as the antithesis of the U.S.'s Glass-Steagall law (which segregates banking from securities), yet in this regard Japan more closely resembles the United States in that financial institutions are legally segregated by function. (This is no coincidence. Article 65 became law in 1948 under the influence of the American occupation.)

Some 5 to 10 years ago, economists were wondering if the Japanese system might not be superior to the Anglo-Saxon one. Their research took both theoretical and empirical forms (Frankel 1993; Hoshi, Kashyap, and Sharfstein 1990a,b,c). The theoretical models assumed asymmetric information between borrowers and lenders. The idea is that from the viewpoint of a firm seeking to finance an investment project, typical investors in the securities markets are strangers who have no way of knowing whether the firm's project will have as high a return as its managers claim it will. Such investors will demand a premium to compensate them. Researchers confirmed that firms were better able to finance their investment projects internally than when they had to go to the securities markets and convince strangers of the worthiness of their projects. Relationship banking was thought to be a possible way around the asymmetric information problems that impeded capital markets. Investigators said that when a firm suffered a temporary setback, the short-sighted American financial system would cut it off from new funds, while Japanese banks had longer time horizons, and would give the borrower the resources to see it through.

The question ultimately was an empirical one. The Japanese system seemed to work extremely well. It produced miracle rates of investment and correspondingly high rates of growth. Observers said that it had helped provide Japan with low cost capital, thereby giving Japanese industry an advantage over American competitors. Versions of this type of financial system in other Asian countries seemed to be working well also, in contrast to the recurrent crises in Latin America.[1]

Now, however, the much vaunted Japanese financial system is looking tarnished. The attribute of the system that previously appeared to be a virtue—banks' willingness to go on lending to firms in distress—now turns out to have led to serious problems. Borrowers who should have been cut off were not, with the result that further billions were lost. The public has had to pay twice, once in the form of slowed economic growth as the result of the prolonged overhang of bad loans (and other aspects of the burst bubble), and then again as taxpayers when the government ends up footing the bill.

Every country encounters bumps in the road, and concluding too much from a single episode is unwise. However, several aspects of the Asian model have been called into question recently. One of them is the close relationship between banks and borrowers, and another is administrative guidance from the government.

East Asian financial systems appear to have been less able to withstand economic shocks than the U.S. system, even though the latter is far from

---

1. The Republic of Korea, for example, achieved remarkable growth rates. In a 1993 paper (Frankel 1993a), I allowed that "one should hesitate before condemning Korean 'financial repression,' given how successful the development process has been over the last thirty years" (p.96). But I did add: "Nevertheless, it may be time to move on to a new stage." Now, four years later, I am prepared to conclude that it is indeed time for Korea to move on.

perfect. Asian systems worked well as long as economies grew fast and steadily. Problems arose when economies slowed or faltered. They include mounting bad loans, overextended property markets, and some scandals. When governments responded by papering over problems rather than addressing them squarely so as to put them in the past, this did not help the situation. By contrast, the U.S. financial system seems to have withstood shocks more readily, for example, the 1990–91 recession, despite the earlier costly procrastination regarding the savings and loan problem.

Increasing the International Focus on Banking Stability

In the last few years, the international focus on banking crises has increased. As with many other international economic phenomena, increased vulnerability to financial crises can be traced to two overarching trends that have swept the world: liberalization and globalization.

Governments everywhere have embraced market liberalization as the path to faster economic growth. This interest in liberalization stems from a wide consensus that the more statist models of development have failed. Governments worldwide have realized that to grow they must rely on markets. Goldsmith (1969), McKinnon (1973), and Shaw (1973) pointed out the drawbacks of financial repression, which both discourages the accumulation of savings and interferes with their efficient allocation. Since then, economists have come to understand that a liberalized, privately focused financial system is a key element of a successful growth strategy. However, as countries liberalize their financial systems, unconstrained financial institutions have more scope for making potentially costly mistakes.

The second overarching trend is globalization. Globalization increases the international effects of domestic financial crises. Private capital inflows have grown in importance in the 1990s, and many of these flows are intermediated through domestic banking systems. This increases the systems' vulnerability to international shocks, and crises can be transmitted from one country to the next.

Some numbers illustrate the increase in private capital flows. In the eight years following the onset of the debt crisis in 1982, net private capital flows into developing countries averaged only US$21 billion a year. Since 1991, however, total private capital inflows have climbed to an average of US$146 billion per year. Portfolio capital flows have grown even faster, from US$6 billion to US$54 billion a year, more than a third of total flows. They tapered off somewhat after the peso crisis in early 1995, but hit a new high in 1996.

Volatile private portfolio flows can interact with liberalized banking systems to increase the likelihood of foreign exchange pressures. Domestic monetary policies must respond to these pressures, especially when a country is attempting to manage or peg its exchange rate, but to do this, monetary authorities must be able to raise interest rates temporarily. If the domestic banking system is already weakened by asset quality problems, raising interest rates will be more costly, and they will hesitate. This hesitation can increase speculative pressures against the exchange rate, leading to a full-fledged speculative attack. A weak domestic banking system was one element that made it difficult for Mexico to defend its peso in 1994.

Recent Banking Crises

A number of prominent banking crises have occurred in recent years. Perhaps the first major one brought about by the current wave of liberalization was the U.S. savings and loan crisis in the 1980s, where a liberalized regulatory regime was grafted onto financial institutions with weak capital positions.

Severe problems also hit banks in some Nordic countries. Policymakers had liberalized the rules for these banks, but supervision had failed to keep up. When macroeconomic volatility hit these countries, banks became deeply insolvent, and state takeovers ensued. State capital guarantees and capital injections ran as high as 8.2 percent of gross domestic product (GDP) for Finland (IMF 1994, p. 75). Clean-up costs following banking problems in Spain were even larger.

In dollar terms, the banking problems that have plagued Japan since 1990 may represent the biggest financial crisis in recent history. The banking practices that looked so attractive in the 1980s proved to depend on a continuously growing economy. They also depended on a stock market bubble, which burst in 1990, sending stock prices plunging more than 50 percent in two and a half years. By 1996, nonperforming loans in Japan had reached 3.3 percent of total loans as officially reported by the major banks (IMF 1996, p. 83). Some signs indicate that Japan's financial problems have lessened recently, partly because banks have begun to get their own houses in order. Nonetheless, for the last seven years a weak financial system has exerted a drag on the Japanese economy.

Two years ago we were reminded of the importance of banking systems in developing countries as well. After the peso crisis hit Mexico in December 1994, a weak banking system became a serious constraint to

Mexican financial policy. Problem loans that had mounted in the three years preceding the crisis had already weakened the banking system. Nonperforming loans rose from 4 percent of total loans in 1991 to 8 percent in mid-1994 (Goldstein 1997, p. 7). Mexico also highlighted the issue of contagion. The peso crisis spread in the form of the famous tequila effect to other Latin American countries—especially Argentina and Brazil—and even translated into foreign exchange pressures on some Asian emerging markets—including Indonesia, the Philippines, and Thailand—as well as some industrial countries with weak economic fundamentals.

Banking problems have also become apparent in other countries recently. To name just a few, Korea is experiencing pressures on its banks in the aftermath of Hanbo's bankruptcy; Russia and other transition economies are being plagued by poorly managed banks, with incestuous relationships between bank owners and bank borrowers; and the Czech Republic and Thailand are also facing pressures.

The cost of banking crises has been severe in many countries. Estimates indicate that since 1980 the costs of resolving banking crises in developing and transition economies have reached almost US$250 billion. According to Goldstein (1997, p. 4), 67 banking systems have encountered crises since 1980, and 52 of these have been in developing countries.

Policy Responses

The prevalence of banking and financial problems calls for policymakers to develop coordinated international responses. The right answer is certainly not to retreat from globalization or from liberalization, because these have both brought many economic benefits. I wonder if even the Greiders who warn of the dangers of the globalized marketplace truly want such a retreat.

Telling banks not to make bad loans is of limited practical use. Banks exist in part to make risky investments, and expecting them to have no bad loans is unrealistic. In an efficient, well-functioning financial system, banks should even fail occasionally. What a financial system should be able to provide is the ability to function efficiently, to support adequate levels of investment smoothly, and to withstand adverse economic shocks.

Elements of a financial system that appear to make it more resilient include transparency, sound accounting practices, strong capital adequacy, and rules-based supervision. While acknowledging such failures as the savings and loan crisis, and without overselling the U.S. financial system, I would suggest that these are key elements of the American approach. The United States has made further moves in recent years to improve rules-based supervision and capital adequacy, for example, "prompt corrective action," though this rule has yet to be tested during a downturn.

Japan has also moved in this direction. The fact that different Japanese banks now pay different borrowing spreads provides evidence that arms-length market transactions are more prevalent in Japan than they used to be. Tokyo's "Big Bang" financial reforms will continue this trend.

International efforts to control banking risks go back to the Basle initiatives of the 1970s. The original Basle Concordat laid down procedures for international banking supervision, to address issues related to the Herstatt failure in 1974. More recently, Basle has provided a forum for bank regulators to coordinate on their capital requirements for international banks (IMF 1996, p. 141). This helps level the playing field between banks in different industrial countries, while also increasing the stability of these banks. The accord on capital to be allocated for credit risk has been followed by an accord on market risks, interest rate risks, and foreign exchange risks. The Basle initiatives generally were intended to cover only the participating industrial countries, and did not cover banks in developing or transition economies. As recent events demonstrate, emerging markets could benefit from more stringent rules. Such rules could also improve international financial stability.

Goldstein (1997) has called for the development of an international banking standard that lays down principles for bank regulation. Emerging market countries that adopted the standard would reap the domestic benefits of a more stable and efficient financial system and would also benefit from international investors' increased confidence in their markets.

Since the Halifax summit of the Group of Seven countries in 1995, the United States has encouraged efforts to improve financial stability in emerging markets more or less along these lines. In the past year the industrial country members of the Basle Committee on Banking Supervision, which includes the United States, have worked with developing countries to put in place a framework for financial stability in the form of a set of core principles of effective banking supervision. Representatives of G-10 and non-G-10 economies also organized a working party that issued a report in April 1997 detailing key elements of a robust financial system. The principles included a proper legal framework, adequate accounting principles, a strong payments and settlement system, high quality and timely financial disclosure, effective risk management and internal controls, and capital sufficient for the risks taken (Working Party on Financial Stability in Emerging Market Economies 1997). The report also laid out an international strategy to promote financial stability, a strategy that G-10 ministers and governors have endorsed and that received a further push at the Denver Summit in mid-1997.

In mid-1997 the Group of Thirty previewed another proposal that is based on the idea that globally active financial institutions should get together and develop standards for running their businesses safely. This international self-regulation could complement current efforts to coordinate national regulatory regimes. Also relevant is a recent report from a task force of the Institute for International Finance. Such private sector initiatives, not to mention important work at the International Monetary Fund, the Bank for International Settlements, and other international organizations, are welcome.

Conclusion

Some policymakers have suggested that Mexico was the first financial crisis of the 21st century. If the current initiatives bear fruit, however, we can hope to limit the frequency and magnitude of the financial crises of the coming century. With increasing international economic interdependence and the prosperity that comes with it, ensuring that the 21st century sees a minimum of such disruptions is important. The United States and its international partners are working to strengthen the stability of domestic financial systems to contribute to continued international financial stability.

References

Frankel, Jeffrey. 1993. "The Evolving Japanese Financial System and the Cost of Capital." In Ingo Walter and Takato Hiraki, eds., *Restructuring Japan's Financial Markets*. New York: Irwin Press and New York University.

_____. 1995. "Recent Changes in the Financial Systems of Asian and Pacific Countries." In Kuniho Sawamoto, Zenta Nakajima, and Hiroo Taguchi, eds., *Financial Stability in a Changing Environment*. MacMillan Press.

Goldsmith, Raymond. 1969. *Financial Structure and Development*. New Haven, Connecticut: Yale University Press.

Goldstein, Morris. 1997. *The Case for an International Banking Standard*. Washington, D. C.: Institute for International Economics.

Hoshi, Takeo, Anil Kashyap, and David Sharfstein. 1990a. "Bank Monitoring and Investment: Evidence from the Changing Structure of Japanese Corporate Banking Relationship." In R. G. Hubbard, ed., *Asymmetric Information, Corporate Finance, and Investment*. Chicago: University of Chicago Press.

_____. 1990b. "Corporate Structure, Liquidity, and Investment: Evidence from Japanese Panel Data." *Quarterly Journal of Economics* (September).

_____. 1990c. "The Role of Banks in Reducing the Costs of Financial Distress in Japan." *Journal of Financial Economics* 27 (September): 67–88.

IMF (International Monetary Fund). 1994. *International Capital Markets: Developments, Prospects, and Policy Issues.* Washington, D. C.

_____. 1996. *International Capital Markets: Developments, Prospects, and Policy Issues.* Washington, D. C.

McKinnon, Ronald. 1973. *Money and Capital in Economic Development.* Washington, D. C.: The Brookings Institution.

Shaw, Edward. 1973. *Financial Deepening in Economic Development.* New York: Oxford University Press.

Working Party on Financial Stability in Emerging Market Economies. 1997. "Financial Stability in Emerging Market Economies: A Strategy for the Formulation, Adoption, and Implementation of Sound Principles and Practices to Strengthen Financial Systems." Bank for International Settlements, Basle, Switzerland.

2

Regulatory Efforts to Prevent Banking Crises

Michael H. Moskow

I am pleased to have this opportunity to discuss, from the regulator's perspective, ways to prevent banking crises. I believe this conference serves as an excellent forum for sharing information available on the causes and consequences of past crises. Why repeat avoidable mistakes of the past? It also allows for a discussion of alternative methods to resolve banking crises once they occur. For example, how have the Latin American countries addressed this challenge? Does it differ from the approach taken in the United States? Are there advantages of one approach over another? Finally, this forum permits sharing ideas as to how best to structure the industry and its regulatory oversight to prevent future crises. All three elements of this discussion—a historical description of past crises, a critique of alternative means of resolving crises, and an evaluation of methods to prevent future crises—are important and I believe can prove valuable in efforts to improve the stability of the industry in the future.

This chapter stresses various ways to prevent banking crises, emphasizing the role of regulation. While prompt resolution of any crisis is necessary, and is an important function of any public regulatory agency, it is not its major responsibility. I believe we spend an inordinate amount of time positioning ourselves to be able to pick up the pieces when and if a crisis occurs. Once we get to the point where we are cleaning up a crisis, the system has failed. My objective, therefore, is to emphasize preventive action. I do not believe that banking crises are inevitable. The more time spent on prevention, the less the need for crisis resolution.

In my remarks I will (a) examine why banking supervision and evaluation is necessary in a market-oriented financial system and discuss the objective of this supervision and of evaluation; (b) discuss the causes of financial crises; (c) discuss steps that I believe could be taken to prevent these crises, emphasizing the key components required for an efficient banking system (that is, the infrastructure) and the principles that I believe should drive bank regulation; (d) comment briefly on the organization of bank supervision and the role for international coordination of banking supervision, evaluation, and reporting requirements.

The Need for Supervision and Performance Evaluation

Let me quickly review why we need bank supervision and evaluation in market economies. I emphasize that this is for private market economies. If the state is in control of banks' assets or asset allocation decisions, history has shown that resources will not be efficiently allocated. In other words, credit allocation in response to market forces differs significantly from credit allocation in response to political forces. This chapter deals only with regulation in private banking markets. I will restrict my comments to address regulation in private banking markets.

Banking systems serve a vital intermediary function in a market economy. Banks collect savings from individuals and businesses and make loans to other individuals and enterprises that need longer-term funds to finance investments in plant and equipment and shorter term financing for inventories and working capital. In making loans, banks undertake a credit analysis of the borrower and assure themselves that the borrower has sufficient capability to repay the loan. In this way, banks allocate a scarce resource, financial capital, to its most productive uses.

The importance of a strong banking sector to a country's economic growth and development is well known. Efficient financial systems help countries to grow, partly by mobilizing additional financial resources, and partly by allocating those resources to the best uses (see, for example, Evanoff and Israilevich 1990; Jayaratne and Strahan 1996; King and Levine 1993; Schumpeter 1969). Banks are the primary mechanisms for the transmission of monetary policy and they play an important role in determining the supply of money in the economy. They also typically form the backbone of the payments system.

Why is regulatory oversight needed? Arguing for government intervention or regulation in markets that are perfect and efficient is difficult. In the absence of distorting factors, the decisions of individual agents in the economy should promote the public interest in general. That is, agents acting in their own self-interest and weighing the costs and benefits of their decisions would make the same decisions as a benevolent, omnipotent social planner. However, instances may occur where the costs and benefits to an individual agent associated with a particular action may diverge from the costs and benefits to society. This is where regulation has a part to play to ensure that the actions individual agents take reflect the costs and benefits to the public in general. Such characteristics are typically associated with banking.

Relative to other types of firms, banks have low capital to asset and cash to asset ratios and are highly leveraged, making them more prone to severe liquidity problems. As bank assets are typically somewhat opaque, investors may not have as much information on the condition of banks as does bank management. This asymmetric information between the banks and investors—a form of capital market imperfection—raises the possibility that during stress, as they are unable to determine whether banks are healthy, funds may be withdrawn from a number of banks, thereby creating liquidity problems (Diamond and Dybvig 1983). Banks within a system are closely intertwined via interbank borrowing, interbank balances, and payment clearing activity. Therefore the potential for spillover effects is typically thought to be worse in banking than in other industries. The failure of one bank may cause depositors at another bank to suspect that their bank could also be the victim of financial distress. The classic regulator fear is that such behavior may feed on itself and the failure of one important bank may trigger runs on other banks. In addition, decisions made at one bank may take into account the risk implications for its own portfolio, but not the spillover effects on other banks. Thus entire payments systems may be adversely affected instead of individual transactions between banks. The fear is that the whole process can multiply until it results in a full-fledged banking panic that has an adverse impact on economic activity.

As banks are so important to the functioning of the economy, to the extent that the externalities described exist, banking supervision and evaluation are equally important. However, regulations aimed at resolving the problems generated by market failure can become the root cause of industry problems. Numerous countries have demonstrated that moral hazard problems, regulatory forbearance, and incentive distortions resulting from the mispricing of the safety net are the underlying causes of banking industry problems. The United States, for example, is currently paying dearly for poorly structured regulations and inadequate supervision and evaluation of its savings and loan associations (for a summary of events see Barth

1991; Barth, Bartholomew, and Bradley 1990; Benston and Kaufman 1997). Estimates indicate that the failure of hundreds of these savings and loan associations may have cost American taxpayers anywhere from US$175 billion to US$225 billion. Inadequate supervision can also have less direct, though no less painful, costs. Institutions that extend poor quality loans in speculative attempts to earn higher returns will take on higher risks. Generally, such loans do not allocate capital to its best use. The rapid run-up in American real estate prices in the 1980s is a recent case in point. Fueled by imprudent bank lending, the rapid increase in real estate values was one of the primary reasons for the so-called credit crunch in the United States. It also contributed to the deterioration in the financial condition of many large U.S. commercial banks and to the U.S. economic recession of the early 1990s.

So how should supervision and regulation be used as preventive medicine against financial crises? I will address this question, first, by examining the causes of financial crises, and then by discussing the regulatory principles and required industry infrastructure necessary to prevent such crises.

The Causes of Financial Crises

The causes of financial crises can generally be divided into two categories: those induced by macroeconomic factors and those caused by poor microeconomic infrastructures. The two are interdependent.

By far the major cause of financial crisis is an unstable economy. This results in deteriorating asset quality, asset price bubbles, and wide swings in asset prices and exchange rates that strain the fundamental business of banking and can lead to systemwide problems. A feedback process may also occur. During upswings banks tend to become "excessively exuberant" and exacerbate the business cycle by driving up asset prices beyond those characterized by prudent lending. In the United States, in the absence of severe macroeconomic shocks, the banking industry has been impressively stable, almost void of crises.

Although macroeconomic shocks may initiate most banking problems, they can be made significantly worse by microeconomic structural problems. These include corporate governance problems; distorted incentive systems generated by poorly structured regulatory arrangements; and poor management practices, including inside lending, fraud, and general ineptness induced by poor internal controls and information infrastructures. These shortcomings allow what may be relatively minor problems to grow into major problems.

The resolution of these problems not only enhances social welfare, but it also generates benefits for most elements of society. Better market or supervisory oversight prevents the failure of poorly managed banks from spilling over and leading to failures at healthy banks as a result of banking panics or runs. Rigorous market and self-evaluations allow bank managers to spot potential problem areas and to take action to address these before additional problems develop. When all banks carry out such evaluations and disclose them in a form that preserves proprietary information, bank managers then have standards of performance by which they can better manage their firms. Similarly, from the perspective of bank stockholders and investors, market and supervisory evaluations provide needed information on the quality of the bank's management and the riskiness of its investments, and gives information useful in comparing these investments to alternative investments.

Means for Addressing the Industry's Problems

So how do we address these potential causes of banking crises? What is needed to avoid financial crises? I believe the solutions fall into three interdependent categories:

- Sound macroeconomic policy
- Minimum infrastructure requirements
- Bank regulatory principles.

Sound Macroeconomic Policy

The need for sound macroeconomic policy is self-evident. Some would argue that in preventing financial crises, creating the environment for stable growth is the single most important solution policymakers can bring to the table. It is also typically the major responsibility of central banks around the world. Yet macroeconomic instability continues to be the major cause of financial crises.

Infrastructure Requirements

Whether the regulator is the market or the public sector regulator, adequate information is necessary if it is to succeed. Thus some fundamental infrastructure requirements are called for if banking is to be a stable, functioning industry. The following are among the key components that underpin efficient banking systems:

- A system of laws and rules for corporate governance and property rights, including bankruptcy laws, and laws that describe the rights of creditors in seizing or disposing of borrowers' assets
- A uniform set of transparent accounting standards, statements, and supporting schedules and reports
- A facility that provides for external bank auditors and examiners
- A set of rules for public disclosure of nonproprietary financial information.

It should be noted that most of these components fall outside the direct control of banks and bank supervisors, because they are frequently the responsibility of another sector of the government. Even so, they are vital to the work of bank supervisors and to the bank performance evaluation process. Without these elements in place the banking system's efficiency is certain to be impaired. Thus in the case of developing countries and transition economies, these items must be properly structured before the banking system is privatized. Note that for industrial countries, having some, but not all, of the components in place is a recipe for trouble.

The accounting system is perhaps the component that is most basic to the efficiency of financial markets. The rules all firms must follow in preparing their financial statements must be clearly specified. These statements—balance sheets, income statements, and various schedules—communicate vital information about the enterprise to creditors, investors, commercial counterparts, and regulators alike.

A set of consistent, structured, and well-defined standards for financial reporting forms part of the core of the resource allocation process. Banks need dependable financial statements from borrowers to be able to perform adequate credit analysis. Uniform accounting standards allow banks to compare borrowers' relative merits. Similarly, bank supervisors, investors, and managers need dependable bank financial statements to make informed judgments about banks' financial health and performance. For a bank, a vitally important component of an accounting system is a consistent set of rules relating to valuation of assets. Assets need to be valued in a bank's books at their true worth, particularly where this is less that the price paid for them. Without such rules, the bank accounting system is of limited value.

Dependable financial information is necessary not only to gauge the health of individual institutions, but also to make comparisons between different banks. In this way bank supervisors can identify those banks in need of attention. Similarly, bank investors can identify those banks most deserving of their capital. To ensure that users of financial statements can be confident that the accounts are prepared according to the proper principles, some form of external check is necessary. In market economies, this added comfort is typically secured by the services of an external auditor.

Closely related to the standardization of accounting principles is the need for public disclosure. The question is not whether financial statements be made available to the public, but how often they should be provided and the appropriate amount of information that should be given.

As stated earlier, if markets possess both the relevant information and the capability to discipline banks adequately, additional regulation has a limited role. If markets possess the disciplining capabilities but incomplete information, regulations should provide the market with adequate disclosure about firms' characteristics. The general level of public disclosure has risen as financial markets have demanded more and better information. This is particularly true in banking, where there is a need for additional and better information on hidden reserves, provisions for loan losses, and nonperforming loans. The benefits of disclosure are one of the lessons that emerge from the derivatives debacles of the last few years. If regulatory structures could ensure that firms had to disclose both their ex ante rationale for their hedging positions as well as the ex post performance, many derivatives' positions would have been unwound much sooner (for example, the Gibson, P&G, and Dharmala cases), thereby preventing the large losses that occurred. Adequate levels of disclosure allow market forces to create strong incentives for banks' management, boards of directors, and regulators to behave prudently.

Disclosure is not, however, a cure-all. Not everyone agrees that depositors can interpret disclosures appropriately. The conventional notion that more disclosure is better ignores the fact that some of this information might be useless to the market; that it might make the task of extracting useful information more difficult for market participants; and that it might have a significant effect on the efficient operation of firms, for example, because of the forced disclosure of strategic and proprietary information by firms. These effects must be considered in the design of the appropriate level (and content) of disclosure requirements for firms. Having said that, I believe that more disclosure is generally preferable to less disclosure as long as it does not produce negative external effects. Disclosure and market discipline represent powerful complements to the direct regulation of institutions, and must be considered an important part of the regulator's arsenal.

(See Moser and Venkataraman 1996 for a discussion of the appropriate role of disclosure in financial services.)

A publication recently released by the Bank for International Settlements (1997) notes that disclosure complements effective bank supervision. The Bank's Committee on Banking Supervision has set up a subgroup to study issues related to disclosure and to provide guidance to the banking industry. In the United States the Securities and Exchange Commission's and the Financial Accounting Standards Board's proposals on disclosure and accounting for derivatives take important steps in the provision of information to the market.

Principles Driving Bank Regulation

As noted earlier, regulatory interference with the marketplace is warranted under certain circumstances. Obviously, an industry's regulatory framework can have a major impact on the efficiency and direction in which the industry evolves. For example, in the United States limitations on geographic expansion have led to a relatively fragmented banking industry with a higher bank per capita ratio than in any other industrial country. One can cite numerous other examples where regulation resulted in firms innovating to exploit a regulatory loophole rather than innovating in a direction that is socially optimal. Therefore, we should be extremely careful in developing bank regulations. Policymakers should take three overall principles into account when devising bank regulations, namely:

- Regulation should be goal-oriented.
- Regulation should accomplish its stated goals efficiently.
- Regulation should evolve as technology and market structure change and should not discourage these developments.

Let us consider each of these principles in turn. First, regulation should be goal-oriented, not process-oriented. We should start by asking the following questions: Why are we regulating? What fundamental public policy objective do we want to accomplish? Why is this an essential principle for regulation? We ask these questions because the fundamental goals of regulation typically do not change, even though the industry, technology, and market structure may change radically.

Thus, not being wedded to approaches used in the past is important. They are just attempts to achieve the goal, not the goal itself. While this may seem obvious, it is remarkable how often this basic principle is ignored. As an observer of the regulatory process (both from the inside and from the outside) for more than 25 years, I would say that most regulatory bodies take whatever regulatory framework is currently being applied as given. Regulatory innovation usually takes the form of looking for better ways to apply the current framework. Rarely, in my experience, do regulatory agencies take as their primary concern the fundamental goal. Thus the new regulatory proposals being introduced around the world are encouraging.

Second, regulatory goals should be accomplished in the most efficient way possible. A regulatory approach is efficient if it accomplishes the desired goal with the least amount of collateral damage to the industry's activity. That is, one wants to use the least intrusive approach that achieves the goals. Efficient regulation often either relies on market mechanisms or has the property of incentive compatibility. Note that the infrastructure discussed earlier is required before we can rely on these market-driven mechanisms. Let us review these alternatives for efficient regulation.

- *Maximum reliance on market mechanisms.* The first question must always be: Is government regulation even necessary? Are market incentives sufficient and available information adequate to ensure that market participants, acting in their own self-interest, effectively achieve the regulatory goals? If the answer is yes, then the market itself is the best dynamic regulator and no further government action is needed. If the answer is no, then we must look for the barriers to self-regulation by market forces. Perhaps government action can remove these barriers, in which case that would be the direction to look for the optimal regulatory strategy.
  — If the main barrier to market self-regulation is lack of information, the best role of government regulation may simply be to provide information. Presumably a bank's credit rating, and thus its cost of funds, would be adversely affected if the information were unfavorable. This may be sufficient to induce prudent behavior without additional regulatory intervention.
  — If the main barrier to market self-regulation is market incompleteness, the government's role would be to encourage the development of additional markets.
  — If the main barrier to self-regulation is the existence of barriers to free entry into the industry, the focus of regulation should be to remove these barriers, given that whenever possible, regulation should encourage, not restrict, market competition. Ironically, these barriers are often created by the government in the first place.

- *Incentive-compatible regulation.* To clarify the concept of incentive compatibility, let us contrast the command approach with the incentive compatible approach. Under the command approach the government simply states what actions are desired of the regulated firm, what actions are permitted, and what actions are prohibited. Under the incentive compatible approach the regulator seeks to align firms' incentives with social goals. In other words, this approach makes it in the firms' own self-interest to achieve the regulatory objectives efficiently. In this context note that the word deregulation, which is often used to describe the process of replacing inefficient regulation with more efficient approaches, is somewhat misleading. The regulatory goals have not changed, so in that sense deregulation is not taking place. The change involves "smart regulating," that is, achieving the same regulatory goals in a better way.

The third principle is that regulation should evolve as technology, market structure, and the industry change and should not discourage these developments. While this principle seems obvious, it is rarely applied. Rather, we often see regulatory approaches in place long after technological changes have rendered them obsolete.

If possible, regulation should be self-evolving. If regulatory change must pass through cumbersome national or international political bodies, then changes may be difficult to implement. Having a structure that is designed to evolve as the industry evolves is better. This is a two-way street: innovations within the industry can affect the viability and appropriateness of certain regulatory schemes, and similarly, regulations themselves can stifle or encourage innovation.

Let us consider some applications of these regulatory principles tied to proposed bank regulatory structures. In the process I want to emphasize the incentive compatible nature of these proposals. The moral hazard problems created by a mispriced safety net have engendered much debate and a number of regulatory proposals aimed at resolving these problems. In the United States, now that banking conditions are relatively good, many proponents are arguing for implementing additional deposit insurance reform. (Earlier reforms were implemented in the early 1990s, when various means to ensure prompt corrective action during banking crises were legislatively introduced. See Benston and Kaufman 1997.) How do some of these proposed reforms fit into the infrastructure requirements and regulatory principles discussed earlier?

Let us consider three reform proposals: (a) decreasing the safety net significantly and increasing the role of disclosure, (b) introducing the narrow bank concept, and (c) altering the capital structure to expand the role of subordinated debt.

Proposals to decrease the safety net and increase the role of disclosure and market discipline are based on the contention that the systemic implications of banking failures are relatively limited and, if given adequate information, the private sector could adequately oversee the activities of the banking sector. This approach is currently being evaluated in New Zealand (see Calomiris 1997). The Reserve Bank of New Zealand decided that from mid-1996, banks in New Zealand would be required to make detailed disclosure statements, including information about credit ratings, guarantees, impaired assets, material exposure, and capital adequacy. In return, the Reserve Bank removed a number of previous regulatory structures. Every bank branch displays a two-page summary of these disclosures to allow depositors to assess the institution's creditworthiness. The Reserve Bank is not responsible for bailing out depositors. The presumption is that with full disclosure, depositors are capable of assessing the risk inherent in using a particular institution and no longer need government protection. This approach obviously requires a well-developed infrastructure with a free flow of information.

The narrow bank proposal would limit insurance coverage to a narrow class of deposits that would be covered by extremely safe and liquid assets. The insurance fund would not cover activities outside this narrow class of deposits. The market would discipline all other activities (see chapter 17 by Geoffrey Miller in this volume). This proposal satisfies the regulatory principles laid out earlier, but depends critically on the completeness of the infrastructure and the government's credibility to avoid expanding the safety net beyond the stated limits. To my knowledge no country has implemented this proposal to date.

The third proposal involves increasing the role of subordinated debt in the capital structure of banks to decrease the moral hazard problem, increase market discipline, and provide for an improved failure resolution process. A command regulation approach to solving the moral hazard problem would have regulators mandate a maximum level of risk for any insured bank. This approach has the typical problems associated with command regulation. First, it is difficult for regulators to measure accurately the risk associated with a bank's loan portfolio. Second, any credible effort to measure this risk accurately is likely to be extremely intrusive. Finally, a one-size-fits-all restriction on bank risk may actually prevent capital from flowing to valuable investment projects. Using the favorable characteristics of subordinated debt may resolve these problems. Proponents argue that debt holders serve as a superior buffer against income variations for both depositors and the insurance fund, because in contrast to equity holders, they do not have the potential to realize up-side gains from having banks hold riskier portfolios. In addition, instead of having uninsured depositors run the bank when asset quality is questioned—thereby disrupting the bank resolution process—debt holders cannot run, but only walk away from the bank as their issues come due. Thus an orderly resolution process could take place. This proposal is consistent with the regulatory principles discussed earlier and requires a sufficient infrastructure, including mature capital markets, to allow for the required market discipline. Countries without this infrastructure may want to use some form of prompt corrective action to substitute for the disciplining role of subordinated debt. Argentina has recently adopted a somewhat similar approach, one that requires debt issues to submit banks to the forces of the marketplace. It has also been proposed in the United States as an extension to a reform proposal that emphasizes market discipline recently released by the Bankers Roundtable (1997). (For a comparison of alternative regulatory schemes with one that relies more heavily on the use of subordinated debt in the capital structure see Evanoff 1993.)

Each of these proposals meet the principles outlined earlier and warrant additional consideration.

Organization of Bank Supervision and the Role of International Coordination

Let me conclude my remarks with a few observations concerning market discipline and international coordination among banking regulators around the world.

The organization of bank supervision differs from country to country. In England (until very recently) and Italy, for example, this is a central bank function. Other countries such as Canada and Switzerland have bank supervisory authorities that are separate from and independent of the central bank. Still others like Germany, Japan, and the United States have mixed systems, where the central bank shares bank supervisory responsibility with other government agencies. Thus no agreed upon best system exists. However, in countries beginning the transition to a market economy, the function should probably be part of the central bank's responsibilities. In these economies it is easier to ensure the supervisor's independence and the chance for informational synergy is higher when the two functions are housed together, and it is important that the two functions work closely together to resolve crises.

As with the central bank, the supervisor must be free from undue political pressure or control. The bank supervisor should have enough authority to supervise the banks, but these powers should not lead the supervisor into managing the banks. This task belongs to banks' managers and directors.

The Basle Committee on Banking Supervision has produced a set of principles to guide bank supervisors in regulating and interacting with the branches of foreign banks operating in the domestic economy. Its report on the topic (Bank for International Settlements 1997) will undoubtedly become required reading for all bank supervisors. It is imperative that banks and banking supervisors around the world abide by sound principles if the global banking system is to remain healthy.

Conclusion

Financial and economic liberalization, combined with the globalization of markets, have clearly changed the contours of the world's financial system. Interest rate and exchange rate volatility has increased; competition among financial institutions, both bank and nonbank, has intensified; and new financial products are continuously being developed. In the face of these changes, banks worldwide have had to develop new markets and services to maintain their market shares and to meet the growing needs of customers.

The changing financial environment has also presented important supervisory challenges, most notably, adapting laws and regulations to changing market realities, improving the infrastructure undergirding the financial system, and recognizing the need for international coordination of supervisory and regulatory efforts. It is therefore important that discussions such as these we are having at this conference continue in order to ensure stability of the global financial system.

References

Bank for International Settlements. 1997. "Core Principles for Effective Banking Supervision." Basle Committee on Banking Supervision, Basle, Switzerland.

Bankers Roundtable, The. 1997. "Deposit Insurance Reform in the Public Interest, Partnering for Financial Services Modernization." Report of the Subcommittee and Working Group on Deposit Insurance Reform Retail Issues and Deposit Insurance Committee. Washington, D. C.

Barth, James R. 1991. *The Great Savings and Loan Debacle*. Washington, D. C.: University Press of America.

Barth, James R., Philip F. Bartholomew, and Michael G. Bradley. 1990. "Determinants of Thrift Institution Resolution Costs." *Journal of Finance* 45(3): 731–54.

Benston, George J., and George G. Kaufman. 1997. "FDICIA after Five Years." *The Journal of Economic Perspectives* 11(3): 139.

Calomiris, Charles W. 1997. "Designing the Post-Modern Bank Safety Net: Lessons from Developed and Developing Economies." The Bankers' Roundtable Program for Reforming Federal Deposit Insurance, May 23, American Enterprise Institute, Washington, D. C.

Diamond, Douglas W., and Philip H. Dybvig. 1983. "Bank Runs, Deposit Insurance, and Liquidity." *Journal of Political Economy* 91(3): 401–19.

Evanoff, Douglas D. 1993. "Preferred Sources of Market Discipline." *Yale Journal on Regulation* 10(2): 347–67.

Evanoff, Douglas D., and Philip R. Israilevich. 1990. "Regional Regulatory Effects on Bank Efficiency." Regional Economic Issues Working Paper Series, WP-1990/4. Federal Reserve Bank of Chicago, Chicago.

Jayaratne, Jith, and Philip E. Strahan. 1996. "The Finance-Growth Nexus: Evidence from Bank Branch Deregulation." *The Quarterly Journal of Economics* 111(3): 639.

King, Robert, and Ross Levine. 1993. "Finance and Growth: Schumpeter Might Be Right." *Quarterly Journal of Economics* CVIII (1993b): 717–38.

Moser, James T., and Subu Venkataraman. 1996. "The Economics of Disclosure Requirements for Derivatives." *Chicago FedLetter* October(110): 1–3.

Schumpeter, Joseph. 1969. *The Theory of Economic Development*. Oxford: Oxford University Press.

3

The Role of the
International Monetary Fund

Karin Lissakers

Why should the International Monetary Fund (IMF) have a role in avoiding banking crises at all? Why should an institution designed to promote international monetary stability and to help its member governments avoid or cope with balance of payments crises be concerned with banking regulation and banking crises? Chapter 2 gave at least part of the answer when it noted that there are three keys to preventing bank crises: having a sound macroeconomic policy, possessing an effective financial infrastructure, and following guiding regulatory principles. The Fund's role in the first area is obvious. Advising governments on macroeconomic policy, on monetary and fiscal policy, is the IMF's bread and butter, what the Fund does most day to day. The Fund's involvement in the other two areas—financial infrastructure and guiding regulatory principles—is somewhat more surprising and a far more recent undertaking.

Group of Seven to Modernize International Architecture

The Fund's new mission in the banking area is an outgrowth of a broad international policy debate. During the Group of Seven (G-7) heads of state economic summit in Naples in 1994, President Clinton challenged his Canadian, European, and Japanese partners to begin to "modernize the international architecture" for the 21st century. This marked the beginning of a systematic, international effort led by the United States, particularly the Department of the Treasury and the Federal Reserve Board of Governors, first, to identify threats to international economic and financial stability that required cooperative international solutions; and second, to ensure that the institutional framework to develop and implement such cooperative solutions exists.

The globalization of financial services has been a particular focus of the G-7's efforts during the past two years. The G-7 deliberations are part of an ever widening national and international dialogue that includes the Group of Ten, the Bank for International Settlements with its enlarged membership, the Basle Committee on Banking Supervision, and new regional central bank and supervisory group forums that have been formed in the Americas and more recently in Asia. At the G-7 summit President Clinton hosted in Denver in July 1997, the leaders announced the following:

- Steps toward the establishment of a multilateral network of supervision appropriate to today's global markets and global institutions
- Progress toward a framework of strong supervisory principles for the major globally active financial institutions
- New steps to improve transparency
- Steps to reduce risk in payment and settlement systems
- Endorsement of a concerted international strategy to help emerging economies strengthen their financial systems, including a new, universally applicable set of core principles for effective banking supervision.

These initiatives will help reduce the risks and costs of future crises. As part of this exercise, major industrial countries have asked, and the full 182 country membership has agreed, that the IMF should augment its traditional macroeconomic advisory and balance of payments support role with more concerted activity in the banking and bank regulatory area. It will work closely with the World Bank, which is also building up its capacity in this field.

The IMF's activities in the banking area could be summarized as "evangelical," "prophesying," and "salvaging." The IMF will undertake to spread the gospel to member governments of sound regulatory and supervisory principles that bank supervisors and other regulatory groups have endorsed. The Fund has already begun to collaborate with various expert groups in drafting policy guidelines for IMF staff to incorporate in their annual macroeconomic consultations with member governments. The Fund will also try to alert member authorities to weaknesses or risks to financial stability; to issue warnings of emerging banking problems;

and if disaster strikes, to help governments manage crises in banking systems, which it can do by incorporating banking rehabilitation in Fund-supported stabilization programs, providing technical assistance, and helping mobilize other sources of expertise and financing as the IMF did recently for Mexico and Venezuela.

How Does Preventing Banking Crises Fit with Traditional IMF Activities?

The Fund's new banking role is a more natural fit with its traditional macroeconomic activity than one may think. The G-7 turned to the IMF because it offers several features no other international institution does. It has a unique mandate for universal surveillance: it is the only institution that goes in and "looks at the books" in 182 countries once a year. Its annual detailed economic consultation mandated under Article IV of the IMF's Articles of Agreement involves a close dialogue with monetary and finance officials at both the technical and policymaking levels. These consultations already cover key fiscal and monetary policy issues, including some regulatory matters. Adding banking and financial supervisory policy to the Fund's surveillance exercises will require some beefing up of its expertise in this area, but nevertheless, it seems a natural extension of existing surveillance activities. Indeed, one could argue that it is a necessary extension, because left unaddressed, weaknesses in a country's banking system can trigger or compound the fiscal and monetary problems the Fund seeks to prevent through its surveillance.

The IMF has a second channel to member countries through its conditional lending, that is, Fund financing tied to corrective policy measures. While in the past the Fund has not consistently recognized the importance of incorporating banking issues into its macroeconomic adjustment programs, it now has a better understanding of the links between the banking regulatory system and balance of payments and macroeconomic instability, and that those linkages become more potent in liberalized, internationally exposed financial markets. Banking and macroeconomic problems can feed off each other in what Myrdal often referred to as "circular causation with cumulative effects."

Failure to take into account the impact on the banking system of necessary macroeconomic policy adjustment can cause IMF-supported adjustment programs to fail. Fund-supported macroeconomic adjustment programs to eliminate unsustainable current account deficits typically include monetary and fiscal tightening, and often involve exchange rate adjustment. If higher interest rates and currency depreciation mandated under the program create distress in the banking system and the government responds with emergency provision of liquidity to distressed banks through central bank credit, this can undermine price stabilization. A fiscal bailout of the banking system can blow a huge hole in the government budget, as demonstrated by both industrial and developing country banking crises, that leaves both the banking system and the Fund's stabilization plan in a shambles. However, Fund conditionality through a well-designed adjustment program that also addresses banking problems can be an effective means of permanently improving the performance of member countries' financial sectors.

Emerging Markets Pose a Special Challenge

Emerging markets, including the former communist states, pose special challenges. These markets are characterized by extremely short maturities on financial liabilities, so interest rate shocks are transmitted almost immediately through to borrowers. Heavy dependence on foreign borrowing to finance high levels of investment loads exchange rate risk on banks or their customers—risks that because of hubris or limited market options may be largely unhedged. A political commitment by the government to hold the exchange rate firm will, of course, exacerbate the tendency to take unhedged exchange rate positions. Compounding the problem is the fact that banks in these markets may have poor asset quality to begin with because of insider dealing and weak supervision. Low public confidence in banks and in the authorities can quickly trigger bank runs and capital flight. A lack of transparency in these markets feeds the worst fears of both domestic and foreign depositors and investors. Consequently, banks in emerging markets are both more likely to be subjected to macroeconomic shocks—internal and exogenous—and less able to absorb them.

The first task for the Fund and its partners is to develop regulatory and policy guidelines tailored to these emerging market conditions. As already mentioned, the IMF and the World Bank are working closely with the Group of Ten, the Bank for International Settlements, and the Basle group to do just that. Once these guidelines are agreed, the IMF will begin to proselytize.

Strengthening banking systems in the emerging markets is not just a matter of fine-tuning regulation and beefing up supervision. Poor supervision and lack of transparency in the financial sector often reflect more endemic weakness in the legal order generally and a poor quality of governance.

All emerging markets, by definition, are undergoing rapid change. The transition from a government-directed, relationship-based economy to a market-driven, rules-based system is difficult. In Asia, for example, deregulation may be extensive on paper, but governments remain reluctant really to let go, and economic actors may operate on the assumption that they will not, and therefore take excessive risks. In former communist states, Russia, for example, the old legal order has been destroyed, but a new order is not yet fully formed. Thus nonpayment of obligations is endemic and contracts are unenforceable. Many African countries have weak administrative capacity and corruption is rampant in both the public and private sectors.

The international establishment's attitude toward governance issues has undergone a profound change, from benign tolerance to recognition of governance as an economic factor with strong macroeconomic and microeconomic effects, including on the financial sector. Both the IMF and the World Bank are actively pressing member governments to root out corruption, improve the management of public funds, and increase the transparency and accountability of public management generally. The IMF has interrupted financial support for governments that fail to respond. Fund adjustment programs are also putting greater emphasis on the legal infrastructure, including property law, contract enforcement, and payments settlement. Such measures are obviously critically important in transforming former centrally planned systems into successful market-based economies. The Fund is beginning to apply the lessons learned in these transition countries to its work in other emerging markets and in developing countries generally, paying particular attention to banking supervision and regulation.

The IMF's biggest challenge will be to integrate financial market and regulatory expertise with its macroeconomic work on a day-to-day basis. This will require both some retraining and bringing in new people. However, the Fund's management and board are fully committed to this endeavor. Its importance will only grow as the IMF becomes more deeply engaged in capital account liberalization.

Part II. Bank Failures
in Latin American Countries

4

The Argentine Banking Crisis: Observations and Lessons

Danny M. Leipziger

The Argentine banking crisis, which followed closely on the heels of the Mexican crisis, was caused largely by factors that were external to Argentina. That is not to say that the system had no weaknesses, and certainly the Convertibility Plan and the quasi-Currency Board added additional risks, but Argentina's economy was not mismanaged.

Argentina seems to be of those rare cases of a country whose macroeconomic fundamentals were basically sound, yet which suffered a banking crisis. It had a current economic deficit that was in the range of 3 to 4 percent of gross domestic product. It had stable political and economic structures. It had relatively high reserves. Its debt structure was long term. Argentina had also completed the bulk of its reforms, for example, in terms of privatization, and was therefore unlike Mexico. It did have one major weakness, the Currency Board itself, insofar as it had limited lender of last resort capacity. Seen differently, however, this limitation gave the peso its credibility.

The Crisis

In any event, the crisis in Argentina was extremely swift. Between December 1994 and the first quarter of 1995 the banking system lost about 16 percent of deposits, and the Central Bank lost about US$5 billion in reserves, one-third its total. Table 4.1 depicts the chronology of events in Argentina.

Table 4.1. *The December 1994–April 1995 Argentine Banking Crisis*

Event	Outcomes
Initial shock	• Domestic minicrisis following failure of bond trading house shakes confidence and causes banks to cut lines to these *mayoristas*. • Tequila effect shakes confidence in Latin America and investors re-evaluate Argentine exposure. • Stock and bond markets suffer large losses. • Banks call in loans extended to dealers and provincial banks, now largely insolvent because of earlier mismanagement.
Aftershock	• Sensing increased risks to convertibility, deposit withdrawals begin that amount to US$2 billion in two weeks. • Liquidity crisis forces banks to cut credit lines. • Central Bank persuades top five banks to provide US$250 million safety net. • Central Bank establishes second net via reserve requirement reduction of top 25 banks, yielding US$790 million.
Continuing crisis	• Deposits fall further during January–March 1995, reaching 16 percent reduction or US$8 billion. • Interbank interest rates skyrocket. • Dollarization increases. • Central Bank extends extraordinary liquidity assistance above limits of bank capital and for longer than 30 days, totaling US$1.7 billion rediscounts and US$300 million repos. • Some banks fail.
Freefall stops	• International package (International Monetary Fund, World Bank, Inter-American Development Bank) plus domestic and international bond issues restore confidence. • Strong commitment to convertibility maintained, although reserve level falls by US$5 billion, close to minimum possible. • Deposit insurance (limited, privately financed) announced. • Dual bank restructuring funds to private provincial banks and to restructure private banks established with aid of multilateral banks. • Fiscal strengthening plans announced. • Bank consolidation as 28 cooperative and 5 wholesale banks close.
Results	• Provincial banks moribund, 15 in process of privatization or closure or are acquired. • Top 10 private banks increase market share as deposits begin to return.

Source: Caprio and others (1996).

The initial crisis started in a particular segment of the banking system, the wholesale banks, many of which were overextended. Jittery investors began to withdraw from Argentina. Falling stock and bond prices created difficulties for some banks, liquidity was affected, resulting in enormously high interbank rates. Provincial banks lost their sources of distress financing and many became technically insolvent.

The Central Bank reacted quickly and tried to establish an effective safety net, basically drawing on the stronger banks and relying on the mandated extremely high reserve requirements. The Central Bank tried to recycle some of the excess liquidity, inevitably from stronger to weaker commercial banks, but legal and political issues limited its ability to act on provincial banks.

The crisis reached tremendous proportions, with a reduction of deposits of US$8 billion in the course of three months and a flight to quality, for instance, people moving accounts not only into U.S. dollars, but also to foreign branch banks. The Central Bank again responded with some extraordinary liquidity assistance, which allowed it to give liquidity to banks for longer than 30 days and in excess of their net worth. This required emergency legislation to amend the Central Bank's charter. Nevertheless, some banks did fail and a crisis of confidence ensued.

You can imagine being in Argentina, looking at the newspaper every day, and comparing the stock of international reserves and the money supply, and when they got very close, under the Convertibility Plan it was clear what could happen, as the money supply was fully backed by reserves. The free fall was finally stopped by a change in these expectations, a firm policy announcement by Domingo Cavallo, the minister of finance, and external assistance. First, the government announced fiscal austerity measures, unusual in a crisis, but important for Argentina, and issued some international bonds to restore confidence and provide additional liquidity. Second, it did finally obtain an international package from the International Monetary Fund, the World Bank, and the Inter-American Development Bank. Third, the government announced a deposit insurance scheme, which was extremely limited, but was meant to allay the fears of smaller depositors, and it did let some banks fail. (The choice facing Minister Cavallo at that juncture was either to let banks fail or to lose the Convertibility Plan itself.)

A major factor that influenced this crisis was that the Argentine banking system had a tremendous proportion of its assets in public banks, roughly half of the system's assets. Within that public sector, assets were split approximately 50-50 between the Banco de la Nación de Argentina (BNA), the large federal public bank, and a whole host of provincial and municipal banks. Initially, weaknesses in the provincial and municipal banks, as well as some wholesale traders, exacerbated the difficulties in the banking system, resulting in a contagious loss of confidence.

The economic fundamentals in Argentina wère quite good at the time, and banking supervision was reasonably good. Capital requirements were higher than elsewhere, at 11.5 percent, 8 percent in Tier One capital. Nevertheless, during this crisis the wholesale banks lost 70 percent of their deposits, the provincials lost 40 percent, and the commercial banks lost 30 percent, so the system suffered a tremendous shock. The remarkable thing is that in the end the system was able to rebound, with some banking failures and some losses, but basically within a year deposits were up to their original levels and the system survived, albeit with a smaller number of banks (table 4.2).

Vulnerability to Crisis

The following five aspects of the Argentine banking system made it susceptible to banking crises:

- The provincial banks were extremely weak. Estimates indicated that they had nonperforming portfolios of about 40 percent before the crisis.
- The BNA, although reasonably well-managed, was basically "too large to fail," a dangerous state of affairs. Admittedly, the BNA was a useful instrument for the government during the crisis, because the government was able to use it to recycle liquidity. Nevertheless, in the aftermath of the crisis the BNA itself restructured many of its loans, and no one knows exactly either its condition or the true cost of that restructuring.

Table 4.2. *Consolidation of the Argentine Financial Sector, 1990–97*
(number of institutions)

Institution	Month/Year				
	12/90	12/94	12/95	12/96	03/97
Government owned	36	33	31	20	20
Private sector, domestic	57	66	56	64	61
Private sector, foreign	31	31	30	28	27
Cooperative	45	38	10	8	7
Other financial companies	51	37	30	26	26
Total financial system	220	205	157	146	141

Source: Banco Central de la Republica Argentina (1996).

- The questionable lending activities by some of the wholesale banks and quasi-banks also contributed. Many of these institutions took in high-rate deposits and lent money to weak provincial banks who were saddled with their own nonperforming loans, many to the provinces that were also their owners. This was the segment of the banking sector that was not easy for the superintendency to supervise because of Argentina's federal structure, and it was clearly in trouble.
- The phenomenon of veteran depositors was yet another contributing factor. Everyone in Argentina has the equivalent of an MBA in finance based on the history of the last 30 years, so that people read risk signals very quickly, and these produce rapid asset shifts.
- The quasi-Currency Board places significant restrictions on the lender of last resort capacity of the Central Bank. That capacity is not zero, because a portion of the currency can be backed by bonds, so it has a limited capacity to act as lender of last resort, but it is quite circumscribed and the Central Bank cannot add to its resources in a crisis unless it can borrow from other central banks or the Bank for International Settlements. (The former is difficult in a regional crisis and the latter proved to be largely unavailable.)

Resiliency in Crisis

A number of other factors contributed to Argentina's resiliency. One, as already mentioned, was the high capital requirements, well above the Basle norms. Reserve requirements were required to be at 32 percent of deposits, which was extremely high, but related to the Currency Board concept. Another important factor was that supervision had improved tremendously in Argentina in the previous few years, with new hirings in the superintendency, many more qualified people, and an active training relationship with the New York Federal Reserve Bank. To this some would add that the lack of deposit insurance was something in Argentina's favor: people had to be much more alert about where they put their funds.

Crisis management is clearly critically important. The Central Bank's quick response took the form of conditional liquidity and active encouragement of mergers and acquisitions. The economic team of Minister of Finance Cavallo, Central Bank Governor Rogue Fernandez, and the executive branch were able to work swiftly with the National Assembly to pass key legislative changes at the time of the crisis, first on the fiscal side to increase revenues and cut expenditures, but also to provide greater flexibility for the Central Bank to deal with suspended banks, basically by segregating their assets and being able to restructure and deal with troubled banks without getting caught up in the courts. The idea was to avoid putting a failed bank through the legal process, because that would take 10 years and not lead anywhere. The practical policy alternative was to give additional powers to the Central Bank to enable it to segregate parts of the balance sheet, place a certain proportion of the assets and liabilities of banks with other banks, and allow losses to be taken in the other areas.

Policy Lessons

Let us take a look at the lessons of the Argentine crisis and extract policy observations for other developing or transition countries. First, the government should keep a watchful eye on public sector banks, be they the provincial or municipal banks in Argentina, the state banks in Brazil, or the banks in Mexico, which in the end can carry implicit national or sub-national guarantees. None of Argentina's provincial governors wanted to see their banks fail, as they would be unable to explain to their constituents that the state government did not stand behind those deposits. Nevertheless, a number of provincial banks in Argentina did close, and many cooperatives were merged with the help of World Bank and Inter-American Development Bank loans.[1]

Second, the general consensus is that governments should let banks fail if that can be dealt with in a normal commercial fashion. Public policymakers tend to try to prevent bank failures, but in the end weaknesses tend to accumulate, and if a standard failure resolution process is not available, the outcome is structural weaknesses that can be detrimental when a crisis, such as the tequila effect, materializes. Systemic failure then becomes a possibility.

Third is the question of how to judge portfolio quality in a more dynamic sense. Portfolios that appear perfectly healthy one day can look quite unhealthy the next day depending on the external circumstances. In transition economies the situation may depend on what is happening with enterprise privatization, and in other developing countries on what is going on in the external environment, or so-called contagion.[2] This was the case in Argentina. Looking at the quality of the portfolio under various assumptions would therefore be helpful.

---

1. During 1996 at least nine provincial banks were privatized (that is, deals completed), following intervention in 1995. Many cooperatives were either acquired or merged.

2. Portfolio quality in East Asia, for example, has tended to be highly correlated with real estate prices.

Fourth, having the appropriate regulation and legislation in place, and giving the Central Bank enough power so that banks know that it means business, is key. An extremely important factor in Argentina (in contrast to Mexico) was that bank owners knew they would lose their equity. This forced many banks to look for acquisition partners and other ways to re-capitalize, but they only did so with the implicit threat of the Central Bank hanging over them. Bank closures have some positive demonstration effects, and that was a pretty clear lesson for the ensuing spate of mergers and acquisitions.[3] Of course, the Central Bank, in its eagerness to see mergers and acquisitions rather than outright closures, may sanction the consolidation of weak banks, either creating larger weak banks or increasing the risks of the stronger banks. Interestingly, the largest, strongest banks in Argentina refused to absorb many troubled banks in the aftermath of the crisis, despite inducements to do so.

Finally, the fiscal side is important as an indicator of how serious the government is in its actions. The entire rescue package for Argentina would not have succeeded had the government not been able to convince (a) the international community, that is, the International Monetary Fund and capital markets, that it was serious in its commitment to the convertibility plan and this required fiscal control; and (b) the multilateral development banks, namely, the World Bank and the Inter-American Development Bank, that it was serious about privatizing or closing moribund provincial banks and promoting the closure or acquisition of unviable commercial banks. In the end, therefore, successful crisis management depended on strong policy leadership.

References

Banco Central de la Republica Argentina. 1996. "Estados Contables de las Entidades Financieras." Buenos Aires.

Caprio, Gerard, Jr., Michael Dooley, Danny Leipziger, and Carl Walsh. 1996. "The Lender of Last Resort Function Under a Currency Board: The Case of Argentina." *Open Economies Review* 7: 195–220.

---

3. Between January 1995 and September 1995 eight banks were liquidated.

5

Lessons Learned from the Chilean Experience

Jorge Marshall

This chapter discusses the main lessons learned from the Chilean banking crisis of the 1980s, the basic principles of the regulatory framework that have been applied since the crisis, and banking regulation and supervision issues that still need to be dealt with.

Lessons Learned from the Crisis

The Chilean banking crisis took place in 1982–84. Its estimated cost ranges from 30 to 40 percent of GDP.

The ingredients of the crisis were a combination of erroneous macroeconomic policies and weak regulation. In the years before the crisis, the exchange rate was fixed, domestic inflation was running above international levels, and wages were indexed. This resulted in a significant misalignment of key prices, in particular, of domestic asset prices, the exchange rate, and wages.

The inconsistent macroeconomic policies also led to rapid credit expansion and large capital inflows into a banking sector that had been recently deregulated and whose supervision was weak. Nonfinancial conglomerates owned the banks, which lent to the companies that owned them, and connected lending was widespread throughout the Chilean banking sector. This led to situations in which the banks increased their capital base using money lent to banks by their owners. This type of connected lending has played an important role in most banking crises in Latin America. The only difference is that in the 1980s most of these operations were domestic, and in the 1990s some international counterpart was involved. In the later cases, where a conglomerate owns both a domestic and an off-shore bank, identification of the corporate structure and regulation are more difficult.

Although deposits were not insured according to the law, previous bailouts of banks by the government resulted in full insurance of depositors. This led to the belief that deposit insurance was generalized. This implicit deposit insurance and the lack of transparency about banks' financial conditions exercised a considerable role in depositors' complacent behavior in regard to the risks that the banks were taking. This exacerbated moral hazard problems in the banks, thereby increasing risk taking in credit and investment.

For example, some banks went bankrupt when they borrowed abroad to finance credit to the nontradables sector, like real estate. Even when a balance sheet shows that the values of assets and liabilities are equal, the underlying values at "normal" prices may not be equal. The difference is usually excessive risk taken by the bank. If there is a change in the interest rate or exchange rate to normal values, the correction in the value of credit is much larger in the nontradables sector. Also, as prices change, the net value of the firm or the market value of collateral of banks' loans also change, with an additional negative effect on adverse selection and moral hazard problems.

Principles of Prudential Regulation and Stability

After the 1982–84 debt crisis in Latin America, new ideas about prudential regulation spread to several countries. Chile was one country that learned the lessons of the crisis rapidly and approved a completely new approach to banking regulation and supervision. Several other Latin American countries have also adopted the same approach toward prudential regulation.

The first element of the new standards was capital adequacy. The General Banking Law enacted after the 1982–84 crisis did not require banks to follow the capital adequacy guidelines outlined by the Basle regulations, but a banking bill passed in the Congress during 1997 does contain such standards. The new capital requirement will take the Basle Committee guidelines as a minimum, and will incorporate incentives for banks to have stringent capital-asset ratios.

Most Latin American countries have adopted standards for capital-asset ratio superior to the Basle recommendation of 8 percent based on the notion that banks in emerging markets face higher risks than banks in industrial countries. The minimum ratio in Brazil is 8 percent, in Argentina it is 11.5

percent, and in the Chilean legislation it is 8 percent, but the law also encourages a ratio of 10 percent by offering more expeditious treatment in the supervision process for international operations. Debate on what is the optimal capital-asset ratio for Latin American banks continues.

The second component of the new standards was a limited deposit insurance scheme, which was introduced in the 1980s. More recently other countries, such as Argentina, have also introduced such insurance schemes, although with different characteristics.

The case of Argentina is interesting in the importance that policymakers have given to the liquidity standards of banks. Today, total liquid assets over liabilities in Argentinean banks amount to 11 to 20 percent, and if one takes into account the new system of international repurchasing agreement, liquid assets are close to 30 percent. The emphasis on liquidity is due to the currency board arrangement, which is linked to the free convertibility regime of the Argentinean peso at a fixed exchange rate. The more restricted the deposit insurance and the maneuverability of the lender of last resort, the larger the role of banks' liquidity standards. In these circumstances, any loss in confidence by depositors that may lead to liquidity problems is first addressed using liquidity held by the banks, rather than by a liquidity facility, as may be the case in countries that use their central bank's lender of last resort facility. More recently, the Argentinean government created a private deposit insurance fund and a contingent international liquidity with private foreign institutions. The liquidity requirement played an important role in the Argentinean banking sector after the contagious effect of the Mexican crisis. While liquidity is an adequate tool for dealing with contagion problems, capital and strong regulatory tools are the only solution for the kind of distorted behavior that leads to losses in the value of bank assets.

Other tools of prudential regulation are limits on connected lending and single borrowers; loan assessment and provisioning (this is an early warning system for banks); and standards on market risk exposures, especially for foreign currency risk, that establish that net foreign denominated assets may not exceed in absolute value 20 percent of capital and reserves.

Information generation and disclosure are other components of reforms of the regulatory framework in Chile and in other countries. The use of private risk-rating systems and the increasing role of institutional investors, such as pension funds, are complementary to the disclosure policy. Also, directors of public companies are considered responsible for the main boards' decisions. These are all steps Chile took after the banking crisis. Subsequently, Argentina has been moving fast in the same direction.

Limiting the scope of banks' activities may restrict risk taking. In Chile the 1986 Banking Law allowed banks to conduct a series of new businesses in addition to traditional banking. At that time banks were not allowed to keep shares in their portfolios except for completing the repayment of a nonperforming loan or for investing in their own subsidiaries. Capital assigned to subsidiaries must be deducted from the capital of the bank. The 1986 law authorized banks to conduct several financial businesses through subsidiaries such as leasing, factoring, financial advisory, mutual funds, closed-end funds, and securities brokerage.

In Chile the 1986 Banking Law established a prompt corrective action mechanism for solving insolvency in financial institutions. First, when a bank is detected to have solvency problems (measured through relevant indicators established by law), its director has to call the shareholders to vote for or against preventive capitalization. If it does not work, a creditor agreement mechanism may operate as a private solution device to bankruptcy. The agreement may consist of the capitalization of debt, debt forgiveness, and extension of debt maturity. The agreement will not affect the deposits guaranteed by the Central Bank (demand deposits). Only if the creditor agreement is finally rejected by the superintendency or the creditors themselves, the bank gets into a situation of forced liquidation.

These criteria occurred during a period when macroeconomic stability started to be followed and when structural and institutional reforms were conducted, such as tax incentives to stimulate investment and savings, debt-equity swaps to reduce overindebtedness, trade reform to open the economy more, and changes in the institutional framework for corporations to enhance corporate governance.

Most Latin American countries are now introducing these principles of prudential regulation. The performance of the Chilean banking sector demonstrates the benefits of learning the lessons and applying the right preventive measures. Table 5.1 presents an overview of the Chilean banking sector. It indicates that during 1985–97 the performance of the banking system has become more sound as a result of the new regulatory principles, macroeconomic stability, and the development of an adequate institutional framework. Provisions are the allowances for the estimated loan losses, which are based on a system that categorizes loan portfolios. These provisions have been decreasing over time. The leverage ratio is the debt-equity ratio. Under the 1986 Banking Law, which was recently amended, a bank's obligations to third parties (including deposits) could not exceed 20 times the bank's capital and reserves. However, to get the highest rating the leverage ratio needed to be less than 17. This ratio has averaged around 11 or

12 in the recent years, with some fluctuation. The Chilean legislation has now introduced the Basle regulations for capital adequacy. Nonperforming loans have been declining from about 3.5 percent of all loans in the mid-1980s to less than 1 percent in recent years. Credit growth has been substantial; however, given the levels of bank penetration into new markets and clients and the economy's high growth rate, credit growth is within safe bounds. Finally, banks' profitability has been high for international standards, although it has been diminishing in recent years.

Overall Chile's banking sector is performing well. Financial stability faces no important risks or significant dangers. This behavior is also related to the economy's achievements, which are higher growth rates and lower inflation than in the past.

Bank Regulation

Bank regulation is a dynamic issue. Technology changes, new competitive forces arise, and new financial products replace old products. This requires an evolving approach to banking regulation. The following paragraphs discuss three important issues in bank regulation in Latin America: international banking, disclosure and market discipline, and capital market development.

Table 5.1. Bank Performance in Chile, 1985–96

Year	Provisions (percentage of loans)	Leverage (ratio)	Nonperforming loans (percentage of loans)	Credit (percentage of growth)	Profit (percentage of capital)
1985	8.1	11.8	3.5	21.1	19.6
1986	7.3	9.2	3.5	18.2	13.5
1987	5.5	9.8	2.7	26.6	20.0
1988	5.0	9.9	2.0	22.5	28.4
1989	4.3	10.6	1.9	33.5	26.3
1990	4.7	9.8	2.1	18.4	22.9
1991	4.5	10.2	1.8	22.4	16.8
1992	3.2	11.1	1.2	34.6	17.6
1993	2.7	11.2	0.8	29.4	22.1
1994	1.6	11.1	1.0	14.3	20.1
1995	1.4	12.1	0.9	27.6	20.0
1996	1.3	11.8	1.0	18.8	18.3

Source: Central Bank of Chile data.

International Banking

International banking introduces new issues into the regulation of banks. Most of them are already in practice in industrial countries, but few are practiced in emerging markets. The whole topic of international banking has changed in such markets, from the receipt of lending that originated in industrial countries to a number of new situations, including investment in subsidiaries and branches abroad and cross-border banking.

It is important to distinguish between two stages in the process of bank internationalization. The first stage consists of the participation of cross-border lending into Chile and the physical installation of foreign banks in Chile. That process has already taken place since the 1970s, with beneficial effects on competition, technology, and improvements in risk controls. Moreover, the country benefits from fewer problems of connected lending, good supervision from abroad, and greater stability of financial flows. A second stage of development occurs when domestic banks start to go international through cross-border operations or investment in subsidiaries and branches abroad.

Many Latin American banks now have a regional strategy that covers their operations in several countries. Others may want to lend from one country to another. Regulations must cover these new types of operations, but given their novelty, policymakers must accumulate experience and proceed cautiously. Chile, for example, has recently authorized banks to finance international trade contracts to third countries and to do commercial lending abroad. Another new challenge is the supervision of branches or subsidiaries of domestic banks in other Latin American countries.

International banking introduces new dimensions in the management of risk: country and exchange rate risk. In addition, international banking gives rise to increased competition, which may mean more entries into and exits from the domestic banking sector. These new risks demonstrate the limitations of uniform capital-asset ratio criteria and pave the way for debate of more comprehensive, detailed, and firm-specific methods for measuring and monitoring risk.

Parallel and off-shore banks introduce other types of issues into international banking. These are domestic banks owned by a financial conglomerate or banks whose headquarters are located in countries that do not have strong regulatory frameworks or good information gathering and disclosure systems. Similar problems may arise when a domestic bank or the owners of the bank own a branch or a subsidiary abroad not subject to good supervision from the country of origin. This type of parallel banking has recently been present in Ecuador, Peru, and Venezuela, and was the case in Chile in the 1980s.

Another recent trend is the burgeoning growth of regional financial networks or organizations. Currently owners of Chilean, Mexican, and Spanish banks are buying banks in other Latin American countries.

The international dimension of banking represents an important opportunity for introducing more efficient financial services, technical innovations, and sounder competition; however, it is also a source of new risks that the regulatory framework needs to take into account. Under the traditional framework Chile had branches of foreign banks with industrial country supervisors doing most of the work. Now Chile needs to do the same work locally. This topic is the most important part of the new banking bill.

Perhaps the main concern in international banking is that a low risk country, with the lowest financing costs of any foreign country in the region, but still more expensive than international funds from industrial economies, funds other countries where the risk is higher. Chile does not have an advantage of low cost funds when compared to industrial economies, so the question is, what is the advantage of a Latin American country with respect to its neighbors? The cost of funds in any Latin American country is higher than the cost of funds in a world financial center. However, the advantage lies in having better information for companies closely linked to the domestic economy. Monitoring borrowers' behavior, producing and gathering information, and designing financial products may be more efficient when closer to the borrower, but the regulatory framework needs to distinguish between these real advantages and pure country risk intermediation.

Disclosure and Market Discipline

Another issue that will become important in emerging markets is the introduction of disclosure standards and market discipline criteria in the regulatory process. Everyone agrees that this is essential, and most Latin American countries are moving in this direction by asking for more information on banks' policies and performance. Moreover, banks are satisfying this requirement. However, market discipline is linked to the quality of the institutions that read and process the information, which include financial news media, financial analysts, investment advisers, and the institutions participating in the financial system. In emerging markets these actors are less developed than in industrial economies. Under these conditions, the supply of more information will have an effect over time as the market increases its interest in banks' financial condition.

The movement toward requiring increased disclosure of information is apparent, as well as the concern about the quality of that information. In this connection Chile has an efficient accounting system for banks and publicly traded corporations, and Argentina is also moving in this direction.

Complementary to the disclosure of information, Argentina set up a system in which banks have to issue subordinated bonds as a way to increase the discipline obtained from the market. This recently launched initiative will provide a device to monitor the financial condition of each bank.

In Chile, private rating agencies and the official system of bank rating are playing an important role. The experience with subordinated bonds may also provide a market assessment of banks' risk and constitute an early warning indicator. While a private rating classification industry is good, a market assessment is better.

The assumption behind these initiatives is that market capacity to assume a new role in the supervision process is available. In Chile this market capacity has been developed by the pension funds, which are active institutional investors. The pension funds have a demand for information and the professional capacity to process it. Insurance companies play a similar role. Thus the demand for information is associated with the development of a long-term capital market. If a well-developed, long-term capital market exists, there will be a demand for information, and disclosure will lead to market discipline.

The development of market capacity to help supervise Latin America banks is in an intermediate stage of development. Some countries are more advanced, but the institutional framework in which markets operate needs to be improved. This is also important given that market discipline encourages the introduction of new technologies and products into the financial system.

Capital Market Development

The final issue is the relationship between the relative decline of commercial banking and the expansion of other financial institutions in the capital markets. This is a process that started more than a decade ago in the industrial countries and is more recent in emerging markets, although Chile has experienced this disintermediation phenomenon for almost a decade.

The changes in the financial market structure raise several issues for banking regulation, leaving aside the effects on monetary policy. First, there are operations that both banks and nonbank financial institutions can carry out, but in a different regulatory setting. The consequences are usually that banks start to increase their scope of activities, which implies that they face new risks that need to be analyzed and supervised.

Second, banks and nonbank financial institutions are frequently connected by a holding company or a conglomerate. Thus Chile is likely to see an increase in the creation and expansion of financial conglomerates. This requires guidelines and supervision. The existence of financial conglomerates without strict regulation increases the moral hazard and adverse selection problems in the behavior of banks and related parties. This feature of financial conglomerates is prominent in most Latin American countries, including Chile, Colombia, Mexico, and Peru. The general rule should be consolidated supervision of financial conglomerates, with global standards of capital adequacy, according to a conglomerate's risks.

Another topic in capital market development is licensing criteria. Currently most countries are experiencing a reduction in the number of banks and a consolidation in their structure. Some countries will probably see an increase in the number of licenses granted and in banking competition. In the 1990s in Chile the number of banks has fallen from 40 to 33 as a result of no new entrants, exits, and mergers. In the future, however, as a result of the application of the new law, Chile will have more explicit entry conditions, and hence more competition.

6

Lessons from Recent Global Bank Failures: The Case of Brazil

Paul L. Bydalek

This chapter is written from the perspective of a leading Brazilian rating agency with easy access to the executive management of Brazil's principal banks. These insights are different from those of regulators or consultants. Bankers provide rating agencies with confidential insights into their operations and describe their competitive strategies, plans, and problems. By inference, the rating agency learns about the foibles of their competition. Dozens of due diligence sessions give rating agencies intimate knowledge about institutions and the system.

Brazil's transition in three years from hyperinflation to predictable stability put pressure on the financial system. Action by the monetary authorities and about 50 bank failures and other mergers provide extraordinary raw material for analyses and hypotheses. Observing these events gives us abundant suggestions on how to predict banker behavior, and possibly how to prevent failures. The observations that follow are based exclusively on empirical observation of the Brazilian "laboratory." What becomes evident is that Brazil's experiences, while apparently unique, are similar to those of most other countries, only taking place more rapidly.

Classic central bank monitoring can no longer work. Banks are too complex; transactions are now multidimensional and transnational; and market circumstances are too dynamic for government agencies to follow, understand, and discipline. The regulator's role has changed to providing a level playing field, to preventing catastrophic disruptions, and to feeding the marketplace with sufficient data to permit effective regulation and natural selection by the market.

Brazil is different from the typical Latin American country in a number of ways, and one must try not to compare Brazil with Argentina and Mexico. By most economic measures, Brazil accounts for about half of Latin America. Exports and imports each represent less than 10 percent of GDP, thereby permitting Brazil the luxury of little dependence on outsiders, except for financing. There is also a vast cultural difference between Brazil and the rest of Latin America, partly because of Brazil's Portuguese roots, and partly because of its size and complexity. A grassroots democracy in place since the mid-1980s with more than a dozen significant political parties means the need for endless political negotiation to accomplish any reforms. Change is slow, but lasting.

Laws governing economic activity and the financial markets are many and changing, and need continuing interpretation, which reflect the country's Portuguese heritage. The business model, however, is that of the United States, where most leaders are educated. The letter of the law, not the spirit, is the rule. Exploiting loopholes spells success and accolades. Enforcement of most laws is weak, with impunity common for the privileged. White-collar crime is rarely disciplined.

Contrary to many countries, the Central Bank does not publish data on individual banks, and gathering homogenous data over several years is troublesome. Horizontal comparisons over years require reclassification of accounts and careful selection of data. All banks must publish audited financial statements with June 30 and December 31 data and an accompanying auditor's opinion and explanatory notes in widely circulated newspapers. Collecting and collating data from the bottom up is almost the only method of monitoring the system available to analysts outside the Central Bank.

Until mid-1994 intense inflation provided banks with most of their revenues and enabled them to enjoy extraordinary profits. Inflation in 1993 was more than 2 percent per working day. Currently inflation is running at less than 8 percent per year. In 1993 float income represented more than 50 percent of revenues for most branch banks, but float is now less than 2 percent. In 1993 GDP data showed that financial activity represented 16 percent of all activity. In 1995 this figure fell to 7 percent, is much lower today, and is falling. These events forced a contraction in the size of the financial system.

Tables 6.1 and 6.2 show changes in the system during recent years and form the basis for the rest of this chapter.

Table 6.1. *Number of Brazilian Banks, 1980–96*

Year	Number of banks [a]
1980	116
1981	116
1982	119
1983	118
1984	116
1985	112
1986	110
1987	108
1988	111
1989	184
1990	219
1991	216
1992	233
1993	245
1994	246
1995	241
1996	234

a. The definition of what constitutes a bank is unknown.
Source: Federacaõ Brasileira de Bancos' – Febraban.

Table 6.2. *Number of Licenses Granted to Brazilian Financial Institutions by Type of Institution, June 1994 and April 1997*

Type of institution	June 1994	April 1997
Commercial banks	34	38
Multiple banks	212	189
Development banks	6	6
Investment banks	17	23
Savings banks	2	2
Cooperative societies	853	984
Finance companies	42	46
Securities brokers	244	205
Exchange brokers	43	39
Securities dealers	371	266
Investment societies	4	2
Leasing companies	67	74
Mortgage companies	24	20
Savings and loan companies	2	2

Source: Banco Central do Brasil.

The 1982 Mexican crisis had little effect on Brazil's local banking system, reflecting the country's self-sufficiency. In the mid-1980s three major banks closed. At the time, rumors about problems at Bamerindus, Econômico, and Nacional were circulating. Only in late 1994, with stabilization, did the number of banks begin to fall.

Before the 1988 constitutional reform the number of banks was roughly constant, with virtually no new licenses granted. The new constitution of 1988 permitted anyone with reasonable credentials and less than US$5 million in capital to open a new bank. Many brokers became bankers, and given the prevalent intense inflation and instability, the primary activity of banks and brokers was trading in government securities and interest arbitrage.

As frequently occurs in Brazil, data sometimes conflict, and data from the Central Bank inexplicably differs from that shown in table 6.1. Part of the difference resides with the definition of banks. Brazil has both privately owned banks and government owned banks. Each can be divided into other categories, particularly multiple (or universal), commercial, savings, and investment banks. As table 6.2 shows, during 1980–96, on a net basis, 23 multiple banks closed, while 4 commercial banks and 6 investment banks opened. Brokerage operations suffered the greatest attrition, falling by 148 to 510. Brazilian securities are now traded in New York, international securities firms are now operating in Brazil, and larger Brazilian banks are spreading into brokerage.

Since mid-1994, about 50 banks have closed, most with intervention by the authorities. Others have merged. Simultaneously, new banks have been opening, some sponsored by private Brazilian capital, but most with international backing. Although the 1988 constitution freezes foreign participation in the system, if national interests are well served, the president can grant special licenses to international banks. President Cardoso has authorized Rabo, Banque National de Paris, Morgan Stanley, CS First Boston, Merrill Lynch, and Ford, among others, to open wholly owned operations and granted joint venture approvals to others.

The disappearance of inflation and the return to traditional banking caused many disruptions and consolidations within the local system. The arrival of international competition will narrow margins further. Banks without a well-defined strategy and niche will disappear during the next few years.

During 1985 through mid-1997 the Central Bank had 11 presidents managing monetary policy for Brazil. Thus during the period of intense inflation and numerous new bank openings, the turnover of Central Bank presidents was high. In 1989, when 73 new banking licenses were granted, the

Central Bank had two presidents, each of whom served for six months. Continuity of management is a valid business principle that was ignored during these turbulent years. It is foolish to expect a political appointee, whose career might be short-lived, who is injected into a complex managerial situation and subject to myriad pressures from politicians and business people, to introduce long-term discipline and lasting change. Only when the second and third echelons of government are convinced and receive strong leadership will lasting change actually occur.

Five years ago the Banco do Brasil, Banespa, Bamerindus, Econômico, and Nacional were among Brazil's most prominent banks, but all have suffered in the intervening years. Since 1995 the government controlled Banco do Brasil has conducted itself much like a private bank, avoiding political involvement and loans. Cleaning up the prior abuse caused the write-off of billions of dollars in loans and the need for a capital injection of US$8 billion in early 1996. The Central Bank intervened in Banespa, owned by the state of São Paulo, in December 1994, and no published financial statements have been available since then. Losses exceed US$25 billion, with ownership now being transferred to the federal government for privatization. The government seized Bamerindus, Econômico, and Nacional and passed them on to private investors. In addition, the government used more than US$20 billion for bailouts for seven private banks under a special program.

During 1992–96, as seen in tables 6.3 and 6.4, private banks at least doubled their equity, basically by retained earnings. Citibank was the largest international bank. The performance of Excel was phenomenal, with equity expanding fivefold following its acquisition of the defunct Econômico together with minority investors. Since 1994 Banespa and other government owned banks have been withering, losing market share, facing up to enormous bad asset problems, with most destined to become defunct.

Note that in the mid-1980s a banking crisis forced the closing of several institutions. Bancos Bamerindus, Econômico, and Nacional were cited as fragile and as targets for a takeover or intervention. Politically connected owners bought support and a second life. A decade later the inevitable occurred and all three closed.

Even before the onset of stability in July 1994, loans were expanding as dollar funding into Brazil began, with the largest increase occurring during the second half of 1994. Deposits plateaued, with major growth occurring off balance sheet as money market funds. These funds, always managed by banks, currently total about US$120 billion. All government owned

Table 6.3. *Largest Brazilian Banks by Equity, December 1992*

Bank	US$ millions
Banco do Brasil	6,178
Bradesco	2,508
Itaú	1,818
Banespa	1,212
Real (group)	711
Unibanco	603
Bamerindus	602
Mercantil de São Paulo	484
Econômico	437
Nacional	418
Excel	48
Total	15,019
Total less Banco do Brasil	8,841

Source: Atlantic Rating.

banks and many mid-sized commercial banks have encountered difficulty in changing with the macroeconomic situation. Many bank owners would like to sell, but buyers are few and selective. As time passes, these owners must decide how to abandon banking, retrieving their capital and redeploying it elsewhere. Postponement of this decision will cause future bank failures.

Table 6.4. *Largest Brazilian Banks by Equity, December 1996*

Bank	US$ millions	Growth since 1992 (percent)
Bradesco	5,384	114.7
Banco do Brasil	5,380	-12.9
Itaú	3,868	112.8
Unibanco	2,085	245.5
Real (group)	1,543	116.9
Bamerindus	1,270	111.0
Mercantil de São Paulo	985	103.7
BCN	937	145.3
Safra	715	150.9
Citibank	569	142.1
Excel Econômico	510	962.5
Total	23,246	54.8
Total less Banco do Brasil	17,866	102.1

Source: Atlantic Rating.

System Weaknesses

System weaknesses include the following: protected activity until 1994, loose enforcement, impunity, a strong lobby, and no credit culture.

Until 1989 virtually no new banks could be formed, with the Central Bank being extremely selective about licenses sold, even auctioned, or awarded. The constitutional reform in 1989 permitted virtually anyone to start a bank. Until 1994, banks faced few challenges beyond inflation, and most reported handsome profits during these years. Inflation suspended classical banking. Lending in local currency was short term, 30 days, to match certificate of deposit funding. Inflation camouflaged problems; delinquencies would wither and disappear. Banking was money brokering.

With few problems, system monitoring was lax and enforcement of regulations loose. Until 1986 no legislation defined crimes against the financial system. A government official recently reported (*O Globo* newspaper, May 18, 1997) that during 1986–95 the Central Bank identified 682 crimes against the financial system sufficient for reporting to the justice system for prosecution. Only three crimes resulted in condemnation.

Impunity exists today for the bankers involved in bank failures since 1994. While several investigations by the justice system are under way, only one banker is under house arrest pending completion of investigations. In general, white-collar crime goes unpunished.

Another characteristic of Brazilian banking is that the Central Bank maintains a tight and complex net of regulations over the system, but bankers are encouraged to find and exploit loopholes. Bankers are expected to fulfill the letter of the law, not the spirit. Loopholes are windows of opportunity. Creativity is rewarded with profits. The bankers' agility is far greater than that of the regulators.

Bankers also enjoy an unusually strong lobby in Congress and with the executive branch of government. The banking associations are effective in obtaining favorable legislation for activities. Nonetheless, banks pay higher income taxes than other commercial and industrial activities.

Inflation prevented the development of a credit culture. Financial projections were deemed nearly worthless, borrowers' financial statements were considered to be unreliable, and funding was short term. Cash flow lending did not exist. As stability arrived in mid-1994, banks expanded loan assets, usually to the consumer or to the middle market. Money managers became lenders. Many subsequent bank failures were caused by foolish lending by inexperienced bankers.

System Strengths

System strengths can be summed up as follows: bankers tested by 2 percent per day inflation; technology denial until 1991, followed by catch-up activity; a society that embraces change; a cashless society with all payments in banks; few loans, high Basle ratios; no dollarization ever; a crawling peg exchange rate; audited statements twice a year; and grass-roots change.

The Brazilian commercial and financial system (universal banks) is largely patterned after the U.S. model. A major difference is that banks with multiple licenses can engage in virtually any capital market, commercial banking, investment banking, credit card issuance, stock exchange brokerage, or leasing activity. Most banks are now acquiring life and casualty insurance subsidiaries and moving into pension fund management. The banks manage all money market mutual funds.

The country is sufficiently large and diversified so that connected lending inside Brazil is uncommon. While abuse does occur, enforcement is efficient.

The intense inflation of the 1980s and early 1990s, combined with churning politics, tested all private entrepreneurs. Most survived by cutting their dependence on the government and cultivating self-sufficiency. Those bankers who are prospering today are generally the same professionals that operated during those turbulent times and are proven, competent managers.

Until 1991 Brazil barred imports of software and hardware. With the relaxation of barriers, state-of-the-art technology was imported, always for the front office and sometimes for the back office. Substantial gains from float motivated high investment in technology to control money flows. The technology of some institutions is now superior to that of their northern hemisphere counterparts. Possibly because of this prior denial of imported technology, the culture embraces change. Cellular telephones, the Internet, and home banking are everywhere. The absence of obsolete equipment to discard has meant that local companies and individuals crave the most modern technology and are almost oblivious to its cost.

Individuals and companies make payments for most account receivables and payables through banks. Checks are rarely sent by mail for account settlement. Salaries and collections are credited by banks. Banks also collect rents, tuition, utility bills, and taxes as well as other predictable payments. Salaries of low-income workers are credited to bank accounts and accessed by ATM machines. People use checks to pay for very small purchases. Inflation created a cashless society.

Until the advent of stability, loan assets were a small proportion of total bank assets, and consequently capitalization ratios were lofty. Loans are now climbing and represent about 50 percent of the system's assets.

Correspondingly, capitalization ratios are falling. Nonetheless, Bank for International Settlements ratios for some banks exceed 20 percent, and for most banks exceed 12 percent. The loan delinquencies of early 1995 and the various subsequent failures intimidated bankers, who now undertake growth of loan assets more carefully.

Most Latin American economies permit transactions within their borders in local currency or in dollars. Even bank deposits are in both currencies. Brazil has always avoided dollarization of in-country transactions. With few exceptions, transactions must be in local currency. Since the introduction of the real in mid-1994, it has been the consistent measure of value, with the dollar used as a remote reference. Brazilians measure value in their own currency, and most people ignore the dollar exchange rate.

The crawling peg exchange rate dissipates pressure for devaluation. Currently the currency is devaluing against the dollar at a rate close to changes in the domestic wholesale price index and price indexes of international trading partners. Authorities insist that despite building pressure, there will be no sudden change in the exchange rate to avoid rekindling an inflationary psychology.

Banks publish complete financial statements twice a year along with opinions by outside auditors, thereby enhancing credibility. Unfortunately, the Central Bank does not provide individual data on any bank to the marketplace, as is common elsewhere.

Change is occurring within all segments of Brazil, from the ground up, and not by decree. Society is negotiating change, with lobbies active everywhere. While this seemingly endless discussion results in slow forward movement, change is lasting. The various bankers' and industry associations constantly discuss with the authorities how to improve the system and to prevent new failures. Dialogue, negotiation, and a bottom-up democracy have replaced the dictatorial years of the past.

Management Strengthening

Proposals for improving management call for the following: lower turnover of senior staff and greater stability, freedom from political pressures, clear mission and immediate objectives, power to attain most objectives, and accountability.

Administration of the monetary system is a complex undertaking that requires unusual talents. For many years a hiring freeze on new government staff has been in place, so the actual number of staff is falling at a time when needs are greater than in the past. The high turnover rate of Central

Bank directors is the primary issue. The handful of directors and their support staff set policy and liaise with other parts of the government and the public. The remuneration paid to Central Bank directors is small compared to their earning potential in the marketplace and insufficient to compensate for the harassment from politicians and the public when they announce unpopular decisions. Besides, as their track record shows, a few months in office is a guarantee for later financial success. Managerial stability by professionals must be structurally encouraged.

The centralization of economic powers in the Central Bank and other executive and congressional departments encourages lobbying. Every municipality, state, agency, and economic association knows that intense pressure on the few decisionmakers can dilute new executive acts. The sheer number of executive orders issued offers unusual potential for lobbyists. Central Bank policymakers should be exempt from political pressures, possibly by fixed mandates, and by not serving at the mere pleasure of the executive branch.

Also needed is a clear, long-term mission with concise objectives that transcends individuals and directorates. Removing the personality factor from decisionmaking would permit the monetary machine to operate more efficiently. Today, the personality of the finance minister and the president of the Central Bank often determine policy and its method of execution. As people change, policies change.

Brazil's Central Bank both monitors monetary aggregates, fine-tuning macroeconomics, and supervises institutions. Political pressures spill over into the supervisory function. A split-off of the supervisory function into an autonomous unit will not automatically solve the political issue. Banks with strong patronage, all government banks, and some commercial banks with political connections will still be protected from discipline. The authorities should have dealt with Bancos Bamerindus, Econômico, and Nacional severely in the mid-1980s, but because of strong political and regional pressures, each escaped to explode later on a much grander scale. Central Bank inspectors could not enforce discipline, thus problems festered and grew. Without power to enforce regulations for all institutions, those with political protection are free to continue abusing the system. After an institution reaches the point of too big to fail, the government loses control totally. Later, the owners of failed institutions are rarely held responsible for their professional negligence, and retire from banking wealthy, leaving society to bear the onus of their behavior.

As government enforcement is lax and white-collar crime occurs with impunity, possibly the marketplace could address these cultural failings. If sources of funding for institutions—large depositors, debenture holders, and banks financing international trade—were to hold score cards for each bank, these sophisticated investors could monitor and induce change. As small problems occur within an institution, for instance, as the volume of renegotiated loans without cash inflow increases, the marketplace should somehow be notified. Subtle differences in delinquencies among institutions during a business slowdown would permit an entry on the score card. Investors should also monitor management actions to cure incipient problems. Variations between institutions would affect the cost of funding, penalizing the less professional organization and squeezing it back into conformity. The informational flow to the marketplace must be constant and thorough, permitting early identification of changes. Sudden discovery of problems when they are already pronounced could damage confidence in that institution, causing continuity problems. An increased flow of facts to the marketplace will permit efficient regulation via liability pricing to banks.

Reduced Political Pressure

Political pressure on the system needs to be reduced through long-term, staggered mandates; clear quantitative limits imposed on the system; automatic, reactive discipline if limits are breached; public censure, fines, and suspension for breachers; and early public disclosure of problems.

Professionalizing and depoliticizing management of the monetary system can cure the high turnover of top executives. The system should look for professionals serving long-term, staggered mandates who are protected from political caprice.

The need for constant interpretation of the multitude of regulations imposed in trying to close the windows of opportunity found by agile private bankers provides unusually great opportunities for abuse. Numerous and ever changing regulations, coupled with lax enforcement, cause bankers to test their limits, to push opportunities to the point of resistance of monetary authorities, who respond with subjective judgments and censures. Some limits, if breached, should have automatic and predictable consequences, for instance, nonperforming loans that exceed predetermined limits should automatically impede the expansion of total loans or bring about a tightening of loan-to-equity ratios, and should not require negotiation between authorities and the bank.

If automatic corrective action does not follow small breaches of limits, then banks and bankers should suffer veiled public censure, thereby permitting the marketplace to sniff out improprieties. Continued breaches should result in changes in management, overt public censure, fines, and suspension of selected activities. As the justice system is slow, the Central Bank should be empowered to discipline breaches of Central Bank regulations, with denial of access to the system and other internal measures. Gradual and continual disclosure to the market of improper conduct, with early veiled criticisms later transformed into loud action, in a highly predictable format, would pressure bankers. The efficiency of gradual market pressure is far greater than the quiet and invisible action that supposedly results from traditional Central Bank discipline.

Deposit Insurance

A deposit insurance scheme with a small deductible would put pressure on deposit authorities and cause depositors to be vigilant and not passive. Until 1994 Brazil had no deposit insurance, but with the many failures it was introduced. The new system is laudably managed by the banks themselves, with mandatory monthly contributions calculated on deposits, insuring 100 percent of all deposits up to about US$20,000. The government covers shortfalls at the insurance authority. The knowledge that their deposits are insured reduces the need for vigilance by small depositors. A coinsurance feature that requires even small depositors to suffer a slight loss would be healthy. With the general public oblivious to bank problems, smaller depositors operate in confidence. The three large failed banks cited earlier suffered little loss in savings deposits during the months preceding their closing, even with newspapers aggressively calling attention to their problems. Some migration of even small deposits from weaker to stronger institutions would cause bank management to be more responsive to the need for quality stewardship and worry the deposit insuring authority. Pressure from the market by small and sophisticated depositors and by peers should focus on institutions with deviant performance. The deposit insurance authority should pressure both the Central Bank and the problem institution to take prompt remedial action before losses occur.

Transparency

Transparency would be increased by semi-annual and quarterly updates, specially trained public auditors, standardized scope of audits set by authorities, personal liability placed on auditors and bank directors, standardized form of disclosure, concise and forward looking provisioning regulations, restructuring reported when problematical, and encouragement of rating agencies.

The marketplace discipline needs information to operate. A continuing flow of abundant, reliable data from each institution will permit the market to compare institutions, rewarding and penalizing as appropriate. Currently, all financial institutions must publish half-year financial statements, with accompanying explanatory notes and an auditor's opinion. Only banks with shares listed on stock exchanges must publish quarterly data. The quality of this reporting varies. A few confident and solid banks offer quarterly consolidated data audited by international auditors. Most offer unconsolidated data, with data about on-shore and offshore subsidiaries reported as investments. They offer virtually no data about the size or quality of these investments.

The complications of auditing a bank demand specially trained auditors, yet banks can use any of hundreds of auditors, many of whom lack the requisite specialized qualifications. While the audits fulfill the minimum standards set by the authorities, the scope of audits and the transparency of reporting vary widely. The scope of audits and the financial disclosure to the market should be standardized, with the common denominator substantially above current levels. A large, solid, and liquid institution should abide by the same criteria as a small, struggling institution, with both providing abundant, standardized disclosure. Quarterly, detailed, consolidated financial statements with opinions by auditors would permit efficient market regulation. The banks would bear the cost of the increased disclosure and auditing requirements.

Standardized disclosure will facilitate comparison to peers. Sophisticated investors will be empowered to price funding objectively and accurately. Any deterioration of basic ratios, such as the risk-asset-based capital ratio, would have immediate impact on funding costs.

Coupled with disclosure should be concise quantitative benchmarks. Bank management and directors and sophisticated investors can measure data against these benchmarks. Outsiders can make realistic judgments about performance. Subjectivity for provisioning for doubtful assets should be reduced, with basic rules for recognizing deteriorating assets clear, with little interpretation required. Cash inflow from a loan should be a basic quality criterion. Doubtful loans performing only on an accrual basis (no cash received) should be booked in financial statements clearly and separately. In addition, restructured loans, where management is concerned about ultimate payment, must be specially recognized on the balance sheet. Loans performing normally should be separated from those with signs of loss.

The wealth of data made available by banks could overwhelm depositors and investors, thereby camouflaging problems. Large institutional investors have the manpower to track complex data. To help less sophisticated investors, the authorities should encourage the presence of rating agencies. A rating agency specializing in banks soon acquires an in-depth understanding of the game playing bankers can indulge in. Peers call attention to their relative strengths and successful strategies, giving the insightful agency hints about where to search for problems elsewhere. Agencies meet with top executives of banks several times a year, and are able to query management about the confidential circumstances surrounding decisions. The agency with this confidential information, and after visits to peers to obtain other interpretations of market events, enjoys a unique perspective on the system. Conclusions expressed as ratings reinforce judgments made by sophisticated investors and are benchmarks for smaller investors.

Summary

Chemotherapy is required, but not life-threatening surgery. The adage "an ounce of prevention is worth a pound of cure" is appropriate in this instance.

Many of the problems of the Brazilian system could have been avoided with better disclosure by authorities and by banks. If enforcement by the authorities is lax or impossible, then let the market undertake part of this discipline. With continuous, standardized, and reliable disclosure, the market will reward and penalize. Nonstandardized and unreliable disclosure is the responsibility of the authorities. The market will never detect deceit, at least in the early stages. Clever accounting practices and smooth talking management will delude the market until problems become too significant to hide. When an efficient market cannot function, the problem becomes one that needs a Central Bank solution. Full transparency all the time should be a requirement. Treating small problems as they develop and appear reduces the danger of catastrophes later. When bank management is under the scrutiny of the market and peers, poor performance will be challenged early. Complex banking and modern informational technology change the historic regulatory role of the Central Bank.

Part III. Bank Failures
in Transition Economies

7

Restructuring Distressed Banks in Transition Economies: Lessons from Central Europe and Ukraine

Michael Borish and Fernando Montes-Negret

The collapse of central planning in Central and Eastern Europe (CEE) and the former Soviet Union (FSU) and the opening of their formerly socialist economies to the West presented enterprises and banks in these countries with an inescapable imperative: the need to undergo radical restructuring—by means of privatization, divestiture, liquidation, and/or reorganization. This had a number of consequences for the countries' banking sectors.

Macroeconomic Transition from Socialism and Implications for Banking Sectors

One outcome was that state-owned enterprises (SOEs) were suddenly and simultaneously faced with imported consumer goods of higher quality from the West, sharp reductions in state subsidies, the disappearance of traditional Council for Mutual Economic Assistance (CMEA) markets for output, and interruptions in the supply of critically needed energy imports for their top-heavy industrial sectors. In the worst case scenarios, economies experienced dramatic cuts in output because of the collapse of markets. These cuts were characterized by an initial period of inventory sell-offs and barter trade that ultimately culminated in arrears on most liability accounts (for example, wages, benefits, taxes, social security, bank debt, trade debt) as inventories and output subsequently diminished.

Faced with insufficient working and investment capital, many SOEs turned to banks to obtain credits that allowed them to escape hard budget constraints temporarily and to defer needed restructuring or liquidation. In some cases, hyperinflation mitigated the balance sheet effect, rewarding enterprise debtors for taking on obligations in currencies that were depreciating on a daily basis. However, the effect on the loan portfolios of state owned commercial banks' (SOCBs) was rapid deterioration. SOCBs had already inherited the burden of risky portfolios from the former monobank system.[1] The second stage of lending to SOEs led to a significant growth in nonperforming loans—in many cases unrecognized until new accounting standards and prudential regulations were in force—and a contraction of liquidity as monetary policy became restrictive to rein in the sometimes devastating and always damaging effects of inflation.[2] In CEE countries that were not part of the FSU, the banks' deteriorating position resulted in an increasing, but unquantified, liability for the state, as implicit deposit insurance and vested SOE interests looking to banks for financing precluded the closure of large SOCBs. In FSU countries, hyperinflation eliminated asset-liability values, but continued patronage of loss-making enterprises, initial major refinancings from central banks, and the run-up of arrears failed to provide the needed resources and confidence to put transactions on an efficient market basis.

In practice, governments pursued a range of approaches to deal with these problems. This chapter assesses banking sector restructuring (or the lack thereof) under distressed conditions in four countries: the Czech Republic,[3] Hungary, Poland, and Ukraine. All four of these countries have taken different approaches, although broad differentiations are apparent between

---

1. These portfolios were risky in three general ways: (a) heavy concentration of exposure to SOEs with large arrears to SOCBs, other SOEs, workers, and even to the state (taxes, pensions); (b) geographic risk, given the fragmented and specialized way in which the monobank system was split up; and (c) product risk (financing of industrial and arms exports to and construction projects in countries that sometimes proved to be significant credit risks).

2. Annualized inflation rates were as high as 4,735 percent in Ukraine in 1993 and 586 percent in Poland in 1990. Peak inflation rates were much more moderate in Hungary, 35 percent in 1991, and in the Czech-Slovak Federal Republic, 57 percent in 1991.

3. At the time of transformation, the Czech Republic was actually part of the Czech-Slovak Federal Republic. On January 1, 1993, the republic was officially disbanded and two independent countries were established: the Czech Republic and the Slovak Republic. This paper refers to the Czech Republic, but events prior to 1993 refer to the Czech-Slovak Federal Republic or to the earlier period of central planning of Czechoslovakia.

most FSU and CEE countries, which are highlighted in table 7.1. However, even within these categories, major differences exist. Ukraine differs widely from Estonia, and more recently Latvia, in its approaches and results, even though all three belong to the community of FSU countries. Likewise, approaches taken by the Czech Republic, Hungary, and Poland differed in the early 1990s, although they are now converging in some ways as the countries address structural, institutional, and policy weaknesses.

The Socialist Incentive Structure

At the outset of transformation, the CEE and FSU economies were highly distorted. The level of distortion varied, and was probably much less in Hungary, Poland, and the former Yugoslavia as reflected in levels of trade with Western markets in the 1980s and the higher proportion of private farming and land ownership compared with other CMEA countries.[4,5] However, as a general rule, the sectoral distribution of economic output was highly focused on industry. While agriculture was important for food security and as input into the agro-industrial sector, services were virtually nonexistent except in the form of transportation of and warehousing for inventories.[6] (Common to all transition countries has been the rapid emergence of the private sector in services, which has made up for this vacuum without having to compete with vested industrial and state farm interests from the socialist period [see Borish and Noël 1996].) Market-based consumer criteria in the domestic economy were subordinated to central planning prerogatives, although some exposure to global standards and quality requirements was evident, insofar as trade with non-CMEA markets existed. Market-based production and costing systems were absent because of constraints imposed on commercial competition. These characteristics reflected the organization, operations, and incentive structures of centrally planned economies whose primary focus was on production and specialization based on predetermined physical targets and plans, which were driven by Communist Party criteria and disregarded financial performance.

---

4. For instance, in 1989, exports of goods and services from Hungary and Poland to the European Community approximated US$3.2 billion and US$4.6 billion in value, respectively. Since the transformation, trade with the European Union has typically come to account for two-thirds of total exports. These values are now generally about three times the export values achieved in 1989–90.

5. In Poland, small farm plots remained private during the communist era. Likewise, the former Yugoslavia permitted private ownership of small farm plots and housing.

6. Yugoslavia had an active tourist trade in the 1980s, as did some of the Black Sea countries. Nevertheless, these were more of an exception than a rule throughout the CMEA.

Table 7.1. Initial Effects and Approaches to Banking Reform in Formerly Socialist Countries

Category	Central and Eastern Europe	Former Soviet Union
Inflation	Less problematic in Hungary and Czech Republic; shock therapy in Poland	Erased real balance sheet values
Privatization	Gradual in most cases; rapid but partial in the Czech Republic; recent acceleration in Hungary	Changed ownership structure, but not governance
Entry	Proliferation in Poland by 1992, slowdown thereafter; increase in Czech Republic and Hungary	Few new banks net of monobank spinoffs
Liquidations	Implicit deposit insurance; small bank failures only, and these have been few	Banks allowed to fail in some cases; sometimes depositors assumed costs, in other cases banks continue to operate even after revocation of their licenses
Recapitalization	Single (Poland)[a] and multiple (Czech, Hungary) recapitalizations, usually via fiscal methods (bonds)	Infrequent
Enabling environment	Reasonably open competition; foreign investment materialized (mainly in Hungary); some protection of specialized banks (savings, housing, agriculture)	Local monopolies in some regional markets; weak court systems, bankruptcy, and collateral laws
Regulation and supervision	Improving licensing and supervision through significant technical assistance in Poland; weaker performance in Czech Republic and Hungary; limited resolution capacity	Weak legal framework and licensing standards; insufficient supervisory enforcement
Banking skills	Limited but improving quickly with foreign investment (Hungary), technical assistance (twinning in Poland); contracts with West European banks	Weak or absent, but improving
Motivation	Accession to the European Union	Quick profitability; speculative period with significant "gray" economy

a. Recapitalization in Poland refers to the state commercial banks, but not to the specialized banks, namely BGZ (agriculture), PKO BP (local currency savings and housing), Bank Handlowy (foreign commercial trade), PKO SA (foreign currency savings), PBR (the Polish Development Bank), and BRE (export finance).

Few CMEA countries deviated from the general tenets of this model, although the extent of centralization, of exposure to non-CMEA markets, and even of private ownership varied.

Consistent with such a model, socialist economies lacked banks in the market sense. Banks were institutions that served as accounting control and cash disbursement vehicles in support of larger economic planning and investment requirements. The role of state owned banks—which until the late 1980s were usually part of the monobank system—was twofold: (a) to disburse funds or transfer payments passively through the noncash circuit to other SOEs upon instruction from line ministries, and (b) to provide basic pension entitlements and other savings services to enterprises and their employees. Disbursements to SOEs were made without regard to creditworthiness or riskiness. For liquidity, state enterprises reimbursed banks upon instruction from government ministries, but only after enterprise allocations were made for production and the provision of benefits and social services to employees and their communities. When SOEs lacked resources to reimburse banks, the government balanced the account. When the government failed to replenish bank resources from the national treasury, banks accumulated and rolled over large stocks of loans that would have been technically in default under market conditions. Likewise, associated interest income from such loans accrued and was capitalized, adding to the size of the overall refinancing. This mode of operation distorted the management and pricing of monetary and fiscal resources, failed to instill financial discipline in banks and SOEs with regard to resource scarcity, ultimately led to a collapse of socialist economies, and made the interim transition more difficult. Box 7.1 highlights key characteristics of the overall collapse, recognizing that these effects differed across countries and were less damaging in many Central European countries that had begun to open up to the West than in other socialist economies that had not.

Reduced Liquidity and the Run-Up of Arrears

Macroeconomic decline (table 7.2) manifested itself in a general deterioration of loan quality, particularly in Poland and the FSU countries. These problems, all brought to light by initial reforms, represented a combination of external factors (inflation rates, foreign exchange rates and reserves, trade liberalization, removal of subsidies, collapse of the CMEA) that were sufficient by themselves to erase portfolio values, as occurred in the FSU countries. Hyperinflation wiped out real household savings (in Ukraine; in Poland, households held more foreign currency), and household distrust or limited liquidity kept savings out of the banking system (FSU, Poland), causing a disintermediation effect. The Czech Republic

Table 7.2. Macroeconomic Indicators of Decline in Transitional Countries, Selected Years

Indicator	Czech Republic 1989	Czech Republic 1991–92	Hungary 1989	Hungary 1991–92	Poland 1989	Poland 1991–92	Ukraine 1992	Ukraine 1993
Average inflation rates (%)	1.4	56.6	17.0	35.0	245.6	70.3	—	4,734.9
Average exchange rate[a]	15.1	29.5	59.1	74.7	0.1	1.1	749.0	25,000.0
Unemployment (%)	0.0	3.4	0.0	10.4	0.0	11.5	0.3	0.4
Foreign exchange reserves (year end)[b]	—	2.8	2.2	5.0	2.1	3.2	2.7	2.0
Merchandise trade (US$1 billions)	—	32.2	26.3	24.9	28.3	28.9	23.2	28.1
M2/GDP (%)	—	75.7	41.1	46.9	81.1	31.8	—	—
Fiscal deficits/GDP	—	0.4	1.3	5.4	6.0	6.7	24.2	11.7

— Not available.

a. Local currency units to the U.S. dollar.

b. Expressed in terms of months of imports of goods and nonfactor services.

Source: International Labour Office, International Monetary Fund, and World Bank data.

Box 7.1. Characteristics of the Collapse of Socialism

Regional Trade

Domestic, regional, and CMEA trade relations collapsed, resulting in drastic interruptions in production and distribution. This was particularly the case with energy, where critical supplies of power were reduced because of countries' inability to provide hard currency in exchange. For Ukraine, this led to barter trade, which was less efficient and reliable. For the Czech Republic, Hungary, and Poland, merchandise trade (exports and imports) was more stable, and eventually increased because of the shift in trade patterns away from the centrally planned economies to those of Western Europe.

Output, Employment, and Incomes

Domestic output, formal employment, and real incomes all declined sharply. Allowing for weaknesses in statistics, GDP fell nearly 15 percent in real terms from 1989–92 in non-FSU countries, and even more in the FSU region. In most transitional countries, industrial employment has fallen by at least one-third, and unemployment rates still range in the 10 to 20 percent range. (Official rates may overstate unemployment because of the growth of the informal sector in transition countries. However, significant underemployment among those officially employed is often not captured.) The Czech Republic remains a noteworthy exception, with unemployment rates in the 3 to 4 percent range, although this may be due to the absence of deep industrial restructuring. Ukraine's official unemployment rate had not exceeded 0.4 percent by 1994 despite economic collapse, reflecting anachronistic statistical indicators.

Pricing and Production

Energy prices increased sharply because of reduced subsidies, which resulted in explicitly higher production costs and output prices.

Inflation Rates and Purchasing Power

Inflation rates increased dramatically in Poland and Ukraine, while in the Czech Republic and Hungary inflation rates were more moderate. In the FSU (Ukraine included), this resulted in reduced purchasing power and reduced values of real fixed income. In Poland, fiscal deficits reached nearly 7 percent of GDP from 1991–92, largely because of social assistance payments.

Source: World Bank data.

---

experienced greater stability because of a disciplined macroeconomic framework and the public's confidence in implicit deposit insurance. Hungary was similarly less "shocked" because of its gradual opening to Western markets that dated back to the 1960s. However, in all four countries, production declines and limited trade with hard currency markets led to a decrease in foreign exchange resources. Meanwhile, domestic currencies lost value, particularly in ruble-based economies. The zloty likewise lost value in Poland. This prompted a chain of events in which cash payments diminished, lack of creditworthiness and competitiveness became more apparent, and the introduction of hard budget constraints became a necessity for renewed stability and improved resource allocation at firm levels.

Governments imposed hard budget constraints on banks and enterprises in varying degrees and at varying times for a number of reasons. From a policy standpoint, the objective was to introduce a measure of disciplined financial management under market conditions to restore macroeconomic balance and to reverse structural weaknesses so that companies (and countries) could compete. From a fiscal standpoint, it was a necessity because of the shrinking tax base. Profits taxes assessed earlier were no longer generating sufficient revenues, so governments had to cut subsidies and support (see Barbone and Marchetti 1994). Another contributing factor in CEE countries was the need to make benefits payments (pensions, social security). These were particularly high in Hungary and Poland, and were reflected in fiscal deficits. FSU countries including Ukraine were unable to honor these commitments: inflation wiped out real savings and fiscal resources were far scarcer than in CEE countries. In Ukraine, scarce fiscal resources were instead used for subsidies and directed credits for agriculture and industry in an attempt to maintain production and jobs.

As budget constraints were eventually imposed, enterprises increased the use of barter in their dealings, and ran up arrears on their debts (arrears were particularly pronounced on trade debt to domestic and foreign suppliers, tax and social security payments to the government, wage payments to employees, and both principal and interest to banks). These problems were particularly severe in Poland and Ukraine, although problems emerged in the Czech Republic and Hungary as well. In Poland and Ukraine this led to an interruption of production and distribution flows, as the quality of receivables diminished, cash was short, price increases were built in to products to cover for some anticipated delays and losses, and orders were taken to utilize capacity and keep people partly employed instead of reducing excess capacity and overheads. (Fewer disruptions occurred in the Czech Republic and Hungary, because of greater investment and remittance flows into these economies.) In countries where disruptions were the greatest, a broad deterioration in the market for bank services resulted, and this prompted a tightening of lending conditions. In the case of Ukraine (and other FSU countries), these developments were particularly severe, affecting trade relations with FSU countries and prompting the need for a series of debt restructurings (debt restructuring with Russia and Turkmenistan were required to permit needed energy resources to flow into the country). Meanwhile, real household incomes and savings declined, leading to diminished confidence and flight from local to hard currencies. This slowed bank deposit mobilization, except in the Czech Republic, where confidence remained high despite negative real rates paid on deposits. Table 7.3 summarizes some of the structural weaknesses that persisted during the early stages of transition.

The Deterioration of Bank Portfolios

While on a stock basis many of these banks appeared liquid, on a flow basis they were not. Excess liquidity on a stock basis was derived from the predominance of short-term assets (securities, loans) on their balance sheets, but earnings from these assets were often low (securities) or negative (funding the cost of large portions of nonperforming loan portfolios), thereby reducing cash flow and constraining liquidity for ongoing operations. These financial weaknesses were symptomatic of larger operational flaws related to governance, management, and incentive structures typically found in state banks in CEE and FSU countries. This manifested itself in poor lending decisions based on noncommercial criteria, which ultimately led to portfolio declines as economies collapsed and new, increasingly market-based, conditions were introduced.

Against this backdrop, a second wave of bad loans materialized after the first wave inherited from the central planning era was recognized.[7] This occurred for several reasons, namely, weak legislation and regulations, the absence of institutional capacity, and significant political pressure to loosen monetary and fiscal policy to restore production and reduce spiraling unemployment. Neither banks nor enterprises were able to manage resources properly under such risky conditions, particularly as the environment was changing so quickly. The effect of hard budget constraints was to limit the quantity of funds available to banks to be able to grow out of their financial problems. Meanwhile, many of the loans made were poorly selected, further weakening the quality of their portfolios. These developments point to the importance of macroeconomic stability and the sequencing of reforms as transition countries were introducing an enabling environment for financial and private sector development. Also of considerable importance was the role of governance and management at the firm (bank) level, and the continued distortion of incentives despite nominal changes in laws and regulations.

---

7. While the inherited bad loans were recognized, the magnitude of the problem was not fully recognized. This was due to the lack of proper accounting and to delays in institutionalizing prudential regulations that properly classified loans and required banks to provision adequately for losses. These reforms occurred later, generally after 1991–92 in the most advanced CEE countries.

Table 7.3. *Structural Factors Responsible for Poor Loan Quality*

Area influence	Bank weaknesses	Enterprise weaknesses
Political	• Central planning and control preempted incentives for active governance and resource management	• Planning and control substituted for market in determining economic needs, distorted incentives
Legal	• Inadequate legal framework for loan recovery • Weak court systems with untrained staff • Incomplete property registries	• Weak bankruptcy laws that favor debtors, provide no legal recourse to creditors for run-up of arrears • Property ownership rights and contractual obligations not clear • Weak collateral laws reduce lending
Regulatory	• Limited or no bank supervision • No risk management capacity	• Weak enforcement of anti-monopoly provisions and protectionism, which limits competition • Unreliable accounting or no disclosure
Financial	• Poor or no credit risk assessment • Lack of portfolio diversification • Inadequate security or collateral • Poor accounting standards • Limited or nonexistent asset-liability management	• Uncompetitive productivity levels • Rising labor costs and overstaffing • Rising hard currency input costs (energy) • Outmoded technologies • Poorly received products • Thin consumer markets • Inadequate cash management • Weak strategic planning capabilities
Operational	• Inappropriate governance structures and ownership patterns • Inexperienced bank management • Lack of risk analysis and controls • Weak incentives for better risk management	• Conflict of interest in terms of enterprise ownership, management and governance of banks • Inexperienced or inappropriate management (in a market context)

By 1991 estimates indicated that nonperforming loans amounted to up to 25 percent, possibly more, of GDP in CEE countries. Lower estimates reflected inaccurate accounting, unsuitable regulations concerning provisioning for losses and writing off of loans, and so on. Table 7.4 shows estimates of bad loan values for some of the largest banks. (In many cases, information was not provided to the public because of the size of the problem.) Many of these loans represented new lending flows in the early 1990s to large industrial companies that were overstaffed, uncompetitive, and unlikely to emerge as sound credit risks even with the introduction of some operational changes. As these new flows were in addition to what had been inherited from the earlier period (CEE) or had been eliminated because of hyperinflation (FSU countries), it was evident by 1993–94 that initial reforms were insufficient to improve the quality of loan portfolios.

Early Banking Sector Reforms and Institutional Responses

A first round of reforms in transition countries involved a flurry of new legislation to break up monobank systems, reintroduce the concept of private property, and encourage the privatization of state assets. Nevertheless, as already noted, economic reality was that of spiraling decline. This put pressure on newly elected officials to respond quickly to the needs of those displaced by the old system before new laws and regulations were effectively implemented and market-based institutions were fully functioning. This resulted in continued state ownership of major banks (CEE countries), bank privatization without operational restructuring in the Ukraine, and direct (state) or indirect (national property funds, state pension funds) state ownership of major companies in all four countries. In the three CEE countries examined, state banks routinely accounted for about 60 percent of total assets and total loans, and about 70 percent or more of total deposits at the end of 1995.

Ongoing state ownership practically ensured that the implementation of reforms would be slowed. In fairness to Poland, the slowdown in reform was partly a reaction to problems associated with the rapid opening of the market to competition (low capital requirements, liberal licensing standards) prior to developing sufficient capacity for oversight. Likewise, in fairness to Hungary, all but one bank has been privatized since 1995 in a market that today is dominated by prime-rated institutions. By contrast, in the Czech Republic, interlocking directorates and structural weaknesses at the firm and bank levels have undermined overall

Table 7.4. Estimates of Nonperforming Loans in Transition Countries, 1991 and 1992

Category	Czech Republic 1991	Czech Republic 1992	Hungary 1991	Hungary 1992	Poland 1991	Poland 1992	Ukraine 1991	Ukraine 1992
NPLs as a percentage of total bank loans	29	15–20	9	15–28	>33	25–60	—	—
NPLs as a percentage of total bank assets	15	10	7	8	>13	13–30	—	—
NPLs as a percentage of GDP	21	14	6	9	>7	7–20	—	—

— Not available.

NPLs Nonperforming loans.

Note: Banks included in 1991 are KB, VUB, Konsolidacni, Investicni, and CSOB (Czech-Slovak Federal Republic); Budapest Bank, OTP, MHB, MKB, K&H, and Postabank, based on total classified portfolio at end 1992 (Hungary); and seven SOCBs not privatized by the end of 1993 (Poland). Figures for 1992 represent figures and estimates of national sources and the International Monetary Fund for all banks. Figures are not available for Ukraine.

Source: Dittus (1994); World Bank data.

competitiveness and raise serious questions about governance, management, and the depth of initial reforms. The Czech Republic is now in the process of dealing with many of these problems. In Ukraine, while "ownership" changed, governance and management practices did not (until very recently), and top managers of the state enterprises that had been majority shareholders of banks prior to share redistribution still made most major policy and personnel decisions.[8] The following paragraphs discuss major reforms.

Movement to Market-Oriented Systems

One of the first banking sector reforms the transition countries implemented was to break up the monobank system into two tiers: a central bank responsible for the conduct of monetary affairs and state owned commercial and specialized banks responsible for mobilizing deposits, lending, and carrying out other commercial banking activities. Hungary did this in 1987, followed by Poland in 1989 and Czechoslovakia in 1990. Ukraine moved in this direction as part of the FSU, and then did so as an independent country in 1991. In general, the break-up of the monobank system was accompanied by subsequent legislation that opened up the banking market to competition. Key features included the following:

- *Clarifying the central bank's role and responsibilities in connection with monetary and banking matters.* These responsibilities often involved determining monetary policy, safeguarding currency stability, managing clearinghouse and payments systems, licensing and supervising commercial banks, and approving mergers and acquisitions.
- *Setting up the legal basis for the establishment and existence of commercial banks.* More often than not, this led to the initial creation of (a) larger, specialized banks with nationwide and global coverage focused on savings, housing finance, agriculture, and international trade; and (b) smaller, diversified commercial banks with limited geographic markets.
- *Establishing a regulatory framework for commercial banking.* This included basic elements of legal and prudential regulatory systems and new accounting frameworks.

---

8. "Private" ownership of banks was established by reclassifying some of the banks' liabilities (for example, savings, deposits) as equity, triggered by a government stipulation in 1993 that the Ministry of Finance should control state enterprise equity. Meanwhile, as of the end of 1994, two large banks—Oschadny Bank (the savings bank) and Exim Bank (foreign trade)—remained state owned and continued to be tools of government policy, while also "commercializing" their operations.

The process of breaking up the monobanks also created confusion with regard to the role of the second tier—commercial and specialized banks—largely because these reforms were not automatically or sufficiently accompanied by changes in incentive structures (legal and regulatory frameworks, institutional development) or the financial discipline necessary for effective transformation to a market-based system. In some countries, the management of second-tier banks knew that the break-up of the monobank system was going to require them to operate according to commercial criteria. However, time and expertise were needed for the legal, regulatory, and institutional changes to take hold for a smooth transition. These developments and weaknesses prompted different responses in terms of how governments, banks, and enterprises adapted themselves to the new commercial system, and how banking systems have evolved since the termination of the monobank system. Key developments were as follows:

- *Specifying the types and scope of activities permitted.* Most CEE countries have moved toward universal banking structures common to continental European Union (EU) systems. Directives from the EU have served as a basis for determining allowable activities in which banks and financial institutions may engage and the modalities of competition, supervision, diversification, and accounting. Ukraine has provided clarification of commercial banking and other financial sector activities, although these efforts have not been shaped by EU directives.
- *Defining methods of regulatory enforcement.* Laws generally specified the need for regulatory enforcement. Responsibility for enforcement has differed across countries. The central bank is prominent in most cases, although Hungary has differed in this respect.
- *Establishing basic regulatory guidelines.* Transition countries, including CEE countries and Ukraine, have spelled out minimum capital and capital adequacy requirements, loan classification systems, limits on exposures (for instance, large, total large, insider lending, foreign exchange), and other fundamentals of banking regulation, although actual enforcement remains uneven.
- *Establishing deposit insurance funds.* More recently, CEE countries have moved to establish explicit deposit insurance funds.

While the privatization of state banks has been slow in CEE countries with the exception of Hungary since late 1995, the number of private banks has grown rapidly in both Central European and FSU countries. In the case of the former, this has largely involved the attraction of prime-rated foreign banks, particularly in the Czech Republic and Hungary, and more recently in Poland after an initial surge through 1992. Smaller private domestic banks have also formed to meet local financing needs, particularly in Poland. In the case of the FSU countries, including Ukraine, privatization has largely involved "ownership transformation" without sufficient restructuring or foreign entry to be competitive.

These countries adopted liberal licensing policies (low minimum capital, flexible business plan requirements and management standards and skills) at the beginning of banking reform. Moreover, they initially granted the same set of licensing requirements to foreign and domestic applicants. As a result, many new private banks were established in the first years of transition. Subsequently, the authorities replaced the initial liberal licensing policies with more restrictive policies, primarily in the form of increased minimum capital requirements and the introduction of differential requirements for foreign applications. Rightly or wrongly, changes were motivated by concerns about (a) the increasing financial problems state banks experienced because of their exposure to deteriorating state enterprises; (b) the difficulties associated with bank supervision given the countries' limited supervisory capacity and a large number of small private banks; and (c) the belief (based partly on the problems with bank supervision) that bank fraud and failure were more likely to occur if the number of banks was too high, except in Ukraine, which until recently did little to rein in "privatized" banks, which are difficult to regulate. In CEE these licensing changes led to a slowdown in the number of new domestic private banks, an abeyance of foreign investment in the sector (Poland), and some geographic and functional diversification of domestic banking activities.

In some cases, the dominance of state banks has restricted the scope of expansion for private banks. For example, the size of private banks, measured by their shares in total banking sector resources on a stock basis, is small. At the end of 1995, private banks' average assets were US$420 million to US$470 million in the three CEE countries. Private banks accounted for nearly half of banking assets in Hungary at the time (more now), but only 30 to 40 percent in the Czech Republic and Poland. In other cases, the protection of state banks through uneven deposit insurance schemes (true today in Ukraine), protection via implicit guarantees (Czech Republic, Poland), and recapitalization (CEE countries) put private banks in a disadvantageous position. Average SOCB deposits were US$0.6 billion to US$3.9 billion in 1995, compared to an average of only US$135 million to US$190 million for private banks.

Table 7.5. *"Large" Banks' Assets, Capital, and Returns, 1994*

Country and banking subsection	Tier one capital (US$ millions)	Total assets (US$ millions)	Capital as a percentage of assets	Risk-adjusted capital (percent)	Pre-tax profits (US$ millions)	Return on capital (percent)	Return on assets (percent)
Czech Republic	3,439	44,020	7.8	10.9	433	15.5	0.99
of which SOCB	3,175	38,826	8.2	11.2	420	16.2	1.07
of which private	264	5,194	5.7	8.3	13	3.9	0.40
Hungary	970	22,307	4.8	12.8	273	32.5	1.25
of which SOCB	523	16,013	3.9	11.9	131	29.1	0.85
of which private	447	6,294	7.1	15.1	142	36.3	2.25
Poland[a]	1,931	37,505	5.1	15.2	787	53.5	1.93
of which SOCB	1,386	30,371	4.8	13.2	355	25.6	1.21
of which private	545	7,134	7.6	17.0	432	93.9	6.04

Note: "Large" here means tier one capital of at least US$12 million. Figures for Ukraine were not available.

a. Figures for Poland do not include BGZ, which would significantly reduce SOCB ratios. Private banks' profit indicators are probably overstated because of insufficient provisioning for loan losses, which is being corrected with increasing use of on-site inspections.

Source: Annual reports; *The Banker*, September 1995; *Bank (Poland)*, 1995 bank survey issue; World Bank data.

The three CEE governments also provided about US$15 billion to re-
capitalize SOCBs, equivalent to 5 percent of same year GDP.[9]

Despite this protection, private banks have grown steadily in CEE markets in the last five years, capturing many of the blue chip lending accounts
and providing fee-based advisory services. In addition to not having the
burden of inherited nonperforming loans from the past, these banks are
often more profitable, because they are better able to provide services in
trade finance, corporate bond issues, custodial and trustee services, advisory services regarding international markets, and mergers and acquisitions. Only Ukraine has failed to accomplish this.

Most CEE banks are stronger today than they were at the beginning of
the transition. Capital ratios more accurately reflect solvency on a book-
valued basis, as new accounting standards, stricter prudential regulations,
and strengthened bank supervision have pressured banks to treat problem
loans with more discipline.[10] Whether enough discipline has been exercised in certain countries is now a topic of serious concern in the Czech
Republic. However, as a general rule, these reforms contrast with the beginning of the transition, when state banks were not even aware of the
existence and magnitude of problem loans. Table 7.5 highlights key capital
and return measures in 1994. Since then, Polish banks have shown improvement, particularly since late 1995, having benefited from earlier bank portfolio and operational restructuring, and bolstered by 6 to 7 percent real
economic growth. Hungary has similarly shown improving performance,
having benefited from privatization and additional foreign investment.

---

9. Total nominal GDP for corresponding years in which recapitalizations occurred
was US$315 billion (including the Slovak Republic as part of the Czech-Slovak Federal
Republic figures for 1991 and 1993). Thus recapitalizations of about US$16 billion ap-
proximate 5 percent of GDP. Interest charges have added to the cost, estimated to be
comparatively low in Poland (0.6 percent), but up to 2.6 percent in the Czech-Slovak
Federal Republic and 2.0 percent in Hungary at the end of 1993. Hungary's additional
recapitalization in 1994 would add to this cost, as well as adding to intermediation
costs for borrowers (see Dittus 1994; OECD 1993).

10. While capital adequacy ratios were only 6.3 percent at the end of 1994, risk-
adjusted capital was 12.6 percent. In 1995 capital adequacy ratios were about 9.6
percent at year end, with private banks showing far higher ratios than SOCBs. Private banks, in particular, show a growing proportion of assets and capital and rising
income figures and return ratios. However, private banks' returns may have been
overstated in some countries. For instance, in Poland private domestic banks reported inordinately high returns on assets, which might reflect the overstatement of
income and distort other ratios. Few of these banks were audited by international
accounting firms in 1994.

Deposit Insurance Trends

Explicit deposit insurance is becoming increasingly prevalent in transition economies, particularly in those CEE countries that aspire to join the EU (Czech Republic, Hungary, Poland). As the EU standard for explicit insurance approximates per capita incomes (up to ECU 20,000), CEE countries have introduced measures along comparable lines: explicit insurance limits in Hungary are higher than per capita incomes, comparable in Poland, and lower in the Czech Republic. Perhaps more important during the transition, the Czech Republic was able to sustain a high level of confidence among depositors in the banking system. This had more to do with a reasonably stable macroeconomic framework than with anything structural. The Czechs accomplished this despite depositors receiving negative real rates of interest—that were as high as -11.3 percent in 1993, stabilizing at -1.9 percent from 1995 through September 1996. Hungary and Poland provided implicit insurance to depositors, although confidence appeared to be a bit lower there when looking at comparative intermediation rates (see table 7.2). This may have been more a function of firm- and household-specific liquidity needs, and less of an issue of actual banking capacity. Hungary and Poland, like the Czech Republic, paid negative real rates on deposits, although Hungary's real rates were less negative than the other countries' rates, and were positive in 1994. In the FSU, ruble-denominated savings lost value, and confidence will be more difficult to restore. Ukraine is still struggling to build a viable deposit base for its banking system.

Banking Supervision and Accounting Standards

Bank supervisory frameworks have improved in recent years, but they continue to experience weaknesses in trained personnel, information systems, and overall risk management. Other key issues relate to the independence of banking supervision, which is often housed in the central bank, but frequently requires permission from the ministry of finance to enforce regulations. Nevertheless, capacity in Poland is clearly significantly greater than that which existed in the early 1990s, with improved information and analysis and a growing corps of trained personnel for off-site surveillance and on-site inspection. This has been reinforced by movement toward international accounting standards. All the CEE countries have introduced new accounting frameworks essential for regulation, governance, management, and overall development of a market economy. These are broadly consistent with international standards, and their introduction represents an institutional success, as the accounting and auditing professions did not exist in the same manner just a few years ago. Domestic and international accounting firms have developed, supplemented, and reinforced local resources. Problems still remain regarding accuracy of information, consolidation of statements, and levels of disclosure. However, improvements have also clearly been made. Key developments include the following:

- *Differing supervisory approaches have been introduced.* Poland has shown the most comprehensive improvement, including the use of on-site inspections, detailed off-site surveillance and early warning systems, and strict monitoring and reporting standards. The other three countries have less capacity and a far greater distance to go in enforcing Basle capital-based standards, let alone meeting standards assumed by the more pioneering risk-based approaches many of the more advanced economies are implementing.

- *Accounting standards have been introduced in CEE countries to provide increasing information and disclosure.* These new standards are still being developed, as are domestic accounting and auditing professions. Nevertheless, CEE countries have structured their frameworks to be consistent with international standards. Often these have been based on specific legislation. However, institutional capacity is still comparatively weak in many cases, both in the origination of the information provided as well as in the analytical use of this information for regulatory, managerial, and investment purposes. Above all, crisis prevention, contingency planning, and crisis management need strengthening, and more complex risk management techniques will also need to be devised over time. This is likely to require continued and significant levels of technical assistance. In Ukraine progress in introducing accounting reforms has been slow. Lack of an acceptable chart of accounts—a hurdle CEE countries overcame several years ago—remains a major drawback in the production of meaningful financial statements in many FSU countries.

Governance and Management

One of the more critical banking sector reforms has been the change in governance and management. Performance in this domain has varied. Poland has done well with the transformation of governance and management standards at many of the state commercial banks in preparation for privatization; however, continued political and financial support for weaker specialized banks (for instance, BGZ in Poland) and resistance to accelerated privatization of "strategic" and politically powerful enterprise sectors has undermined governance in these areas, even if management in some cases has improved. In Hungary, performance has improved significantly over the years, and has been given greater impetus since 1995 with the decision to privatize banks and impose hard budget constraints on loss-making enterprises. The Czech Republic's governance and management record is spotty, partly because of the linked ownership structure of the state (via the National Property Fund), banks, enterprises, and investment funds, as well as problems of information disclosure and accounting standards. Many of the recently proposed reforms to reinvigorate the economy reflect the economy's structural weakness, much of which emanates from lax governance requirements and management standards. In Ukraine, governance still remains weak, and in some ways continues to resemble practices during the period of central planning. Key trends in the banking sector have included the following:

- *Differing ownership patterns and governance practices.* In the Czech Republic, the role of interlocking directorates and the prominence of banks—particularly given the state's continuing ownership role—raises questions about the allocation of resources and the degree of restructuring in the enterprise sector. Notwithstanding the structural change in the Czech Republic's labor market in the early 1990s (approximately 500,000 woman, usually mothers with children, or some 10 percent of the labor market, left the labor force once the authorities offered incentives for early retirement) and the fact that most heavy industry (where labor shedding was most needed) was located in the modern-day Slovak Republic, official unemployment rates of 3 to 4 percent were for a long time an aberration in the region. The government announced a series of proposed reforms in early 1997 intended to reduce the 8.6 percent current account deficit, which partly reflected weak competitiveness. In Poland, the Ministry of Finance introduced strengthened governance practices in 1993, pointing to the importance of privatization as a strategic objective. While privatization has not proceeded rapidly in Poland, state commercial banks (as opposed to some of the specialized banks) are considered eminently more privatizable today than they were in 1993–94. In Hungary, bank management was already strong, and the prominence and profitability of prime-rated banks established high governance standards. The shortcomings of state bank and state enterprise recapitalization in 1993–94 has given way to the most aggressive bank privatization program in the four countries. In fact, Hungary's privatization in banking is more complete than in many EU countries. In Ukraine, governance is weak irrespective of ownership, although current signs indicate that regulators are likely to be more active to contain systemic risks and to support macroeconomic improvements.

- *Growing recognition of the need for transparency and accountability.* This is driven by bankers' needs to determine creditworthiness, regulators' needs to be able to rely on effective supervision, and capital markets' needs to make investment decisions. Increasingly, government policymakers similarly need better information to determine the efficiency of the use of monetary and fiscal resources for budgetary and planning purposes, as well as for potential lender of last resort scenarios and deposit safety in the banking system. The last point has been critical in tightening regulatory oversight and liquidating banks in the Czech Republic and Ukraine, accelerating privatization in Hungary, and pursuing regular on-site inspections in Poland.

Bank Restructuring and Approaches to Sectoral Reform

Initial reform efforts have sought to achieve long-term growth objectives while mitigating some of the social costs associated with transition, adjustment, and stabilization in the short term. In this context, the design of reform programs emphasized restructuring and privatizing banks and state enterprises. In practice, macroeconomic stabilization measures (hard budget constraints, fiscal balance, restrictive monetary policy) induced significant financial restructuring at the bank and enterprise levels in all four countries, with some operational restructuring resulting from less direct access to public resources. Most countries have at least partly privatized or liquidated most of their SOEs, often small and medium size enterprises that lacked strategic value of any sort. Nevertheless, privatization in the banking system has generally lagged behind privatization in the enterprise sector, slowing progress toward a market economy. Hungary is the one notable exception, because of its consistently sustained openness to private and foreign investment and its commitment since mid-1995 to privatize the state banking sector fully.

Originally, reform programs anticipated that with appropriate assistance, state banks would play a leading role in enterprise restructuring efforts. Program designers expected banks to be able to conduct the needed analysis of their troubled borrowers, determine which enterprises should continue as going concerns and borrowers of the banks, provide financing and improved governance for surviving enterprises, and initiate liquidation procedures against those that were unlikely to be creditworthy in the future. [11] They perceived this role to be appropriate for banks because of their familiarity with individual enterprises. Policymakers also believed that bank-led restructuring could be more efficient in resolving debt disputes than centralized, nonbank (government agency) channels.

However, because of their traditionally passive and noncommercial role, state banks lacked the institutional capacity and experience to restructure enterprises financially, physically, and operationally and to provide effective governance. [12] Ukrainian (and FSU in general) banks and enterprises were financially restructured by hyperinflation, but their operations and productivity levels lag behind those found in CEE countries. Meanwhile, CEE countries have taken a more gradual approach, restructuring their bad loans financially through recapitalization and operationally through banks' collection efforts, which have prompted some efficiencies, reorganizations, and changes in enterprise ownership, governance, and management.

In some cases, such as the Czech Republic, governments used the "carve-out" approach to clean up bank balance sheets rapidly. In other cases, Poland, for example, banks retained responsibility for recovery, even after recapitalization (see Montes-Negret and Papi 1997). In yet other cases, such as Hungary, recapitalization was intended to help banks and enterprises adapt to changing market conditions and grow out of their problems in a more disciplined and competitive way without inducing major social dislocation. However, in all cases restructuring needs persisted in banks (and enterprises) well after recapitalization.

A sustained political commitment to and proper sequencing of reforms; a continuation of progress in creating an enabling environment; the introduction of suitable incentives for a wide range of stakeholders; the

---

11. Bank-led restructuring of the enterprise sector originally anticipated banks assuming a comprehensive role. This included (a) conducting an analysis of problem debtors to determine the level of debt owed and how to have principal repaid and interest serviced; (b) restructuring the debt of potentially viable enterprises; (c) financing the physical restructuring of potentially viable enterprises; (d) exercising corporate governance over these enterprises; and (e) writing off the debts of, curtailing new credit to, and in some cases liquidating nonviable enterprises. Thus the decentralized bank-led approach assumed that banks would take the lead in the financial (debt), physical (property, plant, equipment, inventories), and operational (governance) restructuring of viable enterprises, and accelerate the liquidation of nonviable enterprises. This proved to be an overly ambitious conceptualization of banks' roles and capacity in general enterprise restructuring in transition countries.

12. This should not be surprising, as even in the most affluent economies, commercial banks are often poorly equipped to lead enterprise restructurings. Investment banks and specialized consulting firms are often the turnaround experts in these markets.

importance of "strategic" investment from, training by, and correspondent linkages with prime-rated institutions from market economies; and the prominent role of governance and management have emerged as critical ingredients for successful reform. The following sections discuss specific country experiences. Box 7.2 highlights the depth of illiquidity and insolvency in each country, which set the stage for restructuring. [13]

Czech (and Slovak) Republic: The Problem of Partial Privatization and Weak Governance

The Czech Republic has pursued a dual approach to privatization and private sector development: voucher distribution for the vast majority of citizens who had previously been unable to accumulate much in the way of savings because of the level of control and centralization that prevailed during the communist period, combined with efforts to attract investment from and joint ventures with Western companies. These efforts were backed by a commitment to macroeconomic stability to keep inflation and interest rates comparatively low, the currency stable (and strong), and fiscal accounts largely in balance. Until recently, results appeared to be positive at the macroeconomic level, although significant structural weaknesses have long been evident and culminated in deteriorating 1996 current account figures.

In the banking sector, the Czech (and Slovak Federal) Republic opted to pursue an up-front carve-out of bad debts in the major banks as an integral part of the bank privatization program under the country's general mass privatization program. At the time, nonperforming loans were estimated to approximate 36 percent of total credit to nongovernment entities and 25 percent of GDP. As with challenges faced in the enterprise sector, the government believed that swift and mass privatization combined with a stable macroeconomic environment would be sufficient to work out structural problems. A carve-out of bad assets was intended to make the banks more amenable to privatization on a stock basis (more attractive value based on a clean balance sheet)—as well as on a flow basis—by not burdening management with the overhang of bad debt from the central planning era, and giving banks the opportunity to become more profitable under new incentive structures.

---

13. This chapter refers to liquidity and illiquidity on a cash or funds flow basis, not on the basis of current assets and liabilities on the balance sheet. Hence, liquidity problems or illiquidity reflect limited earnings flows to banks available for new lending, investments, and operations. This may occur despite bank balance sheets holding substantial net current asset positions.

Box 7.2 Bank Portfolio Restructuring: Causes and Approaches

Magnitude of the Problem

In the Czech Republic, nonperforming loans accounted for about 20 to 30 percent of total banking system loans. Hungary had a lower amount of nonperforming loans, but the amount increased quickly with the passage of new legislation in 1991–92, which led banks to recognize more of their bad loans.[1] Poland's bad loans were as much as 60 percent of total bank loans. In Ukraine, nonperforming loans are high and remain a problem today because of the absence of serious structural reform.

The Problem of the State Sector

Bad loans were highly concentrated in the state banking sector, which held 85 to 100 percent of nonperforming loans. Also, at least in the early stages, state enterprises represented the bulk of nonperforming borrowers. This problem was particularly severe in Poland, where more than 60 percent of the seven SOCBs' loans were nonperforming, and where the loan portfolios of some of the larger specialized banks were in even worse shape. In the Czech Republic, where 30 percent or more of state owned banks' portfolios were nonperforming, individual state banks often carried much higher proportions of such loans than the average. In Hungary, state banks' loans were 64 percent nonperforming once new laws were adopted in 1991–92. In Ukraine, problem loans were in both state and "private" banks, the latter being generally controlled by SOE managers.

Impact on Solvency and Liquidity

The concentration of bad debts among a number of state owned banks meant that these banks faced severe problems of solvency and had low capital adequacy ratios. At the end of 1990, VUB (Czech-Slovak Federal Republic) reported a capital adequacy ratio of less than 2 percent. At the end of September 1992, 7 of the 14 largest Hungarian banks had negative capital adequacy ratios and 5 others had capital adequacy ratios that were below the 7.25 percent targeted by the end of 1992. These low capital adequacy ratios were more problematic (more so than would have been reported according to Basle standards) in that more rigid loan classification standards observed by market economies were not yet in place. The introduction of these standards led to widespread provisioning and write-offs in CEE countries, prompting the need for recapitalizations to counter solvency problems (negative capital). Ukraine is now in the process of implementing comparable regulations. Only 14 banks currently meet relatively low minimum capital requirements, and most have low or negative capital.

Approaches

CEE governments faced two main alternatives in dealing with the bad debt problem: (a) they could pursue a decentralized approach—as in Poland with commercial banks (but not specialized banks) and Hungary with commercial banks—whereby individual banks lead the financial restructuring process (or more modestly retain responsibility for loan recovery), with assistance from the state; or (b) they could follow a centralized approach—as in the Czech Republic, and to some extent in Hungary—by carving out bad debts and recapitalizing the banks. (For an overview of the major options see Saunders and Sommariva 1993. Also see Borish, Long, and Noël 1995 for a review of country-specific restructuring programs in the banking and enterprise sectors.) Other options included debt cancellation or forgiveness; liquidation of insolvent state banks, with government assumption of banks' liabilities; and hyperinflationary elimination of banks' liabilities. In Ukraine, hyperinflation and liquidation have been used as tools, but serious restructuring still needs to occur.

---

1.   Key factors were (a) the Act on Financial Institutions of 1991, which created three categories of nonperforming loans (substandard, doubtful, bad) and mandated provisioning for these loans (20, 50, 100 percent provisioning, respectively); (b) the Accounting Act of 1992, which allowed banks to create provisions out of pretax profits; and (c) the Bankruptcy Act of September 1991, which imposed bankruptcy proceedings on any firm that was in arrears by more than 90 days.

Such a carve-out was thus considered an effective tool in accelerating the privatization of state banks.

Within this context, the Czech-Slovak Republic established the Konsolidacni Banka in March 1991 as a "loan hospital" or "bad bank" to clean up the balance sheets of the commercial banks and to work out nonperforming loans without burdening the other banks with the clean-up effort. The carve-out, recapitalization, and partial privatization were carried out in four steps as follows:

- *Carve-out.* The government carved out K 110 billion (US$4 billion) in substandard and nonperforming assets from three of its major banks (in exchange for matching liabilities in the redistribution of credit and deposits of the savings banks), and placed them on the balance sheet of the newly created Konsolidacni Banka (which assumed more than 6,000 nonperforming loans granted prior to 1989 from the balances of the banks participating in the carve-out). The K 110 billion taken over came from a total of K 180 billion (US$6 billion) of permanently revolving loans, the so-called TOZ credits, which were originally given to enterprises at 6 percent interest and without a specified maturity date. At the beginning of 1991 the authorities abolished all TOZ credits, and the credits taken over by Konsolidacni Banka were renegotiated at 13 percent interest (300 basis points above the discount rate) with an eight-year maturity. When the two republics separated in January 1993, Konsolidacna Banka Bratislava was created in the Slovak Republic to assume Sk 30 billion (US$1 billion) in nonperforming loans, while Kč 80 billion (US$2.8 billion) were allocated to the Czech Konsolidacni Banka.

- *New bond financing (first recapitalization).* Also in 1991, the National Property Fund issued K 50 billion (US$1.7 billion) in bonds. Of this bond issue, K 12 billion (US$400 million) was made available for capital (repayable in currency), and K 38 billion (US$1.3 billion) was provided in bonds with a five-year maturity (repayable in the form of shares in privatized enterprises). Proceeds were transferred to the banks for the carve-out of bad loans and to recapitalize the banks. Capital adequacy ratios for these banks consequently increased from 1.5 to 4.5 percent.

- *Inclusion in mass privatization program.* The banks were immediately included in the mass privatization program. After the first wave of mass privatization, all the major banks of the system had been partially privatized, including Komercni Banka, Investicni Banka, Zivnostenska Banka, and Ceska Sporitelna. However, the largest shares of these banks remained with the state through the National Property Fund.

- *Assumption of additional nonperforming assets (second recapitalization).* The carve-out and recapitalization were followed in 1993 with the assumption by the Czech and Slovak ministries of finance of K 95.5 billion (US$3.2 billion) of Obchodni Banka's (the Foreign Trade Bank's) assets and K 74.4 billion (US$2.5 billion) in liabilities in nonconvertible currencies from the central planning era. By the end of 1993 both governments had injected K 4.05 billion (US$135 million) into Obchodni Banka and transferred K 40 billion (US$1.3 billion) in bad or doubtful loans to separate collection units, thereby raising Obchodni Banka's capital adequacy ratio to 6.25 percent.

Most observers believe that the carve-out helped the remaining banks clean up their balance sheets instead of bogging them down with problem loans that would have continued to be a burden for them. These measures were taken at the time to deal forthrightly with stocks of nonperforming loans during the Czech-Slovak Federal Republic period in advance of bank privatization. In mid-1997, Konsolidacni itself had about US$4 billion in assets, more than US$1 billion in reserves (reflecting the nature of its portfolio), and access to the Euromarkets. Meanwhile, since that time smaller banks have been merged and liquidated as problems in their portfolios have come to light.

Nevertheless, given the still high levels of nonperforming loans currently held in other banks' portfolios after the recapitalization, serious questions remain about (a) the mixed ownership structures (banks, funds, enterprises), interlocking directorates, and lack of transparency; (b) the impact these structural weaknesses have had on the governance and management of banks; and (c) the impact of these banking sector weaknesses on the enterprise sector, given the prominent role of banks and bank debt in the economy. As the Czech Republic had one of the highest levels of domestic credit provided by the banking sector to GDP in the world as recently as 1995 (and presumably in 1996), the quality of such lending is critically important to the economy at large.[14]

Problems remain with regard to ongoing high levels of nonperforming loans, as well as with SOCB governance, internal bank supervision, levels of information disclosure and accountability, and general risk that has manifested itself in the need for continuing high levels of provisions for loan losses. Some shortcomings are also apparent in the way that bank

---

14. Domestic credit provided by the banking sector was 93.4 percent of GDP in 1995, higher than in all other transition countries and higher than in most countries of the world (see World Bank 1997).

privatization was handled, namely, the partial privatization and blocking shares of banks that the National Property Fund has retained (through the fund, the government has kept 30 to 45 percent blocking shares in the four major banks). Corporate governance weaknesses remain as a result of cross-ownership between the state, investment privatization funds, banks, and large state enterprises. Investment privatization funds are among the largest shareholders in the banks, yet banks are among the largest shareholders in the biggest enterprises. Thus weaknesses with the approach appear to include inadequate governance and management in financially restructured banks caused by ownership structures, inadequate enforcement of prudential regulations or weaknesses in the framework, and lack of interest in some of the technical assistance that was previously available to strengthen bank operations.

Hungary: The Triumph of Structural Reform and Rapid Privatization

After the acceleration of reforms in 1990, the Hungarian authorities became progressively aware of the weak financial situation of most Hungarian state banks. (As of the end of 1995, the government still held significant, and usually majority, ownership in 10 banks, including the country's largest banks.) Above all, with the introduction of new banking and accounting standards combined with a strict bankruptcy law, it was apparent by 1993 that a significant portion of banks' loan portfolios were nonperforming—more than 40 percent of large state banks' loans were classified as such—and that the largest state banks were generally insolvent. Meanwhile, because of Hungary's long-standing commitment to an open environment that dated back to the late 1980s, foreign investment from prime-rated banks that maintained high levels of competitiveness was significant, and in some cases siphoned off the best companies in the Hungarian market.

In 1993–94, when the fiscal deficit was beginning to balloon out of control because of high social entitlements and a weakening economy, the government opted to recapitalize its troubled state banks to restore solvency and make them more privatizable. It implemented a series of bank recapitalization programs each year from 1991 through 1994, small in the early years, and more costly in 1993–94, when the magnitude of the problem was more fully recognized. The direct cost of Hungary's bank recapitalizations was US$3.5 billion, with an additional estimated US$1.0 billion to US$1.5 billion in interest charges passed on to customers. These interest charges approximated 2 to 3 percent of year-to-year GDP from 1991 to 1994. The various recapitalizations took place as follows:

- *1991 consolidation agreement (US$0.1 billion).* Government guarantee for Ft 10.5 billion (US$100 million) for bad loans made before 1987 during the monobank period, mainly to coal mines. This was accompanied by the drafting of new accounting rules and bankruptcy and banking laws.
- *1992 loan consolidation scheme (US$1.1 billion).* New accounting standards led to a dramatic increase in recognition of nonperforming loans, prompting the 1992 loan consolidation scheme. Nonperforming loans made to resident enterprises before September 1992 were swapped for 20-year, variable coupon government bonds at market rates. Swaps were made for 50 percent of loan values for loans made before 1992 and at 80 percent replacement for loans made during 1992. Fourteen banks and 60 savings cooperatives participated in the scheme. In total, Ft 120.5 billion of bad debt was swapped for Ft 98.6 billion in government bonds. Bad debts were placed in the Credit Consolidation Fund managed by the Hungarian Investment and Development Corporation, which got a license to operate in 1993. The debt swap involved 1,885 companies, of which 116 went bankrupt and 549 were liquidated. Three-quarters of the swapped bad debt involved 110 companies, of which about 100 went bankrupt or were liquidated.
- *"13+1" program (US$0.6 billion).* This recapitalization involved swapping Ft 57 billion in bonds for 90 percent of the book value of bank loans to 13 large industrial enterprises and the state railway company. The two state property funds were expected to turn these "strategic" enterprises around based on a strategy of short-term loss containment and financial restructuring.
- *1993/1994 consolidation agreement (US$1.65 billion).* In 1993, Parliament voted a bank recapitalization program to raise banks' capital adequacy ratios from -15 percent to zero by the end of 1993, and to 8 percent in 1994. Eight banks (and some savings cooperatives) received government bonds worth Ft 114.4 billion in 1993, of which MHB received about half (Ft 56 billion), K&H received about one-third (Ft 37 billion), and Budapest Bank received Ft 6 billion. A second injection of Ft 50 billion in 1994 brought the total to Ft 165 billion and capital adequacy ratios to 4 percent. The Ministry of Finance ended up with 75 percent of voting shares until the end of 1995.

In the first recapitalization effort, the 1991 consolidation agreement, the government issued a guarantee of 50 percent of Ft 10.5 billion (US$100 million) in doubtful loans that had been transferred to the banks in 1987.

This should have reduced the burden on the banks of bad loans to enterprises, but it covered only 2 percent of the bad loans the banks were holding at the end of 1990. The 1992 loan consolidation scheme was launched in 1992, but took effect in May 1993. The program involved the exchange of Ft 98.6 billion (US$1.1 billion at the time) in government bonds for loans with a carrying value of Ft 120 billion (US$1.3 billion). The loans were carved out from the banks, with the goal of executing separate workout arrangements. However, workout attempts achieved limited success, and the plan failed to remedy the problem of recurring credit quality deterioration. In late 1993 the authorities introduced the "13+1" program, which involved the exchange of Ft 58 billion (US$620 million) in bonds for 90 percent of the book value of bank loans to 13 large industrial enterprises and the railways. The Ministry of Industry and Trade selected these enterprises based on their strategic importance. The hope was to turn them around through loss reduction measures and financial reorganization without significant physical restructuring. The program achieved moderate success.

The inadequacy of the first recapitalization schemes led the government to launch the 1993 bank consolidation program, intended to be a comprehensive solution to bank problems. The government contracted Crédit Suisse First Boston to evaluate the banks' portfolios. The evaluation revealed that (a) three of the five largest banks, all SOCBs, were technically insolvent; (b) a number of cooperatives were inadequately capitalized; (c) OTP's capital was deficient, a highly risky situation given its importance to depositors' confidence and the financing of the interbank market; and (d) ongoing SOCB operating losses would erase remaining capital in one year. Capital deficiency at the end of 1993 was estimated at Ft 139 billion (US$1.4 billion), the equivalent of 7 percent of nominal SOCB assets. This left little more than Ft 18 billion (US$179 million) in capital, or less than 1 percent of assets, showing that SOCBs had little net worth in the aggregate, even after four recapitalizations that had exceeded Ft 320 billion. Nonperforming loans were expected to continue to reduce SOCB capital, particularly at two of the largest banks (MHB, K&H), where estimates indicated that nonperforming loans were as high as 87 percent of total loans. Meanwhile, annual operating losses at 16 banks approximated Ft 20 billion (about US$200 million), which would have eliminated SOCB capital in about one year if nonperforming loans and the Ft 139 billion capital deficiency were taken into account.

Immediate action to deal with solvency issues was warranted, given the risk of a liquidity crisis and high interest spreads. Estimates of the contribution of loan portfolio deterioration on the level of intermediation spreads suggest that banks raised interest rates to sound borrowers by nearly 400 basis points to offset the effect of nonperforming loans (see OECD 1993). This contributed to real margins of 7 to 8 percent through 1993, although these have come down steadily since 1994 as net margins tightened due to increased competition (real net margins were 6 percent in 1994, 5 percent in 1995, and 4 percent in 1996, and are very narrow today in the hotly contested blue chip sector). This subsequently resulted in reduced profits for SOCBs. Meanwhile, more competitive private and joint venture banks, with their stronger balance sheets, lower cost structures, and superior profitability, were able to offer better rates and be more precise in selecting creditworthy borrowers.

The government recapitalized SOCBs to a zero percent capital adequacy ratio at the end of 1993. Two additional infusions followed in May and December 1994 to increase the capital adequacy ratios of the troubled banks to 8 percent. This 1993 consolidation program marked a shift in the government's strategy from the centralized approach more characteristic of the Czech Republic to a bank-led decentralization scheme more similar to that followed by Poland. To effect the capital infusion, the state issued 20-year bonds paying semi-annual interest at an annualized rate of 5 percent. The value of these bonds totaled Ft 165 billion (US$1.65 billion), about the same as all earlier recapitalizations combined (on a dollar basis).

The banks were asked to evaluate their financial and operational positions, prepare corrective action plans, develop special workout units, and improve key operational functions. However, these agreements were often ineffective, because they failed to (a) specify quantitative performance criteria and targets, leaving the extent of restructuring open to interpretation; (b) provide adequate incentives to owners, managers, and bank personnel for improved governance and performance; and (c) impose penalties for noncompliance. The lack of strong regulatory oversight resulting from fragmented supervision aggravated the problem. [15]

While the first recapitalizations were limited in their cost, the final consolidation plan was costly in its timing, coinciding with a period when the government was running up large fiscal deficits in 1993–94 to cover high social welfare costs. Perhaps more damaging was the notion that government efforts at least indirectly created a moral hazard by precipitating expectations of future assistance among large enterprise loss makers, particularly

---

15. The Ministry of Finance established the Bank Control Unit in January 1994 to monitor compliance with the consolidation agreements, although its authority was unclear. This lack of clarity was rooted in the fragmentation created by the 1991 Banking Act, which split responsibility for regulation, supervision, and enforcement between the Bank Supervisory Committee and the state banking supervision agency.

in strategic sectors with high employment levels. Such an approach undermined bank management, as government intervention undercut attempts to enforce financial discipline.

Even though the 1993 bank consolidation program increased capital adequacy ratios to acceptable levels, true capital adequacy ratios were still uncertain because of the incomplete scope of audits. The SOCBs were still struggling to maintain adequate capital levels in 1995, which ultimately contributed to the decision to privatize the banks under the May 1995 Law on Privatization. The state banks accounted for the major share of losses and nonperforming loans. By September 1994 the stock of bad loans had reached Ft 597 billion (US$5.5 billion), or 26 percent of total loans (69 percent of the total stock of enterprise loans). The stock of bad loans not serviced for more than a year was Ft 268 billion (US$2.5 billion), or 12 percent of outstanding loans.[16] The proportion of troubled loans in the portfolios of the four large SOCBs increased from less than one-third at the end of 1993 to nearly 40 percent by September 1994. The progressive deterioration of their portfolios meant that the 1993 consolidation program may not have been sufficient in achieving an 8 percent capital adequacy ratio based on end 1994 balance sheets, as it was based on end 1993 data (see IMF 1995). Large state banks generated pretax profits in 1994, but these were thin—return on average assets was only 0.85 percent—and well below levels the SOCBs needed to achieve 8 percent capital adequacy ratios.

In light of these weaknesses, the Ministry of Finance initiated policies to improve the financial positions of the large state owned banks by focusing on hard budget constraints and privatization. It initiated the process in 1995 with the partial privatization of several SOCBs, including the acquisition of Budapest Bank by General Electric Capital and EBRD for US$87 million, and the partial privatization of OTP, which raised more than US$140 million in new capital. MHB, which is now majority private, made strong efforts to reduce problem loans in advance of full privatization.[17] It succeeded

---

16. Annual operating losses approximated Ft 20 billion at 16 banks, most of which were SOCBs. Nonperforming loans were estimated to be (a) Ft 186.4 billion (US$2.2 billion), or 11.5 percent of outstanding loans at the end of 1992; (b) Ft 229 billion (US$2.5 billion), or 13 percent of outstanding loans in mid-1993; and (c) Ft 352 billion (US$3.5 billion) at the end of 1993, before recapitalization; (d) Ft 143.8 billion (US$1.4 billion), or 11.1 percent of outstanding loans at the end 1993, after recapitalization. Classified loans were mostly to large SOEs.

17. Between mid-1995 and March 1996, K&H resolved more than half of its troubled credit portfolio (a reduction in nominal value from Ft 45 billion to Ft 22 billion), while MHB launched a subsidiary ("Risk Kft") to restructure Ft 82 billion of its troubled assets (Ft 16.8 billion of book value, net of provisions). More than half of the assets transferred to Risk Kft were resolved of approximately two-thirds of the net value of the assets.

in attracting investment from ABN-Amro in 1996, partly because of these efforts. In the case of ABN-Amro's investment, another US$200 million to US$250 million or more are expected to be invested to strengthen the bank's position in the retail banking market.

The strengths of Hungary's new approach include the restored commitment to macroeconomic stabilization, the sustained political commitment to an enabling macroeconomic environment, the improved governance and management at banks and firms, the recognition of the need to be competitive as markets become increasingly linked, and the establishment of a timetable for full privatization. Notwithstanding some of the weaknesses of the recapitalization approach, Hungary is well on its way to being the most fully privatized and competitive banking sector in Central Europe.

Poland: From Shock Therapy to Gradualism

In Poland, the banking system's portfolio deteriorated substantially in 1991, at which time the government was confronted with the fiscal implications of the loss of some 40 percent of bank assets. The government wanted to find a solution that minimized the loss of jobs and productive capacity. After an initial period when licensing requirements encouraged the entry of private banks to stimulate competition (but for which Poland's legal and regulatory framework and supervisory capacity were unprepared), Poland's bank reform program stressed the gradual restructuring of nine regional SOCBs and several specialized banks prior to privatization. The government originally decided to delegate to the nine SOCBs the task of restructuring the enterprises that had failed to adapt to new market conditions, and to recapitalize the commercial banks for that purpose. After two banks (Bank Slaski and Bank Wielkopolski) were partly privatized with foreign investment, the number was reduced to seven commercial banks.

The Law on Financial Restructuring of Enterprises and Banks became effective in March 1993, and established the basis for a program not only to recapitalize the banks and restructure their balance sheets, but also to deal with state enterprises with bad debts. Key features of the plan were as follows:

- *Classifying loans.* The authorities instructed the state banks to separate out loans classified by auditors as loss and doubtful, and to create provisions amounting to 100 percent for the loss category and 50 percent for the doubtful category on the basis of a December 1991 portfolio analysis conducted by international accounting firms.
- *Setting up workout units for loan restructuring.* The SOCBs set up internal workout units to manage their bad loan portfolios and to restructure

these loans within about a year. Banks refrained from lending to borrowers with doubtful or unrecoverable loans unless they presented a clear and acceptable plan to the bank (and to the Ministry of Finance, the banks' owner) to enhance their creditworthiness and justify new lending. Each workout unit had 15 bank staff, although not all bad debts were assigned to these units.

- *Issuing bonds (recapitalization).* The government recapitalized seven SOCBs with about US$600 million in 1993, approximating 12 percent capital adequacy after provisioning for loan losses and accrued interest. Poland also recapitalized three specialized banks, although the restructuring of these banks differed considerably from that of the SOCBs, in that it follows a more centralized approach. The cost of these recapitalizations thus reached about US$1.1 billion.
- *Establishing the Bank Privatization Fund.* Poland established the Bank Privatization Fund at the end of 1992 to service the bonds issued to the SOCBs in 1993. It established this fund to reduce prospective investors' fears of debt service complications that would interfere with bank privatization. Resources from the fund were to be transferred to the government to service the Treasury bonds any SOCB held as a result of its recapitalization. As an incentive to privatize as rapidly as feasible, funds are made available only after a bank has been privatized.

By the March 1994 deadline spelled out in the law, the commercial banks had financially restructured the 800 or so enterprises that accounted for most of their bad loan portfolios. About 200 of these enterprises, which accounted for more than half of the bad loans, entered into conciliatory agreements with their creditors under an out-of-court reorganization procedure modeled on the U.S. bankruptcy code (Chapter 11). The agreements typically entailed (a) transforming state enterprises into joint stock companies; (b) rationalizing and reorienting troubled enterprises' activities by reshaping product lines, closing unproductive units, and trimming the work force; (c) rescheduling financial obligations to make repayment financially feasible; and (d) diluting state ownership through debt-equity swaps in about 150 cases. Other enterprises underwent liquidation, had their collateral executed, regained their creditworthiness, or had their debts auctioned off by banks.

The recapitalization of the seven SOCBs enabled them to recognize their losses and work out their bad loans. The results are still hard to gauge, as many enterprises have shown improved performance that might not have occurred if the economy had not grown at 6 to 7 percent real rates. However, the process helped to "commercialize" the banks prior to privatization based on the adoption of strengthened corporate governance and management, a program to restructure loan portfolios, and incentives for employees through the issuance of shares. The enterprise and bank restructuring program has strengthened financial discipline and forced commercial banks to develop risk-assessment capacity. By most accounts, the commercial banks have succeeded in restructuring their loans and strengthening their financial condition.

As of March 1994, the SOCBs had effectively dealt with 98 percent of their larger bad loans, and by some estimates, their average capital adequacy ratios stood at 27 percent, well above international standards. They significantly reduced their stocks of bad loans, from 30 percent of portfolios in 1993 to about 8 percent in 1995. About 83 percent of classified SOCB loans have been or are being restructured, while 17 percent have been declared unrecoverable. Regional SOCBs are currently extremely profitable, largely because of the large net interest spreads they have enjoyed between government securities and deposits—these rates were in the 8 to 9 percent range until 1996—as well as from efficiency improvements. Since late 1995 lending has increased, while spreads have narrowed as competition has intensified.

The strengths of the Polish approach include the sustained political commitment to improved bank governance and management; the introduction of suitable incentives to stakeholders, that is, shares for bank employees and retained proceeds by banks from recoveries after recapitalization; the beneficial institutional effects of internal workout units, which have contributed to better credit management and operations after the restructuring period (see Montes-Negret and Papi 1997); the extensive use of training and technical assistance from internationally recognized Western banks; and the recognition that recapitalization should be up-front, one-time, fiscally feasible, and focused on privatization. All this has been reinforced by a steadily improving macroeconomic context characterized by 6 to 7 percent real growth rates, declining inflation rates, and reduced fiscal deficits.

However, questions remain about the extent of SOEs' operational and physical restructuring and their ability to compete as the market opens up. Some of the financial restructuring of bad loans to long-term status may have delayed loss recognition, because some enterprises have yet to undergo sufficient operational restructuring to demonstrate real competitiveness and positive cash flow in open market conditions. This contributes to a level of nonperforming loans in the range of 15 to 20 percent of loan portfolios.

With regard to the bank privatization that has occurred, it has been partial, largely because of fears of the domestic banking sector being overrun by more competitive foreign institutions without ample time being provided to allow Polish banks to become competitive. Signs that this attitude is changing are encouraging, as shown in the increasing stakes held by ING of the Netherlands and Allied Irish Bank in the two state banks that did not require recapitalization under the program, and the initial privatization of Poland's most profitable bank, Bank Handlowy, in mid-1997. However, the privatization of five SOCBs has been put on a consolidation track, which may be complicated by remaining questions about the (a) degree of expertise SOCBs have attained regarding internal and managerial controls, loan evaluation, risk management, and overall service delivery, although here technical assistance in the form of twinning arrangements with West European banks has led to vast improvements; (b) basic bank governance, particularly for those banks that still hold troubled SOE loans in important industrial sectors; (c) general levels of SOCB competitiveness without protection from greater foreign entry; and (d) impact on changing portfolios as net spreads on government securities decline, and as interest income from lending increases as a share of the income stream. Polish banks were partly shielded from foreign competition during 1992–95 to give Polish banks time to recover, reduce bad debts, and increase capital in advance of more open competition. Such protection is not likely to recur. Another major challenge is the reform of the specialized banks—BGZ and PKO BP—which still accounted for more than a third of banking system assets in 1996. Thus weaknesses to the Polish approach include continued weaknesses in the enabling environment (although these are steadily improving), slow privatization after several years of institutional strengthening, and still low levels of financial intermediation.

Ukraine: The Perils of Delayed Economic Reform

Since 1992 the number of "private" commercial banks in the Ukraine has proliferated; however, most of these banks have long been in serious financial trouble, many are unable to meet minimum capital requirements, and some are still managed according to noncommercial criteria. In general, banks' profits are weakened by the persistent accumulation of nonperforming loans to enterprises. Thus Ukraine did not pursue structural reforms as intently as its counterparts in CEE countries.

The first commercial banks with private ownership were registered in 1989. In 1990 three of the five sectoral banks in Ukraine—Bank Ukraina (agriculture), Prominvest (heavy industry), and Ukrsotsbank (social investment bank)—transformed themselves into joint stock companies. These three banks accounted for more than 80 percent of Ukraine's banking activity from 1991–93. By the end of 1994, the banking sector consisted of the National Bank of Ukraine, five specialized banks, (two state owned and three majority owned by state enterprises), and about 350 locally owned commercial banks. The number of commercial banks had shrunk to around 220 by early 1995 because of widespread insolvencies, including some of the larger "private" banks, which failed because of foreign exchange losses and fraud. Among the remaining banks, nearly half (about 100) were reported to be in serious financial trouble in 1996 because of the large share of nonperforming loans in their portfolios. Only 14 banks were sufficiently strong to meet Ukraine's minimum capital requirements. Meanwhile, as of the end of 1994, two large banks—Oschadny Bank (the savings bank) and Exim Bank (foreign trade)—remained state owned, although under more commercialized incentive structures. Fundamental problems facing the Ukrainian banking sector have been both structural and macroeconomic in nature, although the country's macroeconomic circumstances have improved in the last few years and it has made some progress at the structural level in terms of building institutional capacity and skills. The current situation can be summarized as follows:

- *Ownership, management, and governance.* Many of the commercial banks were formed to raise funds for specific enterprises. Thus their criteria for resource management were usually captive to the prerogatives of enterprise owners, and were often noncommercial. For these banks the introduction of hard budget constraints altered incentives and decisionmaking, thereby helping to contain some of the problem after significant damage had already been done to the economy.
- *Funding sources.* Banks' liabilities consisted mainly of enterprise deposits that have contractual maturities of three months or longer, with an option to withdraw funds and forfeit interest. In 1991–92 newly formed commercial banks had to respond to enterprises' demands for cash. This shortage of cash forced enterprises and state banks to write IOUs to their employees rather than pay wages in cash. Enterprise and household deposits have diminished since as local currency values depreciated, and as foreign currency holdings were kept outside the banking system to meet liquidity needs. Banks have tried to restore deposits since that time, but with little success. Meanwhile, Ukraine has a limited capital market to tap as a source of funding, with most of this market dominated by trading in short-term government securities. At great risk, only the National Bank of Ukraine and the Savings Bank are meaningful in the

interbank market. Here too, resources are scarce. Through the interbank market, the Savings Bank has suffered significant losses and has been forced to reschedule what were originally short-term loans to other banks, some of which have failed.

- *Lending.* Liabilities are matched by 3- to 12-month loans to state enterprises or new, privately owned firms. These short-term loans have been priced at variable interest rates that can be reset every three months. Long-term lending is virtually nonexistent. The introduction of the karbovanetz in January 1992 enabled the National Bank of Ukraine to create currency that was channeled into the economy through commercial banks. Commercial banks lent aggressively through 1993 with little or poor security, and paid no attention to cash flow in a market sense. This was subsequently followed by a period when banks recognized bad debts, triggering a decline in new lending flows. Since then, enterprises have had fewer incentives to place deposits with banks, which has added to the cycle of resource scarcity in the banking system.

- *Pricing.* Commercial bank spreads on local currency (loans against deposits) were as high as 45 to 85 percent in 1995, although they have fallen since. High interest rate margins on loans have partially compensated for large classified debt levels since 1994, although they may not actually cover the full range of costs associated with portfolio problems, taxes, reserve requirements, and other features that undermine banks' profitability (see Montes-Negret and Papi 1996). However, these high nominal rates were unsustainable for many enterprises, and weakened their cash flow and their ability to service interest fully and ultimately repay principal. (Effective interest rates on U.S. dollar loans ranged from 30 to 60 percent, and interest rates on Ukrainian currency loans were also high.) These high nominal margins were primarily a function of a lack of deposits to fund loans, the poor quality of banks' loan portfolios, and the undeveloped level of competition within the banking system. Today, Ukraine's commercial banks are not a major source of investment or working capital financing.

Until 1994, foreign exchange transactions were the major source of income for banks. Spreads on these transactions ranged up to 10 percent, although margins had dropped to 2.4 percent by late 1994. Banks that had a greater capacity to obtain funds or approval for transactions from the National Bank of Ukraine prospered. Contacts in the government played a significant role in this process.

Today, the Savings Bank with its extensive national network of about 15,000 branches is possibly the most important bank functioning in the market. It has served as a conduit for public payments such as households' accounts and pensions, and as a keeper and distributor of privatization certificates. Since May 1991, the Savings Bank has actively tried to develop the asset side of its operations by making housing loans and by extending loans to small enterprises owned by people who hold deposits with it. It has also solicited commercial banks for loans and negotiated more favorable rates with them than what it could earn on credit to the National Bank of Ukraine. This has helped to develop the interbank market, whose size was constrained by regulatory lending rate ceilings. The Savings Bank remained the only bank that could offer its clients government guaranteed deposit insurance. This prompted an aggressive pricing strategy—lower interest rates on deposits than other commercial banks—the outcome of which was a decline in its share of household deposits to less than 60 percent by the end of 1994 despite the government insurance guarantee. The majority of savings deposits accumulated during 1991–94 were forwarded to the National Bank of Ukraine for its own internal use or for on-lending to commercial banks. The Savings Bank incurred large losses as a result of its aggressive pricing and diversification strategy.

In general, Ukraine's banking sector has yet to experience meaningful restructuring. This was both a cause and a consequence of Ukraine's weak economy. Since 1995–96 the authorities have made some progress in strengthening the banking sector, largely through efforts to build supervisory capacity, reform accounting standards, and enforce regulations when capital is severely impaired or when gross violations occur. Along with the moderate improvement in macroeconomic conditions, this represents a step forward. However, as seen elsewhere, macroeconomic stabilization is necessary, but not sufficient. Ukraine will ultimately have to make faster and greater progress at the structural level to achieve competitiveness in the banking sector. This

Table 7.6. *The Distribution of Responsibility for Successful Banking Sector Reform*

Ingredient	Governments	Banks
Macroeconomic environment	Provide sound monetary, fiscal, and exchange rate framework to contain inflation rates, limit fiscal deficits, and maintain stable current and capital accounts	Respond with efficient, well-managed, diversified operations as net interest margins shrink
Links to markets	Encourage linkage across markets, products	Should be focused on feasible "universal" options

Table 7.6. (*Continued*)

Ingredient	Governments	Banks
Recapitalization	Should have little or no adverse macroeconomic impact	Should be one-time, up-front, linked to privatization timetable, and focused on strong governance and management to attract strategic domestic and/or foreign investment
Enabling environment	Build on stable macroeconomic framework with open markets, well-functioning institutions for oversight, and supportive infrastructure	Take advantage of opportunities, including joint ventures with experienced specialists; be innovative, stress open information and recognize that markets are subject to constant change
Political commitment	Sustained commitment to reform with long-term vision; rejection of short-term political pressures	Sustained commitment to marketplace competitiveness based on global standards, not interim distortions
Stakeholder incentives	Better banking performance strengthens macroeconomic fundamentals	Rewards (financial and otherwise) for improved performance
Technical assistance and training	Assistance and training essential for policymakers and regulators for safe and sound banking in support of a stable macroeconomic framework	Training to professionalize standards and personnel; correspondent links with prime-rated banks formalize competitive systems
Sequencing of reforms	Institutional capacity and financial sector infrastructure needed; links between macroeconomic framework and structural issues should be recognized from the start; should include liquidation	Restructuring should be as rapid as is feasible within the context of prudential standards for safety and soundness
Governance and management	Incentives need to emphasize global standards for sustainability, accountability, safety, and soundness; should reinforce enabling environment efforts	Should be focused on share appreciation and long-term competitiveness based on global standards
Privatization	Institutional capacity and financial sector infrastructure needed; links between macroeconomic framework and structural issues should be recognized from the start	Privatization should be as rapid as is feasible within the context of prudential standards for safety and soundness and the ability to attract strategic investment

Table 7.7. *Evaluation of Banking Sector Restructuring Results*

Item	Czech Republic	Hungary	Poland	Ukraine
Approach	Centralized; up-front carve-out and recapitalization; "good bank-bad bank"; partial SOCB privatization	Decentralized; multiple recapitalizations; rapid privatization since 1995; most competitive banking sector in region because of enabling environment, foreign investment	Partly decentralized, up-front recapitalization and slow, partial privatization of SOCBs; partly centralized for large enterprises in sensitive sectors	No recapitalization; rapid ownership transformation, but lacking in transparency and unaccompanied by needed changes in incentive structures
Technical assistance and foreign participation	Limited assistance; more needed at state banks, regulatory agencies	Some; high levels of foreign investment accelerated competitiveness	Significant via twinning and other forms	Some; more needed in absence of significant foreign investment
Financial impact on banks	Bank solvency restored; balance sheets restructured; more capital needed because of increased recognition of nonperforming loans with introduction of stricter standards in 1994, findings of external auditors with more severe assessment than banks' internal views	Bank solvency restored; balance sheets restructured; recognition of nonperforming loans with introduction of stricter standards in 1993–94; SOCB earnings less than those of private banks despite holding 72 percent of banking system assets (1994); fiscal pressures lead to faster reforms	Bank solvency restored; balance sheets restructured; transparency strengthened by loan loss provisioning, but undermined by doubts about enterprise restructuring and ongoing credit quality; earnings based on securities rather than on lending	Weak capital and liquidity because of high level of nonperforming loans; insufficient provisioning, transparency; limited role and level of financial intermediation in economic development

Table 7.7. (*Continued*)

Item	Czech Republic	Hungary	Poland	Ukraine
Bank operations, management, and governance	Ongoing problems with SOCB loan portfolios; improved supervision required; weak governance because of ownership structures; additional technical assistance needed	SOCBs could not compete with private banks after recapitalizations; rapid privatization since 1995–96; highly competitive standards now in place; weak supervision	Slow privatization; SOCBs partly protected from new foreign competition from 1992–95; SOCBs now have strong capital; SOCBs benefited from twinning, strong governance since 1993	Ongoing loan portfolio problems; supervision improving, but continued risk of weak governance because of ownership structures; increased foreign investment, systems, know-how needed
Financial cost of recapitalizations	US$10 billion (1991, 1993) = 15–20% of GDP in those years	US$3.5–5.0 billion (1991–94) = 2-3% of GDP during the period	Less than US$1 billion for SOCBs (1993) = less than 1% of 1993 GDP; other costs from higher spreads, disintermediation; more for specialized banks	No recapitalization; costs from losses, high net spreads, fiscal subsidies, foregone growth and efficiency
Financial performance of enterprises	Serious questions about degree of restructuring, levels of competitiveness because of governance; serious current account deficit in 1996 prompted emergency proposals for reform in April 1997	Improving performance because of competition, high levels of foreign investment, and hardened budget constraints since 1995–96	Improving performance because of real GDP growth; concerns about delays in privatizing "strategic" firms, potential costs in mining, steel, shipyards, agriculture	Weak performance; need for major overhaul at the structural level; informal sector accounts for 60% of economy, mostly micro and small-scale; foreign investment needed

Source: World Bank.

could be facilitated by a firm commitment to reorganize the banking sector, to impose stricter capital and governance requirements, to change the Banking Law and the Central Bank Act, to provide more thorough oversight of bank management, and to attract the capital and expertise needed from foreign banks to invigorate the banking market.

Summary of Structural Reforms

CEE reform programs have adopted a series of measures to transform existing financial systems to serve a market-oriented economy, restructure and privatize enterprises, and to create stable macroeconomic conditions for growth. Their approaches to reform have met with varying degrees of success. Table 7.6 highlights some of the critical ingredients needed for successful reform. Table 7.7 evaluates results by country and approach.

The Enabling Environment for Successful Banking

All four countries have improved the enabling environment, particularly by restoring macroeconomic stability and confidence in national currencies. With the exception of Ukraine, they have introduced meaningful laws, regulations, and accounting frameworks consistent with market principles, and Ukraine has shown some movement in this direction. The CEE countries have made progress with institution building, for example, banking supervision, credit rating systems, bankers' associations, and training programs (Poland); with overall levels of competitiveness resulting from investment by prime-rated banks and accelerated privatization since 1995 (Hungary); and with capital markets showing increasing investment interest in domestic banks and insurance companies (Hungary, Poland). Underlying all these developments is maintenance of a stable macroeconomic framework, as was the case in the Czech Republic until recently when its current account deteriorated, and is increasingly the case in Hungary and Poland. Accelerating the pace of industrial and financial sector privatization in Poland, sustaining a commitment to stable macroeconomic fundamentals in Hungary, and following through with ambitious structural reforms in the financial banking and enterprise sectors in the Czech Republic should enhance competitiveness and increase the countries' links to regional and global markets. This bodes well for banking, on the condition that they are prepared for global competition, can manage risk properly, and are willing to adopt the kinds of governance and accountability standards investors and regulators increasingly require.

In contrast, Ukraine (and most non-Baltic FSU countries) has failed to provide domestic and foreign investors with sufficient stability for long-term confidence. Notwithstanding modest improvements in the legal framework, recent regulatory interventions, and a generally open commitment to external investment, countries like Ukraine have far to go in establishing an enabling environment. Institutional capacity is weak, financial sector infrastructure is limited, and capital markets activity is limited. Delays in developing basic financial infrastructure have been a serious drawback, particularly in accounting and legal matters. Achieving macroeconomic stability has been a major challenge, and revamping the economy into one that is competitive will require a major overhaul. None of this bodes well for the banking sector in the near term. Adding to these problems is the general weakness of most of Ukraine's traditional trading partners, although its links with Poland and other countries of Central Europe are increasing as are its good relations with countries of the Organisation for Economic Co-operation and Development.

Parameters of Competition for Successful Banking

Transition countries show varying levels of competition in their financial markets. Hungary has long been the most open to foreign investment, and has been the most profitable (along with Poland more recently) among transition countries' banking sectors (see Borish, Ding, and Noël 1996). Privatization of large SOCBs has accelerated quickly since 1995, and Hungary is likely to have virtually no state ownership in the banking sector by late 1998 or early 1999. The Czech Republic has also had an open environment for investment in the banking system, much of it associated with mass privatization and derived from neighboring countries to provide financing and services for joint ventures and direct investment. However, the Czech Republic's interlocking directorates have reduced the importance of the stock exchange and information disclosure as a catalyst for heightened competitiveness (see OECD 1996). The emergency measures proposed in April 1997—full privatization of banks and enterprises, enhanced transparency and disclosure, strengthened regulation—reflect increased recognition of many of the structural weaknesses that need to be reformed. Poland's licensing policy was less open from 1992–95, although foreign banks remained the most profitable during that period. Poland is now increasingly focusing on the consolidation of remaining SOCBs, and banks represented a disproportionate 40 percent or more share of the Warsaw Stock Exchange's market capitalization in late 1996. How long Poland will take to privatize, liquidate, and/or merge its remaining SOCBs and specialized banks, and the potentially distortionary effect these delays might have on further financial sector development, particularly given the depth of problems at the largest specialized banks, remains to be seen. However, Poland has long had a vision of privatization by the end of the century, and understands the need for satisfactory institutions to regulate banks and enterprises properly in an increasingly liberalized environment. The recent privatization of Bank Handlowy and plans for additional banking privatization in 1998–99 reflect continued commitment to this direction.

Noteworthy among CEE countries is the trend toward convergence in real interest rate trends. As they sustain stable frameworks and competition, average real interest margins have increasingly converged.

Ukraine has had an open environment for investment in the banking sector from domestic and foreign sources, but its weak economy and lack of institutional capacity have undermined serious banking development. Along with most of the rest of the FSU, Ukraine is beginning to recognize that safe and sound banking practices are preconditions for stable and orderly growth. Proper oversight by investors and regulators (and later by depositors) is needed to achieve this, but to date Ukraine has lacked such oversight.

Most countries initially had low capital requirements and flexible licensing standards to promote entry and competition. This was particularly evident in Poland and Ukraine, where the number of banks increased quickly, but was also true in the Czech Republic and Hungary. However, this exemplifies an error in the sequencing of reforms, that is, liberalizing markets before establishing adequate legal, regulatory, supervisory, and enforcement capacity for stable market development. Recognizing this error, CEE countries tightened minimum capital requirements. The Czech Republic and Hungary have capital standards higher than EU minimums, while Poland's criteria are currently consistent with the EU. However, a second key point is the development of capacity for regulatory enforcement in a forward-looking manner to contain systemic risks that could have a contagion effect and prompt lender of last resort or other emergency scenarios with significant macroeconomic implications. Such risk management on the part of banks, investors, and regulators involves a range of variables that, if exposed to excess volatility, could have a significant adverse impact on individual banks' capital and earnings and spread to the system at large. Regulatory capacity to prevent such problems is currently relatively weak in the Czech Republic. The view in Hungary is that foreign investment into the sector partly externalizes these risks. Poland has focused on developing domestic capacity in these areas. Ukraine, which is not likely to become a member of the EU in the foreseeable future, has greater capacity needs. As CEE countries make progress toward accession to the EU (having already joined the Organisation for Economic Co-operation and Development), they have begun to implement recommendations from the Basle Committee. This will need ongoing strengthening as the Basle Committee itself begins to incorporate new risk-based techniques that go beyond traditional rules-based approaches.

Proper application of prudential regulations has been a key institutional priority for orderly financial sector development. As systems become more open to competition, more rather than less regulation is needed. Poland discovered this in the early 1990s after following extremely flexible licensing practices. Ukraine faced a similar set of circumstances and is now beginning to deal with these problems. However, in all countries, effective supervision and oversight is a dynamic process that must take the changing, interrelated, and increasingly complex features of financial sector development into account. For transition countries this requires time to develop, particularly as these countries have only recently introduced new laws, regulations, and accounting frameworks and moved away from passive, compliance-based oversight to more active forms of oversight.[18] Poland has made great strides toward effective supervision of banking. However, supervision requires strengthening in Hungary. In the Czech Republic banking supervision has limited preventive capacity given that structural weaknesses may be deeper than previously thought, fraud may be more prevalent than can be tolerated, and bank debt represents a central part of economic financing. Ukraine has slowly moved to improve supervision, although enforcement may be more difficult than in CEE countries. Ongoing development in this area will be needed to protect depositors and to manage risk for those issuing debt and equity. This will also require coordination with supervisory authorities across national borders.

Methods of Recapitalization

The performance of CEE countries and the methods chosen to recapitalize banks has varied. In some cases, such as the Czech Republic, the macroeconomic environment appeared to be stable until late 1996–early 1997, when structural weaknesses were disclosed more openly. Despite high levels of economic growth, high and growing levels of nonperforming loans continued to

---

18. Most transition countries have only recently begun to introduce rules-based supervision consistent with international standards. Some countries, such as Poland, are also introducing more recently pioneered risk-based supervision techniques in varying degrees, particularly as they move closer to integration with more affluent EU countries through international agreements.

weaken the financial condition of the large SOCBs in the Czech Republic. Recognition of a massive 8.6 percent current account deficit exposed the magnitude of structural weaknesses and demonstrated that macroeconomic stability is not sufficient for successful reform. Thus the up-front carve-out may have helped with the initial partial privatization of banks, but it does not appear to have been sufficient to create the conditions and incentives required for necessary structural reforms.

In other cases, Hungary, for instance, has benefited from a strong enabling environment and high levels of investment, which have raised the level of banking sector competition. However, macroeconomic fundamentals deteriorated in 1993–94, demonstrating that macroeconomic stability enhances structural reforms and competitiveness, while macroeconomic deterioration weakens or undermines them. The recapitalizations Hungary pursued largely reflected the recognition of losses at state banks and enterprises and the government's desire to restore bank solvency prior to privatization and limit some of the more drastic restructuring requirements, for instance, layoffs, of loss-making enterprises. In the end, the government recognized that accelerated privatization and strategic investment were more efficient than recapitalization. Fortunately for Hungary, ongoing reforms dating back to the 1980s and a favorable enabling environment made this approach feasible.

Meanwhile, Poland has pursued a gradual approach to privatization, but a steady approach to institutional strengthening, development of regulatory capacity, and improvement of macroeconomic fundamentals. Reform of state commercial banks was fairly swift and time-bound, leading to internal changes that made these banks more privatizable than in 1993. However, privatization has taken place more slowly. Poland's efforts to reform its SOCBs were relatively low-cost in terms of GDP, although intermediation rates remain low and questions persist about the ability of these banks to manage credit in an increasingly competitive environment. Poland's approach to the SOCBs points to much of what is necessary in terms of increasing macroeconomic stability and improving structural capacity. However, how these banks will fare in more open markets remains to be seen.

Most recapitalization has involved the issuance of bonds (and guarantees in the case of Hungary) to replace nonperforming loans on bank balance sheets, thereby strengthening banks' solvency positions. Where these were interest-bearing bonds, carve-outs eased some of the liquidity problems banks experienced as a result of nonperforming loans. In the Czech Republic, the carve-out was conducted prudently so as to not create macroeconomic imbalances. In

Hungary, the highest financial costs coincided with worsening fiscal deficits, and thereby may have contributed to macroeconomic imbalances. However, even more worrisome at the time was the risk of moral hazard and the institutional weaknesses of Hungary's supervisory system. The government of Hungary reacted successfully in 1995 with a vibrant commitment to privatization in the banking sector. In Poland the recapitalization had less of an adverse effect on macroeconomic imbalances, although it did not address the two largest and most troubled specialized banks. Ukraine did not pursue recapitalization. Table 7.8 presents a review of CEE country performance.

Restructuring, Privatization, and the Importance of Governance and Management

In all three CEE countries, recapitalization occurred prior to privatization. In the Czech Republic, privatization was rapid as part of the 1992 mass privatization program, but only partial. In Poland, privatization was more gradual. Several SOCBs remain in state hands, although this is likely to change in the next two years. In Hungary, no timetable for privatization existed until 1995, although sustained commitment to reform and firm commitment to privatization from 1995 on has been successful. All the examples point to the need for improved bank governance, management, skills, systems, and competitiveness, and show the limitations of recapitalization as a panacea for banking sector problems. Some of the more persistent problems reflect the need for further and significantly greater investment in bank automation and skill development.

In the Czech Republic, improved management and governance relate to the ongoing role of the state and the cross-ownership structure of banks, insurance companies, investment funds, and enterprises. While restrictions on the concentration of ownership and on lending to shareholders do exist, these restrictions are probably insufficient to maintain disciplined financial management, to avert arm's length deals, and to prevent wider systemic risk in the banking and financial sector. Much of the current weakness in the economy relates to these structural weaknesses, which are now more openly reflected in the macroeconomic data that had previously presented a picture of stability and competitiveness.

In Hungary, the authorities made significant efforts to impose financial discipline on loss-making enterprises through strict bankruptcy laws and procedures. Likewise, their recapitalization efforts included revised business plans, performance indicators, and operational reforms that were meant to make companies more competitive and creditworthy. However, even if bank management was satisfactory in its credit decisionmaking, government ministries

Table 7.8. *Review of Bank Restructuring Results in CEE Countries*

Country, costs, benefits, and results	Positive	Negative
Czech Republic	Considered only partly successful, with serious structural weaknesses remaining to be resolved.	
Costs	Fiscally responsible. To pay for the recapitalization, offsetting cuts in public expenditure were made to achieve fiscal balance.	
Benefits	Five major banks were privatized (up to 63 percent private share ownership) along with enterprises in the 1992 mass privatization program.	Continued large share of assets held by SOCBs, partial (not full) privatization of SOCBs, and limited growth of private Czech banks reflect the limitations of the Czech approach to bank privatization. Governance still a major concern.
Results	Some improvement in the financial sector enabling environment combined with initial macroeconomic stabilization, fiscal balance, and benefits of investment in the enterprise sector.	Large banks still only partly privatized. Konsolidacni still needs high capital because of portfolio weaknesses. Major concerns about cross-ownership risks (National Property Fund, banks, insurance, funds). Weak supervision. Limited use of bankruptcy and liquidation to force serious restructuring.

116

Table 7.8. (*Continued*)

Country, costs, benefits, and results	Positive	Negative
Hungary		
	Recapitalization considered less successful than general commitment to enabling environment and strong commitment to privatization after recapitalizations occurred.	
Costs		US$3.5 to US$5.0 billion in recapitalization averaged more than 2 to 3 percent of GDP per year from 1991–94. Main risk was a moral hazard. Coincided with period of costly fiscal deficits. May have crowded out some private investment.
Benefits	Policy of ongoing recapitalization from public resources reversed in 1995 in favor of a policy based on accelerated privatization.	
Results	Hungary has created a favorable enabling environment for banks. The rising number of private and foreign banks has added enhanced banking sector capacity and competition.	Failed to make SOCBs profitable or competitive, although they were privatizable. Uncertain whether recapitalization (restored solvency) directly assisted privatization, as acquisition prices would have been discounted relative to individual bank insolvency.

(*Table continues on the following page.*)

Table 7.8. *(Continued)*

Country, costs, benefits, and results	Positive	Negative
Poland		
Up-front recapitalization for SOCBs considered successful. Recapitalization of specialized banks not successful.		
Costs	Comparatively low cost in terms of GDP. Hard budget constraints helped clean up state commercial bank portfolios.	US$2 billion, most of which was for specialized banks that should probably be liquidated or downsized. Weak or inadequate legal framework for specialized banks in housing and agriculture.
Benefits	Restored solvency, strengthened governance and management, tightened lending criteria, introduced incentives for employees and other stakeholders.	Some of the cost associated with bank restructuring was imposed on the private sector, because of foregone investment resulting from difficulties in accessing credit from banks. Banks recapitalized from the purchase of government securities, a safe route to profitability that has helped finance fiscal deficits at the expense of private sector investment.
Results	SOCBs sufficiently recapitalized, and credit management strengthened. Supervision improved. Fast transfer of know-how through twinning arrangements with prominent West European commercial banks.	Poland's approach to banking reform has been gradual. Intermediation rates remain low. The portfolios of the troubled specialized banks remain problematic. Management skills are sometimes thin; seniority is often more important than performance. Restrictions on foreign bank entry from 1992–95 may have slowed progress. Weak automation.

responsible for the banks and loss-making enterprises sometimes overruled such decisions. Today, such risks appear to have vanished due to the strong commitment to privatization that has left all but one bank in the hands of the state. Privatization has been accompanied by strategic investment, which has shored up governance and management standards, thereby increasing confidence in the competitiveness of Hungary's financial sector in the long term.

In Poland, governance in SOCBs has been fairly strong under the direction of the Ministry of Finance. The Enterprise and Bank Restructuring Law made provisions for strict governance and management, set timetables for portfolio restructuring, and included incentives for banks in their recovery and collection efforts. This included shares to employees so that they could benefit from capital appreciation once privatization occurred, as well as sophisticated training from Western institutions, which gave these individuals greater value in the marketplace as the banking sector continued to open up to competition. Hard budget constraints were employed to clean up state commercial bank portfolios. However, the portfolios of the troubled specialized banks remain problematic, and intermediation rates remain low.

Lessons Learned

The following represent key lessons learned from banking reform in transition countries and their approaches to distressed banking sectors.

- *Macroeconomic and structural issues are linked.* Macroeconomic stability is essential for savings mobilization, investment, and growth. Likewise, governments' willingness and ability to impose hard budget constraints on loss-making banks and enterprises is critical to promote the larger objectives of macroeconomic stabilization, fiscal and external balance, and economic growth. Hungary is now benefiting from improvements in its macroeconomic fundamentals, which are reinforced by more prudently managed banks and more creditworthy enterprises. Poland has shown progress at the structural level largely because of the imposition of hard budget constraints and strong governance in the banking sector. All this has occurred while macroeconomic fundamentals have steadily improved. Enhanced competitiveness in the Czech banking sector will depend on improvements at the structural level, and this should be reinforced by the Czech Republic's long-standing emphasis on macroeconomic stability. Ukraine shows that achieving meaningful structural reform in the absence of macroeconomic stability is difficult or impossible.

- *An enabling environment is essential for successful banking reform.* Legal and regulatory reform are necessary, but not sufficient for banking reform. Also needed are court and out-of-court processes that are effective in resolving debt disputes; property registries that provide needed information related to prospective collateral properties; effective supervisory enforcement of prudential regulations; credit rating agencies that provide needed information and risk assessment; analysts who review bank operations for investment purposes; banking associations that help to professionalize and maintain standards; accounting firms that audit banks; and financial media that actively cover financial sector issues for the public. Having an enabling environment for competitive, market-based banking includes equal treatment on issues of entry (licensing) and exit (liquidation, consolidation). Transparent criteria need to be established and implemented for bank resolution to maintain standards of competitiveness and service delivery. The enabling environment is positive in Hungary and is getting better in Poland. The Czech Republic will likely need to implement much of the package proposed in April 1997 to provide the needed transparency, accountability, and institutional framework for long-term stability and growth. Ukraine lags behind these countries in virtually all categories, although it is making progress in terms of institutional capacity building, for example, banking supervision.

- *Sustained political commitment for banking reform is indispensable.* Governments, budgets, and the economy benefit from a safe, sound banking system. Conversely, an unstable banking system is detrimental to governments, budgets, and the economy. Nevertheless, some of the draconian measures required during transition undercut public sector determination to accelerate reform and privatization in the banking sector. Countries that have pursued incomplete approaches to banking reform have incurred high costs in the form of unrestructured banks and enterprises, deferred problems, and foregone competitiveness, all of which can result in continuously poorly performing portfolios, the run-up of arrears, and efforts to tap scarce monetary and fiscal resources that could be better allocated elsewhere. Ukraine represented many of these characteristics until recently. Hungary and Poland represent good examples of ongoing commitment to reforms. Hungary since 1995 in particular represents a good example of commitment to rapid reform. Governments must sustain the political commitment needed for banking reforms. This will be important in the Czech

Republic as it closes the circle on a number of ownership, governance, management, and regulatory issues.

- *The sequencing of reforms is important.* Most transition countries have raised their capital requirements and tightened their licensing standards in the banking sector after an early burst of liberalization. Poland represents the best example of this among the three CEE countries, with a proliferation of private banks before the authorities put in place the necessary laws, regulations, and institutions to monitor for risk. Since then, Poland has tightened requirements, and is now poised to privatize, liquidate, and/or merge most of its large state commercial banks by the end of the century. Profits are up, the stock exchange is heavily invested in banks (compared to other sectors), market participants and regulators are more confident that renewed commitment to open competition can be launched. Hungary already has sound institutions, which is one of the reasons why private investment has steadily flowed into the financial sector. However, banking supervision still needs some strengthening to assist with overall financial sector modernization. The Czech Republic will need to strengthen standards and establish enforcement capacity that is more preventive and forward looking. To date, standards in the Czech Republic have been somewhat lax. All these challenges and developments point to the need for sufficient institutional capacity for safe and sound banking and orderly markets. Ukraine is beginning to commit to institutional strengthening and an enabling environment for financial sector development, having recognized that ownership transformation does not work without new capital, market-based governance and management, adequate legislation and regulations, and institutions that support and reinforce market development.

- *In a competitive environment governance and management must be market-based for banks to be financially viable on a sustainable basis.* The application of noncommercial criteria in an environment of scarce resources (hard budget constraints, run-up of arrears) usually leads to a misallocation of resources that ultimately reduces liquidity and solvency. Even if resources are not scarce, the emergence of market-based investors requires that banks manage resources efficiently to meet return targets. If not, their funding will decline and their position in the market will erode. Accountability and transparency are essential for strengthened governance and management, and for continued expansion of banks' funding bases. Hungary and Poland have faced up to this reality now that hard budget constraints are generally in place.

The Czech Republic will likewise need to focus on this as an extension of reforms already initiated to add liquidity to its capital markets and to reduce the centrality of bank debt as a means of financing in the economy. Ukraine is also facing up to this because of the weakness of its banks and the recognized need for a major transformation that has yet to occur.

- *Market-based privatization, not share-based ownership transformation or privatization using vouchers, is the best way to ensure market-based governance.* Private investors have more incentives to manage their real cash capital prudently (or to have it managed) than do public officials or coupon holders. Ukraine's "privatization" of banks was conducted without serious governance and management changes, and cash capital put at risk was limited. This approach failed, as it has in many other parts of the FSU. While Poland has demonstrated that private ownership is not necessary for adequate governance, the temptation public sector officials face to soften budget constraints to increase the franchise value of their banks or to ensure lending to preferred firms, friends, and political allies on noncommercial bases jeopardizes macroeconomic fundamentals and safe banking practices. This is in evidence in Poland in some strategic sectors, and was true in Hungary on the justification of protecting jobs in an economy with official double-digit unemployment rates. There is concern that this is also the case with some of the Czech Republic's largest state banks and enterprises, particularly since 1996, when the current account deficit started spiraling to worrisome levels.

- *Suitable incentives need to be in place for a wide range of stakeholders for banking reform to succeed in the long term.* Investors, lenders to banks, and depositors all represent the funding base of banks. The extent to which banks can generate confidence relative to the competition in earnings, debt service capacity, and overall safekeeping of deposits is the degree to which banks will provide needed incentives for long-term success. To make that happen, management and employees at all levels need to have incentives for competitive performance. In Poland, many bank employees (and employees of SOEs) were awarded shares at discounted prices to make privatization an acceptable alternative and to promote improved performance for share appreciation purposes. Likewise in Hungary, significant training has been provided to improve professional skills. In addition, both countries have improved their standards for accountability in recent years, which was made possible with increasing disclosure as investment and stock market activity intensified.

- *Technical assistance and training from experienced market-based practitioners are essential building blocks for institutional development.* The fastest approach to developing the financial sector is to accelerate institutional development predicated on a viable legal and regulatory framework and to promote competition among world-class institutions. However, this takes time. Poland's impressive enhancement of SOCB competitiveness (in contrast to that of its large, specialized banks) and achievements in developing supervisory and enforcement capacity reflect the importance and value of technical assistance and training. Similarly Hungary has benefited significantly from foreign investment in the banking sector, and this has had a beneficial effect on overall competitiveness. By contrast, while the Czech Republic has attracted foreign investment, it has de-emphasized the role of technical assistance. Consequently, the Czech Republic may have missed out on some essential building blocks for structural competitiveness along the way, particularly in the area of banking supervision and regulation. In Ukraine, foreign investment has been sparse, including in the banking sector. For Ukraine to become competitive, several changes will have to be made. One of the most important will be developing institutional capacity for safe and sound banking, which will require continued technical assistance in banking as well as in supervision.

- *Links to regional and global markets are becoming increasingly crucial to financial sector competitiveness and economic growth.* While banks in transition countries are sometimes just emerging from decades of central planning, the world market is becoming increasingly intertwined. CEE countries will have the benefit of joining the EU in the near future, and this is serving as an anchor for reform. FSU countries generally lack this kind of anchor. In all cases, foreign investment would greatly assist with new capital, management, systems, technologies, and market linkages. Hungary is the most noteworthy beneficiary to date, and benefits have also accrued in the Czech Republic and Poland. Attracting foreign investment into the banking sector is even more crucial for Ukraine (and other FSU countries) to make up for greater weaknesses, and because accession to the EU is not likely to occur any time soon.

- *Banking reform is closely linked to capital markets development.* Banking and other financial sector activities are increasingly converging. Most of the world has followed universal banking practices, and international norms to address risk management across financial subsectors are gradually evolving. In terms of financing, the establishment of viable bond markets would ease demand on banks for riskier, long-term investment (project) financing. More active stock exchanges would improve bank funding, enhance overall risk management capacity and oversight, and improve the capital structure of companies to which banks might lend and/or provide services. Poland and Hungary are moving forward in this respect, with prospects improving as their macroeconomic fundamentals improve and their governance requirements match international standards. However, stock market capitalization still remains relatively small as a percentage of GDP. In the Czech Republic, stock market turnover is limited and high levels of capitalization were based on a number of false premises. Ultimately, greater transparency and accountability will be required to increase liquidity and to provide more accurate measures of capitalization.

- *Recapitalization of banks should be up-front, one-time, fiscally balanced, institutionally focused, and linked to timetables for full privatization.* The Czech recapitalization, while the most expensive, was partly successful in that it was generally up-front and one-time (the 1993 recapitalization related to ruble-based debt), and fiscally balanced. However, its weakness is that it failed to achieve full privatization, and institutional strengthening was insufficient to impose market-based governance and management structures. In Poland, recapitalization of SOCBs was successful in most cases, but privatization has still not occurred in several of the banks. With regard to the specialized banks, Poland should consider a liquidation or downsizing scenario for nonsalvageable assets as part of its privatization strategy. The case of Hungary, the most successful in the region, shows the importance of timetables for full privatization supported by an enabling environment and strong institutions. While Ukraine did not recapitalize its banks, its efforts should focus on the above principles.

References

Barbone, Luca, and Dominico Marchetti, Jr. 1994. "Economic Transformation and the Fiscal Crisis: A Critical Look at the Central European Experience of the 1990s." Policy Working Paper no. 1286. Europe and Central Asia Country Department II, World Bank, Washington, D. C.

Borish, M., and M. Noël. 1996. *Private Sector Development during Transition: The Visegrad Countries.* Discussion Paper no. 318., Washington, D. C.: World Bank.

Borish, Michael S., Wei Ding, and Michel Noël. 1996. *On the Road to EU Accession: Financial Sector Development in Central Europe*. Discussion Paper no. 345., Washington, D. C.: World Bank.

Borish, Michael S., Millard F. Long, and Michel Noël. 1995. *Restructuring Banks and Enterprises: Recent Lessons from Transition Countries*. Discussion Paper no. 279., Washington, D. C.: World Bank.

Dittus, Peter. 1994. "Bank Reform and Behavior in Central Europe." *Journal of Comparative Economics* 19 (December): 335–61.

IMF (International Monetary Fund). 1995. "Hungary. Recent Economic Developments and Background Issues." Washington, D. C.

Montes-Negret, F., and L. Papi. 1996. "Are Bank Interest Rates too High?" Policy Note. World Bank, Financial Sector Development Department, Washington, D. C.

_____. 1997. "The Polish Experience with Bank and Enterprise Restructuring." Policy Research Working Paper no. 1705. World Bank, Washington, D. C.

OECD (Organisation for Economic Co-operation and Development). 1993. "OECD Economic Survey, Hungary." Paris.

_____. 1996. "OECD Economic Survey, the Czech Republic." Paris.

Saunders, A., and A. Sommariva. 1993. "Banking Sector and Restructuring in Eastern Europe." *Journal of Banking and Finance* 17 (September): 931–57.

World Bank. 1997. *World Development Indicators*. Washington, D. C.

8

Preventing Banking Crises by Supporting the Truth

Ivan Remsik

When analyzing processes that are part of the economic transformations in Central European countries, many believe that problem loans, which are generally accepted as the major contributor to banking crises, are always connected to previous regimes rather than to loans granted in the new market economy era. Therefore they believe that carving out old, bad loans from commercial banks and putting them into loan "hospitals" solves the problem. In the real world, new loan exposures and new securities exposures are just as threatening to the commercial banking sector's stability as inherited loans.

In the early days of economic transformation any process used to identify problem assets is often subjective and exposed to various political and other pressures. Promising assets can become nonperforming later because of changed circumstances, and commercial bankers are often tempted to evergreen inherited loans for certain clients in the hope of cashing in fat interest margins and/or lucrative, fee-based export-import transactions.

The new market economy era brings with it new pressures. In the absence of private capital, commercial banks cannot resist political pressures and have to substitute for missing capital by extending privatization loans to a new generation of "entrepreneurs" who have no money and no idea how to run a business. It is thus understandable that large parts of privatization loan portfolios are today classified as lost. Commercial bankers also have to extend new loans to existing enterprises to pay workers so as to prevent social disturbances in fragile democracies.

Liberalizing banking and creating new, private banks put more pressure on the management of already established banks. They are expected to provide new entrants with money market lines, and some managers agree to do so as not to be labeled as being opposed to competition or reform. A lot of these new banks do not exist any longer, but their unpaid debt does.

Even decisions on new "greenfield" projects using the sophisticated tools of Western project finance analysts is still subjective and open to failure. In the absence of financial data, decisionmaking is often more intuitive than scientific, and monitoring the performance of such projects is difficult.

What has happened in some countries and what will happen in others obviously cannot be changed. However, what they must all do is use financial reporting as a basis for making decisions and measuring progress, and thus assessing the success of the economic transformation process.

As concerns loan loss provisioning, transition economies need to set up well-defined loan classification systems and enforceable loan loss provisioning rules at the beginning of an economic transition. The Czech Republic introduced its first such system and rules in 1994, six years after it had introduced a two-tier banking system. A sound loan classification and loan loss provisioning system should have been in place much earlier to enable the disclosure of old loan exposures or their residuals, as well as of new exposures, at their fair value. This would have helped prevent the over-rating of the success of the Czech economic transformation.

Let us consider a simplified example of the loan loss provisioning rules currently in effect in the Czech Republic to demonstrate some of the problems of the country's banking sector and economy. Banks in the Czech Republic are allowed to set aside a maximum of 1 percent provision per year if a loan is 30 days overdue, a maximum of 5 percent if it is 90 days overdue, a maximum of 10 percent if it is 180 days overdue, and a maximum of 20 percent if it is 360 days overdue. This illustrates sufficiently that the whole concept of loan loss provisioning is not quite correct. Central banks around the world require minimum levels of loan loss provisions to maintain the health of commercial banking systems, not maximum levels. However, in the Czech Republic more provision allowances are permissible if bankruptcy has been initiated, but this is still rare.

Some central banks in transition economies take the tax approach to loan loss provisioning rules as they try to solve two problems at the same time: what is the required level of loan loss provisions and what should their tax treatment be in profit and loss accounts. This creates more problems than it solves: some Czech banks have not built adequate levels of loan loss provisions simply because they have not been required to do so. However their interpretation is different. They say that they have not been allowed to do so. Another point in connection with the tax treatment of loan loss provisions is that the maximum amount of tax allowable loan loss provisions is limited to 3 percent of a loan portfolio per year. Such a low limit is more than conservative for any transition economy.

On the other side there is no limit to loan loss provisions without tax relief. When I was responsible for restructuring the balance sheet of the Zivnostenska Bank when preparing the bank for privatization, the only possibility was to build adequate loan loss provisions out of the bank's equity reserves. This was perfectly legal. However, commercial bankers are reluctant to use their equity reserves as loan loss provisions in the belief that they will lose their negotiating power when trying to convince governments to increase the level of tax allowable loan loss provisions if their balance sheets look fine. They are also afraid that if they build loan loss provisions from their equity reserves, and thus state their assets at fair value, they will not be able to claim tax relief on provisions in subsequent years because additional provisions would no longer be needed. No deferred tax credit system exists. Banks are not allowed to recognize deferred tax assets and claim deferred tax credits in following tax years as they can in the United Kingdom.

Another notable regulation in the Czech Republic is that unpaid interest must be recognized as income and tax must be paid on unpaid interest. Some years ago I refused to sign the Zivnostenska Bank's accounts showing unpaid interest as income, because as far as I know it is considered a crime in some countries. However, I instructed the Finance Department to calculate and pay tax on it so as not to break Czech tax laws.

The Czech banking industry has a track record of attempting to determine realistic asset values. The result is not yet perfect, but the industry is moving in the right direction. The most recent step was in 1997, when the Central Bank introduced a system for classifying securities holdings in investment and trading books with relevant reporting, valuation, and provisioning policies that were in line with international practices. This happened some eight or nine years after the creation of a two-tier banking system and after grandiose privatization that had involved a massive issuance of securities.

Corporate financial reporting in Central Europe is generally far from any accepted standard. Assets are stated at cost, including the assets of newly privatized entities; mark-to-market valuation for any class of assets, including financial assets such as shares or fixed income securities, is not required; and requirements for the provisioning of a debtor's book do not exist. Income statements and audits of such statements are tax driven. Some of the more than 1,000 licensed auditors in the Czech Republic can audit a large company in a single day as they just look at income statements and check whether the company has calculated its taxes correctly. In such an environment, it is difficult for bankers to carry out sensible corporate credit analyses and to make prudent credit decisions. What is even more danger-ous is that industrial holdings and privatization and mutual funds, which emerged as part of the transition economies' transformation, value their assets at cost and are not required to do mark-to-market valuation or to create provisions for undervalued assets.

Thus we need to look at the entire economy: enterprises and compa-nies do not tell the truth; their owners, such as privatization and mutual funds, do not tell the truth; the banks do not tell the truth. So we wonder, can official macroeconomic data be correct? The recent crisis in the Czech banking sector and the less than optimistic economic reality indicate that having had true information available during the various stages of the country's economic transition would have been better. To prevent simi-lar scenarios from occurring again we should do everything to support the truth. Central banks have done something. It was not on time, it is not perfect, but they are on the right track.

I am not so sure about international monetary authorities. When I was in banking most International Monetary Fund and World Bank missions came to see me to find out what was really going on in the country. They would receive a lot of promising information in the morning while visiting government officials and realistic information in the afternoon when visit-ing commercial bankers. The commercial bankers asked for guidance from these missions on how to set up prudential regulations and policies. Un-fortunately, some reluctance to provide such help has been apparent.

However, the most critical period is still ahead of us. For the Czech government, proud of its privatization results, introducing sensible account-ing and valuation policies for the nonbanking sector will be difficult. They are unlikely to tell public shareholders that under their new guidelines the shareholders' securities in company ABC or mutual fund XYZ have no value. The reality is that they are unlikely to do so voluntarily.

International monetary institutions should take a greater role in the process of discovering and telling the truth to policymakers, bankers, and the general public. Progress will not occur without the truth, and support-ing dissemination of the truth is the best way to prevent banking crises.

Part IV. Bank Failures in Industrial Countries

9

Lessons from Bank Failures in the United States

James R. Barth and Robert E. Litan

In mid-1997 the U.S. Congress and the Clinton administration were actively considering proposals to modernize the financial services industry. At the time, support for easing the restrictions separating banks, securities firms, and insurance companies was fairly broad. There was far less support for mixing banking and commerce. Indeed, House Banking and Financial Services Committee Chairman James Leach testified that "Mixing commerce and banking simply doesn't fit our kind of democracy" (Leach 1997, p. 5).[1]

The debate in the United States about the appropriate role of banks in the overall financial system was not occurring in isolation. Many other industrial and developing countries were also assessing various banking laws and regulations to determine which were most appropriate in an increasingly technological and global banking world. The intense and widespread focus on bank regulation at this particular time was largely due to the occurrence of significant banking problems in more than half the world's countries between

---

1. Despite this view, in late June most members of the House Banking and Financial Services Committee voted to permit a limited degree of bank ownership of nonfinancial firms and vice versa. However, many considered the prospect for legislation being enacted in 1997 that contained even a limited amount of such mixing to be doubtful. A majority of members also voted to eliminate many of the barriers separating banks, securities firms, and insurance companies.

1980 and 1997 (see, for example, Caprio and Klingebiel 1996; Lindgren, Garcia, and Saal 1996). These problems were still ongoing in many countries and had developed in both industrial countries and emerging market economies. To prevent future problems, countries were working individually to design regulatory structures that better ensured more stable, efficient, and competitive banking industries. Countries were also working jointly, frequently with the assistance and advice of such international agencies as the International Monetary Fund and the World Bank, to ensure that such structures lessened the likelihood that financial disruptions in one country would spread to other countries (see Goldstein 1997).

This chapter attempts to contribute to our understanding of the relationship between banking problems and bank regulation by examining the banking problems that occurred in the United States during 1980 through 1996. As has been well documented in the literature, many factors were responsible for the problems (see, for example, Barth 1991; Barth and Bartholomew 1992; Barth and Brumbaugh 1994; Barth, Brumbaugh, and Litan 1992; Bartholomew and Whalen 1995; Brewer 1995; Brumbaugh 1988; Kane 1985, 1989b; Kaufman 1995; Kroszner and Strahan 1996; Litan 1987, 1991, 1994; Romer and Weingast 1992; White 1991). Most agree, however, that bank regulation bears an important part of the responsibility for what happened. In particular, overly restrictive laws and regulations contributed to thousands of depository institutions being exposed to substantial interest rate risk in the late 1970s and early 1980s. Subsequently, especially in the early to mid-1980s, lax regulation and supervision enabled many inadequately capitalized institutions to grow rapidly by engaging in high-risk activities.

Bank Failures, Resolution Costs, and Related Developments

Tables 9.1–9.4 and figure 9.1 present selected information about U.S. federally insured banking institutions from 1980 through 1996. In particular, the tables indicate the extent of the problems of commercial and savings banks, savings and loan institutions (S&Ls), and credit unions.

Note the following important points about the information contained in tables 9.1–9.4 and figure 9.1. First, between 1980 and 1996, 5,207 federally insured institutions with US$920 billion in assets failed and cost an estimated US$192 billion in nominal dollars to resolve. (These totals are obtained by simply summing the appropriate figures under the heading "Resolution" at the bottom of tables 9.1–9.3.) When expressed in inflation-adjusted dollars, that is, 1992 dollars, the costs are US$216 billion, or about 3.5 percent of 1992 GDP. Not all the different types of depositories experienced the same degree

Table 9.1. U.S. Federally Insured Commercial Bank Industry, 1980–96

Category	1980	1981	1982	1983	1984	1985
Number of institutions	14,435	14,408	14,446	14,460	14,483	14,407
Number of branches	38,738	40,786	39,783	40,853	41,799	43,293
Number of full-time equivalent employees (thousands)	1,442	1,489	1,499	1,509	1,527	1,562
Total assets (US$ billions)	1,856	2,029	2,194	2,342	2,509	2,731
Equity capital (US$ millions)	107,599	118,241	128,698	140,459	154,103	169,118
Net after tax income (US$ millions)	14,010	14,722	14,844	14,931	15,502	17,977
Taxes (US$ millions)	4,658	3,904	3,037	4,017	4,721	5,629
Percentage of real estate loans to total assets	14.5	14.4	14.0	14.4	15.4	16.1
Percentage of commercial & industrial loans to total assets	21.1	22.4	23.0	22.4	22.5	21.2
Percentage of agriculture production loans to total assets	1.7	1.7	1.7	1.7	1.6	1.3
Percentage of loans to individuals to total assets	10.1	9.5	9.1	9.6	10.6	11.3
National commercial banks						
Percentage of number of institutions	30.7	30.9	31.7	32.8	33.8	34.4
Percentage of total assets	56.9	57.2	57.4	58.0	59.7	59.8
State, federal member commercial banks						
Percentage of number of institutions	6.9	7.1	7.2	7.3	7.3	7.4
Percentage of total assets	17.4	17.0	17.6	16.6	18.2	18.1
Equity capital to asset ratio categories						
More than 8%						
Number	7,981	7,941	7,976	7,674	7,423	7,324
Total assets (US$ billions)	278	300	320	344	353	377
6% to 8%						
Number	5,401	5,411	5,292	5,280	5,441	5,339
Total assets (US$ billions)	434	466	494	560	648	710
3% to 6 %						
Number	1,038	1,041	1,141	1,426	1,507	1,571
Total assets (US$ billions)	1,141	1,260	1,375	1,432	1,498	1,633
1.5% to 3%						
Number	12	16	27	53	61	84
Total assets (US$ billions)	2	4	3	4	7	6
0% to 1.5%						
Number	2	5	12	21	23	36
Total assets (US$ billions)	*	*	1	2	1	2
Less than 0%						
Number	1	2	5	14	11	29
Total assets (US$ billions)	*	*	*	1	*	1
Number of problem commercial banks	—	196	326	603	800	1,098
Assets of problem commercial banks (US$ billions)	—	—	—	—	—	—
Resolutions of commercial and savings banks						
Number	10	10	42	48	80	120
Total assets (US$ millions)	236	4,859	11,632	7,027	3,276	8,735
Estimated present value cost (US$ millions)	31	782	1,169	1,425	1,635	1,044
Number of months rated 4 or 5 before closure	15	19	16	19	15	15

(Table continues on the following page.)

Table 9.1. *(Continued)*

Category	1986	1987	1988	1989	1990	1991
Number of institutions	14,199	13,703	13,123	12,709	12,343	11,921
Number of branches	44,392	45,357	46,381	48,005	50,406	51,969
Number of full-time equivalent employees (thousands)	1,563	1,545	1,527	1,532	1,518	1,487
Total assets (US$ billions)	2,941	3,000	3,131	3,299	3,389	3,431
Equity capital (US$ millions)	182,144	180,651	196,545	204,823	218,616	231,699
Net after tax income (US$ millions)	17,418	2,803	24,812	15,575	15,991	17,935
Taxes (US$ millions)	5,266	5,404	9,988	9,540	7,704	8,265
Percentage of real estate loans to total assets	17.5	20.0	21.6	23.1	24.5	24.8
Percentage of commercial & industrial loans to total assets	20.4	19.7	19.2	18.8	18.2	16.3
Percentage of agriculture production loans to total assets	1.1	1.0	1.0	0.9	1.0	1.0
Percentage of loans to individuals to total assets	11.4	11.7	12.1	12.1	11.9	11.4
National commercial banks						
Percentage of number of institutions	34.3	33.7	35.3	32.9	32.2	31.8
Percentage of total assets	59.3	59.1	58.9	59.7	58.6	56.5
State, federal member commercial banks						
Percentage of number of institutions	7.7	7.9	8.1	8.1	8.2	8.2
Percentage of total assets	18.2	17.6	17.1	16.4	16.5	16.9
Equity capital to asset ratio categories						
More than 8%						
Number	6,699	6,790	6,646	6,741	6,377	6,422
Total assets (US$ billions)	384	438	437	488	554	615
6% to 8%						
Number	5,169	4,944	4,703	4,407	4,540	4,309
Total assets (US$ billions)	755	846	944	1,113	1,088	1,377
3% to 6 %						
Number	2,028	1,604	1,401	1,295	1,234	1,048
Total assets (US$ billions)	1,776	1,588	1,680	1,572	1,684	1,421
1.5% to 3%						
Number	124	165	158	109	92	66
Total assets (US$ billions)	14	111	39	76	41	13
0% to 1.5%						
Number	88	108	96	73	66	43
Total assets (US$ billions)	6	5	10	26	6	3
Less than 0%						
Number	71	76	104	82	35	32
Total assets (US$ billions)	4	10	21	23	15	2
Number of problem commercial banks	1,457	1,559	1,394	1,092	1,012	1,016
Assets of problem commercial banks (US$ billions)	286	329	305	188	342	528
Resolutions of commercial and savings banks						
Number	145	203	221	207	169	127
Total assets (US$ millions)	7,638	9,231	52,683	29,402	15,729	62,524
Estimated present value cost (US$ millions)	1,728	2,028	6,866	6,215	2,889	6,037
Number of months rated 4 or 5 before closure	20	21	24	28	34	29

Table 9.1. (Continued)

Category	1992	1993	1994	1995	1996
Number of institutions	11,462	10,958	10,451	9,940	9,528
Number of branches	51,935	52,868	55,145	56,513	57,215
Number of full-time equivalent employees (thousands)	1,478	1,494	1,488	1,484	1,489
Total assets (US$ billions)	3,506	3,706	4,011	4,313	4,578
Equity capital (US$ millions)	263,403	296,491	312,088	349,578	375,295
Net after tax income (US$ millions)	31,987	43,036	44,624	48,749	52,390
Taxes (US$ millions)	14,481	19,838	22,426	26,176	28,227
Percentage of real estate loans to total assets	24.8	24.9	24.9	25.0	25.9
Percentage of commercial & industrial loans to total assets	15.3	14.5	14.7	15.3	15.5
Percentage of agriculture production loans to total assets	1.0	1.0	1.0	0.9	0.9
Percentage of loans to individuals to total assets	11.0	11.3	12.2	12.4	12.4
National commercial banks					
Percentage of number of institutions	31.5	30.3	29.4	28.8	28.6
Percentage of total assets	57.2	56.7	56.3	55.7	55.3
State, federal member commercial banks					
Percentage of number of institutions	8.4	8.8	9.3	10.5	10.7
Percentage of total assets	18.2	19.6	21.1	22.8	24.6
Equity capital to asset ratio categories					
More than 8%					
Number	6,857	7,542	6,969	7,497	7,104
Total assets (US$ billions)	994	1,365	1,160	1,719	1,757
6% to 8%					
Number	3,924	3,151	3,074	2,281	2,261
Total assets (US$ billions)	1,894	2,090	2,185	1,998	2,116
3% to 6%					
Number	624	263	398	159	158
Total assets (US$ billions)	626	250	667	59	709
1.5% to 3%					
Number	24	7	8	3	4
Total assets (US$ billions)	2	1	0.5	*	*
0% to 1.5%					
Number	14	6	4	2	1
Total assets (US$ billions)	3	1	*	*	*
Less than 0%					
Number	23	2	0	0	0
Total assets (US$ billions)	8	*	0	0	0
Number of problem commercial banks	787	426	247	144	82
Assets of problem commercial banks (US$ billions)	408	242	33	17	5
Resolutions of commercial and savings banks					
Number	122	41	13	6	5
Total assets (US$ millions)	45,485	3,527	1,402	753	190
Estimated present value cost (US$ millions)	3,707	655	208	104	—
Number of months rated 4 or 5 before closure	32	—	—	—	—

— Not available.

* Less than US$500 million.

Source: Barth and Brumbaugh (1994); Federal Deposit Insurance Corporation, Office of the Comptroller of the Currency, Bank Research Division data. The format is adapted from Barth, Brumbaugh, and Litan (1990, p. 25).

Table 9.2. *U.S. Federally Insured Savings and Loan Industry, 1980–96*

Category	1980	1981	1982	1983	1984	1985
Number of institutions	3,993	3,751	3,287	3,146	3,136	3,246
Total RAP assets (US$ billions)	604	640	686	814	978	1,070
GAAP capital (US$ billions)	32	27	20	25	27	34
Tangible capital (US$ billions)	32	25	4	4	3	9
Net after tax income (US$ millions)	781	(4,631)	(4,142)	1,945	1,022	3,728
Net operating income (US$ millions)	790	(7,114)	(8,761)	(46)	990	3,601
Net non-operating income (US$ millions)	398	964	3,041	2,567	796	2,215
Taxes (US$ millions)	407	(1,519)	(1,578)	576	764	2,087
Percentage of home mortgages to total assets	66.5	65.0	56.3	49.8	44.9	42.4
Percentage of mortgage-backed securities to total assets	4.4	5.0	8.6	10.9	11.1	10.4
Percentage of mortgage assets to total assets	70.9	70.0	64.9	60.7	56.0	52.8
Stock institutions						
Percentage of number of institutions	20	21	23	23	30	33
Percentage of total assets	27	29	30	42	52	56
Federally-chartered						
Percentage of number of institutions	50	51	51	53	54	53
Percentage of total assets	56	63	70	69	66	65
Tangible capital to asset ratio categories						
More than 6%						
Number	1,701	1,171	787	661	643	806
Total assets (US$ billions)	181	101	59	84	62	95
3% to 6%						
Number	1,956	1,766	1,202	1,091	945	1,009
Total assets (US$ billions)	379	348	190	222	227	259
1.5% to 3%						
Number	230	524	592	569	526	460
Total assets (US$ billions)	39	113	136	185	168	212
0% to 1.5%						
Number	63	178	291	310	327	266
Total assets (US$ billions)	4	50	81	88	153	135
Less than 0%						
Number	43	112	415	515	695	705
Total assets (US$ billions)	0.4	29	220	234	336	335
Conservatorships at Resolution Trust Corporation						
Number	—	—	—	—	—	—
Total assets of institutions taken over (US$ billions)	—	—	—	—	—	—
Number of problem savings and loans	330	499	744	689	748	679
Assets of problem savings and loans (US$ billions)	43	104	182	189	265	270
Resolutions						
Number	11	28	76	54	27	36
Total assets (US$ millions)	1,458	13,908	27,748	19,655	5,783	7,066
Estimated present value cost (US$ millions)	167	1,018	1,213	1,024	833	1,025
Number of months reporting tangible insolvent before closure	5.4	5.2	12.9	16.4	23.4	25.9

Table 9.2. (Continued)

Category	1986	1987	1988	1989	1990	1991
Number of institutions	3,220	3,147	2,949	2,616	2,359	2,110
Total RAP assets (US$ billions)	1,164	1,251	1,352	1,187	1,029	895
GAAP capital (US$ billions)	39	34	46	52	52	53
Tangible capital (US$ billions)	15	9	23	—	—	42
Net after tax income (US$ millions)	131	(7,779)	(12,057)	(6,783)	(3,817)	1,195
Net operating income (US$ millions)	4,562	2,850	907	(8,308)	(4,022)	2,265
Net non-operating income (US$ millions)	(1,290)	(7,930)	(11,012)	2,198	1,347	1,356
Taxes (US$ millions)	3,141	2,699	1,952	673	1,142	2,426
Percentage of home mortgages to total assets	38.9	37.8	38.6	41.2	43.0	45.6
Percentage of mortgage-backed securities to total assets	13.1	15.6	15.4	14.2	14.5	14.2
Percentage of mortgage assets to total assets	52.0	53.4	54.0	55.4	59.5	59.8
Stock institutions						
Percentage of number of institutions	37	40	43	43	44	45
Percentage of total assets	62	65	68	69	74	76
Federally-chartered						
Percentage of number of institutions	53	56	59	61	64	65
Percentage of total assets	66	66	72	76	83	84
Tangible capital to asset ratio categories						
More than 6%						
Number	972	1,113	1,136	1,180	1,132	1,148
Total assets (US$ billions)	156	188	196	206	195	227
3% to 6%						
Number	995	891	864	813	837	763
Total assets (US$ billions)	316	356	418	480	484	468
1.5% to 3%						
Number	354	277	281	245	163	105
Total assets (US$ billions)	191	196	244	206	154	104
0% to 1.5%						
Number	227	194	160	120	101	47
Total assets (US$ billions)	144	143	182	59	83	36
Less than 0%						
Number	672	672	508	239	109	33
Total assets (US$ billions)	324	336	283	192	89	41
Conservatorships at Resolution Trust Corporation						
Number	—	—	—	318	207	123
Total assets of institutions taken over (US$ billions)	—	—	—	142	127	70
Number of problem savings and loans	637	574	—	404	450	340
Assets of problem savings and loans (US$ billions)	249	217	—	202	235	224
Resolutions						
Number	51	47	222	327	213	144
Total assets (US$ millions)	24,182	10,921	113,965	146,811	134,766	82,626
Estimated present value cost (US$ millions)	3,605	4,509	52,203	51,140	21,473	10,823
Number of months reporting tangible insolvent before closure	30.6	35.7	42.0	36.0	43.0	41.0

(Table continues on the following page.)

Table 9.2. *(Continued)*

Category	1992	1993	1994	1995	1996
Number of institutions	1,871	1,669	1,543	1,437	1,334
Total RAP assets (US$ billions)	807	775	774	771	769
GAAP capital (US$ billions)	56	58	58	62	61
Tangible capital (US$ billions)	52	54	55	57	56
Net after tax income (US$ millions)	5,103	4,917	4,275	5,360	4,750
Net operating income (US$ millions)	6,855	7,141	6,597	7,460	—
Net non-operating income (US$ millions)	1,047	595	422	835	—
Taxes (US$ millions)	2,779	2,819	2,744	2,935	1,748
Percentage of home mortgages to total assets	45.7	45.8	47.0	47.4	49.9
Percentage of mortgage-backed securities to total assets	14.5	15.4	16.5	16.3	14.4
Percentage of mortgage assets to total assets	60.2	61.2	63.5	63.7	64.3
Stock institutions					
Percentage of number of institutions	49	54	56	59	60
Percentage of total assets	80	82	86	86	90
Federally-chartered					
Percentage of number of institutions	70	75	78	82	82
Percentage of total assets	87	90	93	95	96
Tangible capital to asset ratio categories					
More than 6%					
Number	1,246	1,342	—	—	—
Total assets (US$ billions)	310	397	—	—	—
3% to 6%					
Number	559	323	—	—	—
Total assets (US$ billions)	435	372	—	—	—
1.5% to 3%					
Number	39	2	—	—	—
Total assets (US$ billions)	33	4	—	—	—
0% to 1.5%					
Number	7	2	—	—	—
Total assets (US$ billions)	13	3	—	—	—
Less than 0%					
Number	3	0	—	—	—
Total assets (US$ billions)	4	0	—	—	—
Conservatorships at Resolution Trust Corporation					
Number	50	8	0	0	—
Total assets of institutions taken over (US$ billions)	35	6	0	0	—
Number of problem savings and loans	203	101	53	41	29
Assets of problem savings and loans (US$ billions)	134	77	30	11	5
Resolutions					
Number	59	9	2	2	1
Total assets (US$ millions)	45,980	6,339	142	456	—
Estimated present value cost (US$ millions)	4,741	532	14	66	—
Number of months reporting tangible insolvent before closure	38.0	—	—	—	—

— Not available.

GAAP Generally accepted accounting principles.

RAP Regulatory accounting practices.

Source: Barth (1991); Barth and Brumbaugh (1994); Resolution Trust Corporation (various years); data from the Federal Home Loan Board, the Office of Thrift Supervision, and the Office of the Comptroller of the Currency.

Table 9.3. U.S. Federally Insured Credit Union Industry, 1980–96

Category	1980	1981	1982	1983	1984	1985
Number of institutions	17,350	16,960	16,424	15,804	15,180	15,033
Total assets (US$ billions)	61	65	70	82	93	120
Capital (US$ billions)	3.7	4.3	4.7	5.3	6.2	7.8
Net income (US$ millions)	314	677	714	747	1,131	1,303
Net operating income (US$ millions)	502	882	922	930	1,316	1,538
Net non-operating income (US$ millions)	0.8	7	1	12	11	66
Provision for loan losses (US$ millions)	190	212	209	194	195	301
Federal income taxes (US$ millions)	0	0	0	0	0	0
Percentage of 1st mortgages to total assets	4.7	4.4	3.3	3.7	3.9	4.8
Percentage of mortgage-backed securities to total assets	—	—	—	—	—	—
Percentage of total real estate assets to total assets	—	—	—	—	—	—
Federally chartered						
Percentage of number of institutions	71.7	70.8	69.4	69.1	69.4	67.3
Percentage of total assets	65.8	65.9	65.3	66.5	68.6	65.3
Federally insured state-chartered						
Percentage of number of institutions	28.3	29.2	30.6	30.9	30.6	32.7
Percentage of total assets	34.2	34.1	34.7	33.5	31.4	34.7
Capital to asset ratio categories						
More than 6%						
Number	10,286	11,282	11,134	10,460	10,763	10,552
Total assets (US$ billions)	26.2	30.7	34.2	38.1	46.2	58.3
3% to 6%						
Number	4,563	3,811	3,725	3,894	3,490	3,676
Total assets (US$ billions)	24.3	22.8	27.4	34.4	39.2	52.6
1.5% to 3%						
Number	1,357	1,083	944	960	612	560
Total assets (US$ billions)	4.8	5.4	4.9	6.3	5.2	6.7
0% to 1.5%						
Number	872	582	481	347	208	172
Total assets (US$ billions)	5.1	4.5	2.7	1.7	1.1	1.0
Less than 0%						
Number	272	202	140	143	107	73
Total assets (US$ billions)	0.6	1.1	0.4	1.4	1.3	1.2
Number of problem credit unions	1,180	1,174	1,192	1,124	872	742
Assets of problem credit unions (US$ billions)	2.4	3.0	4.6	4.7	4.1	4.1
Resolutions						
Number	239	349	327	253	130	94
Total shares (US$ millions)	—	136	156	102	208	47
Estimated present value cost (US$ millions)	33	44	79	55	20	12
Number of months rated 4 or 5 before closure	—	—	—	69.6	80.8	64.9

(Table continues on the following page.)

Table 9.3. *(Continued)*

Category	1986	1987	1988	1989	1990	1991
Number of institutions	14,687	14,335	13,878	13,371	12,860	12,960
Total assets (US$ billions)	148	162	175	184	198	227
Capital (US$ billions)	9.2	10.6	12.0	13.5	15.0	17.4
Net income (US$ millions)	1,366	1,464	1,659	1,653	1,691	2,066
Net operating income (US$ millions)	1,746	2,074	2,310	2,445	2,609	3,026
Net non-operating income (US$ millions)	113	(36)	38	21	28	36
Provision for loan losses (US$ millions)	494	574	688	813	946	996
Federal income taxes (US$ millions)	0	0	0	0	0	0
Percentage of 1st mortgages to total assets	7.4	10.1	11.9	12.6	12.3	11.5
Percentage of mortgage-backed securities to total assets	—	—	—	—	—	—
Percentage of total real estate assets to total assets	12.4	16.5	19.6	21.7	21.9	20.6
Federally chartered						
Percentage of number of institutions	66.4	65.6	65.7	66.0	66.2	63.5
Percentage of total assets	64.6	64.9	65.4	65.7	65.6	63.4
Federally insured state-chartered						
Percentage of number of institutions	33.6	34.4	34.3	34.0	33.8	36.5
Percentage of total assets	35.4	35.1	34.6	34.3	34.4	36.6
Capital to asset ratio categories						
More than 6%						
Number	9,719	9,673	9,984	10,496	10,367	10,399
Total assets (US$ billions)	66.9	81.3	101.7	121.4	139.7	168.0
3% to 6%						
Number	4,156	3,875	3,257	2,370	2,032	2,141
Total assets (US$ billions)	69.9	69.6	64.5	54.2	50.3	50.7
1.5% to 3%						
Number	575	549	413	294	255	262
Total assets (US$ billions)	8.0	8.1	6.0	4.1	3.7	5.6
0% to 1.5%						
Number	175	188	155	130	133	102
Total assets (US$ billions)	1.4	2.6	1.9	2.5	2.5	1.0
Less than 0%						
Number	62	50	69	81	74	56
Total assets (US$ billions)	1.5	0.6	1.2	1.5	2.1	1.8
Number of problem credit unions	794	929	1,022	794	678	685
Assets of problem credit unions (US$ billions)	6.6	8.1	10.6	8.4	9.4	10.4
Resolutions						
Number	94	88	85	114	164	130
Total shares (US$ millions)	116	327	297	285	339	267
Estimated present value cost (US$ millions)	29	52	33	74	49	77
Number of months rated 4 or 5 before closure	55.4	44.1	30.1	24.0	17.5	—

Table 9.3. *(Continued)*

Category	1992	1993	1994	1995	1996
Number of institutions	12,594	12,317	11,991	11,687	11,392
Total assets (US$ billions)	258	277	290	307	327
Capital (US$ billions)	20.9	24.9	27.7	31.7	35.2
Net income (US$ millions)	3,364	3,743	3,438	3,377	3,530
Net operating income (US$ millions)	4,148	4,419	4,181	4,172	4,620
Net non-operating income (US$ millions)	95	76	(59)	(20)	15
Provision for loan losses (US$ millions)	879	752	684	775	1,105
Federal income taxes (US$ millions)	0	0	0	0	0
Percentage of 1st mortgages to total assets	11.3	11.9	12.9	12.8	14.0
Percentage of mortgage-backed securities to total assets	—	3.5	3.6	3.1	2.8
Percentage of total real estate assets to total assets	19.0	18.7	20.0	20.1	21.6
Federally chartered					
Percentage of number of institutions	62.8	62.5	62.5	62.7	62.8
Percentage of total assets	62.7	62.4	63.1	63.2	63.2
Federally insured state-chartered					
Percentage of number of institutions	37.2	37.5	37.5	37.3	37.2
Percentage of total assets	37.3	37.6	36.9	36.8	36.8
Capital to asset ratio categories					
More than 6%					
Number	10,356	10,901	11,074	11,146	10,990
Total assets (US$ billions)	208.5	250.9	268.1	296.6	321.0
3% to 6%					
Number	1,971	1,279	824	465	321
Total assets (US$ billions)	46.1	24.3	20.1	9.6	5.6
1.5% to 3%					
Number	178	80	54	37	35
Total assets (US$ billions)	1.5	1.4	0.4	0.4	0.1
0% to 1.5%					
Number	59	39	24	16	30
Total assets (US$ billions)	1.7	0.5	0.2	0.1	0.1
Less than 0%					
Number	29	17	14	23	15
Total assets (US$ billions)	0.6	0.2	0.1	0.1	0.03
Number of problem credit unions	608	474	319	267	—
Assets of problem credit unions (US$ billions)	7.4	4.3	2.4	2.0	—
Resolutions					
Number	114	71	33	26	19
Total shares (US$ millions)	223	265	255	545	19
Estimated present value cost (US$ millions)	107	20	36	13	2
Number of months rated 4 or 5 before closure	—	—	—	—	—

— Not available.

Note: Capital includes undivided earnings, regular reserves, and other reserves, but excludes allowances for loan and investment losses. As of 1996 the allowance for investment losses no longer exists. Effective January 1, 1995, the National Credit Union Share Insurance Fund insurance year changed from October 1 through September 30 to January 1 through December 31.

Source: Barth and Brumbaugh (1991, 1994); National Credit Union Administration (1995); correspondence with Dr. Tun A. Wai, National Association of Federal Credit Unions.

Table 9.4. *Selected Performance Measures for Commercial Banks and Savings and Loan Institutions, 1950–96*

Year	Commercial banks			Savings and loan institutions		
	Return on assets (%)	Return on equity (%)	Equity capital to assets (%)	Return on assets (%)	Return on equity (%)	Equity capital to assets (%)
1950	0.67	9.80	6.75	1.19	16.60	7.18
1951	0.61	9.04	6.71	1.22	16.71	7.30
1952	0.59	8.73	6.73	1.01	13.89	7.25
1953	0.57	8.73	6.93	1.02	14.51	7.05
1954	0.75	8.30	7.11	1.06	15.40	6.87
1955	0.64	10.72	7.16	1.10	16.41	6.73
1956	0.69	9.03	7.04	1.02	15.20	6.74
1957	0.72	9.55	7.70	0.95	13.84	6.85
1958	0.91	11.82	7.65	0.97	14.06	6.92
1959	0.65	8.31	7.89	0.97	14.08	6.92
1960	0.90	11.33	8.05	0.86	12.49	6.92
1961	0.89	11.11	7.97	0.98	14.16	6.93
1962	0.82	10.24	8.02	0.98	14.07	6.95
1963	0.79	9.78	8.08	0.70	10.26	6.81
1964	0.79	10.04	7.72	0.72	10.83	6.69
1965	0.79	10.43	7.53	0.67	9.82	6.82
1966	0.78	10.45	7.42	0.50	7.24	6.88
1967	0.82	11.34	7.09	0.38	5.52	6.88
1968	0.80	11.40	6.89	0.60	8.80	6.85
1969	0.85	12.02	7.18	0.68	9.73	6.99
1970	0.88	12.36	7.12	0.57	8.17	6.98
1971	0.87	12.37	6.95	0.71	10.86	6.53
1972	0.83	12.24	6.62	0.77	12.16	6.36
1973	0.85	12.75	6.68	0.76	12.18	6.22
1974	0.76	12.43	5.70	0.54	8.65	6.21
1975	0.68	11.78	5.90	0.47	8.09	5.81
1976	0.69	11.50	6.11	0.63	11.14	5.68
1977	0.70	11.72	5.92	0.77	13.99	5.70
1978	0.76	12.94	5.77	0.82	14.21	5.77
1979	0.80	13.96	5.73	0.67	11.55	5.80
1980	0.79	13.77	5.75	0.11	2.61	5.47
1981	0.76	13.18	5.82	-0.75	-17.28	4.34
1982	0.71	12.18	5.84	-0.65	-20.44	3.18
1983	0.64	11.11	6.00	0.27	8.11	3.33
1984	0.65	10.52	6.14	0.11	3.97	2.77
1985	0.69	11.12	6.19	0.39	12.30	3.17
1986	0.61	9.92	6.19	0.08	2.40	3.34
1987	0.09	1.55	6.02	-0.59	-21.69	2.72
1988	0.81	13.16	6.28	-0.96	-44.24	2.17
1989	0.48	7.76	6.21	-0.54	-13.17	4.10
1990	0.48	7.55	6.45	-0.35	-6.97	5.02

Table 9.4. *(Continued)*

	Commercial banks			Savings and loan institutions		
Year	Return on assets (%)	Return on equity (%)	Equity capital to assets (%)	Return on assets (%)	Return on equity (%)	Equity capital to assets (%)
1991	0.53	7.97	6.75	0.13	2.25	5.94
1992	0.92	12.93	7.51	0.61	9.33	6.93
1993	1.20	15.50	8.01	0.63	8.66	7.50
1994	1.17	14.61	7.78	0.56	7.36	7.48
1995	1.17	14.61	8.11	0.70	9.00	8.01
1996	1.19	14.46	8.20	0.62	7.78	7.92

Source: Federal Deposit Insurance Corporation and Office of Thrift Supervision data.

of difficulties, however. Tables 9.1–9.3 show that the major contributors to the total failure resolution costs were failed S&Ls. These institutions alone accounted for 80 percent of the total costs, whether the costs are expressed in nominal dollars or in 1992 dollars. Indeed, when all figures are expressed in 1992 dollars, S&L failure resolution costs from 1980 through 1996 actually exceed the losses borne by all uninsured depositors in both commercial and savings banks and in S&Ls from 1921 through 1933, although they are smaller as a percentage of GDP, and they are only slightly less than these losses plus the total losses borne by both uninsured depositors and the insurance funds for these institutions from 1934 through 1940. (This particular comparison is made because some might consider the later losses to be carried over from the period before insurance was in effect.)

The losses associated with banking failures, in other words, were less without federal deposit insurance, but with market discipline, than those with federal deposit insurance and regulatory discipline. Even including the losses for the first several years after the implementation of federal deposit insurance to the calculations does not alter the conclusion one draws. The evidence clearly indicates that the regulatory structure for S&Ls that existed during most of the 1980s and early 1990s was inadequate in assuring that the industry would operate safely and soundly. Worse yet, the federal deposit insurance fund for S&Ls itself reported insolvency in 1985 for the first time since its establishment in 1934 and was replaced with a new insurance fund in 1989. As a result of this insolvency, taxpayers were required to help pay for resolving failed S&Ls.[2]

---

2. The enormity of the failure resolution problem led to the establishment of the Resolution Trust Corporation in 1989 to dispose of failed S&Ls and/or their assets. It ceased operations in 1995. Table 9.2 presents information on the conservatorships the Resolution Trust Corporation handled during its existence.

Figure 9.1. Return on Assets and Equity and Equity Capital to Assets, 1950–96

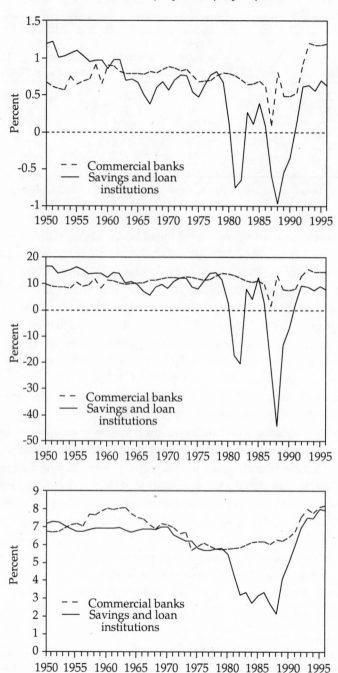

By contrast, the regulatory structure for credit unions worked much better during the same period. By recapitalizing their own federal deposit insurance fund, credit unions themselves provided more than enough resources to cover all failure resolution costs. Note that unlike in the case of S&Ls and commercial and savings banks, there was no widespread concern being expressed in the 1980s that taxpayer funds would be needed to resolve failed credit unions.[3]

Second, despite the serious problems federally insured depositories experienced during the 1980s and the early 1990s, they were nonetheless temporary and, most important, did not significantly disrupt aggregate economic activity.[4] The temporary nature of the problems is evident in figure 9.1, which shows the rate of return on assets, rate of return on equity, and the equity capital-to-asset ratios for commercial banks and S&Ls from 1950 through 1996. Figure 9.1 and table 9.4 also show that S&Ls experienced far worse problems than commercial banks based upon these three widely used measures of performance. Furthermore, figure 9.1 clearly shows two distinct times when S&Ls suffered severely. The first period was when short-term interest rates rose relative to long-term interest rates in the late 1970s and the early 1980s. The second period was when asset quality deteriorated significantly in the latter half of the 1980s.

A substantial literature documents that the problems experienced by S&Ls were due to a combination of factors, including both sharp declines in energy prices and adverse tax rate changes in 1986.[5] Most observers agree that one of the most important contributors to the S&Ls, problems were laws and regulations that exposed them to substantial interest rate risk in the late 1970s and early 1980s. Subsequently, lax regulation and supervision, especially in the early to mid-1980s, enabled inadequately capitalized institutions to grow rapidly by engaging in high-risk activities. As

---

3. The insurance fund for commercial and savings banks reported insolvency in 1990 and 1991, but then returned to solvency as the financial condition of these institutions significantly, albeit unexpectedly, improved.

4. In this sense, federal deposit insurance accomplished its goal of preventing widespread runs and the associated disruption in the credit system and payments mechanism. Disruptions in the latter, of course, also disrupt aggregate economic activity. The failures of federal deposit insurance during this time were that taxpayers were not adequately protected because of excessively costly failure resolutions and that economic resources were misallocated.

5. With respect to tax rate changes, the Economic Recovery and Tax Act of 1981 shortened depreciable life from 40 to 15 years for real property and increased the depreciation rate from 125 to 175 percent declining balance for real property. The Tax Reform Act of 1986, by contrast, lengthened depreciable life from 19 to 27.5 years for residential property and to 31.5 years for commercial property. Also, the depreciation rate was decreased from a 175 percent declining balance to straight-line for real property, and a passive loss rule was added that prevented the direct offset of most real estate losses against ordinary income.

table 9.2 shows, even though several hundred institutions holding about US$200 billion or more in assets were reporting insolvency or were known by the regulatory authorities to be problem institutions during 1982 through 1986, total industry assets grew by 70 percent, or US$478 billion.

Although the banking problems were severe, tables 9.1–9.3 and figure 9.1 show that they were clearly over by the mid-1990s. Indeed, at that time the regulatory authorities of all three types of federally insured depository institutions were issuing reports on the overall healthy condition of institutions. This situation reflected a combination of largely unanticipated factors, including a favorable interest rate environment, widespread and noninflationary economic growth, and a significant shift away from traditional banking activities as institutions essentially reinvented themselves through their own efforts and the efforts of both the regulatory authorities and Congress. Gilbert (1997, p. 1), an economist with the Federal Reserve Bank of St. Louis, reports that: "Almost all of the rise in profitability of the banking industry from 1992 to 1996 can be attributed to the relatively low interest rates paid on savings and small time deposits."

Third, several important changes have occurred in the structure of the federally insured depository industry. Since 1980, the number of all types of depository institutions has fallen substantially. Indeed, the total number of institutions has declined by 36 percent. This reduction has been due not only to failures, but also to consolidation through mergers and acquisitions brought about by increased domestic and global competition, improved information technology, and eased restrictions on both geographical expansion and intradepository industry entry.

At the same time, as table 9.5 and figure 9.2 show, the depository institutions' share of total financial assets held by all U.S. financial service firms declined from 65 percent in 1950 to 30 percent in 1996. During the same period the share accounted for by only U.S.-chartered commercial banks declined from 50 to 17 percent. The U.S.-chartered commercial banks' share today is nearly the same as the share accounted for by money market and other mutual funds. This latter development emphasizes the declining role of banks in the traditional intermediation function as the U.S. financial system has evolved over time. Similarly, the role of S&Ls has also diminished in terms of its traditional intermediation function, but in a more fundamental way.

As table 9.6 shows, as recently as 1980 S&Ls were the major holder of home mortgages. The securitization of such mortgage loans, however, has contributed to the decline in the traditional role of S&Ls as major holders of home mortgages. Indeed, the share of home mortgages accounted for by all savings institutions declined from 50 percent in 1980 to

Table 9.5. *Percentage Distribution of Total Financial Assets Held by All U.S. Financial Service Firms, Selected Years, 1950–96*

Institution	1950	1960	1970	1980	1990	1995	1996
Depository Institutions [a]							
Commercial banks	50.9	37.8	38.2	34.1	27.5	24.4	23.0
U.S.-chartered	50.3	37.1	36.1	29.1	21.8	18.0	16.8
Foreign offices in the U.S.	0.4	0.6	0.7	2.3	3.0	3.6	3.5
Bank holding companies	—	—	1.1	2.4	2.5	2.5	2.5
Banks in the U.S. possessions	0.3	0.1	0.3	0.3	0.2	0.2	0.2
Savings institutions	13.7	19.6	19.7	18.2	11.2	5.5	5.1
S&Ls	5.9	11.8	12.8	14.4	9.1	—[e]	—[e]
Savings banks	7.7	6.8	5.9	3.8	2.1	—[e]	—[e]
Credit unions	0.3	1.0	1.3	1.6	1.8	1.7	1.6
Contractual intermediaries							
Life insurance companies	21.3	19.2	14.8	10.7	11.3	11.4	10.9
Other insurance companies	4.0	4.3	3.7	4.2	4.4	4.0	3.9
Private pension funds [b]	2.4	6.3	8.3	11.6	13.4	14.3	14.8
State and local government retirement funds	1.7	3.3	4.4	4.5	6.8	8.3	8.5
Others							
Finance companies	3.2	4.6	4.7	4.7	5.0	4.5	4.4
Mortgage companies	—	—	—	0.4	0.4	0.2	0.2
Mutual funds [c]	1.1	2.8	3.5	1.4	5.0	10.1	11.5
Money market mutual funds	0.0	0.0	0.0	1.8	4.1	4.0	4.4
Closed-end funds	—	—	—	0.2	0.4	0.7	0.7
Security brokers and dealers	1.4	1.1	1.2	1.0	2.2	3.1	3.1
Real estate investment trusts	—	—	0.3	0.1	0.1	0.1	0.2
Issuers of asset-backed securities	—	—	—	0.0	2.3	3.7	4.0
Bank personal trusts [d]	—	—	—	5.6	4.3	4.0	3.7
Total assets (US$ billions)	294	605	1,356	4,349	12,152	18,414	20,482

— Not available.

a. Commercial banks consist of U.S.-chartered commercial banks, domestic affiliates, Edge Act corporations, and agencies and offices in U.S. possessions. Foreign banking offices in the United States include Edge Act corporations and offices of foreign banks. International banking facilities are excluded from domestic banking and treated like branches in foreign countries. Savings and loan associations include all savings and loan associations and federal savings banks insured by the Savings Association Insurance Fund. Savings banks include all federal and mutual savings banks insured by the Bank Insurance Fund.

b. Private pension funds include the Federal Employees' Retirement Thrift Savings Fund.

c. Mutual funds are open-end investment companies (including unit investment trusts) that report to the Investment Company Institute.

d. Bank personal trusts are assets of individuals managed by bank trust departments and nondeposit, noninsured trust companies.

e. The flow of funds accounts were restructured in the second quarter of 1993, thereby omitting this breakdown.

Source: Board of Governors of the Federal Reserve System, flow of funds accounts.

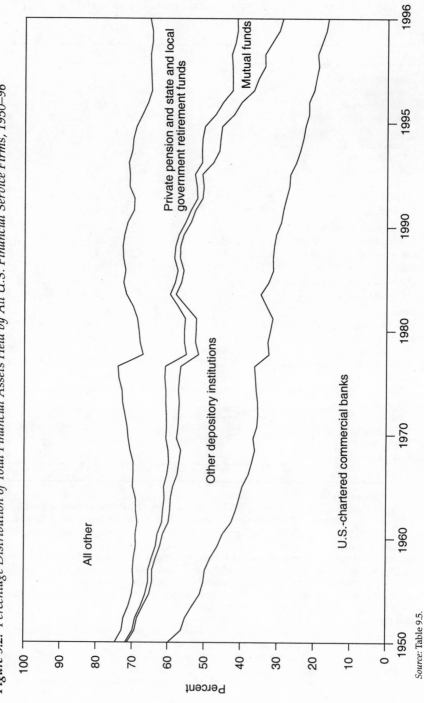

Figure 9.2. Percentage Distribution of Total Financial Assets Held by All U.S. Financial Service Firms, 1950–96

All other

Private pension and state and local government retirement funds

Mutual funds

Other depository institutions

U.S.-chartered commercial banks

Percent

100

90

80

70

60

50

40

30

20

10

0

1950 1960 1970 1980 1990 1995 1996

Source: Table 9.5.

150

Table 9.6. *Percentage Distribution of U.S. Real Estate Mortgage Loans by Lender, Selected Years, 1950–96*

Lender	1950 HM	1950 MM	1950 CM	1960 HM	1960 MM	1960 CM	1970 HM	1970 MM	1970 CM
Commercial banks	21.0	10.2	18.1	13.6	5.4	20.4	14.4	5.5	27.2
Savings institutions	38.5	32.0	11.8	53.5	28.5	15.2	56.2	36.9	22.6
S&Ls	29.0	2.5	2.5	39.0	10.5	7.5	41.9	22.9	13.4
Savings banks	9.5	29.5	9.3	14.5	18.0	7.7	14.3	13.0	9.2
Credit unions	1.0	0.0	0.0	0.3	0.0	0.0	0.3	0.0	0.0
Life insurance companies	18.8	28.1	29.4	17.5	18.6	30.1	9.1	26.6	30.4
Private pension funds	0.1	0.3	0.2	0.4	1.7	1.0	6.0	2.0	1.4
State and local government retirements funds	0.1	0.3	0.1	0.6	2.2	0.5	1.0	3.3	1.1
Finance companies	0.8	0.4	0.1	1.0	0.8	0.2	2.0	2.0	0.4
Real estate investment trusts	0.0	0.0	0.0	0.0	0.0	0.0	0.2	2.1	2.4
Mortgage pools	0.0	0.0	0.0	0.0	0.0	0.0	1.0	0.1	0.0
Government-sponsored enterprises	0.0	0.0	0.0	2.0	0.0	0.0	5.3	0.5	0.0
Issuers of asset-backed securities	0.0	0.0	0.0	0.0	0.0	0.0	0.0	0.0	0.0
U.S. government	3.3	0.4	0.1	3.0	4.9	0.1	2.1	5.1	0.5
State and local governments	0.5	0.0	0.0	1.0	0.1	0.0	0.6	3.3	0.2
Households	16.8	28.2	39.2	7.2	37.9	32.1	7.6	13.2	13.7
Total assets (US$ billions)	45.0	9.0	13.0	142.0	21.0	33.0	294.0	60.0	86.0

(Table continues on the following page.)

Table 9.6. (Continued)

Lender	1980 HM	1980 MM	1980 CM	1990 HM	1990 MM	1990 CM	1996 HM	1996 MM	1996 CM
Commercial banks	16.8	9.1	31.6	17.5	12.0	44.5	18.4	15.8	52.7
Savings institutions	50.1	38.1	24.1	24.0	29.7	14.4	13.5	20.8	7.5
S&Ls	43.0	26.8	17.7	—	—	—	—	—	—
Savings banks	7.1	11.3	6.4	1.9	—	—	—	—	—
Credit unions	0.5	0.0	0.0	0.5	—	—	1.9	—	—
Life insurance companies	1.9	10.0	31.6	0.3	9.4	28.4	0.2	8.1	24.3
Private pension funds	0.1	0.3	0.7	0.3	1.3	1.5	0.1	0.3	2.0
State and local government retirements funds	0.4	2.7	1.4	0.1	1.6	1.0	0.1	1.6	1.0
Finance companies	2.6	1.5	1.2	2.5	—	—	2.6	—	—
Real estate investment trusts	0.0	1.1	0.9	0.0	0.7	0.7	0.1	3.8	0.6
Mortgage pools	11.2	4.2	0.0	37.9	9.5	—	44.0	11.0	—
Government-sponsored enterprises	6.1	4.7	0.0	4.4	4.3	—	5.6	6.5	—
Issuers of asset-backed securities	0.0	0.0	0.0	2.3	1.6	0.3	6.5	11.4	9.0
U.S. government	1.9	7.3	2.2	1.4	7.4	1.8	0.4	4.9	1.1
State and local governments	2.1	7.5	0.7	2.3	13.2	0.9	1.6	15.3	1.1
Households	6.3	10.1	2.9	4.6	6.9	3.2	5.1	0.6	0.9
Total assets (US$ billions)	955.0	142.0	256.0	2,616.0	309.0	758.0	3,818.0	297.0	706.0

—Not available.
HM Home mortgages.
MM Multifamily mortgages.
CM Commercial mortgages.
Source: Board of Governors of the Federal Reserve System, flow of funds accounts.

14 percent in 1996. At the same time, as tables 9.1 and 9.3 show, real estate assets have increased in importance for commercial banks and credit unions. These and other recent developments are continuing to blur many of the distinctions among the different types of financial service firms as they all attempt to adapt to the changing, competitive, domestic, and increasingly global, financial marketplace.[6]

Lessons from U.S. Banking Problems

As the experiences of the 1980s and early 1990s demonstrate, despite the existence of an elaborate regulatory structure, significant banking problems can develop. In trying to understand how to design bank regulation to prevent future problems, deriving some lessons from actual problems of the past is helpful. The lessons discussed here are based on U.S. banking problems, and therefore may not be applicable to other countries at different stages of development and with different cultures and financial systems.

Banks' Participation in a Wider Range of Activities

The ongoing debate over whether to allow banks to engage in a wider range of activities highlights the fact that regulation has significantly limited federally insured depositories in what they can do and when they can do it. This necessarily means that depository institutions have been unable to adapt freely to changing, competitive financial markets. The situation of the S&Ls in the late 1970s and early 1980s represents the most extreme case in which institutions were unable to adapt to a changing environment in a timely manner. As table 9.7 shows, despite repeated attempts to broaden their range of permissible activities, prior to the early 1980s S&Ls could essentially offer only long-term, fixed rate home mortgages. Only the threat of their very survival prompted Congress to grant S&Ls, albeit too late for many of them, greater freedom to reduce their interest rate risk exposure. This was largely done by permitting institutions to diversify away from home mortgages, authorizing the use of various derivative instruments, and allowing variable rate home mortgage loans.

---

6. A commercial bank is legally defined to be an institution that accepts demand deposits, makes commercial loans, and whose deposits are insured by the Bank Insurance Fund of the Federal Deposit Insurance Corporation. Yet today only about 15 percent of the assets of commercial banks are commercial loans and only about 15 percent of their assets are funded with demand deposits. In other words, by 1997 legal rather than market factors were needed to distinguish a commercial bank from many other types of firms in the financial marketplace.

Table 9.7. *Evolution of Federal S&L Powers, 1933–82*

Power	Enacted Home Owner's Loan Act, 1933	Enacted Housing Act, 1959	Enacted Housing Act, 1961	Enacted Public Law 87-779, 1962	Enacted Public Law 88-560, 1964	Proposed Administration's Federal Savings Bank Bill, 1965[a]
Home mortgage	Yes ($20,000 loan limit)					Yes ($35,000 or 2% of assets)[h]
Nonresidential mortgages	Yes (15% of assets)			Yes (20% of assets)		Yes
Land development		Yes (Loans up to 5% of assets)				Yes (Loans)
Direct investment			Yes (5% of assets in bus. dev. corp.)		Yes (2% of assets in urban renew. area)	Yes (Up to 50% of capital)
Service corporation					Yes (1% of assets)	Yes (No limit)
Construction loans						
Corporate bonds						Yes
Education loans						Yes (Up to 5% of assets)
Consumer loans						Yes (Up to US$5000)
Commercial loans						
Leasing of personal property						
Investment in commercial paper						
Credit cards						

Table 9.7. *(Continued)*

Power	Proposed Hunt Commission Study,[b] 1972	Proposed Admini- stration's proposed "Financial Institution Act," 1973[c]	Proposed "Fine study" legislation passed Senate 1975[d]	Proposed House Banking Committee print, 1976[e]	Enacted Public Law 95-630, 1978
Home mortgage	Yes (Statutory loan limit dele.)		Yes (Statutory loan limit dele.)	Yes (Statutory loan limit dele.)	**Yes ($60,000 loan limit)** [i]
Non-residential mortgages	Yes	Yes	Yes (30% of assets)	Yes (20% of assets)	**Yes (20% of assets)**
Land development	Yes		Yes (Loans)		**Yes (5% of assets)**
Direct investment	Yes (Up to 3% of assets)	Yes (For community development)	Yes (For community development)	Yes (For community development)	**Yes (2% of assets for community development)**
Service corporation			Yes (1% of assets)	Yes (1% of assets)	**Yes (1% of assets)**
Construction loans	Yes	Yes	Yes	Yes (20% of assets)	**Yes (5% of assets)**
Corporate bonds	Yes	Yes (Up to 10% of assets)	Yes	Yes	
Education loans	Yes (Up to 3% of assets)		Yes (30% of assets)	Yes (20% of assets)	**Yes (5% of assets)**
Consumer loans	Yes (Up to 10% of assets)	Yes (Up to 10% of assets)	Yes (30% of assets)	Yes (20% of assets)	
Commercial loans	Yes (Up to 3% of assets)				
Leasing of personal property					
Investment in commercial paper	Yes (Up to 3% of assets)	Yes (Up to 10% of assets)	Yes (30% of assets)	Yes	
Credit cards	Yes	Yes	Yes		

(Table continues on the following page.)

Table 9.7. (Continued)

Power	Proposed Administration proposal, 1979[f]	Enacted Depository Institutions Deregulation Act, 1980	Proposed Administration proposal, 1981[g]	Enacted Garn-St. Germain, 1982	Year first authorized
Home mortgage		Yes (90% loan-to-value limit)	Yes (Statutory loan-to-value limit dele.)	Yes (Statutory loan-to-value limit dele.)	1933
Non-residential mortgages		Yes (20% of assets)	Yes (No limit)	Yes (40% of assets)	1933
Land development					1959
Direct investment		Yes (2% of assets for community development.; 5% business development)	Yes (In small business investment corporation)	Yes (1% assets in small business investment corporation)	1961
Service corporation		Yes (3% of assets)	Yes (5% of assets)		1964
Construction loans		Yes (5% of assets)			1978
Corporate bonds	Yes (10% of assets)	Yes (20% of assets[j])	Yes (No limit)	Yes [k]	1980
Education loans		Yes (5% of assets)	Yes (No limit)		1978
Consumer loans	Yes (10% of assets)	Yes (20% of assets)	Yes (No limit)	Yes (30% of assets)	1980
Commercial loans			Yes (No limit)	Yes [l] (10% of assets)	1982
Leasing of personal property			Yes (10% of assets)	Yes (10% of assets)	1982
Investment in commercial paper	Yes (10% of assets)	Yes (20% of assets)			1980
Credit cards	Yes	Yes			1980

Table 9.7. *(Continued)*

Note: Enacted legislation in bold, everything else is proposed legislation.
a. H.R. 14 and H.R. 11508, 89th Congress
b. Report, Presidential Committee on Financial Structure and Regulation (1972)
c. S. 2591, 93rd Congress (1973)
d. S. 1267, 94th Congress (1975)
e. Financial Reform Act of 1976, 94th Congress (1976)
f. Depository Institutions Deregulation Act, 96th Congress (1979)
g. S. 1703, 97th Congress (1981)
h. The bill also provided an 80% loan-to-value limit that could be waived by regulation.
i. The limit was raised to $75,000 in 1979, Public Law 96-161
j. By regulation, up to 1% unrated bonds
k. While the Garn-St. Germain Act continues the placement of corporate bond investments in the 20% of assets basket, the Bank Board interpreted the Act to permit up to 100% of assets in corporate bonds, with up to 1% in unrated bonds.
l. By regulation, the Bank Board interpreted this authority to include investment in unrated corporate bonds up to 10% of assets.
Source: Barth (1991).

Figure 9.3 presents a broader perspective on bank regulation by providing information on some of the more important developments that affected all depository institutions from 1781 through 1996. Based on studies of various aspects of this historical record, one learns that most bank regulation has not been proactive, but rather a reaction to actual or perceived banking problems. Yet the attempts to resolve the identified problems all too often created new and potentially even more serious problems. The reason for this is that changes in the regulatory structure not only change the opportunities for banking institutions to engage in what they consider to be the most profitable activities, but also change their incentives with respect to risk-taking behavior. Their proponents view changes in the range of opportunities available to institutions to pursue various activities as necessary to achieve a safe and sound banking industry. Viewed in a static context, such changes may appear to be able to achieve their goal, but financial markets must be viewed in a dynamic context. Financial markets are subject to changes that the regulatory authorities cannot control, or even anticipate. In such a situation changes in the regulatory structure may breed new and unanticipated problems. This was the case when S&Ls were first required to specialize in fixed rate home mortgages and then encouraged to diversify into new activities, many of which they were allowed to do without either sufficient expertise or adequate equity capital contributed by owners.

In view of this situation, there is considerable merit to Federal Reserve Bank of Cleveland President Jerry Jordan's (1996) view that: "Banking companies should not be required to get permission from regulators before doing

Figure 9.3. *Timeline of Banking Developments in the United States*

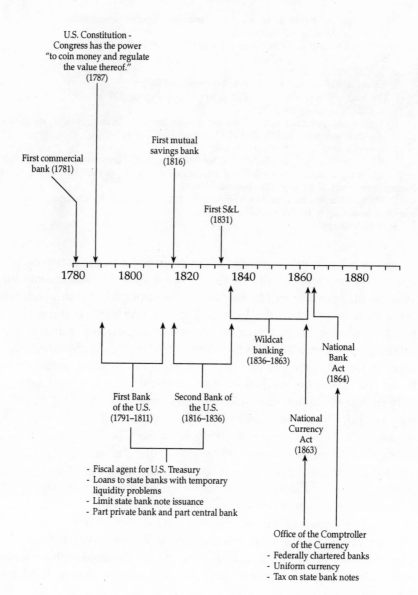

Figure 9.3. *(Continued)*

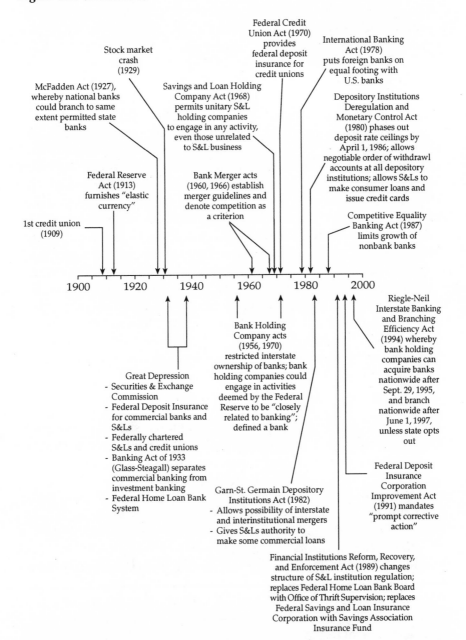

Note: Before the Civil War the federal government only issued coins, and only these were legal or lawful money. During the Civil War "greenbacks" were added, and finally in 1933 federal reserve notes were added.

something new. Rather, they should notify authorities of their intentions. If regulators want to prevent the action, the burden should be on them to intervene in a timely way to demonstrate that the costs exceed the benefits." There is also considerable merit to Federal Reserve Bank of Kansas City President Thomas Hoenig's (1996, p. 11) view that: "In light of the costs and difficulties of implementing prudential supervision for larger institutions who are increasingly involved in new activities and industries, the time may have come to sever the link between these institutions and the safety nets, making it feasible to significantly scale back regulatory oversight of their operations." Of course, if banks were permitted unrestricted access to new activities, the authorities would want to be sure that they conducted such activities under appropriate conditions. In this regard, the authorities could require that new activities, whether conducted in a subsidiary of a bank or in a holding company, be capitalized by funds other than those used to meet the bank's required capital standards. The authorities could also impose interaffiliate lending restrictions on banks and any new nonbank affiliates. Moreover, they could prohibit nonbank affiliates that are creditors from reaching banks' assets by "piercing the corporate veil." In short, any expansion by banks into new activities should be accompanied by prudent limitations on the overall way in which such activities are conducted. This qualification also applies to the design of an appropriate bank regulatory structure for the emerging market economies.

Federal Safety Net

Many individuals believe that banking institutions should be restricted to a fairly narrow range of activities because they have access to the federal safety net, that is, deposit insurance, discount window borrowing, and the Fedwire payments system. Indeed, much of the debate about whether or not to ease, if not eliminate, the restrictions separating banks and nonbank firms relates to the safety net. A specific concern is that any subsidy associated with the safety net could flow from banks to any affiliated nonbank firms. Yet disagreement exists about whether any such subsidy even exists. Federal Reserve Chairman Alan Greenspan has testified that a subsidy does exist (Greenspan 1997); Comptroller of the Currency Eugene Ludwig has testified that "no net [taking into account the cost of the regulatory burden imposed on banks] subsidy exists" (1997, p. 2); and Federal Deposit Insurance Corporation Chairman Ricki Helfer has testified that "if a net subsidy exists, it is very small" (1997, p. 2). Outside the bank regulatory agencies, the Shadow Financial Regulatory

Committee has concluded that the net subsidy is "probably not particularly large" (1997, p. 2).

Obviously some effort should be made to measure the net subsidy, and if a net subsidy is found to exist, it should be eliminated in an efficient and timely manner. Once eliminated, the danger of the subsidy spreading to other affiliates is also eliminated. The more important point, however, is that the mere existence of a subsidy should not be used to deny banks the opportunity to engage prudently in a wider range of activities, and correspondingly, for other firms to own banks. As table 9.8 shows, the United States is clearly out of step with almost all the other 19 nonoverlapping Group of Ten and European Union countries with respect to the extent to which banks are permitted to engage in securities, insurance, and real estate activities. The United States is also out of step with respect to permitting banks to own nonfinancial firms and vice versa (see Barth, Nolle, and Rice 1997 for further international comparisons regarding these and related banking issues).

Adverse Selection and Moral Hazard

Various types of adverse selection, principal-agent, and moral hazard problems arise in banking. It is therefore incumbent upon the regulatory authorities to examine, supervise, and regulate federally insured depositories to promote a stable, efficient, and competitive banking industry. The authorities must also, of course, resolve troubled institutions in a timely and cost-effective manner so as to limit losses to the insurance funds and thereby better protect taxpayers and minimize the misallocation of resources. As the S&L situation so vividly demonstrates, regulatory forbearance can exacerbate an existing problem. In the early 1980s, when virtually the entire S&L industry was deeply troubled, the authorities lowered regulatory capital requirements and broadened the measurement of capital for meeting the requirements to include items unacceptable under generally accepted accounting principles. As figure 9.4 shows, these actions were taken by the regulatory authorities (the Federal Home Loan Bank Board at that time) after the U.S. Congress first lowered the minimum statutory capital requirement and then eliminated it entirely. As a result of these and other regulatory actions, many institutions engaged in high-risk activities with little, if any, equity contributed by owners at stake. As table 9.2 shows, S&Ls were publicly reporting tangible insolvency for several years before being resolved. Indeed, the institutions resolved in 1988 had been reporting tangible insolvency on average for three-and-a-half years prior to resolution.

Table 9.8. *Permissible Banking Activities and Bank Ownership in the European Union and Group of Ten Countries, 1995*

Power and country	Securities	Insurance	Real estate	Commercial bank investment in nonfinancial firm	Nonfinancial firm investment in commercial banks
Very wide powers					
Austria	Unrestricted	Permitted	Unrestricted	Unrestricted	Unrestricted
France	Unrestricted	Permitted	Permitted	Unrestricted	Unrestricted
Netherlands	Unrestricted	Permitted	Permitted	Unrestricted	Unrestricted
Switzerland	Unrestricted	Permitted	Unrestricted	Unrestricted	Unrestricted
United Kingdom	Unrestricted	Permitted	Unrestricted	Unrestricted	Unrestricted
Wide powers					
Denmark	Unrestricted	Permitted	Permitted	Permitted	Unrestricted
Finland	Unrestricted	Restricted	Permitted	Unrestricted	Unrestricted
Germany	Unrestricted	Restricted	Permitted	Unrestricted	Unrestricted
Ireland	Unrestricted	Prohibited	Unrestricted	Unrestricted	Unrestricted
Luxembourg	Unrestricted	Permitted	Unrestricted	Unrestricted	Restricted
Portugal	Unrestricted	Permitted	Restricted	Permitted	Unrestricted
Spain	Unrestricted	Permitted	Restricted	Unrestricted	Permitted
Somewhat restricted powers					
Belgium	Permitted	Permitted	Restricted	Restricted	Unrestricted
Canada	Permitted	Permitted	Permitted	Restricted	Restricted
Greece	Permitted	Restricted	Restricted	Unrestricted	Unrestricted
Italy	Unrestricted	Permitted	Restricted	Restricted	Restricted
Sweden	Unrestricted	Permitted	Restricted	Restricted	Restricted

Table 9.8. (Continued)

Power and country	Securities	Insurance	Real estate	Commercial bank Investment in nonfinancial firm	Nonfinancial firm investment in commercial banks
Restricted powers					
Japan	Restricted	Prohibited	Restricted	Restricted	Restricted
United States	Restricted	Restricted	Restricted	Restricted	Restricted

Unrestricted	A full range of activities in the given category can be conducted directly in the bank.
Permitted	A full range of activities can be conducted, but all or some must be conducted in subsidiaries.
Restricted	Less than a full range of activities can be conducted in the bank or subsidiaries.
Prohibited	The activity cannot be conducted in either the bank or subsidiaries.

Note: Securities activities include underwriting, dealing, and brokering all kinds of securities and all aspects of the mutual fund business. Insurance activities include underwriting and selling insurance products and services as principal and as agent. Real estate activities include investment, development, and management.

Source: Barth, Nolle, and Rice (1997).

163

Figure 9.4. *Federal Savings and Loan Insurance Corporation Insured Institutions, Capital to Asset Ratios, 1940–88*

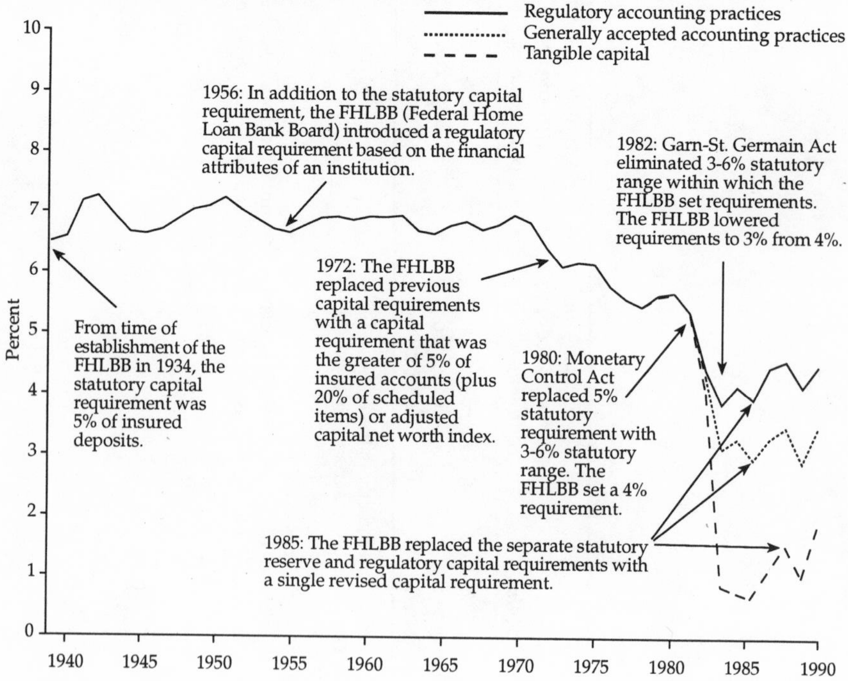

Source: Barth (1991).

The enormous failure resolution costs discussed earlier reflect the consequences of allowing insolvent institutions to remain open for lengthy periods. Figure 9.5 shows the relationship between regulatory delay and failure costs for S&Ls during the 1980s.

Many believe that the enactment of the Federal Deposit Insurance Corporation Improvement Act in 1991 eliminates the possibility of any similar regulatory forbearance in the future. While the act certainly has its desirable features, one should not be overly optimistic that it will always work as intended. The reasons for some healthy skepticism are twofold. First, when adverse movements in interest rates in the late 1970s and early 1980s devastated the S&Ls, existing statutory and regulatory capital standards were deemed to be too stringent, and were therefore simply eased, with the effect of papering over the problem. Second, as table 9.2 shows, sufficient information was publicly available that documented the severity of the problems in the S&L industry throughout the 1980s, and yet decisive action to resolve the situation once and for all was not taken until the end of the decade. This suggests that even

Figure 9.5. Failed S&Ls: Regulatory Delay and Failure Costs, 1980–92

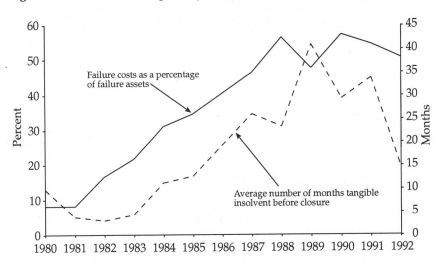

statutorily mandated regulatory discipline may be less than a perfect substitute for market discipline. Attempts should therefore be made to rely as much as possible on stable market discipline and less on regulatory discipline, not vice versa, to prevent future banking problems (see Calomiris 1989, 1992, 1997; Kane 1989a, 1992).[7]

The Perspective of Policy Decisions

All too often policy decisions about bank regulation seem to be made from a relatively narrow perspective. To demonstrate this point, figure 9.6 shows that funds from savers do not flow to investors only through banks. Instead, funds may flow from savers to investors through money and capital markets and through a variety of financial intermediaries. Given the importance of investment for long-term economic growth, and hence for improved living standards, the flow of funds from savers to investors must not be disrupted. Yet, as indicated in the center of the figure, problems arise that may indeed impede the flow of funds from savers to investors. As also indicated, however, private and public methods exist that are used to try to resolve problems that impede the flow of funds. The important point that nonetheless remains is that disruptions in the credit system and payment mechanism, or more generally, in the entire financial system, can

---

7. Note that Argentina, for instance, has recently implemented a subordinated debt requirement for its banking system.

Figure 9.6. Designing a Financial System

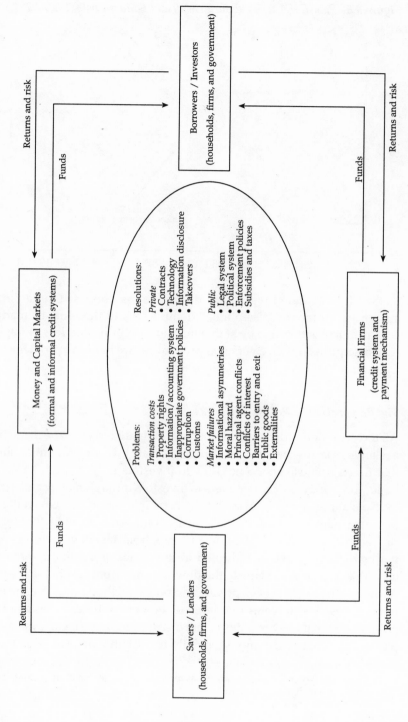

interfere with the smooth and efficient flow of funds from savers to investors. This in turn can adversely affect economic growth.

Based on a broad perspective, as illustrated by figure 9.6, designing appropriate bank regulation should be viewed as part of the process of designing an appropriate overall financial system (see, for example, Barth and Brumbaugh 1997; Herring and Litan 1995; Kaufman and Kroszner 1996). As the different entities identified in the figure are interrelated, the authorities should not focus exclusively on any one entity or subset of entities, such as depository institutions, when designing regulatory structures. Furthermore, this figure can be viewed from either a domestic or a global perspective. In any event, by focusing too narrowly on just banks, for example, the authorities might consider certain regulations as appropriate that from a broader perspective would be inappropriate. A few examples might be useful to help make this point clearer.

First, as figure 9.3 shows, prior to 1956, the mixing of commercial banking and commerce was permitted through holding companies. In that year and subsequently in 1970, however, legislation was enacted that permitted commercial banks only to be affiliated with nonbanking firms that were "closely related to banking." Thus the mixing of commercial banking and commerce was effectively terminated. Yet in 1968 Congress enacted legislation that permits a holding company that owns a single S&L to engage in any activity, even activities unrelated to the S&L business. As a result of this freedom and other important differences (such as unrestricted nationwide branching and an eased qualified thrift lender test in 1996), the value of an S&L charter has been enhanced relative to a commercial bank charter; however, the relative enhancement has resulted from legislative and regulatory actions, not market forces. By focusing too narrowly on one particular type of depository institution, in other words, policymakers can enact legislation that unintentionally alters the competitive landscape in significant ways.

Second, when the authorities recognize that many different types of financial firms exist, they naturally must ask the question: what is a bank? Legally, a U.S. bank is defined to be a firm that makes commercial loans, accepts demand deposits, and whose deposits are federally insured by the Bank Insurance Fund of the Federal Deposit Insurance Corporation. Yet, today, as noted earlier, commercial loans and demand deposits each only amount to about 15 percent of the total assets of commercial banks. What was once a traditional bank no longer exists. Banks have been reinventing themselves in recent years to remain viable in a changing financial marketplace. They now compete with a variety of other less-regulated financial and nonfinancial firms, as well as the money and capital markets, by increasingly offering more services that generate fee income and by relying less on net interest income.

Who would have thought only a few years ago that an automobile firm and an electric company would be direct competitors of banks. Today, however, more than half of Ford Motor Company's net income comes from its financial services operations, and General Electric Company earns about 40 percent of its net income from its capital services operations. In view of this situation, the authorities must broaden their focus beyond the legal definition of a bank to encompass the functions banks actually perform when designing appropriate bank regulation. As the saying goes, "we need banking services, not banks," and laws and regulations can prevent legally chartered banks from offering banking services.

Third, various restrictions on banks undoubtedly contributed to the development and growth of competing nonbank firms and capital markets. For example, the branching restrictions on banks in the 1800s limited their size (see Roe 1997). This in turn limited banks' ability to provide bigger loans to the large-scale commercial firms that were coming into existence. Together with the prohibitions on nonbank ownership by banks, this situation undoubtedly contributed to the growth of U.S. capital markets as commercial firms increasingly sought outside funds to support their growth. Of course, this development has produced desirable, albeit unanticipated, benefits; however, when the regulatory barriers to nationwide branching were finally reduced in 1995, banks were of diminished importance in the overall financial system.

Conclusions

The United States has recently experienced its worst bank problems since the Great Depression. The problems occurred despite an elaborate bank regulatory structure. The obvious conclusion is that the existing structure was not appropriate for fulfilling its assigned responsibilities. Although banking institutions are now in overall good financial condition and the authorities have significantly improved bank regulation, debate about the exact way to modernize the legal definition of a bank persists. Perhaps the most important lesson from the recent past in the United States is that the most appropriate way for all countries to proceed is by viewing banks not in isolation, but instead as an integral part of a much larger financial system: a financial system that is increasingly global in nature and constantly evolving in response to new developments. Such a broader perspective suggests that relying less on extensive bank regulation and more on market discipline is the best way to proceed.

References

Barth, James R. 1991. *The Great Savings and Loan Debacle*. Washington, D. C.: The American Enterprise Institute Press.

Barth, James R., and Philip F. Bartholomew. 1992. "The Thrift Industry Crisis: Revealed Weaknesses in the Federal Deposit Insurance System." In James R. Barth and R. Dan Brumbaugh, Jr., eds., *The Reform of Federal Deposit Insurance: Disciplining the Government and Protecting Taxpayers*. New York: Harper Business.

Barth, James R., and R. Dan Brumbaugh, Jr. 1991. *The Credit Union Industry: Financial Condition and Policy Issues*. California Credit Union League.

_____. 1994. "Moral Hazard and Agency Problems: Understanding Depository Institution Failure Costs." In George G. Kaufman, ed., *Research in Financial Services*, vol. 6. Greenwich, Connecticut: JAI Press.

_____. 1997. "Development and Evolution of National Financial Systems: An International Perspective." Latin American Studies Association meeting, April 17–19, Guadalajara, Mexico.

Barth, James R., R. Dan Brumbaugh, Jr., and Robert E. Litan. 1990. *The Banking Industry in Turmoil: A Report on the Condition of the U.S. Banking Industry and the Bank Insurance Fund*. Report of the Subcommittee on Financial Institutions Supervision, Regulation, and Insurance of the Committee on Banking, Finance, and Urban Affairs. Washington, D. C.: Government Printing Office.

_____. 1992. *The Future of American Banking*. Armonk, New York: M. E. Sharpe.

Barth, James R., Daniel E. Nolle, and Tara N. Rice. 1997. "Commercial Banking Structure, Regulation, and Performance: An International Comparison." Economics Working Paper no. 97–6. Office of the Comptroller of the Currency, Washington, D. C.

Bartholomew, Philip F., and Gary W. Whalen. 1995. "Analysis of Bank Failure Data: Commercial Bank Resolutions: 1980–1994." Office of the Comptroller of the Currency, Washington, D. C.

Brewer, Elijah. 1995. "The Impact of the Deposit Insurance System on S&L Shareholders' Risk/Return Tradeoffs." *Journal of Financial Services Research* 9 (1): 65–89.

Brumbaugh, R. Dan, Jr. 1988. *Thrifts under Siege*. Cambridge, Massachusetts: Ballinger.

Calomiris, Charles W. 1989. "Deposit Insurance: Lessons from the Record," *Economic Perspectives* (Federal Reserve Bank of Chicago) (May/June).

_____. 1992. "Getting the Incentives Right in the Current Deposit-Insurance System: Successes from the Pre-FDIC Era." In James R. Barth and R. Dan Brumbaugh, Jr., eds., *The Reform of Federal Deposit Insurance: Disciplining the Government and Protecting Taxpayers*. New York: Harper Business.

_____. 1997. "Designing the Post-Modern Bank Safety Net: Lessons from Developed and Developing Economies." Conference paper from the Bankers' Roundtable Program for Reforming Federal Deposit Insurance, May 23, American Enterprise Institute, Washington, D. C.

Caprio, Gerard, Jr., and Daniela Klingebiel. 1996. "Bank Insolvency: Bad Luck, Bad Policy, or Bad Banking?" World Bank, Development Research Group, Washington, D. C.

Gilbert, R. Alton. 1997. "Banks Profit from Low Rates on Time and Savings Deposits." *Monetary Trend* (Federal Reserve Bank of St. Louis) (June).

Goldstein, Morris. 1997. *The Case for an International Banking Standard*. Washington, D. C.: Institute for International Economics.

Greenspan, Alan. 1997. Statement before the Subcommittee on Financial Institutions and Consumer Credit of the Committee on Banking and Financial Services, United States House of Representatives, February 13.

Helfer, Ricki. 1997. Oral Statement before the Subcommittee on Capital Markets, Securities, and Government Sponsored Enterprises, Committee on Banking and Financial Services, United States House of Representatives, March 5.

Herring, Richard J., and Robert E. Litan. 1995. *Financial Regulation in the Global Economy*. Washington, D. C.: The Brookings Institution.

Hoenig, Thomas M. 1996. "Rethinking Financial Regulation." *Economic Review* (Federal Reserve Bank of Kansas City) (Second Quarter).

Jordan, Jerry L. 1996. "The Future of Banking Supervision." *Economic Commentary* (Federal Reserve Bank of Cleveland) (April 1).

Kane, Edward J. 1985. *The Gathering Crisis in Federal Deposit Insurance*, Cambridge, Massachusetts: MIT Press.

_____. 1989a. "Changing Incentives Facing Financial-Services Regulators," *Journal of Financial Services Research* 2, September, 1989.

_____. 1989b. *The S&L Insurance Mess: How Did It Happen?* Washington, D. C.: The Urban Institute Press.

_____. 1992. "The Incentive Incompatibility of Government-Sponsored Deposit Insurance Funds." In James R. Barth and R. Dan Brumbaugh, Jr., eds., *The Reform of Federal Deposit Insurance: Disciplining the Government and Protecting Taxpayers*. New York: Harper Business.

Kaufman, George G. 1995. "The U.S. Banking Debacle of the 1980s: An Overview and Lessons." *Financier* 2 (2): 9–26.

Kaufman, George G., and Randall S. Kroszner. 1996. "How Should Financial Institutions and Markets Be Structured? Analysis and Options for Financial System Design." Working Paper no. WP-96-20, Federal Reserve Bank of Chicago.

Kroszner, Randall S., and Philip E. Strahan. 1996. "Regulatory Incentives and the Thrift Crisis: Dividends, Mutual-to-Stock Conversions, and Financial Distress." *Journal of Finance* 51 (4): 1285–319.

Leach, James A. 1977. Statement before the Subcommittee on Capital Markets, Securities, and Government-Sponsored Enterprises, United States House of Representatives, March 22.

Lindgren, Carl-Johan, Gillian Garcia, and Matthew I. Saal. 1996. *Bank Soundness and Macroeconomic Policy*. Washington, D. C.: International Monetary Fund.

Litan, Robert E. 1987. *What Should Banks Do?* Washington, D. C.: The Brookings Institution.

_____. 1991. *The Revolution in U.S. Finance.* Washington, D. C.: The Brookings Institution.

_____. 1994. "U.S. Financial Markets and Institutions in the 1980s: A Decade of Turbulence." In Martin Feldstein, ed., *American Economic Policy in the 1980s.* Chicago: The University of Chicago Press.

Ludwig, Eugene A.. 1997. Oral Statement before the Subcommittee on Capital Markets, Securities, and Government-Sponsored Enterprises, Committee on Banking and Financial Services, United States House of Representatives, March 5.

National Credit Union Administration. 1995. *Annual Report.* Alexandria, Virginia.

Resolution Trust Corporation. Various years. *Statistical Abstract.* Washington, D. C.

Roe, Mark J. 1997 "The Political Roots of American Corporate Finance." *Journal of Applied Corporate Finance* 9 (4): 8–22.

Romer, Thomas, and Barry R. Weingast. 1992. "Political Foundations of the Thrift Debacle." In James R. Barth and R. Dan Brumbaugh, Jr., eds., *The Reform of Federal Deposit Insurance: Disciplining the Government and Protecting Taxpayers.* New York: Harper Collins.

Shadow Financial Regulatory Committee. 1997. Statement No. 137. May 5.

White, Lawrence J. 1991. *The S&L Debacle.* New York: Oxford University Press.

10

The Banking Crisis in Japan

Thomas F. Cargill, Michael M. Hutchison, and Takatoshi Ito

In the 1970s many industrial and developing economies embarked on a transition of financial institutions and markets from administratively controlled to more open and competitive structures. The transition was driven by conflicts between existing financial structures, inflationary macroeconomic policies, and the emergence of a new economic and technological environment.

Despite considerable progress toward liberalized financial structures, the transition has not progressed smoothly, marked in many cases by severe financial disruptions and banking problems (see Borio, Kennedy, and Prowse 1994; *Economist* 1997; Lindgren, Garcia, and Saal 1996). Japan initiated financial liberalization in the mid-1970s, and until the mid-1980s it proceeded at a slow, steady pace with few disruptions to the real or financial sectors, especially when compared to the United States (Cargill and Royama 1988). What started as a smooth transition changed dramatically in the second half of the 1980s, however, with the sharp run-up in asset prices and the booming economic and monetary growth that characterized the "bubble economy" (Cargill, Hutchison, and Ito 1997). The bubble economy followed the pattern of a classic speculative bubble, and the subsequent fall in asset prices in the early 1990s and the associated recession had an adverse impact on banks' balance sheets. Financial institutions were saddled with a massive nonperforming loan problem estimated at some US$500 billion (as of late 1995), with some estimates putting the figure at more than twice that amount.

Regulatory inertia, forbearance, and forgiveness despite awareness of the same policy failures earlier in the United States have exacerbated Japan's banking crisis and nonperforming loan problem. The piecemeal and tentative approach the Japanese Ministry of Finance initially followed in dealing with the banking crisis exhausted the deposit insurance funds'—the Deposit Insurance Corporation (DIC) and the insurance agency for small institutions—limited resources without confronting the underlying problems.[1] Against the background of a nonperforming loan problem, depressed asset markets, and the weakened condition of financial institutions, Japan has been confronted with its most serious financial crisis since the early 1950s.

The turning point was reached in 1995–96, when the authorities took more decisive action. They departed from the official no failure of financial institutions policy, committed public funds explicitly to problem institutions, restructured the two deposit insurance agencies, and passed legislation to deal with the special problems of the *jusen* (largely insolvent financial institutions that had mainly provided credit for real estate) and the credit cooperatives.

Moreover, in November 1996 Prime Minister Ryutaro Hashimoto—at the head of a newly reorganized Liberal Democratic Party elected following a campaign heralding broadly based reform—announced extensive deregulation of Japan's financial system by the year 2001. Senior officials have likened this proposal to the "Big Bang" financial deregulation in the United Kingdom more than a decade ago. The far-reaching objective of the initiative is to make Tokyo a global financial center that rivals New York and London, based on three basic principles of reform: market mechanisms, global in nature, and transparency. Acting on this initiative, the Diet passed legislation in mid-1997 that, among other things, created the new Financial Supervisory Agency (FSA), thereby greatly reducing the role of the Ministry of Finance in monitoring and supervising the financial system and further deregulating the foreign exchange market (see Choy 1997 for a summary of these legislative events).

The changes enacted and those proposed for future legislation, even if they resulted in major benefits to the economy as a whole, necessarily entail losers as well as winners. The potential losers, long protected by regulation from market competition in Japan's compartmentalized financial services industry, are likely to oppose further change vigorously. Financial deregulation has been on the agenda for many years, has proceeded only gradually, and some skeptics argue that a sense of *dèja vu* surrounds the present push for deregulation.

---

1. The DIC is the major deposit insurance agency in Japan. Organized in 1971, the DIC insures the deposits of banks and nonbank depositories.

Japan's financial system, however, is at a juncture today that is not comparable to any other episode during the past 45 years. Stress in the financial system, especially failure to resolve the nonperforming loan problem quickly, continues to hold back the economy, and a large part of the real estate market has stagnated as a result. The shortcomings of the existing regulatory and supervisory structure, especially in the context of the major changes in financial institutions and markets during the past 15 years, are readily apparent. Market forces and competition among financial institutions make the existing financial structure incompatible with Japan's regulatory and supervisory structure. The recent legislation creating the FSA recognizes this and attempts to address the problem. Moreover, economic and political pressure for fundamental reform will likely continue, even if the present wave of popular opinion against Japan's financial institutions and regulators, especially the Ministry of Finance, wanes.

This chapter discusses the conflict between the existing financial system and regulatory structure, and focuses on whether recent changes are likely to resolve this problem. Our research suggests that a central element of any successful reform is the introduction of a new policy approach that avoids past mistakes, especially regulatory delays, moral hazard, and inadequate funding, when dealing with insolvent financial institutions burdened with nonperforming loans. A more explicit and transparent accounting, supervisory, and regulatory framework would help to avoid future banking problems, and the creation of the FSA appears to be an important step in this direction.

Financial Deregulation and the Bubble Economy

In the second half of the 1980s asset inflation was evident in many countries, though not to the same extent as in Japan. Indexes of real asset prices for 13 industrial countries consisting of equity, residential real estate, and commercial real estate components illustrate a broadly based process of asset inflation during this period (Borio, Kennedy, and Prowse, 1994).

The international character of asset inflation suggests common explanatory factors. The coincidence of financial liberalization and asset inflation and deflation has led a number of observers to argue that liberalization played a major role in the financial disruptions of the 1980s and in the problems that the 1990s inherited from the boom and bust period. In the context of liberalization in the 1980s, the removal of binding portfolio constraints permitted banks and other depositories to take on riskier investment and loan portfolios, including high loan to value ratios.[2] Banks, directly or indirectly, provided imprudent levels of credit to real estate and equity markets in an effort to offset declining profit margins and declining market shares and to maintain the franchise value of commercial bank charters supported in the past by a regulated and administratively controlled financial environment.

The following features of Japan's financial system in the mid-1980s made asset inflation more probable in the context of a newly liberated financial structure and accommodating monetary policy:

- Market participants had more portfolio flexibility than they had ever had in the past. This was especially true for small depositories like savings and loan institutions. In the 1980s small depositories of the credit union type aggressively pursued lending in speculative real estate ventures during the bubble phase, and like their U.S. counterparts, did so without oversight.
- The shift to a slower growth path after the first oil price shock in 1973 reduced the corporate sector's reliance on bank credit and services. As a result, banks sought out new markets outside traditional corporate finance and were willing to assume new, and often higher, risks for which they had little previous experience.
- The main bank system began to unravel in response to financial liberalization. In the past, this system had served as an effective tool for evaluating and monitoring risk. No widely available financial disclosure framework was available to replace the main bank system.
- Despite a common perception that Japanese banks were subject to a Glass-Steagall type of rule, they actually have considerable authority to purchase and hold equities directly, thereby allowing bank credit to flow easily into equity markets. In addition, banks' hidden reserves were tied directly to the fortunes of the stock market.
- The regulatory monitoring system lagged behind market developments and administrative guidance could not keep pace with the rapidly changing financial environment.

---

2. "In those countries where the asset price boom was most marked in the 1980s (Finland, Sweden, Norway, Japan and the United Kingdom) or where the disruption caused by the downward correction in valuations has caused great concern (Australia and the United States) there is a relatively close correlation between the ratio of private credit to GDP and asset price movements...To a large extent, the major expansion of credit during the past decade reflected a relaxation of credit constraints in the financial industry in wake of both market-driven and policy-determined structural developments" (Borio, Kennedy, and Prowse 1994, pp. 27–28).

- Complete deposit guarantees encouraged risk taking at the very time the Bank of Japan provided the liquidity and financial liberalization provided the asset diversification powers.

The risk incentive nature of government deposit guarantees (the moral hazard problem) plays an important role in accounting for the coincidence of asset inflation and financial liberalization in Japan and elsewhere (see Iwamura 1993 for a simulation study of the effects of moral hazard on portfolio choice). In most cases liberalization failed to change the system of government deposit guarantees, which had been designed for a more regulated and administratively controlled financial environment. As a result, government deposit guarantees provided incentives to assume risk, while at the same time, regulatory and market innovations permitted depositories to manage and assume more risk. In addition, regulatory authorities responsible for administering the government deposit guarantee system were subject to perverse incentives in how they dealt with troubled institutions, which in turn encouraged greater risk taking on the part of depository institutions.

Financial Liberalization, Other Fundamentals, and Bubbles

Table 10.1 summarizes the factors that generated the asset price bubble and the consequent nonperforming loan problem. The initial jump in stock and land prices during 1985–86 was probably related to changes in fundamentals: aggregate productivity gains in Japan were extremely strong at the time; demand for real estate, particularly in the Tokyo area as a direct result of liberalization, increased significantly; and expansionary monetary policy pushed interest rates to low levels.

Financial deregulation, changes in the flow of funds, and banks' increased risk taking activity also played a role at the beginning of the run-up in asset prices, but whether these factors were fundamental determinants or speculative activities is unclear. The increased risk taking was rational in the sense that banks aggressively expanded into the real estate business given the newly expanded powers over asset allocation, the changes in traditional business relationships, and so on. In addition, financial deregulation combined with lax supervision and extensive deposit guarantees allowed expanded lending into real estate on a speculative basis.

At some point, probably in late 1986 or 1987, the asset inflation process became a speculative bubble with little restraint shown by the financial institutions, the regulatory authorities, or the Bank of Japan. Expectations

Table 10.1. *Factors that Created the Asset Price Bubble and Economy Contributing to the Nonperforming Loan Problem*

Factor	Outcome
Financial liberalization starting in the mid-1970s and continuing to the present.	Increased asset diversification powers for bank and nonbank depositories; increased ability to manage and assume risk unequaled in the postwar period.
Downward shift in potential GDP growth path after 1973 oil price shock reduced corporate dependence on the banking system as the rate of investment fell from rates prevalent during the high-growth period.	Banks sought out new markets to re-establish and enhance their market share. Specifically, banks moved aggressively into real estate lending and competed with *jusen* in the 1980s.
The decline of the main bank system and the overall reduced role of banks in enterprise groups.	Reduced banks' ability to monitor risk.
Banks were permitted to hold equities in nonfinancial businesses as part of the enterprise group framework. Banks could apply 45 percent of the appreciation of equity holdings to capital referred to as hidden or latent capital.	Banks' capital position became dependent on the equity market, so that during equity price increases banks would expand loans and investments, and during equity price declines banks would contract loans and investments.
Reliance by the regulatory authorities on administrative guidance to monitor bank and nonbank depositories.	Regulatory authorities became less able to monitor risk as bank and nonbank depositories engaged in greater asset diversification than in the past. Bank and nonbank depositories had few incentives to limit risk.
Pervasive system of government deposit guarantees.	The reduced oversight and enhanced asset diversification powers became more sensitive to the risk incentives embedded in the deposit guarantee system.
Monetary easing in 1987 and 1988 as the Bank of Japan placed greater emphasis on exchange rate objectives than on domestic considerations.	The Bank of Japan provided liquidity that supported the asset inflation.
Incentives for regulatory authorities to adopt forbearance and forgiveness in dealing with troubled institutions.	Incentives to assume risk were enhanced.

Source: Cargill, Hutchison, and Ito (1997).

of asset price increases fed upon themselves, and price to dividend and price to rent ratios increasingly deviated from fundamental values until the crash in the 1990s. Speculators typically believed that even though the levels of stock and land prices were abnormally high and would eventually fall, they believed that further investment was warranted as long as other investors thought that prices would continue to rise. Many speculators assumed that they would be among the first to sell their asset holdings, thereby realizing large capital gains, when the market started to fall. This kind of behavior has been termed as stochastic bubbles, herd instinct, momentum trading, or bandwagon behavior.

Eventually asset prices reversed course, and declined rapidly in the early 1990s. The Nikkei 225 stock price index reached its peak of 38,915 on the last business day of 1989, and then tumbled. By October 1, 1990, the Nikkei stood barely above 20,000, having lost almost 50 percent of its value in nine months. The Nikkei fell below 15,000 in mid-1992, and only broke the 20,000 point again in 1996. Land prices began to fall in late 1991, and by 1996 prices were frequently only half of their peak values. At that time, the land prices averaged those prevalent 10 years earlier.

A combination of policy actions and the self-correcting mechanism of the speculative process (deflating the bubble) were responsible for the asset price decline. By mid-1989 the monetary authorities became fully aware of, and concerned about, asset price inflation and started to raise interest rates. The Ministry of Finance also introduced several measures to slow land price rises. The Iraqi invasion of Kuwait on August 2, 1990, further weakened the world economic outlook, and the prospects for oil-dependent Japan in particular. Furthermore, once the decline in asset prices began, banks had an incentive to reduce lending for real estate and other purposes. When the Basel risk-based capital ratio was negotiated in 1988 as an international minimum standard for banks with international business, Japanese banks were allowed to count 45 percent of their equity holdings as part of their Tier Two capital. As the value of these equities was devoted to meeting capital asset requirements, the cost of capital increased, reducing banks' incentive to make loans and contributing to the drop in credit expansion.

Despite these factors, the most important reason for the collapse in asset prices was the self-correcting mechanism inherent in stochastic speculative processes. Expectations of further price declines generated selling, which in turn led to price declines. In early 1990, for example, Nikkei futures tended to lead the decline in cash markets. This was responsible for the view that futures transactions were making the stock market too volatile, and led to a tightening of margin requirements in the Nikkei futures market in Osaka in 1991.

Nonperforming Loans, the *Jusen* Problem, and Regulatory Inertia

Asset deflation dramatically affected the profitability of Japanese financial institutions and led to serious concerns about the stability of the entire financial system. Deterioration in the quality of loans to the real estate sector was the primary problem, but was compounded by the drop in the value of banks' large equity holdings and growing loan problems associated with a prolonged recession.[3]

The Ministry of Finance, as the primary regulatory agency, was slow in reacting to the nonperforming loan problem confronting financial institutions. After the initial sharp decline in stock and land prices in 1991–92, the ministry initially adopted a forbearance policy, allowing banks to hold nonperforming loans without special write-offs in the hope of a quick recovery of the economy and the real estate market (Folkerts-Landau, Ito, and others 1995, p. 2). However, smaller financial institutions with large real estate exposure began showing signs of distress in 1993, soon followed by even larger problems for *jusen* or housing loan companies (nonbank subsidiaries of financial institutions specializing in housing loans). At that time the Ministry of Finance arranged a 10-year rehabilitation plan for *jusen*. Rather than recognizing loan losses, however, the plan was predicated upon a land price recovery. When land prices failed to recover, and with nonperforming loans growing in size and number, the ministry quickly abandoned the rehabilitation plan.

As the financial crisis unfolded, in 1994 and 1995 the regulatory authorities launched a new approach for resolving these problems. The Ministry of Finance closed some of the lowest quality institutions, created the Tokyo Kyodo Bank as a bridge bank that would receive the remaining assets of failed smaller institutions, allowed (or encouraged) massive write-offs by some banks, and decided to close down the *jusen*. An infusion of public funds, proposed for the first time in the 1996–97 budget, was earmarked to cover the costs of closing seven *jusen* companies, and a variety of other measures were enacted in the wake of the nonperforming loan and *jusen* problem.

The *jusen* companies had been created in the mid-1970s as subsidiaries of banks, securities firms, and life insurance companies. At that time,

---

3. Japan's most severe postwar recession itself can largely be traced to the decline in asset prices. Consumption fell as households saw the real value of their equity and real estate holdings decline precipitously. The fall in consumption induced a fall in fixed investment, which was further weakened by the overhang of excess capacity accumulated during the asset inflation phase and the credit crunch induced by the decline in banks' hidden capital.

banks were concentrating on corporate lending, and were not generally interested in expanding their operations to household lending, either for mortgage or consumer credit. The *jusen* companies provided consumer credit, and much like consumer finance companies in the United States, borrowed from other institutions, because they were not permitted to accept deposits. As the corporate sector reduced its dependence on bank credit after 1975, however, banks began to turn to consumer finance as a new line of business, and in the 1980s became aggressive lenders to individuals. In response to the competition for personal loans, *jusen* companies turned to real estate lending in the second half of the 1980s to substitute for the lost consumer lending business.

In April 1990 the Ministry of Finance introduced regulations to limit total bank lending to the real estate sector; however, *jusen* lending was exempted. During 1990–91 *jusen* lending increased rapidly as a result of funds provided by agricultural cooperatives and their prefectural federations. Concerns about *jusen* asset quality were raised as early as 1992, and the authorities arranged a 10-year rehabilitation plan for seven of the eight *jusen* companies in early 1993. (The eighth *jusen*, established by agricultural cooperatives, is not considered to be a problem institution and was exempt from the plan.) Lending to *jusen* was restructured so that parent banks (*jusens'* major shareholders) were required to reduce the interest rate on outstanding loans to zero, other banks (nonparent banks that lent to the *jusen*) were required to reduce the interest rate on outstanding loans to 1.5 percent, while agricultural cooperatives and their prefectural federations were to receive interest income of 4.5 percent from *jusen*. These arrangements were designed to provide liquidity to *jusen* until the expected future recovery in land prices permitted the outstanding loans to be paid off in 10 years. Land prices, however, continued to fall, and the nonperforming loans held by *jusen* rose dramatically. For all practical purposes, the rehabilitation plan itself became bankrupt.

The *jusen* problem became the focus of intense policy debate in 1995, and even overshadowed the banks' nonperforming loan problem. In August 1995 the Ministry of Finance conducted a special examination of the *jusen* problem. Of the total ¥ 13 trillion of *jusen* assets, it estimated nonperforming loans to be worth ¥ 9.6 trillion, of which ¥ 6.4 trillion was unrecoverable and ¥ 1.2 trillion was a possible loss. This amounts to more than a quarter of all losses financial institutions had incurred to that date.

The Ministry of Finance and the suppliers of funds to *jusen* companies agreed to dissolve the seven housing loan companies, and in July 1996 the Housing Loan Administration was established to assume ¥ 6.4 trillion of unrecoverable loans extended by failed *jusen* companies.

Financial markets became increasingly concerned about the burden sharing of the *jusen* losses among banks and other financial institutions that further reduced the creditworthiness of Japanese banks because politicians and ministry officials suggested that banks should shoulder more than a *pro rata* share of *jusen* losses. The precedent for this approach had already been set when banks were required to provide a more than *pro rata* share in schemes for dealing with failing institutions in July and August 1995 (Cosmo credit cooperatives, Kizu credit cooperatives, and the Hyogo Bank). Banks unrelated to these institutions were asked to contribute to the loss-sharing scheme by contributing capital or making below market rate loans to banks that assumed the assets of the insolvent institutions. This request was rationalized on the public good character of the financial system and the need to maintain stability. The policy of requiring unrelated banks to contribute directly to bail out schemes was referred to as the all-Japan rescue scheme.

Uncertainty about future bank losses because of doubts about the specific *jusen* resolution scheme and the extent of the all-Japan component, however, led to a downgrading of Japanese banks' creditworthiness. The perception of increased risk in Japanese banks at large resulted in a Japan premium in the Euro-dollar market over the London interbank offered rate. The Japan premium appeared in late July to mid-August 1995, and persisted for several months, even though the Ministry of Finance attempted to reassure the market by announcing a complete deposit guarantee to 2001.

Regulatory Response to the Nonperforming Loan Problem

The first official response to the nonperforming loan problem was a series of uncoordinated actions predicated on a short recession and a rapid recovery of asset prices. On August 18, 1992, the government announced a temporary rule change that allowed corporations to defer reporting their stock portfolio losses until the end of the fiscal year (March 1993); permitted other accounting innovations that delayed or concealed the impact of stock and land price declines on reported assets; allowed banks, in special cases where a loan default would have adverse social effects, not to report interest concessions as taxable income (Packer 1994); directed the Postal Life Insurance System to support the stock market through funds provided to trust banks; postponed sales of government held shares of Nippon Telegraph and Telephone and Japan National Railways; used administrative guidance to encourage institutional purchases of equities and discourage institutional sales of equities; and provided less than candid estimates of the magnitude of the nonperforming loan problem.[4] These actions had little impact on the downward trend in asset prices and the deterioration of the financial system. More specific and aggressive actions followed. These will be considered more or less in chronological order.

Establishment of the Cooperative Credit Purchasing Company

The Cooperative Credit Purchasing Company (CCPC) was the first obvious effort to deal with the nonperforming loan problem. The government established the CCPC in late 1992, and it commenced operations in January 1993. The CCPC uses pooled funds from 162 banks and cooperatives with the active encouragement and involvement of the Ministry of Finance. The CCPC purchases real estate loans at prices determined by a panel of experts, with the institution selling the loan providing the financing. The CCPC then sells the real estate, and any difference between what the CCPC paid for the loan and the selling price is charged to the institution that originally sold the loan.

From the outset the market viewed the CCPC with skepticism (Choy 1992). Concerns were voiced that the planned loan purchases would represent only a small percentage of the nonperforming loans; that the self-financing requirement limited access to only the strongest banks; that only the best of the nonperforming loans would be sold to the CCPC, thereby delaying the inevitable adjustment; and that as the original borrowers continued to manage the properties, their incentives to cooperate were unclear.

These concerns persist despite several years of operation during which the CCPC purchased ¥ 8.7 trillion of loans at face value with an average loss ratio from March 1993 to May 1995 of 55.4 percent. The critical issue, however, is to what purpose the loans have been purchased and how the

---

4. Until March 1993 the Ministry of Finance reported the sum of nonperforming loans only for the 21 major banks combined. The ministry's definition of a nonperforming loan is narrow: those loans for which the principal is not likely to be collected and those for which interest has not been collected in the past six months. This leaves considerable room to exclude loans that are clearly in serious default, for example, restructured loans in which the interest rate has been drastically reduced, or even set to zero, are not regarded as nonperforming. Loans that receive only a fraction of an interest payment can also be excluded from the nonperforming category. Moreover, evidence indicates that banks made additional loans to enable borrowers to pay interest on previous loans, so the nonperforming loan amount is understated. This type of activity on the part of private depositories was widespread in the savings and loan industry in the 1980s, with disastrous consequences. Based on the loss ratios reported by the Cooperative Credit Purchasing Company and experience with insolvent institutions, the ministry's estimates of recoverable loans also appears to be conservative.

CCPC plans to dispose of the loans. Sales of CCPC loans have been only a fraction of total holdings, and the concern is that revenues from loan sales and rental income from properties will be insufficient to repay interest to the funding banks at market rates.

Establishment of the Resolution and Collection Bank

The Tokyo Kyodou Bank was established in March 1995 to assume the assets of several failed credit cooperatives. The bank was reorganized in September 1996 into the Resolution and Collection Bank, which was loosely modeled after the Resolution and Trust Corporation, established in 1989 to dispose of the assets of failed savings and loan institutions.

The CCPC's track record suggests that the Resolution and Collection Bank will have a difficult time liquidating bad loans. Many of these loans are tied to a real estate market that remained depressed during 1997. The fact that at the time of writing the CCPC had sold only a fraction of the loans assumed, which were the "best" of nonperforming loans, is not an impressive indicator of the likely success of the Resolution and Collection Bank. The depressed real estate market, the slow pace of economic recovery, the lack of well-developed foreclosure and bankruptcy procedures, and even the influence of organized crime in some real estate transactions make disposing of nonperforming loans difficult. A possibility is that the CCPC, the Housing Loan Administration Corporation, and the Resolution and Collection Bank will end up being a form of forbearance, that is, merely new warehouses for bad loans, when what the Ministry of Finance really needs is a garage sale.

Provision of Assisted Mergers Using the Deposit Insurance Corporation

In 1991, for the first time in the postwar period, the regulatory authorities officially assisted in the mergers of insolvent depository institutions with stronger institutions using the DIC, the largest of Japan's two deposit insurance agencies. Before 1991 the DIC had never had to pay depositors, although some claim that the Ministry of Finance arranged several unpublicized rescue mergers without DIC assistance. Since 1991, however, the DIC has publicly assisted a small number of problem institutions, and two of the institutions it recently assisted exhausted the DIC's reserves.[5] The details of these assisted mergers, examined in

---

5. This is not surprising, because the DIC was grossly underfunded. To gain an appreciation of the degree of underfunding one can compare the DIC to the Federal

Cargill, Hutchison, and Ito (1997), reveal a disturbing pattern about the ability of Japanese regulatory authorities to administer deposit guarantees and limit moral hazard effectively.

During its short history the DIC has had a turbulent record. The first 20 years were uneventful and few regarded the DIC as an important component of Japan's deposit guarantee system, although a number of commentators pointed to problems that could arise as a result of a poorly funded deposit insurance agency (see, for example, Cargill 1995; Ito and Ueda 1993). Since 1991, however, the DIC has become a focal point of concern for two reasons: first, bailouts in late 1995 rendered the DIC insolvent; and second, the approach to assisted mergers imposed few penalties on shareholders and none on depositors.

Resolution of the Jusen Problem and the Use of Public Money

In December 1995, the government proposed a resolution plan for the seven insolvent *jusen* companies that the Diet passed in early 1996. Of the ¥ 13 trillion in assets of the seven *jusen* companies, ¥ 6.4 trillion was an immediate (primary) loss, ¥ 1.2 trillion was a possible (secondary) loss, ¥ 2.1 trillion was nonperforming but possibly recoverable, and ¥ 2.5 trillion was a normal or performing asset. The primary loss of ¥ 6.4 trillion was to be borne by banks and life insurance companies, by agricultural cooperatives as a "gift" (the agricultural cooperatives insisted that any funds they lent would be repaid in full and that any burden they assumed would be in the form of a gift they would make to the bank that assumed the bad *jusen* assets), and public spending by the government. The *Jusen* Resolution Corporation, now known as the Housing Loan Administration, assumed the remaining assets. The secondary losses will be dealt with in the future using special accounts.

The plan has two problems. First, burden sharing was inequitable and reflected the political strengths of the agricultural sector. The strength of farming interests was revealed, for example, during the debate about sharing the cost burden of the financial crisis when it became public that the Ministry of Finance's Banking Bureau director general had secretly signed a memorandum of understanding with his

---

Deposit Insurance Corporation in the United States. While close to 80 percent of deposits in both countries are insured, the reserve to deposit ratios are significantly lower in Japan. In 1994, for example, the ratio of insurance fund reserves to insured deposits was 0.16 in Japan and 1.15 in the United States (Deposit Insurance Corporation of Japan 1995; Federal Deposit Insurance Corporation 1994).

counterpart at the Ministry of Agriculture, Forestry, and Fisheries that promised the Ministry of Finance's full backing of agricultural cooperatives lending to *jusen* companies. The relatively heavier burden on banks also reflected the public perception that the banks that had set up *jusen* as subsidiaries had a direct involvement in *jusen* operations. These founder banks provided staff to manage operations and maintained business relationships with the *jusen* in the form of referring potential borrowers, who turned out to be high risk customers.

Second, although the proposed amount of public funding was small compared to the magnitude of the nonperforming loan problem, the political opposition to using taxpayer funding was strong and surprised some observers. The resolution plan will spend only ¥ 685 billion of public funds in filling the gap between the primary loss and private sector burdens.[6] The opposition turned out to be so strong, however, that policymakers are likely to be reluctant to propose public funding as part of any solution to deal with financial problems in the future.

Unfortunately, the problem and its resolution were poorly presented by the Ministry of Finance. The plan was actually a reasonable starting point for tackling the financial debacle, but its purpose was lost in the debate about burden sharing, policy errors on the part of the Ministry of Finance, and protection of the agriculture sector.

Lessons for Regulatory and Supervisory Policy

The regulatory response to the nonperforming loan problem and the resolution of the *jusen* problem against the backdrop of widespread deposit guarantees offers several lessons. Any sweeping overhaul of Japan's regulatory and supervisory structure should address each of the issues if Japan is to undertake a serious Big Bang deregulation of its financial system.

The regulatory response was slow, and once regulatory action was initiated, it often made the problem worse. This was due to improper administration of the deposit guarantee system and failure to appreciate the moral hazard inherent in protecting depositors and assisting troubled institutions.

---

6. The amount of ¥ 685 billion figure was derived in a curious manner. During the negotiations between the Ministry of Finance and the Ministry of Agriculture, Forestry, and Fisheries, the Ministry of Finance originally proposed that the agricultural cooperatives share the burden of ¥ 1.2 trillion. Political opposition from the farmers' lobby was so strong that this figure was bargained down to ¥ 530 billion. The difference between the estimate by the Ministry of Finance and the amount accepted by the Ministry of Agriculture, Forestry, and Fisheries, namely, ¥ 685 billion, became the amount of fiscal spending proposed for resolving the *jusen* problem.

This failure is even more striking given that Japanese policymakers were familiar with the problems of and lessons from the U.S. experience.

By 1995 Japan had come under intense international pressure to take decisive action to solve its nonperforming loan problem. An International Monetary Fund report (Folkerts-Landau, Ito, and others 1995), highly publicized in Japan, criticized the authorities for their delayed response. The market's judgment was also critical: the credit ratings of Japanese banks, previously at the top of the industry internationally, were downgraded sharply. The Daiwa Bank scandal and the Ministry of Finance's violation of international bank regulation rules through its failure to inform U.S. regulatory authorities of the problem in a timely manner further weakened confidence in Japanese financial institutions and regulatory authorities.

In the context of growing public awareness of the nonperforming loan and *jusen* problems, as well as intense international pressure, in December 1995 the government initiated a series of reforms to cope with future financial problems. Legislators introduced six bills that the Diet passed in June 1996 that dealt with *jusen* resolution; established corrective actions to limit the operations of weak financial institutions; and strengthened deposit insurance by increasing the system's staff, increasing deposit insurance premiums sevenfold to strengthen the system's reserves, and setting up a special deposit insurance reserve for credit cooperatives during the consolidation process.

This round of actions omitted reform of the supervisory framework. In light of the Ministry of Finance's poor performance in dealing with the country's financial problems, some observers questioned the effectiveness of any reform as long as the Ministry of Finance remained the primary financial regulatory authority. These concerns are largely responsible for the government creating the FSA in mid-1997, which will gradually assume most of the ministry's supervisory and regulatory responsibilities.

Delay in shutting down an insolvent financial institution increases losses that will have to be dealt with when resolving the problem. This is a classical case of the moral hazard problem of deposit guarantees and the administration of those guarantees. Permitting insolvent or almost insolvent institutions to operate provides incentives for the institution to either gamble on high risk, high return projects or to engage in fraudulent behavior, such as lending to top management of related companies. The *jusen* industry had numerous incidents of excessive risk taking and fraudulent behavior.

Indecision by the Ministry of Finance is primarily responsible for the delayed response, especially during 1992 and 1993, as by that time the *jusen* problem had been evident for several years, both to the ministry and to market insiders, before becoming public knowledge. Documents submitted to the Diet in February 1996 show that the Ministry of Finance made the first on-site examinations of *jusen* in 1991–92. Those examinations revealed that 67 percent of loans made to the largest 50 borrowers were already nonperforming; however, the ministry allowed the *jusen* companies to operate on the assumption that land prices would rise in the near future. Instead land prices continued to decline and the *jusen* problem increased in magnitude: in the subsequent four years nonperforming loans in the *jusen* increased by 75 percent.

A number of factors contributed to the delay in regulatory response, namely: (a) the lack of political leadership; (b) the administration of deposit guarantees; (c) the political power of the agriculture sector; (d) the existence of three separate, and in some cases competing, regulatory authorities (the Ministry of Finance; the Ministry of Agriculture, Forestry, and Fisheries; and the Ministry of Posts and Telecommunications); and (e) the general unwillingness to recognize that Japanese financial institutions are susceptible to moral hazard problems.

Moral Hazard in Japan

The moral hazard problem facing Japanese financial institutions is similar in magnitude to its counterparts abroad. The failure of two credit cooperatives in December 1994, Tokyo Kyowa and Anzen Credit Cooperative, offers some insights. The Tokyo Metropolitan Government, the direct supervisor in the case, reportedly became aware of the insolvency of the two credit cooperatives in early 1993, when it conducted a special joint examination with the Ministry of Finance. The delay in closing the two institutions substantially increased the ultimate cost of the bailout.

The two credit cooperatives suffered from a classic case of moral hazard in the last two years of operation (*Asahi Shinbun* February 16, 1995). Deposits at both institutions increased from ¥ 139 billion in March 1992 to ¥ 244 billion in November 1994, an annual rate of 32 percent, while lending increased from ¥ 137 billion to ¥ 225 billion, an annual rate of 22 percent, during the same period. Most new loans made during this time were ultimately classified as nonperforming. The total amount of nonperforming loans of the two credit cooperatives increased from ¥ 250 billion (out of total loans of ¥ 1,371 billion) in March 1992 to ¥ 1,769 billion (out of total loans of ¥ 1,990 billion) in March 1994. Moreover, unrecoverable losses increased from ¥ 65 billion in March 1992 to ¥ 1,118 billion in March 1994. Not only did the two credit unions aggressively expand deposits by offering above market deposit rates to make new, higher risk loans during their decline into insolvency, but the amount of total nonperforming loans increased sevenfold and of unrecoverable losses increased sixteenfold during the same period.

The portfolio behavior of the two credit cooperatives illustrates the incentives facing private depository institutions in the presence of government deposit guarantees when confronted with actual or impending insolvency. Insolvent or close to insolvent institutions have an incentive to take on high risk investments in hopes of earning large returns that would restore them to profitability. Depositors have little incentive to monitor the portfolio shift, because they are protected by the deposit guarantees. The supervisory agencies must assume the monitoring role, and in this respect the Ministry of Finance responded inadequately. The U.S. deposit insurance failure in the late 1980s and the early 1990s and the current difficulties in Japan illustrate the universality of the problem.[7]

The 1997 Legislative Agenda

The collapse of asset prices in the 1990s, the recession, the nonperforming loan situation, and the continued deterioration of the financial system combined with the Ministry of Finance's failed policy response provides the background for the recent flurry of legislative efforts. In March 1997 the government introduced several pieces of legislation to initiate the Big Bang reforms (Choy 1997). The Diet passed part of this legislative package by mid-year, namely:

- The foreign exchange market will be deregulated by eliminating the need to have a license to conduct foreign exchange operations, abolishing the requirement to obtain advance approval for foreign direct investments and overseas capital transfers from the Ministry of Finance, and eliminating the daily limits on positions in any one currency.
- The Ministry of Finance's regulatory responsibilities will be reduced in two areas. First, its current monitoring and supervision of the financial sector will be gradually transferred to the FSA, which reports directly to the prime minister. The FSA will also have the power to monitor and supervise agricultural cooperatives, labor cooperatives, and a wide range of finance and leasing companies that the Ministry of Agriculture, Forestry, and Fisheries; the Ministry of Labor; and the

---

7. Before the series of credit cooperatives failures in late 1994 and 1995, several authors (Cargill and Todd 1993; Kane 1993) had argued that Japan was missing a chance to learn from the U.S. deposit insurance failure when legislators were discussing the Financial System Reform Law prior to its passage in June 1992.

Ministry of International Trade and Industry, respectively, currently monitor and supervise. Second, the operations of the Securities and Exchange Surveillance Commission, now part of the Ministry of Finance, will be shifted to an agency outside the ministry.

- The 1942 Bank of Japan Law will be revised to provide the Bank of Japan, one of the world's most formally dependent central banks, with enhanced formal independence. This is to be accomplished by limiting the Ministry of Finance's role over the bank's Policy Board, restricting the ministry's influence on the bank's budget and personnel matters, and improving the transparency of Bank of Japan policymaking by making Policy Board discussions and decisions public and by requiring the bank to provide the Diet with biannual reports.
- The long-standing prohibition against a holding company structure for industrial organizations will be removed.
- The corporation funded by the government will be required to disclose financial information much like their publicly traded counterparts.
- The Nippon Telegraph and Telephone Corporation will be reorganized along holding company lines to enhance domestic competition in telecommunications.

In addition to these specific proposals, the Liberal Democratic Party's policy committee is introducing a number of reform proposals to effect the government's financial market reforms and to move up the deadline from 2001 to 1998.

The flurry of legislative and reform efforts in the first half of 1997 raises two questions. First, how successful will these reforms be, both in terms of their content and their implementation; and second, do the reforms deal with the immediate problems in the financial system?

Likelihood of Success

The new legislation created the FSA, which is slated gradually to assume most of the regulatory and supervisory responsibilities currently held by the Ministry of Finance. The ministry, however, will still be responsible for drawing up financial policies and creating financial market structures. The FSA must also confer with the finance minister if the FSA's actions are likely to affect the stability of the financial system. Whether this requires the FSA simply to confer with the ministry, or whether the ministry or other supervisory agencies must give their approval before a financial institution is be closed is unclear. Moreover, FSA decisions may not be completely independent of other ministries: its initial staff of 300 people will include around 210 transferred from the inspection offices of the Ministry of Finance and the Ministry of International Trade and Industry, and the others will come from the Securities and Exchange Surveillance Commission. Finally, the FSA needs to petition the Ministry of Finance if it needs public funds to liquidate troubled financial institutions. Choy (1997) notes that these limitations may change the institutional form of supervisory and regulatory policy, but not its substance.

However, other pressures might lead the FSA to take a new and independent approach to regulatory policy given that the old model based on insularity, mutual support, and restraint between the Ministry of Finance, the finance industry, and politicians has not adapted to the new demands and challenges presented by the technological and economic environment of the 1990s. In addition, the FSA is entirely focused on regulatory and supervisory policy, and in principle will not have to deal with the multitude of often conflicting objectives the Ministry of Finance faced.

Resolution of Current Problems

The Big Bang and recent legislative efforts, if they succeed, will move Japan toward a more open and competitive financial structure that will benefit both Japan and the rest of the world. Unfortunately, they do little to confront the current problems. To date Japan has shown little willingness to depart from its extensive system of deposit guarantees. Other concerns also remain, namely: the manner in which depositors and shareholders have faired in the closing of a number of institutions; the continued reliance on improved economic conditions to solve the nonperforming loan problem; the transparent role of politics in dealing with the *jusen* problem; and, most important, the government's inability to convince the public that public funds will be needed to deal with current and forthcoming financial problems.

Conclusion

Whatever the ultimate division of responsibilities among the Japanese government bureaucracy, a central element of any successful reform would be a new approach based on a more explicit and transparent accounting, supervisory, and regulatory framework. While the FSA may facilitate introducing and implementing a new policy, the process itself, as opposed to the specific institution taking responsibility for it, is the most important for successful reform. Successful regulatory reform must resolve the current system's fundamental problems: delays in regulatory responses, moral hazard, and inadequate funding to deal with problem financial institutions quickly.

Reform dealing with these issues would naturally entail greater openness in the sense of adopting standard accounting procedures to value the assets of financial institutions and making this information public. It would also entail less informal administrative guidance and greater reliance on explicit rules in the supervision of financial institutions. This approach would reduce the uncertainty inherent in the present system and allow more rapid resolution of financial problems, such as the current nonperforming loan issue, as they arise. Financial institutions would likely benefit from regulatory reforms of this nature, and the overall economy would also benefit, for instance, sectors such as the real estate market would be revived. Foreign financial institutions would also benefit from a more transparent and explicit regulatory and supervisory structure in Japan. Policy changes along these lines would stimulate growth and development in the financial system and help stem Tokyo's recent decline relative to other leading financial centers.

This paper has focused on events through July 1997. Recent developments, however, make even our cautionary tale for Japan seem optimistic. The currency collapses and banking crises in Indonesia, Korea, Malaysia, the Philippines, and Thailand that emerged in the second half of 1997 further weakened Japan's financial system. On January 12, 1998, the Ministry of Finance officially acknowledged what critics have maintained for years: the nonperforming loan problem is far larger than previous official estimates had indicated. The ministry announced that in the six months to September 30, 1997, problem bank loans totaled ¥ 76.7 trillion (US$592 billion at ¥ 130 to the dollar), and acknowledged that this estimate does not include problem loans at credit cooperatives, insurance companies, and other institutions. Nor does the figure reflect the impact on Japanese institutions from the financial crises in other Asian countries since September 30.

The government announced in early 1998 its intent to push for significant infusions of public money to support the financial system. The Ministry of Finance's policy position is tenuous, however, in light of recent scandals. Several ministry officials have been arrested, and in early March 1998 prosecutors looking into allegations of influence peddling and corruption raided the ministry for a second time. The argument for public infusion of funds to bail out a scandal ridden financial system is likely to continue to face political opposition.

References

Borio, C. E. V. N. Kennedy, and S. D. Prowse. 1994. *Exploring Aggregate Asset Price Fluctuations across Countries.* Economic Papers no. 40. Geneva: Bank for International Settlements.

Cargill, Thomas F. 1995. "A U.S. Perspective on Japanese Financial Liberalization." *Monetary and Economic Studies* (Bank of Japan, Institute for Monetary and Economic Studies) (May 3): 115–61.

Cargill, Thomas F., and Shoichi Royama. 1988. *The Transition of Finance in Japan and the United States: A Comparative Perspective.* Stanford, California: Hoover Institution Press.

Cargill, Thomas F., and Gregory F. W. Todd. 1993. "Japan's Financial System Reform Law: Progress toward Financial Liberalization?" *Brooklyn Journal of International Law* 19: 47–84.

Cargill, Thomas F., Michael M. Hutchison, and Takatoshi Ito. 1997. *Political Economy of Japanese Monetary Policy.* Cambridge, Massachusetts: MIT Press.

Choy, Jon. 1992. "Japanese Banks' Self-Help Questioned." *Japan Economic Institute Report* November 6, no. 42B: 1–3.

_____. 1997. "Hashimoto Fills Diet's Docket With Reforms." *Japan Economic Institute Report* March 21, no. 11B: 4–7.

DIC (Deposit Insurance Corporation of Japan). 1995. *Annual Report.* Tokyo.

Economist. 1997. "Banking in Emerging Markets." April 12.

Federal Deposit Insurance Corporation. 1994. *Annual Report.* Washington D. C.

Folkerts-Landau, David, and Takatoshi Ito, with others. 1995. *International Capital Markets: Developments, Prospects, and Policy Issues.* Washington, D. C.: International Monetary Fund.

Ito, Takatoshi, and Kazuo Ueda. 1993. "Editors' Introduction." In Takatoshi Ito and Kazuo Ueda, eds., "International Comparison of the Financial System and Regulations." *Journal of the Japanese and International Economies* 7 (December): 323–28.

Iwamura, Mitsuru. 1993. "Deposit Insurance and Moral Hazard." *Monetary and Economic Studies* (Bank of Japan, Institute for Monetary and Economic Studies) (July 11): 63–85.

Kane, Edward J. 1993. "What Lessons Should Japan Learn from the U.S. Deposit-Insurance Mess?" In Takatoshi Ito and Kazuo Ueda, eds., "International Comparison of the Financial System and Regulations." *Journal of the Japanese and International Economies* 7 (December): 329–55.

Lindgren, Carl-Johan, Gillian Garcia, and Matthew I. Saal. 1996. *Bank Soundness and Macroeconomic Policy.* Washington, D. C.: International Monetary Fund.

Packer, Frank. 1994. "The Disposal of Bad Loans in Japan: A Review of Recent Policy Initiatives." Paper presented at the conference on Current Developments in Japanese Financial Markets, June 9–10, University of Southern California.

11

Bank Failures in Scandinavia

Sigbjørn Atle Berg

During the 1980s and early 1990s each of the Scandinavian countries faced severe banking crises that have had a substantial impact on their economies. The experience could be described as a watershed event, and has been analyzed in many papers and books (see the list at the end of this chapter). The interpretation of events differs somewhat from author to author, and there is no consensus on the relative importance of the large number of factors that contributed to the crises.

The Scandinavian countries proper include Denmark, Norway, and Sweden. This chapter also treats Finland as part of Scandinavia, but excludes the fifth Nordic country, Iceland, which is too much of a special case to fit into the common framework discussed here.

In the four countries discussed here, nearly all the major banks got into serious difficulties as a result of heavy loan losses. Only two of the larger banks, one in Denmark and one in Sweden, escaped serious problems altogether. This does not mean that most major banks failed in the strict meaning of the word. In reality few outright failures occurred. Most problem banks were either merged with other banks or enabled to continue as independent units through financial support from insurance funds or governments. All large Danish banks and the three largest Swedish banks also managed to get through the crises without receiving direct external assistance.

The four countries differed in the nature of their banking crises. Møller and Nielsen (1995) point out some major differences, in particular, between Denmark and the three other countries. For instance, they stress that mark-to-market accounting rules in Denmark left Danish bankers with fewer opportunities to conceal their problems. While it is true that the Danish banking crises differed in some important respects from the developments in the three other countries, I believe that the similarities between the four countries are more striking. The basic structures of the crises were more or less the same, and proceeded in accordance with well-known theories of financial cycles.

One of the special features of the Scandinavian banking crises was that so many of the largest banks incurred losses of a size that could not be dealt with without government intervention (table 11.1). In Finland the five largest banks and in Norway the four largest all received capital injections from the government. In Sweden the three largest banks came through without direct support, but not the next three. Only in Denmark did all large banks manage without government capital injections. However, even most of the large banks that did not receive government capital sustained heavy losses.

Table 11.2 reports financial support to banks from both governments and bank insurance funds until the end of 1993, when the crises had peaked in all four countries The banking industries are taken to include both commercial and savings banks, along with the many small Finnish cooperative banks. Since the distinction between the activities of the groups are becoming increasingly blurred, they will be treated as one group. Note that table 11.2 includes only bank-specific guarantees, and not the general guarantees issued by the Finnish and Swedish governments. Again, Denmark is a special case, where few banks received support from the government.

The Dynamics of the Crises

The common structure of the four Scandinavian crises included an initial stage with rapid increases in bank lending (table 11.3). This occurred first in Norway, and a couple of years later in the other three countries. The tax subsidy implicit in the deduction of interest payments from taxable income stimulated the growth in all four countries. While the average growth rates hide much higher rates in a number of individual banks, even the averages were sufficiently high that they should have been disturbing to bank managers and regulators.

To some extent people did worry about the rapid extension of new loans. However, in Finland, Norway, and Sweden the growth in lending occurred relatively soon after the abolition of important pieces of bank regulation. The details of the deregulatory processes differed, but in each country the authorities felt that banks needed to adjust to an unregulated

Table 11.1. *Government Capital Injections, Guarantees, and Ownership of the Six Largest Banks in Finland, Norway, and Sweden, End of 1993*

Country and bank	Government capital	Government guarantees	Government ownership (percentage of shares)
Finland[a]			
KOP	1,700	1,800	14.8
Unitas	1,700	1,000	5.8
PSP	900	0	100.0
SKOP	15,700	800	52.9
OKO	400	0	0
Aktia Savings Bank	0	0	0
Norway[b]			
Den norske Bank	7,000	0	87.5
Christiania Bank	8,800	0	68.9
Union Bank	1,000	0	48.0
Fokus Bank	1,900	0	97.9
BN-Bank	0	0	0
Savings Bank of Nord-Norge	700	0	0
Sweden[c]			
SE-Banken	0	0	0
Handelsbanken	0	0	0
Savings Bank of Sweden	1,000	0	0
Nordbanken (including Securum)	50,200	0	100.0
Föreningsbanken	0	2,500	0
Gota Bank (including Retriva)	23,800	0	100.0

a. Millions of Fmk.
b. Millions of NKr.
c. Millions of SKr.
Source: Bank of Finland, Norges Bank, and Sveriges Riksbank.

equilibrium, and that this equilibrium entailed a substantially higher level of bank lending. Initially rapid growth in lending could be rationalized as normal adjustments to a new regime.

In Denmark most of the banking regulations had been abolished earlier, and some of the adjustments to a new equilibrium had been made during an economic recession. Only when economic conditions improved did bank lending really take off. In the other three countries the deregulation of banking coincided with high levels of economic activity, which acted as a further spur to bank lending.

Table 11.2. *Capital Injections or Disbursements to Banks from Insurance Funds or Governments, 1988–93, and Bank Structure before the Crises*

Country	Total equity capital of all banks, end of 1988[a]	Total number of banks, end of 1988	Total disburse- ments, 1988–93	Number of receiving banks, 1988–93
Denmark (millions of DKr)	65,098	206	5,092	7
Finland (millions of Fmk)	22,760	590	54,278	278
Norway (millions of NKr)	22,831	187	24,912	25
Sweden (millions of SKr)	19,414	525	65,000	3

a. Excludes subordinated debt.
Source: Scandinavian central banks.

One important component of deregulation that permitted the growth in bank lending, but which has not drawn much attention, was the withdrawal of some foreign exchange regulations. For most of the postwar period all the Scandinavian countries except Denmark had heavily regulated capital flows. In Finland and Norway the remaining regulations that prevented banks from borrowing funds on international capital markets were lifted before the strong growth in bank lending took place.[1] This deregulation did not have much immediate effect, but international markets proved to be an important source of funding when bank lending took off. Without this access to foreign funding the rapid growth in lending would have been impossible. The banking industries in Finland, Norway, and Sweden became heavily dependent on foreign funding. The ratio between domestic deposits and borrowing and domestic lending also declined in Denmark, and while the Danish banking industry did not become dependent on net foreign funding, the Danish bond market did. While free capital flows are important for long-term economic efficiency, the Scandinavian banking crises illustrate that they have the potential to increase the volatility of small, open economies.

In all four countries the structure of liabilities on balance sheets was changed during the credit expansion, with relatively less weight given to ordinary deposits and more reliance placed on money market borrowing.

1. In Norway banks were free to obtain foreign funding from 1978 and in Finland from 1986. Sweden did not lift formal restrictions until 1989, but banks were in practice free to obtain foreign funding before that time.

Table 11.3. *Growth in Lending Rates by Parent Banks, 1980–96*
(percent per year)

Year	Denmark	Finland	Norway	Sweden
1980	—	18.0	12.7	—
1981	—	14.9	16.7	10.8
1982	—	18.8	17.3	14.8
1983	—	14.5	18.4	9.3
1984	—	14.1	27.5	9.7
1985	—	17.6	31.8	3.4
1986	—	11.9	33.0	15.4
1987	15.0	19.1	18.7	15.9
1988	8.1	31.1	6.1	31.5
1989	10.0	15.2	9.3	25.7
1990	11.5	11.2	3.9	16.6
1991	0.8	1.4	-4.4	-1.5
1992	-7.0	-3.0	1.0	1.7
1993	-1.3	-13.4	0.5	-19.1
1994	-12.6	-8.3	4.1	-3.1
1995	3.5	-6.5	9.1	-3.7
1996	12.0	-0.7	13.9[a]	3.9

— Not available.
a. The growth rate shown is artificially high because during the year some nonbanks were transformed into banks
Source: Scandinavian central banks.

In this sense the banks' funding base became less robust. In particular, the availability of foreign funding proved sensitive to macroeconomic developments and other systemic factors. Most of the foreign funding evaporated when the signs of an imminent crisis appeared.

The regulatory regimes included restrictions on interest rates and lending volumes. These regulations had a cementing effect on the market shares of individual banks. Deregulation was thus also seen as a unique opportunity to capture a higher market share, especially by the larger banks. This perception certainly contributed to the growth in overall lending, and is the only possible explanation for the fact that some banks extended loans at rates below their marginal funding costs. Furthermore, an unusually large number of banks set up new branches to expand their activities into new regions and new market segments, such as real estate financing. Some of the highest loss ratios were generated by such newly established branches, which is in full accord with standard theories of asymmetric information.

The regulations had created a backlog of would-be borrowers, and enabled the banks to give priority to their loyal customers. This simplified credit evaluations at the time, but left banks with little experience in evaluating the creditworthiness of unknown customers. Routines for doing so were often not available at banks that defined market shares as one of their principal objectives.

Table 11.4 reports loss provisions in the four countries. Accounting rules differed slightly among the Scandinavian countries, and the numbers are thus not strictly comparable, but the essential facts stand out clearly. Within a few years after loan growth had peaked, banks began to see heavy losses. Industrywide loss provisions amounted to around 3 percent of total banking assets in 1991 in Norway, in 1992 in Finland, and in 1993–94 in Sweden. This should be compared to levels of equity capital that averaged only about 6 percent of total assets in these three countries. The losses of Danish banks were more evenly distributed over time, and the Danish banking industry had a more solid initial capital base that could absorb the losses.

The high level of losses applied to both household and business lending. In the household sector most of the losses were on real estate loans. Prices of residential and commercial real estate had increased

Table 11.4. *Bank Loss Provisions, 1980–96*
(percentage of total assets)

Year	Denmark	Finland	Norway	Sweden
1980	—	0.3	0.1	0.0
1981	—	0.4	0.1	0.1
1982	—	0.4	0.1	0.2
1983	—	0.3	0.2	0.2
1984	—	0.3	0.2	0.3
1985	—	0.4	0.3	0.2
1986	—	0.4	0.4	0.3
1987	0.5	0.5	0.7	0.2
1988	0.8	0.5	1.5	0.2
1989	0.7	0.6	1.7	0.2
1990	1.0	0.6	1.7	0.7
1991	1.3	0.9	3.6	2.3
1992	1.7	2.8	1.9	3.8
1993	1.5	2.6	1.2	3.2
1994	0.8	2.4	0.1	1.0
1995	0.5	1.6	-0.2	0.6
1996	0.3	0.7	-0.1	0.3

— Not available.
Source: Scandinavian central banks.

Table 11.5. Price Indexes of Residential Real Estate, 1980–96
(1990 = 100)

Year	Denmark	Finland	Norway	Sweden
1980	68.1	28.9	30.7	77.0
1981	64.9	33.2	33.7	69.0
1982	63.4	39.5	53.2	69.0
1983	77.0	47.0	56.9	65.0
1984	88.9	52.9	65.3	65.0
1985	104.1	55.1	78.8	67.0
1986	116.2	57.3	103.4	71.0
1987	107.7	64.0	111.5	74.0
1988	108.9	87.3	114.8	81.0
1989	108.1	106.5	107.0	88.0
1990	100.0	100.0	100.0	100.0
1991	101.3	85.3	93.6	92.0
1992	99.7	69.8	89.5	79.0
1993	98.7	64.7	91.4	67.0
1994	110.7	68.9	102.7	—
1995	119.1	66.2	109.3	—
1996	131.9	70.3	118.1	—

— Not available.
Source: Scandinavian central banks.

as a result of the growth in bank lending, and vice versa: increased access to borrowing led to increased demand and increased prices for real estate, which in turn increased collateral values and gave rise to even more borrowing. Table 11.5 shows developments in the residential real estate markets, demonstrating how the asset price bubble first built up and then burst in each of the four countries. Real estate prices fell dramatically from their peak levels and trapped many borrowers in positions where their loans were substantially higher than the market value of their collateral. When this coincided with higher real rates of interest and economic recession, increased loan losses to banks were an obvious consequence.

In addition to the real estate price bubbles, a stock price bubble contributed to the losses on business lending in Finland. However, most of the losses on commercial lending originated from the concurrent macroeconomic cycle. A large number of loans extended during the boom years turned sour when the recession hit. Total losses on commercial lending far exceeded losses on household lending, thereby confirming the widespread perception that commercial lending is the more risky of the two.

Table 11.6. Household Savings Rates, 1980–96
(percentage of disposable income)

Year	Denmark	Finland	Norway	Sweden
1980	6.2	5.5	3.9	5.0
1981	7.5	4.6	4.4	4.0
1982	9.7	5.3	4.2	0.8
1983	6.8	5.7	3.9	1.6
1984	4.9	4.4	5.0	1.3
1985	-0.2	3.8	0.8	2.3
1986	-4.9	2.5	-5.5	1.3
1987	-3.1	2.9	-6.2	-2.8
1988	0.1	-1.2	-4.0	-4.8
1989	2.6	-0.6	0.3	-4.9
1990	4.6	0.4	0.9	-0.6
1991	6.0	5.1	2.1	3.1
1992	4.8	7.1	4.3	7.7
1993	5.8	5.2	5.8	8.3
1994	3.2	1.5	6.8[a] 3.8	8.6
1995	3.8	4.4	7.0[a]	7.2
1996	3.9	3.0	5.7[a]	—

— Not available.
a. The series was redefined from 1994.
Source: Norges Bank; OECD (various years).

The Relationship between the Macroeconomy and Asset Price Bubbles

A rapid growth in credit volumes will always have an expansionary effect on the economy, far beyond the immediate effect on asset prices. The effect comes through different channels, but one of the most important is probably the wealth effect that follows directly from the higher level of asset prices. People holding these assets will feel that they can comfortably increase their level of consumption, which resulted in the negative household savings rates reported in table 11.6. In the next step the increased consumer spending spurs business investment activities.

The economic stimulus from the credit market was extremely strong in each of the Scandinavian countries. In three of the countries the stimulus worked in an already booming economy. To some extent fiscal policies sought to counteract the monetary influence, but the counterbalancing fiscal effects were too small and came too late to be of much importance during the upturn.

When the asset price bubbles burst, the wealth effect began to work in a contractionary fashion. This occurred in a situation in which consumers had increased their indebtedness to nearly unprecedented levels. Thus a high share of consumers' disposable income was required to pay interest and repay loans, which left less than the normal amount for consumption purposes. This is probably the main reason for the contraction in credit volumes during this phase of the crises. A higher level of real interest rates and the introduction of less lenient treatment of interest expenses in the tax code reinforced the contractionary monetary tendency in some of the countries. In Finland and Sweden a large proportion of loans was denominated in foreign currencies, and these loans became harder to service as the national currencies depreciated during the crises.

During this phase fiscal policies were still contractionary. It took some time before governments realized that the cycle had turned downward, and even more time before they could revise their policies to produce an expansionary effect. In this way fiscal policies also contributed to the recession that occurred in each of the Scandinavian countries after the banking industries collapsed. The recession was particularly deep in Finland, mainly because the Soviet Union and its economy collapsed around the time of the Finnish banking crisis. A high percentage of Finnish exports were to the Soviet Union, but after 1991 the volume of these exports fell to almost nothing.

The main influence on the economic cycle in the Scandinavian countries came from the credit market, both during the upturn and during the downturn. The Scandinavian banking industries claimed that they had been hit by bad economic policies, but even if the cycle had been exogenous to each individual bank, it was certainly not exogenous to the banking industries. This does not imply that individual banks were to blame for the cycle, but it does mean that their collective behavior put governments in an extremely difficult position. This would have been true even if the governments had been more accustomed to strong influences on economic activity originating from the credit market.

Solutions to the Crises

Denmark, Finland, and Norway had established bank insurance funds long before the crises, and in Denmark and Norway these funds helped some of banks that ran into problems early on, but when the major banks needed capital injections, the insurance funds quickly proved to be insufficient, and the governments had to step in. In Finland and Sweden governments were directly involved at an even earlier stage. Government funds for the ailing banks were established in 1991 in Norway, in 1992 in Finland, and in 1993 in Sweden. Solutions to the Scandinavian banking crises were thus largely a question of government policies.

In only three cases did the authorities close problem banks and liquidate their assets. This happened to one small Danish and two small Norwegian commercial banks with limited customer bases. In all other cases they permitted banking operations to continue without interruption, even if some of the problem banks were split up through piecemeal sales of their assets and deposits and shareholders in some banks lost their money. Throughout the crises avoiding interruptions in banking services was a major concern for the Scandinavian governments, who felt that this was essential to limit the negative effect on other industries. The concern was not only to protect the payment system and to avoid a domestic credit crunch, but also to retain foreign banks' confidence in the national banking industries.

Apart from the three bank liquidations, small and medium-size problem banks were invariably merged with or taken over by other banks, and in many cases the transactions were aided by capital transfers from governments. Finland and Sweden made extensive use of "bad banks," that is, asset management companies set up to manage the nonperforming assets of problem banks. These bad banks were mostly funded by the governments, who took this course of action to enable the remaining problem banks to resume normal operations as soon as possible.

The major problem banks posed the greatest challenge to government policies, and the Scandinavian governments met the challenge with somewhat different strategies. Only the Danish government was able to stay behind the scenes and leave solutions to the banking industry and its insurance fund, with some assistance from the central bank.

The three largest commercial banks in Norway had to make loss provisions that wiped out their entire equity capital, and obtaining new equity capital by issuing shares proved impossible. Except for some minor categories of equity capital, the government then required shareholders formally to write down the value of the share capital to zero before it injected new capital. The government thus took control of the three banks through government funds. Bank boards and top managers were replaced by new teams of professional bankers selected by the government. The Norwegian government used its position as owner to impose cuts in balance sheets, branch networks, and staff levels in much the same way private investors would have done.

The Swedish government also took full control of two major problem banks; however, it already had a 70 percent ownership share in the largest of these banks before it became a problem bank. In addition to these two cases of direct intervention, the Swedish government also helped in the merger of a large number of savings banks to create the Savings Bank of Sweden. However, the government's main option was to help the banks indirectly by issuing in December 1992 a blanket guarantee for all their liabilities, including subordinated debt, but not share capital. This guarantee was particularly important for the large banks' operations abroad, and worked as a substitute for equity capital.

Finland's central bank temporarily took over one of the major commercial banks. The government took over almost the entire savings bank sector and initiated mergers to create the Savings Bank of Finland. After transferring bad loans to asset management companies and recapitalizing both the large commercial bank and the Savings Bank of Finland, they were split up and sold in pieces to various other Finnish banks. The other major problem banks in Finland also received government capital transfers, but the government did not take formal control. Convertible loans were offered to and accepted by nearly all banks. As in Sweden, in February 1993 the government issued a blanket guarantee of bank liabilities, mainly to help the banks' international operations.

There is a clear contrast between the strategies of the Norwegian government and those of the Finnish and Swedish governments. The Finnish and Swedish governments allowed some undercapitalized banks to continue operations backed by a blanket guarantee of their liabilities. According to standard banking theory, this would be an invitation to risk taking by bank owners and managers. The Norwegian government preempted this possibility by taking direct control of the major problem banks. Nevertheless, the Finnish and Swedish policies still worked relatively well, perhaps because the risk-taking incentives applied to only a few large banks that either the government owned or whose managers stayed in close touch with the government and the supervisory authorities.

The Current Situation

The banking industries of the four countries have now mostly recovered from the crises. Some banks have recently had low, or even negative, net provisions for losses, as provisions made during the crises have been recovered (see table 11.4). Governments are about to recover a substantial part of their outlay as they reprivatize the banks they took over and sell off the assets from the asset management companies.

The lasting structural impact of the banking crises had much to do with the way the governments handled problem banks. The Finnish and Swedish banking industries became more concentrated during the crises, largely because of the government-led mergers of most savings banks in each country. The Swedish government also merged the two large commercial banks under its control in 1993. These mergers helped reduce banking capacity, which the authorities in all the Scandinavian countries believed was excessively large. The Norwegian government reduced capacity by forcing reductions on the large banks over which it took direct control, i.e. without increasing the degree of concentration.

Norway represents a special case, in that its government became the majority owner of the country's three largest commercial banks. It has resold the third largest of these banks, mostly to foreign investors, and has also sold some parts of the two largest banks, but it still holds more than 50 percent of the shares in these banks. This means that the government is acting both as owner and as regulator in banking markets. While this may work for a limited time, in the long term it might damage the credibility of the government's policy toward this sector. The Norwegian government will probably sell additional shares to reduce its ownership to about one-third. The purpose would be to prevent takeovers and to retain banks' head offices within the country. The government believes that retaining one or two major banks whose management consists mostly of Norwegian nationals is important for the economy's prospects in the long term.

Lessons Learned

The former governor of the Norwegian central bank said that the banking crisis was due to "bad banking, bad policies, and bad luck." To some extent this is true: the crises developed as a result of complicated dynamic processes in which all three factors played a part. However, the description is not quite adequate. With hindsight, the behavior observed was clearly less than optimal, but in most cases it is readily understood given the context in which decisions were taken. Given the decisionmakers' experience and the institutional frameworks they were acting within, the decisions often look reasonably rational, even if lacking in foresight. If placed in similar positions in the future, bankers, borrowers, and politicians might respond in much the same way again.

This is perhaps a negative lesson. It means that the financial system is inherently unstable when it becomes subject to large disturbances. This is the prediction made by well-known theories of financial cycles, and the Scandinavian banking crises are good illustrations of such theories.

Literature about the Scandinavian Banking Crises

Berg, S. A. 1993. "The Banking Crises in the Scandinavian Countries." In *Bank Structure and Competition 1993*. Chicago: Federal Reserve Bank of Chicago.

_____. 1994. "Governments' Strategies: The Nordic Banking Industries after the Crises." In D. E. Fair and R. J. Raymond, eds., *The Competitiveness of Financial Institutions and Centres in Europe*. Dordrecht, Holland: Kluwer Academic Publishers.

Ingves, S., and G. Lind. 1996. "The Management of the Bank Crisis - In Retrospect," *The Quarterly Review* (Sveriges Riksbank, Sweden) (1): 5–18.

Kjellman, A. 1996. *What Can We Learn from the Finnish Banking Crisis?* Åbo, Finland: Åbo Akademi University.

Koskenkylä, H. 1994. "The Nordic Banking Crisis." *Bank of Finland Bulletin* 68 (8): 15–22.

_____. 1995. "The Condition of Nordic Banks and Future Prospects Post-Crisis." *Bank of Finland Bulleti* 69 (8): 9–5.

Llewellyn, D. 1992. "The Performance of Banks in the UK and Scandinavia: A Case Study in Competition and Deregulation." *Penning & Valutapolitik 1992/3 The Quarterly Review* (Sveriges Riksbank, Sweden) (3): 20–30.

Møller, M., and N. C. Nielsen. 1995. "Some Observations on the Nordic Bank Crisis: A Survey." Working Paper no. 95–8. Institute of Finance, Copenhagen Business School, Copenhagen, Denmark.

Nyberg, P. 1995. "The Banking Crisis in Finland." *Journal of the Economic Society of Finland* 48: 115–20.

OECD (Organisation for Economic Co-operation and Development. Various years. *Economic Surveys*. Paris.

Vihriälä, V. 1997. *Banks and the Finnish Credit Cycle 1986–1997*. Bank of Finland Economic Studies no. E:7. Helsinki, Finland.

12

Banking Disasters: Causes and Preventative Measures, Lessons Derived from the U.S. Experience

Richard J. Herring

As recently as 1990, asking why only the United States alone among advanced industrial economies had been plagued by banking disasters was perfectly reasonable. The 1980s were indeed a troubled era for depository institutions in the United States. During the decade more depository institutions failed in the United States than at any time since the Great Depression. Between 1980 and 1991, 10 percent of all banks and 25 percent of all savings and loan institutions (S&Ls) failed, and many more depository institutions were in extremely fragile financial condition. By 1995, however, banks and S&Ls were earning record profits and had greatly strengthened their capital positions. Moreover, by then it was clear that banking disasters were not confined to the United States. Serious banking problems had swept over most of Scandinavia, France, and Japan.

This chapter reviews the U.S. experience with the aim of drawing lessons for preventing future disasters. It focuses on the increasing vulnerability of the banking system to a crisis before a shock occurs where a shock is an event that would cause loss to exposed banks. Note that this chapter treats shocks as if they are exogenously determined. (See Kindleberger 1978 and Minsky 1977 for explanations of financial crises as the consequence of an unsustainable economic expansion and Allen and Gorton 1993 for a discussion of financial bubbles and references to the literature.) It also reviews how policy actions taken after a shock occurs may worsen the damage rather than mitigating it and considers possible parallels between the U.S., Japanese, and Scandinavian experiences drawing from the material presented in chapters 9, 10, and 11 of this volume.

Before a Disastrous Shock Occurs

Uncertainty

A lengthy period when no major shocks have occurred often precedes disastrous shocks. In the United States after World War II, for example, bank failures were extremely rare and were usually the result of idiosyncratic circumstances that often involved fraud.

After a shock has occurred, of course, it is clear that the banks damaged by the shock had assumed excessive insolvency exposure. However, this section focuses on the period before the shock has occurred and poses the question: Why do banks become increasingly vulnerable to the shock? We will consider two possible answers. First, managers may have underestimated the probability that a shock would occur. Second, managers may have perceived the probability of a shock correctly and willingly taken on greater insolvency exposure because they expected it to be profitable.

In earlier work with Jack Guttentag (Guttentag and Herring 1984, 1986), I argued that underestimation of such shocks may be a consequence of the way in which decisions are made under uncertainty (Meltzer 1982 has also emphasized the central role of uncertainty in financial crises). Our ability to estimate the probability of a shock depends on two key factors. First is the frequency with which the shock occurs relative to the frequency of changes in the underlying causal structure. If the structure changes every time a shock occurs, then events do not generate useful evidence regarding probabilities. However, if the shock occurs many times while the structure is stable, one may estimate probabilities with considerable confidence. High-frequency shocks affect many kinds of activities conducted by retail banks. For example, default rates on portfolios of car loans and credit card receivables can be estimated with considerable confidence. Indeed, the degree of predictability of such default probabilities has facilitated the securitization of this kind of lending. In general high-frequency shocks are not a source of insolvency exposure for banks. Banks have both the knowledge and the incentive to price high-frequency shocks properly and to make adequate provisions to serve as a buffer against loss. If they do not, they will quickly incur ruinous losses that will lead to insolvency. By contrast, the causal structure underlying low-frequency economic shocks such as speculative bubbles, shifts in policy regimes, or abrupt changes in relative prices may not remain stable for long enough to permit estimation of shock probabilities with much confidence.

The second is that our ability to predict the probability of a shock depends on our understanding of the causal structure. If we have knowledge of the mechanism that determines an event like the fair toss of a coin, we may be able to predict the probability of an outcome with considerable confidence, even if we have not observed the results of prior tosses. In contrast to the transparent mechanism that generates outcomes in the toss of a coin, our understanding of the economic processes that generate shocks is much less comprehensive, and therefore more likely to be subject to uncertainty.

Banks often lack the knowledge to price low-frequency shocks with uncertain probabilities. How do banks make decisions with regard to uncertain events?

The Disaster Myopia Hypothesis

Researchers in cognitive psychology (Tversky and Kahneman 1982) have found that decisionmakers, even trained statisticians, tend to formulate subjective probabilities on the basis of the "availability heuristic," that is, the ease with which the decisionmaker can imagine that the event will occur. Since the ease with which an event can be imagined is highly correlated with the frequency with which the event occurs, this rule of thumb provides a reasonably accurate estimate of high-frequency events. However, other factors, such as the time elapsed since the last occurrence, also affect ease of recall. Under such circumstances the availability heuristic can give rise to an "availability bias." This is depicted in figure 12.1, where the subjective probability, π, is shown as a declining function of the time elapsed since the last shock at $t = 0$.

At some point, the threshold heuristic (see Simon 1978) exacerbates this tendency to underestimate shock probabilities. This is the rule of thumb by which busy decisionmakers allocate their scarcest resource, managerial attention. When the subjective probability falls below some threshold amount (π^* in figure 12.1), it is disregarded and treated as if it were zero.

Once decisionmakers have reached this threshold, their behavior seldom changes, even in the face of evidence that the actual shock probability has increased; however, the tension between observations and beliefs may give rise to cognitive dissonance. When confronted by evidence that challenges the competence of their decisions, bankers, like other decisionmakers, first tend to ignore it, then reject it, and finally accommodate it by changing other beliefs.

Figure 12.1. Disaster Myopia

The availability and threshold heuristics together cause disaster myopia, that is, the tendency over time to underestimate the probability of low-frequency shocks.[1] To the extent that subjective probabilities decline even though actual probabilities remain constant or increase, banks take on greater exposures relative to their capital positions and the banking system becomes more vulnerable to a disaster. This is an insidious process. Disaster myopia can lead banks to become more vulnerable to a disaster without anyone having taken a decision to increase insolvency exposure.

Disaster myopia is likely to be shared by a large number of banks because uncertainty may also be conducive to herding, in which banks take on largely similar exposures to some shock. Being part of a group provides an apparent vindication of the individual banker's judgment, and some defense against ex post recriminations if the shock occurs. Perhaps even more important, the banker knows that the supervisory authorities cannot terminate all the banks or discipline them harshly. Indeed, the authorities may be obliged to soften the impact of the shock on individual banks to protect the banking system. Keynes (1931, p. 176) perceived this clearly: "A 'sound' banker, alas, is not one who foresees danger and avoids it, but one

---

1. Although in this exposition I have relied heavily on cognitive psychology to explain disaster myopia, Guttentag and Herring (1984) show that the hypothesis is consistent with the Bayesian approach to optimization for low-frequency events.

who, when he is ruined, is ruined in a conventional way along with his fellows so that no one can really blame him."

Disaster myopia may also afflict the supervisors who should constrain the banks' increasing vulnerability. Supervisors, after all, are likely to be subject to the same perceptual biases as bankers, and for that matter, as university professors. The conditions that caused disaster myopia among bankers may also have influenced regulators. For example, one seasoned regulator speculated about why supervision had been so ineffectual in preventing the banking problems of the 1980s, and conjectured that part of the reason had been "the comfort of years of real and financial macrostability with unusually low failure rates in both the banking and the thrift industries" (Ettin 1991, p. 15).

Several institutional factors may reinforce the tendency toward disaster myopia. Managerial accounting systems, for example, may inadvertently favor activities subject to low-frequency shocks. Although generally accepted accounting principles are helpful in monitoring, pricing, and provisioning for high-frequency shocks, they are not so useful in controlling exposure to a low-frequency hazard, because the shock occurs so rarely that it will not be captured in the usual reporting period. Indeed, the absence of bad outcomes in the accounting data may intensify pressures to reduce default premiums and reserves. Moreover, in the absence of appropriate provisions for potential losses, an activity subject to low-probability shocks will appear misleadingly profitable.

The illusion of high profitability creates additional problems. To the extent that salaries and bonuses are based on reported short-term profits without adjustment for reserves against shocks, the line officers who are in the best position to assess such dangers will be rewarded for disregarding them. In the United States the prospect of job mobility often strengthens this incentive to take a short-term view. Managers may expect that they will be elsewhere—in another job, perhaps in another institution—by the time problems emerge. The appearance of high profitability may also impede the effectiveness of the supervisory authorities, who find it very difficult to discipline banks that appear to be highly profitable.

In addition, competition may interact with disaster myopia in two related ways to increase vulnerability. First, competitive markets make it impossible for banks that are not disaster myopic to price transactions as if there were a finite probability of major shock when banks and other competitors that are disaster myopic price them as if that probability were zero. Second, if banks are apparently earning returns above the competitive level (disregarding the need for reserves against future shocks), equally myopic banks will be encouraged to enter the market, thereby eroding those returns. In response, banks can protect target rates of return on equity for a time by increasing their leverage and rationalizing such actions in terms of the need to maintain target returns on equity in the face of shrinking margins, and in terms of similar actions by other banks. Thus when competition interacts with disaster myopia it may accelerate the process through which banks become increasingly vulnerable to a major shock.

The disaster myopia hypothesis cannot be tested directly, because demonstrating ex ante excessive insolvency exposure to shocks of unknown probability is impossible. Nonetheless, one can identify trends that are consistent with and conditions that are conducive to disaster myopia.

Interest Rate Risk and the S&L Industry

This section examines increasing exposure with regard to the interest rate shock that decapitalized the S&L industry. The evolution of the S&L industry in the 1970s is a particularly clear example of rising vulnerability to a shock in the face of increasing probabilities that the shock will occur. The S&L industry prospered following World War II by making fixed rate, long-term, residential mortgages backed by short-term savings deposits. (They were not permitted to issue adjustable rate mortgages until 1982, after the interest rate shock had devastated most of the industry.) Their charter—and the absence of appropriate hedging instruments such as interest rate swaps—gave them a structural, asset-liability mismatch, with the duration of their assets greatly exceeding that of their liabilities. During most of this period, their exposure to interest rate risk generated substantial profits.

Generally, the yield curve was upward sloping so that interest rates on 30-year residential mortgage assets exceeded short-term rates on deposit liabilities (figure 12.2). A series of increasingly severe interest rate spikes that began in 1966 led to temporary yield curve inversions and an erosion of the net worth of S&Ls. More important, this erosion of net worth was greatly exacerbated by the upward trend in interest rates, which obliged S&Ls to reprice their liabilities at higher interest rates much more rapidly than they could reprice their assets. Accounting practices obscured this loss in value because mortgages were reported at historical cost without making any adjustment for their decline in market value as interest rates rose. During the 1970s interest rates became more volatile and the upward trend accelerated. Even without the benefit of hindsight, it seems obvious that the risk of a disastrous interest rate shock was not falling during the 1970s. Indeed, it was probably rising. However, instead of reducing their

Figure 12.2. *Ninety-One-Day Treasury Bill Discount Rate and Long-Term Government Bond Yields, 1945–95*
(percent)

Source: Author's calculations.

vulnerability to an interest rate shock or increasing their capacity to withstand an interest rate shock by increasing their capital, S&Ls let the book value of their capital positions decline steadily throughout the seventies (figure 12.3). Of course, the economic value of their capital positions declined even more sharply, because the book value measures did not reflect the decline in the market values of mortgage portfolios.

An interest rate shock like that which occurred during October 1979 is inherently difficult to predict, because it was the result of an abrupt change in the policy regime: the Fed abruptly switched from targeting interest rates to targeting bank reserves. Such events have been rare, and because we do not have a widely accepted causal model of shifts in policy regimes, the probability of such a shock was subject to uncertainty.

The accounting system, which took no account of the impact on balance sheets of changing market values in response to rising interest rates and created no reserves to deal with an interest rate shock, undoubtedly reinforced the tendency to be disaster myopic. This obscured the erosion of economic net worth from owners, managers, creditors, and regulators and led to an overstatement of profits that sustained the salaries and bonuses of managers who might otherwise have taken measures to reduce exposures.

Increasing competition from other financial institutions may have hastened the process of increasing vulnerability. S&Ls were subject to disintermediation as depositors shifted to money market mutual funds in search of higher returns and as banks and insurance companies became more

Figure 12.3. *The Evolution of the Generally Accepted Accounting Principles Value of S&L Capital Ratios, 1963–87*

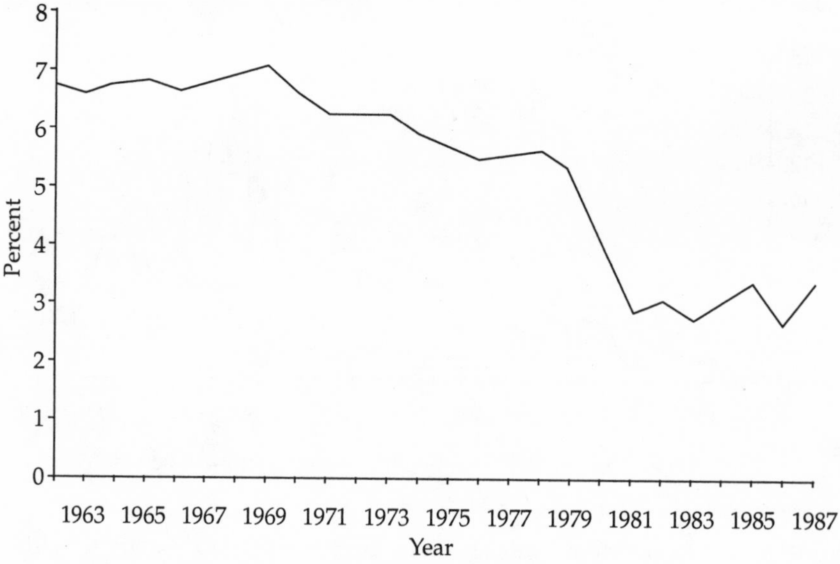

Source: FHLBB *Journal* (Federal Home Loan Bank Board), various issues.

active in the mortgage market and the nationwide market in securitized mortgages developed. In this setting raising mortgage rates to accommodate a sufficient premium to cover interest rate risk uncertainty was not possible, and in the face of shrinking margins, increasing leverage to maintain returns on equity may have seemed tempting. Any residual doubts about the prudence of such a policy may have been eased by herding: managers might have taken comfort from observing that their peers at other institutions were also accepting similar exposures with declining capital positions.

This example illustrates the dynamics of disaster myopia. An activity that appears to be profitable may be subject to a disastrous, low-frequency shock. However, if no persuasive way to estimate the probability of the shock is available—and this will be true for many economic disturbances—managers may rely on decision processes that are subject to disaster myopia. The consequence is that over time, exposures will increase relative to capital. This tendency may be intensified by accounting practices that gloss over signs of increasing vulnerability and by compensation practices that emphasize short-term profits without taking account of reserves for future shocks. Increased competition may lead to increased vulnerability by hastening the decline in shock premiums and by reducing the banks' capacity to withstand the shock. Although this section has focused on an interest rate shock and a transfer risk shock, shocks to agricultural lending, energy lending, commercial real estate lending, or highly leveraged transactions could be analyzed in the same way (see Guttentag and Herring 1986, pp. 5–16, for an application of the hypothesis to transfer risk).

Although the disaster myopia hypothesis as developed here refers explicitly to banks, the story to this point applies in most respects to any firms that are subject to low-frequency exogenous shocks that are difficult to predict. Banks, however, differ substantially from most other firms because they are regulated and protected by a safety net, which makes disaster myopia in banks a public policy concern. In addition, regulation and the safety net may lead to increased vulnerability to disaster.

Restrictions on the Diversification of Bank Activities

Banks are regulated for a number of reasons that have little, if anything, to do with the safety and soundness of the financial system. Indeed, regulations imposed for other reasons may undermine the safety of banks.

U.S. depository institutions are subject to relatively tight restrictions on what they may do and where they may do it. In general, these restrictions constrain their ability to diversify and make them more accident prone than their less-regulated counterparts elsewhere.

The S&L charter was one of the most restrictive in the United States (see table 9.7 in chapter 9 of this volume), and, as we have already seen, in a fundamental sense the S&Ls' vulnerability to an interest rate shock was implicit in their charter. Moreover, their enforced specialization in residential mortgage lending left them vulnerable to the vicissitudes of just one industry.

Banks were also subject to activity restrictions, such as prohibitions on underwriting corporate securities and selling insurance, which impeded their ability to evolve as their customers' needs changed. In addition, both banks and S&Ls were subject to geographic restrictions that constrained their ability to diversify deposits and loan portfolios and made them more vulnerable to local economic conditions.

These restrictions are implicated in a large proportion of failures. Litan (1991, p. 21) calculated that between 1985 and 1989 failures in just three states—Louisiana, Oklahoma, and Texas—accounted for 57 percent of all bank failures and 81 percent of total bank resolution costs. Banks in these states were heavily dependent on energy and agricultural lending and their branching authority was strictly limited. Moreover, out-of-state banks were not permitted to acquire home state institutions.

Although rigid constraints on the activity and branching powers of depository institutions undoubtedly made them more vulnerable to shocks, this need not have resulted in the enormous losses U.S. taxpayers and prudently managed institutions sustained. The magnitude of the losses is directly attributable to the design and implementation of the safety net at that time.

The Moral Hazard Implications of the Safety Net

In most industrial countries, the various circuit breakers that constitute the safety net have succeeded in preventing a disaster at one bank from escalating into a financial crisis that damages the real economy. In an important sense, however, the safety net has been too successful in protecting depositors. Because depositors are confident that they will be protected against loss, they have little or no incentive to monitor and discipline risk taking by their banks. This is the classic moral hazard problem, in which the existence of insurance may undermine the incentive for depositors to be concerned about preventing the insured risk—in this case, the risk of insolvency—from occurring. Bank managers find that if depositors do not demand greater compensation when greater risks are taken, they can increase expected returns to their shareholders by assuming greater insolvency exposure.

Explicit deposit insurance is directly implicated in the moral hazard problem. In the United States deposit insurance covers claims up to US$100,000, and until the Federal Deposit Insurance Corporation Improvement Act (FDICIA) reforms in 1991, institutions were assessed a fixed premium for deposit insurance that did not vary with the risk profile of the institution. Most depositors at small banks and S&Ls were fully protected by deposit insurance.[2]

In addition, depositors at larger banks in the U.S. benefited from implicit deposit insurance that arose from the way in which the other two components of the safety net were deployed. First, the lender of last resort routinely lent to banks long after they became insolvent rather than lending solely to solvent, but illiquid, banks. This gave anxious creditors who were not covered by explicit deposit insurance the opportunity to withdraw their deposits before a bank was terminated. Second, the termination authorities generally did not intervene to terminate a bank promptly before it became insolvent. Instead they usually delayed until the bank was deeply insolvent. Then, rather than liquidating the bank and imposing loss on uninsured depositors and creditors, the authorities provided assistance while keeping the bank open,

---

2. Scott (1991, p.3) notes that Federal Deposit Insurance Corporation regulations made it easy to circumvent the legal limit of $100,000. Families can combine accounts to increase insured accounts well above the US$100,000 limit, and pension funds, "Section 457" plans, and holders of bank investment contracts can get coverage for US$100,000 per participant, thereby boosting the insured amount to several million.

or arranged a purchase and assumption transaction in which the acquiring bank honored all commitments to uninsured depositors and other creditors. This policy applied to all banks with more than US$500 million in assets and gave credibility to the notion that such banks were too big to fail.

Thus explicit deposit insurance fully protected most depositors in small banks, and depositors in larger banks were protected not only by explicit deposit insurance up to the legal maximum, but also by implicit deposit insurance for amounts above the legal maximum. These components of the safety net effectively removed the main constraint on risk taking at most firms. When creditors are indifferent to risk, who else will constrain risk taking? One possibility is managers who have significant human capital at risk if their bank should become insolvent. If they are quite independent from shareholders and do not have a significant equity stake in the bank, they may guard the safety of the bank to protect the value of their human capital.

Shareholders have their equity interest at stake. The possible loss of their equity interest will act as a brake on risk taking so long as the equity stake is high relative to the potential loss. However, as the equity stake falls relative to the potential loss on existing exposures, shareholders will be tempted to take increasingly greater risks because they can keep large returns, while losses larger than their equity stake are passed on to the deposit insurer (and the prudent banks and taxpayers who finance deposit insurance). Thus in the absence of countervailing pressures from the supervisory authorities, banks are likely to take larger risks when the economic value of their capital positions (their ability to absorb losses before defaulting on any of their obligations) falls even if they are not subject to disaster myopia.

Moral Hazard and Declining Franchise Value

During the 1970s the economic value of the capital positions of many depository institutions fell. The economic value of a bank's capital position is equal to the market values of all assets (both on and off the balance sheet) less the values of all liabilities adjusted for limited liability.[3] Assets include

---

3. That is, the value of all liabilities as if they would be repaid by the shareholders even in the event of failure. This measure will differ from the bank's market value of equity, because the market value of equity contains the value of the bank's limited liability, that is, its option to "put" the bank's assets to its creditors.

4. Or more broadly, the present value of opportunities for future growth (Herring and Vankudre 1987). Opportunities for future growth flow from the bank's authorized powers, including the power to engage in a particular kind of business within a particular area, the market structure in such areas, and the customer relationships the bank has developed. Growth opportunities reflect the bank's economic rents or quasi-rents.

not only tangible and financial assets, but also the bank's franchise value.[4] In addition, the franchise value of U.S. depository institutions eroded because of technological advances, financial innovations, and the liberalization of interest rate ceilings on deposits.

During the same period a series of innovations in financial instruments and institutions blurred traditional product line boundaries between financial institutions and undermined the value of the banking franchise. On the liability side of banks' balance sheets, increased interest rate volatility and competition from money market mutual funds made deposit rate ceilings unworkable, and thus depository institutions were obliged to pay market rates on an increasing proportion of their funds in competition with other short-term borrowers. Commercial banks began to lose their monopoly position as providers of transactions services as S&Ls, money market mutual funds, and brokerage sweep accounts, began to compete in offering transactions services. Corporate customers also began to find ways to economize on demand deposits through increasingly sophisticated cash management techniques.

On the asset side of their balance sheets, banks faced increasing competition from other financial institutions and securities markets. With the increased institutionalization of consumer savings, pension funds and insurance companies developed the capacity to assess and diversify credit risk in competition with banks. Unregulated finance companies began to compete for a larger share of consumer lending, some commercial lending, and leasing. Improved disclosure practices and the rising importance of credit rating agencies enabled an increasing number of borrowers to shift from reliance on banks to the securities markets for funding investments. Also, many foreign banks gained entry to the U.S. market at this time and began to compete aggressively for a larger share of corporate lending.

The upshot of these developments was that the value of the banking franchise declined. This loss of franchise value undoubtedly increased the propensity of weakly capitalized firms to take greater risks.

Summary

In sum, the safety net increased incentives to take excessive risks, and thus put greater pressure on the supervisory function to constrain risk taking. At the same time, however, it reduced incentives for regulators and supervisors to take prompt corrective measures. The success of the safety net in preventing bank runs removed the most powerful pressure on the supervisory authorities to act expeditiously. This gave rise to a principal-agent problem between the taxpayer principals and the supervisory agent. Without the market pressure of a bank run, the supervisory authorities were free to engage in forbearance after a shock occurred, which often exacerbated bank disaster.

After the Shock Occurs

Once a shock occurs, disaster myopia may turn into disaster magnification. The availability heuristic may exacerbate financial conditions because, just after a shock has occurred (such as $t + n'$ in figure 12.1), imagining a reoccurrence is all too easy and the subjective shock probability will rise well above the true shock probability. As Guttentag and Herring (1984) show, this will result in sharply increased credit rationing and tiering of interest rates in financial markets as lenders try to reduce exposures and increase risk premiums in response to sharply higher shock probabilities. This might lead to runs on banks if the safety net were not in place, but the safety net has shielded depository institutions from these harsh, abrupt market sanctions and converted the closure of banks from a market-driven phenomenon to an administrative process with lots of scope for the exercise of administrative discretion.

Forbearance

The evolution of the S&L industry after the interest rate shock provides a clear example of the potential costs of such an approach. The interest rate shock that began in October 1979 substantially decapitalized the S&L industry, leading to negative net worth (measured as the difference between the face value of deposits and the market value of assets at insolvent institutions) that was estimated to be nearly US$100 billion at the end of 1981 (figure 12.4). About two-thirds of the federally insured S&Ls had negative net worth.[5] Despite these enormous losses, few insolvencies were recognized and resolved.

The supervisory response to this shock was restrained for three reasons as follows:

---

5. In market value terms the situation was even bleaker. A former chairman of the Federal Home Loan Bank Board (Pratt 1988, p. 4) later testified that the real capital positions of all thrift institutions had been completely eroded, and that virtually all thrift institutions had large negative net worths when their assets and liabilities were valued at actual market rates.

Figure 12.4. *Federal Savings and Loan Insurance Corporation and RTC's Accumulation of Losses*

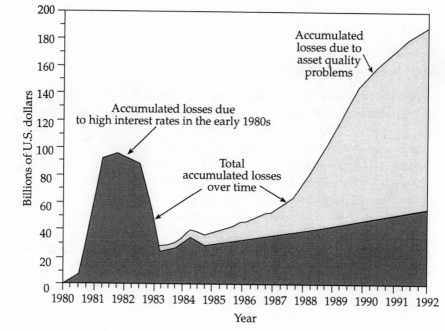

Source: Ely (1993, p. 372).

- The sheer magnitude of the crisis overwhelmed the supervisory authorities. The reserves of the Federal Savings and Loan Insurance Corporation—a mere US$6.5 billion in 1980 (Beaver, Datar, and Wolfson 1992, p. 267)—were wholly inadequate to pay off insured depositors at all institutions with negative net worth. Moreover, the Reagan administration was ideologically committed to deregulation and the reduction of the fiscal deficit, and was not favorably disposed to requests to hire more supervisory personnel or to replenish the deposit insurance fund from tax revenues.
- The supervisory authorities were reluctant to admit to the scale of the crisis. On the one hand, such an admission would raise questions about the quality of oversight they had provided. On the other, they feared that public acknowledgment of the extent of the insolvencies might undermine confidence and ignite a financial crisis.
- The prospect that interest rates might return to preshock levels gave hope that no action need be taken to restore the industry's solvency. Thus the authorities decided to forbear and gamble that the interest

rate shock would be reversed. To a large extent, this gamble paid off. By the third quarter of 1983 interest rates had returned to their preshock levels, and the industry's negative net worth had declined to just under US$25 billion. However, even this amount was too large for the deposit insuring agency to absorb, and so the authorities chose to address the problem by introducing generous new regulatory accounting conventions and by attempting to increase the franchise value of the thrift charter through liberalizing powers.

The S&L industry was in obvious financial distress. When an increasing number of institutions were unable to meet their 5 percent capital requirement under the lenient standards of generally accepted accounting principles (which valued mortgages at historical costs rather than much lower current market values), the regulators responded by reducing capital requirements to 3 percent and by instituting a new, still laxer set of regulatory accounting principles. The latter were designed to boost capital for regulatory purposes by delaying recognition of some losses, accelerating recognition of some gains, and capitalizing assistance from the authorities, thereby enabling some economically insolvent institutions to continue operation.

Private Greed, Public Corruption

The supervisory authorities were subject to strong political pressures to forbear. As Kaufman (1995, p. 25) observed:

> The benefits of forbearance are highly visible and concentrated among a few with strong stakes and the costs are dispersed over the country as a whole and are less visible to each stakeholder. As a result, pressures for forbearance are strong and cumulative and difficult for regulators and legislators to resist.

Owners of faltering S&Ls were often politically powerful in their local communities. They were keenly aware of the gains from regulatory forbearance. Indeed, the opportunity to gamble another round at the taxpayers' expense was their main hope for redemption. Many of them mounted aggressive lobbying efforts that sometimes amounted to thinly disguised bribery.

The damage from the abuse of forbearance was not just financial, but also political. It undermined public confidence in political institutions and cast doubt on the integrity of the financial regulatory system. Moreover, it diverted attention from more important public problems to focus on the largely self-inflicted trauma of the S&L crisis.

Go-for-Broke Behavior

The perverse incentive effects of explicit and implicit deposit insurance become increasingly powerful as an institution's capital erodes. The willingness of banks to take large gambles, even at the cost of a lower total expected return, is greater the lower the bank's capital position (Herring and Vankudre 1987). Shareholders, who were constrained by their capital at risk, find that after their capital is exhausted, extremely risky ventures may offer higher returns to them than less risky ventures with lower expected returns. The reason is that shareholders value a distribution of returns that is truncated at the termination point. They reap all the positive returns above this point, but shift all returns below this point, including the negative returns, to the deposit insurer.

Managers, who may exercise a constraining influence while an institution has positive net worth, find that when capital is exhausted their main hope for survival is also in extremely high risk ventures. Indeed, "When a bank's capital position has been (or is about to be) depleted, incentives increase for self-dealing transactions and fraud. When continuance of the bank is in doubt, the bank's managers face greater temptations to take the money and run" (Guttentag and Herring 1982, p. 108).

Congress addressed the plight of the S&Ls in two important pieces of legislation—the Depository Institutions Deregulation and Monetary Control Act of 1980 and the Depository Institutions Act of 1982—that permitted S&Ls to shorten the maturities of their assets and offer competitive interest rates on their liabilities. The new legislation raised the deposit insurance ceiling from US$40,000 to US$100,000, liberalized Regulation Q interest rate ceilings on deposits, and enabled S&Ls to make consumer and commercial real estate loans as well as variable rate mortgages.[6] This liberalization of powers was long overdue. If these reforms had been instituted a decade earlier, the S&L industry would surely have been less vulnerable

---

6. The Depository Institutions Deregulation and Monetary Control Act began the phased elimination of deposit rate ceilings (which was completed in 1986). It also permitted thrift institutions to offer checking accounts to compensate for their weakened competitive position as Regulation Q ceilings were phased out. The Depository Institutions Act permitted the payment of interest on checking accounts and authorized the introduction of a new money market deposit account. The act also expanded the investment powers of thrifts. Some states, such as California and Texas, broadened the powers of state-chartered S&Ls to include activities that had no obvious link to housing finance, such as commercial real estate development.

to a disastrous interest rate shock. However, liberalization of powers for insolvent institutions provides more opportunities for playing go-for-broke with the deposit insurer's resources, often in activities the supervisors are ill-prepared to monitor. Liberalizing the powers of almost insolvent institutions can lead to a disaster of even greater magnitude.

Once the deposit interest rate ceiling was eliminated, insolvent institutions could attract large sums of money from a national market by offering to pay interest slightly above the going rate. Brokers facilitated the process by accepting amounts well over the new, higher US$100,000 insurance ceiling, dividing them in smaller amounts that would be fully covered by the US$100,000 deposit insurance ceiling, and placing them with the institution promising the highest available interest rate. Of course, as these smaller amounts were fully insured, brokers had no reason to be concerned about the financial condition of the institutions in which they placed deposits. This enabled institutions in a go-for-broke mode to grow rapidly and play with increasingly higher stakes.

All these factors put more pressure on the supervisory authorities to curb excessive risk taking, but instead of strengthening control over risk taking, supervisory efforts faltered. While shielding insolvent institutions from market discipline, the S&L supervisory authorities reduced the frequency of examinations and monitoring and delayed the resolution of insolvent institutions.

Although some institutions rode out the interest rate cycle and were restored to healthy condition, many others played go-for-broke. The consequence can be seen in figure 12.4. In mid-1983 almost all the insolvencies were attributable to the interest rate shock and could have been resolved for about US$25 billion. Instead, the authorities practiced forbearance, S&Ls played go-for-broke, and many of the gambles failed. The result was an increase in losses caused by asset quality problems that totaled about US$140 billion.

In the S&L industry, policy actions taken after the initial shock made a serious problem substantially worse. The increased costs were ultimately paid by the insurance premiums of healthy institutions, taxpayers, and other institutions whose profit margins were eroded by competition from subsidized, insolvent S&Ls.

Lessons from the U.S. Experience

What can one learn about preventing future disasters from the US experience? The remedy depends on the diagnosis, and as we have seen, several pathogens are suspected.

Measures to Counter Disaster Myopia

The traditional bank supervisory process is not well designed to deal with disaster myopia and exposure to major shocks of unknown probability. Instead, the primary thrust of supervision has been to assess the current condition of a bank. While the identification of weak banks is useful for managing crises, it is inadequate for preventing crises. To prevent crises, the supervisory process must identify vulnerable banks before they become weak banks.

For supervisors to constrain a bank in good condition that would be seriously damaged by a shock of unknown probability is extremely difficult, because reasonable people could easily disagree about the probability of such an eventuality. Nonetheless, the central concern of prudential supervision should be to identify banks that are becoming heavily exposed to a major shock to prevent exposures from reaching a point where they constitute a danger to the financial system.

The identification of emerging sources of systemic vulnerability involves a continuing interplay between assessing the exposure of banks to particular shocks and assessing the probability that a particular shock may occur. The process may be broken down into the following three stages:

- Developing a shock hypothesis
- Measuring the shock vulnerability of individual banks
- Measuring the vulnerability of the system.

Once the supervisory authorities have collected the requisite exposure data, they have three basic policy options (see Guttentag and Herring 1989 for more detail). First, they can provide the information to individual banks, perhaps accompanied by supervisory commentary, but permit each bank to determine whether its exposure is prudent. This is a measure and confront approach. An example is the use the U.S. supervisory authorities made of the Country Exposure Lending Survey before the transfer risk shock in 1982. It has the merit of forcing firms to face the issue of whether their exposure is prudent. To the extent that excessive exposure is inadvertent, the result of inattention or poor communications among operating officers, senior management, and directors, this approach may be sufficient to prevent excessive vulnerability. However, the bank may already be aware of its exposure to the shock, having deliberately chosen to accept a larger exposure in the belief that shock probabilities were low and in anticipation of higher expected profits. Indeed, the bank may take comfort in the knowledge that its peers were equally exposed. Under such conditions, the policy of measure and confront may prove wholly inadequate to prevent systemic vulnerability to a major shock, and may actually facilitate herding behavior.

Second, the supervisory agency may release exposure data to the public in the hope that markets will discipline banks viewed as excessively exposed. An example is the requirement the U.S. Securities and Exchange Commission and the bank regulatory agencies established in the wake of the 1982 Mexican debt crisis, that the bank holding companies publicly disclose any concentration of country risk exposure that exceeds three-quarters of 1 percent of their total assets. The disclosure of exposure data, however, may reveal proprietary information, abrogate confidential relationships, and, if disclosure occurs only after the shock, undermine confidence. Moreover, it may not be sufficient to constrain exposures, because creditors may also suffer from disaster myopia or because they anticipate being protected by the safety net in the event of trouble.

Third, the supervisory authorities can specify stress tests that banks should be prepared to meet. This would constitute specifying the minimum shock magnitude that a bank should be able to sustain. The Basle Committee outlines a similar approach in the supervised use of internal risk models to estimate capital requirements for market risk. Banks using this approach must conduct regular stress tests to gauge their vulnerability to low-probability events of several types. Under the stress test approach, if the bank's critical shock magnitude—the shock magnitude that would exhaust the bank's capacity to bear loss—were less than the minimum shock magnitude specified in the stress test, the bank would be required to reduce its exposure or increase its capacity to bear loss until its vulnerability to the shock decreases to the minimum shock magnitude. The basic problem with this approach is that judgments about whether vulnerability to a particular shock is excessive and what minimum shock magnitudes should be are inherently subjective. Moreover, if the supervisory authorities suffer from disaster myopia to the same extent as bankers, they may not identify the appropriate shocks to stress test.

From a regulatory perspective, perhaps the most important reform to counter vulnerability to disaster myopia is to reduce regulatory restrictions on diversification. Liberalization of powers for solvent, well-capitalized banks should help reduce vulnerability to future shocks. The greater the degree of diversification across activities and geographic regions, the lower the vulnerability to any particular shock, even if disaster myopia cannot be corrected.

In addition to these direct supervisory measures to counter disaster myopia, dealing with factors that encourage disaster myopia is also important. Opaque accounting practices that mask deterioration in the market value of exposures to hazards are a fundamental source of vulnerability. They impede the ability of managers, owners, creditors, and supervisors to monitor

insolvency exposure, and they may also make a risky activity appear misleadingly profitable. This problem is compounded when these flawed measures of performance are used to set salaries and bonuses. The line officers
who are in the best position to assess the dangers of increasing vulnerability
should have incentives that encourage them to take a long-term view of the
institution's exposure. This generally means calibrating bonuses to long-term
measures of profitability rather than to short-term returns with no adjustment for reserves against shocks.

Measures to Counter Moral Hazard

In contrast to the measures for countering disaster myopia, the measures
for countering moral hazard are relatively straightforward. The first principle is to refrain from providing full protection for all creditors, especially
large creditors such as corporations, banks that have made interbank place-
ments with the bank in trouble, and institutional investors. This is largely a
matter of ending implicit deposit insurance. A policy of too big to fail places
the entire burden of monitoring risk taking on the supervisory authorities,
and one clear lesson from the 1980s is that supervisory authorities cannot
be counted on to initiate prompt corrective action. Note that this section
focuses on reforms instituted in the United States under the FDICIA. For a
more general discussion that looks at a much broader range of measures to
deal with moral hazard, such as risk-rated deposit insurance and narrow
banks, see Benston and others (1989).

The FDICIA attempted to achieve this by requiring that the Federal
Deposit Insurance Corporation use the least costly method of resolution
under the assumption that its only liability is for insured depositors. The
aim was to deter the use of purchase and assumption transactions that
provided protection to all creditors.

The other channel through which implicit insurance is extended is lender
of last resort assistance to insolvent banks. The FDICIA attempts to deter
such practices by depriving the Fed of the protection of collateral for extended advances to banks near insolvency. A major exception remains if the
Fed and the secretary of the Treasury agree that such advances are necessary
to prevent "a severe adverse effect on…the national economy." Whether this
will be a significant constraint on Fed behavior when a large bank is in jeop-
ardy remains to be seen, but there is at least some reason to doubt whether
protection will be automatic. That alone should enhance market discipline.

The second principle to counter moral hazard is to prevent banks from operating without substantial amounts of shareholders' funds at risk. One clear

lesson from the S&L debacle is that losses surge as institutions become decapitalized and shareholders and managers are tempted to play go-for-broke. The FDICIA attempts to reduce the scope for forbearance by replacing supervisory discretion with rules. These rules are designed to stimulate prompt corrective action as soon as a bank's capital position deteriorates. The sanctions are similar to the conditions that banks impose on their borrowers when their financial condition deteriorates. They become increasingly severe as a bank's capital position erodes from the well-capitalized zone down through three other zones to the critically undercapitalized zone, in which the supervisor must appoint a receiver or conservator within 90 days. If the bank is viable, the threat of increasingly severe sanctions will induce shareholders to recapitalize the bank. The aim is to ensure that prompt corrective action is taken—either by the shareholders or by the supervisory authorities—before the bank's capital is depleted.

Although the FDICIA calls for accounting reforms that would move regulatory measures of capital closer to market values, no clear progress has been made. This is a crucial omission. The rules for prompt corrective action will be effective only to the extent they capture the deterioration in the economic value of capital. If accounting conventions do not reflect changes in market values, then exposures will be more difficult to monitor before a shock, and after a shock the supervisory authorities will retain a significant amount of discretion to exercise forbearance. Under such conditions corrective action is not likely to be prompt. Indeed, it may not be forthcoming at all. Without more transparent accounting practices, it will be difficult for supervisors to monitor the moral hazard incentives of banks and difficult for taxpayers to monitor the performance of their agents, the supervisors.

Parallels to the Japanese and Scandinavian Experiences

To what extent were the causes of the banking crises in Japan and Scandinavia similar to those in the United States? Drawing on chapters 10 and 11 in this volume, this section will first consider the era before the collapse of the bubble in asset prices and ask what factors may have contributed to the increasing vulnerability of Japanese and Scandinavian banks.[7] It will then examine signs

---

7. Although Berg classifies Denmark as having suffered a banking crisis alongside Finland, Norway, and Sweden, I believe that the Danish problem was qualitatively different. Denmark suffered a banking problem—heavy losses in real estate lending—that did not escalate into a crisis. The Danish deposit insurance fund was not exhausted and the Danish government did not intervene in or bail out the banking sector. The relatively favorable Danish experience may have been attributable to more flexible regulation and to the fact that the solvency of Danish banks could be monitored more readily because of Danish mark-to-market accounting conventions.

of disaster myopia, restrictions on diversification, moral hazard incentives from the safety net, and the declining franchise value of banks. Finally, it will consider the extent to which forbearance after the shock may have exacerbated losses and led to go-for-broke behavior.

During the late 1970s into the mid-1980s, Japanese banks were rapidly increasing the concentration of their portfolios in real estate-related loans and investments, while at the same time reducing their capital ratios. In every year from 1975 to 1990, the rate of increase in real estate-related loans and investments in affiliated nonbank subsidiaries was greater than the increase in total loans, often by a substantial margin. Is it plausible that Japanese banks were not consciously increasing their insolvency exposures? With the benefit of hindsight the signs of increasing vulnerability are easy to see, but ex ante, before the collapse of asset prices, were the signs as clear?

Profits in Japanese real estate-related loans and investments were relatively high with few losses. Although the high price of real estate in Japan was the subject of considerable comment, it was rationalized as the consequence of rapidly increasing wealth in a country with relatively little space suitable for economic development.

The eight *jusen*, which are an important part of the current problem, were formed in the 1970s to conduct real estate lending regarded as too risky for banks. However, the *jusens'* relatively high profitability and low losses encouraged banks that had invested in *jusen* to enter the market during the 1980s in competition with their own affiliates (Yoshitomi 1996). In the absence of compelling contemporary evidence about the riskiness of such loans and investment, extrapolating recent favorable experience and increasing exposures relative to capital without consciously accepting greater insolvency exposure may have been tempting.

Real estate-related lending also played a central role in the Scandinavian crises. Table 11.5 in this volume presents time series of real estate price indexes for Denmark, Finland, Norway, and Sweden that the author interprets as evidence of a real estate bubble. An asset bubble is a good example of a low-frequency shock that is subject to uncertainty. Robust economic models that would have enabled us to predict an asset price bubble with a high degree of confidence, particularly in economies with modest inflation in the prices of goods and services, are not available. Empirical evidence regarding such episodes in each country is so sparse that it did not provide a useful basis for setting aside reserves or charging appropriate risk premiums. Nonetheless, international experience with disastrous real estate lending has been growing over the past decade. Real estate lending tends to be self-justifying in the short run, so that increased lending to the real estate sector tends to raise real estate prices, which in turn justifies more lending.

Management information systems did not correct disaster myopia. Japanese accounting practices do not require that real estate be marked to market (and in any event, given the opacity of real estate markets, this would have been difficult to accomplish). This also appears to have been true in the Scandinavian countries (with the important exception of Denmark). To the extent that bonuses were based on profits without adjustment for reserves against defaults in real estate lending, line managers may have been encouraged to ignore signs of impending disaster. Although life-time employment practices undoubtedly lead Japanese managers to take a longer term view than their U.S. counterparts, the practice of rotating managers to new positions every two to three years may have undercut this benefit to some extent.

If Japanese managers were troubled by doubt about the prudence of increasing concentrations of exposure to the real estate sector, they were undoubtedly encouraged that their peers were taking similar positions. Herding has been a prominent feature of the Japanese banking system and had been officially encouraged to some extent by the "convoy approach" to bank regulation and supervision.

Disaster myopia is likely to have played some role in causing the Japanese and Scandinavian banking crises, but regulation and the moral hazard effect of the safety net may also have been contributing factors. Financial regulation in Japan, as in the United States, has imposed tight regulatory restrictions on different kinds of financial institutions. This has led to a highly segmented financial system with extremely specialized institutions. These regulatory constraints on diversification have probably made Japanese institutions more vulnerable to shocks than universal banks in Germany, the Netherlands, or Switzerland. However, regulatory constraints on diversification—with the possible exception of constraints on the *jusen*— did not appear to have played the central role in Japan's banking problems that constraints on S&Ls played in the U.S. crisis. Indeed, what is notable about the current Japanese banking problem is how many different categories of institutions managed to build up heavy exposures to the real estate sector despite the high degree of regulatory segmentation.[8] Among

---

8. The role of the agricultural cooperatives in the *jusen* debacle indicates some of the perils of regulatory attempts to compensate for the declining value of a traditional franchise by permitting entry into what appears to be a highly profitable new sector that is subject to risks that neither managers nor regulators have experience evaluating.

the Scandinavian banks, Finnish, Norwegian, and Swedish banks appear to have been subject to greater restrictions on powers than Danish banks. Chapter 11 in this volume associates the beginning of banking problems in Scandinavia with the transition to a less regulated system.

Although the components of the safety nets for financial institutions differ from those in the United States, the overall protection provided to depositors and other creditors of banks has been at least as powerful as in the United States.[9] From World War II until very recently, the Japanese authorities followed a policy of avoiding all bank failures, and recently, the 21 major banks (city banks, trust banks, and long-term credit banks) were officially designated as too big to be permitted to cause losses to creditors. Although Japan, like the United States, has flat rate deposit insurance, it has played a relatively minor role. As in the United States, the main mechanism for protecting bank creditors has been purchase and assumption operations in which a large institution purchases the assets and assumes the liabilities of a faltering, smaller institution. This process was often guided administratively by the Ministry of Finance. (Financial infusions by the Deposit Insurance Corporation have occurred only recently and infrequently.) The Scandinavian countries also provided effective protection for bank depositors that extended well beyond explicit deposit insurance and dulled incentives for creditors to monitor the insolvency exposure of their banks.

This put much greater pressure on supervisors to monitor and discipline the insolvency exposure of banks. Just like their counterparts in the United States, Japanese bank supervisors had difficulties meeting this challenge. Indeed, Ogawa (1995, p. 4) cites reports of a "woefully inadequate supply of trained bank examiners" that are strongly reminiscent of concerns about U.S. bank examiners during the 1980s.

The task of monitoring the insolvency exposure of banks was made more difficult in Japan by innovations in financial markets and the liberalization of banking regulations, and banking supervisors apparently failed to adapt quickly enough to the new competitive environment. Chapter 11 in this volume also emphasizes the importance of innovations in bank practices and the liberalization of banking regulations in the Scandinavian countries. In Finland, Norway, and Sweden authorities were not particularly concerned

---

9. In particular, the termination function relies more on standard bankruptcy law. This constrains the ability of the Japanese regulatory authorities to close a bank before it is insolvent.

about the rapid expansion of bank lending, because they interpreted it as a normal adjustment to an unregulated equilibrium.

Japanese banks, like their peers in the United States, suffered from declining franchise values before the shock. During the 1970s and 1980s the development of the domestic securities market led to disintermediation from banks on the liability side. Government bond repurchase agreements provided a higher return to corporate and institutional clients than wholesale time deposits, and medium-term government bond funds provided an attractive alternative to retail deposits. This led to pressure to liberalize deposit rates during the 1980s, so that by 1990 nearly 70 percent of the deposits at city banks bore a market-determined interest rate. Scandinavian banks experienced disintermediation and grew more reliant on borrowing in money markets.

On the asset side of their balance sheets, Japanese banks saw traditional, large corporate customers turn increasingly to other sources of funds. With the lifting of capital controls, borrowers turned to the less-regulated Euroyen market, issued securities directly in capital markets, and relied on internally generated funds. Also, a growing number of sophisticated, foreign financial institutions opened offices in Tokyo and competed for large corporate customers. The blurring of regulatory distinctions among financial institutions in Japan also increased competition. Banks attempted to compensate for the decline in net interest margins by lending to smaller firms and to the real estate sector. They appear to have been no more successful than U.S. money center banks in setting lending rates that were sufficient to compensate for higher risks in the new lines of business. New branches that Scandinavian banks established to reach new geographic regions and market segments suffered the heaviest losses. Some new loans were apparently extended at rates below marginal funding costs.

The loss of franchise value could be seen in the erosion of profits from traditional banking activities that had been sheltered from competition. Declining franchise values meant that shareholders had diminished incentives to constrain the risk taking of banks.

The importance of this factor may be open to question in the Japanese context. Close observers of Japanese corporate behavior argue that shareholders' interests seldom rank first in corporate decisions. The interests of other corporate stakeholders, such as managers, employees, and customers, may receive a higher priority, leading to a situation in which growth is often preferred over profitability. From a U.S. perspective this can be characterized as a principle-agent problem, in which the shareholder principles find it difficult to induce agent managers to act in their interests. Thus in Japan the key issue may be how the moral hazard effect of the safety net influences managerial, rather than shareholder, behavior. If creditors and shareholders do not constrain managerial behavior, then the burden falls on the supervisory authorities. The Japanese supervisory authorities, like their counterparts in the United States, have found this heavier burden difficult to bear.

After the shock the Japanese authorities pursued a policy of forbearance. They permitted banks to carry on with their impaired capital positions in the expectation that they would be able to earn their way out of trouble, or that in time, rising asset prices would reverse unrecognized losses. This is precisely the policy that proved to be so costly in the United States, especially in dealing with the S&L crisis.

Some evidence of go-for-broke behavior is apparent in the Japanese experience. A striking example is the case of two credit cooperatives in Tokyo, the Tokyo Kyowa and Anzen credit unions. A special examination in 1993 alerted the authorities to significant nonperforming loans that would render the cooperatives insolvent, but the authorities did not close the cooperatives, opting instead for a policy of forbearance. The two credit cooperatives took advantage of this policy by rapidly expanding their balance sheets, bidding for deposits at above market interest rates and lending to high-risk projects. Most of the new bets turned out badly, with the consequence that the institutions became even more deeply insolvent.

Evidence of fraud is also apparent in the Japanese experience. One notable example was a restaurateur in Osaka who became, for a brief time, the largest individual shareholder in the Industrial Bank of Japan on the basis of forged certificates of deposit from a decapitalized financial institution. These kinds of events have undermined public confidence in banks and the regulatory system. It is too soon to judge how costly the policy of forbearance may be for Japan, but the evidence suggests that some Japanese institutions are capable of playing go-for-broke as aggressively as U.S. institutions.

The Scandinavian countries appear to have avoided most of the costs of forbearance even though bank insurance funds were overwhelmed in Finland, Norway, and Sweden (but not in Denmark). In Norway the government took direct control of the faltering banks, and in Finland the central bank temporarily took control of one of the banks. Close supervision seems to have limited risky behavior by decapitalized banks and averted go-for-broke behavior. Moreover, the Swedish banking system was undoubtedly strengthened by the authorities' relatively rapid response in recognizing losses, recapitalizing banks, and liquidating nonperforming assets.

In sum, many of the factors that caused banking disasters in the United States also appear to have been implicated in the Japanese and Scandinavian experiences. Looking beyond the rich industrial nations, indications of disaster myopia and go-for-broke behavior can be discerned in the many developing countries that have sustained banking crises during the past 20 years. History may not repeat itself, but with regard to banking disasters, as Mark Twain once observed, it almost certainly rhymes. Failure to learn from these painful experiences can be costly. In the last 20 years at least a dozen countries years have sustained banking losses or government bailouts of the banking sector that amounted to 10 percent or more of GDP.

References

Allen, Franklin, and Gary Gorton. 1993. "Churning Bubbles." *Review of Economic Studies* 60 (4): 813–36.

Basle Committee on Banking Supervision. 1994. *Risk Management Guidelines for Derivatives*. Basle, Switzerland.

Beaver, William H., Srikant Datar, and Mark A. Wolfson. 1992. "The Role of Market Value Accounting in the Regulation of Insured Depository Institutions." In J. R. Barth and R. D. Brumbaugh, Jr., eds., *The Reform of Federal Deposit Insurance*. New York: Harper Business.

Benston, George, Daniel Brumbaugh, Jack M. Guttentag, Richard J. Herring, George G. Kaufman, Robert E. Litan, and Kenneth E. Scott. 1989. *A Blueprint for Reforming The Financial System*. Washington, D. C.: The Brookings Institution.

Ely, Bert. 1993. "Savings and Loan Crisis." In David R. Henderson, ed., *Fortune Encyclopedia of Economics*. New York: Warner.

Ettin, Edward C. 1991. "The Moral Hazard Hypothesis: Opening Comment." In R. J. Herring and A. C. Shah, eds., *Reforming the American Banking System*. Philadelphia: The Wharton Financial Institutions Center.

FHLBB (Federal Home Loan Bank Board). Various issues. *FHLBB Journal*.

Guttentag, Jack M., and Richard J. Herring. 1982. "The Insolvency of Financial Institutions: Assessment and Regulatory Disposition." In P. Wachtel, ed., *Crises in the Economic and Financial Structure*. Lexington, Massachusetts: Lexington Books.

_____. 1984. "Credit Rationing and Financial Disorder." *Journal of Finance* 39 (December): 1359–82.

_____. 1986. *Disaster Myopia in International Banking*. Essays in International Finance no. 164. Princeton, New Jersey: Princeton University.

_____. 1989. "Prudential Supervision to Manage Systemic Vulnerability." In *The Financial Services Industry in the Year 2000: Risk and Efficiency*. Proceedings of the Conference on Bank Structure and Competition. Chicago: Federal Reserve Bank of Chicago.

Herring, Richard J., and Prashant Vankudre. 1987. "Growth Opportunities and Risk-Taking by Insured Intermediaries." *Journal of Finance* 42 (July): 583–99.

Kaufman, George. 1995. "The U.S. Banking Debacle of the 1980s: An Overview and Lessons." *Financier* 2: 9–26.

Keynes, J. M. 1931. "The Consequences to the Banks of the Collapse in Money Values." In *Essays in Persuasion, Collected Writings of J. M. Keynes*, vol. xiii. London: Macmillan.

Kindleberger, Charles. 1978. *Manias, Panics, and Crashes*. New York: Basic Books.

Litan, Robert E. 1991. "Could Broader Powers—Geographic and Product—Have Saved the Banks?" In R. J. Herring and A. C. Shah, eds., *Reforming the American Banking System*. Philadelphia: The Wharton Financial Institutions Center.

Meltzer, Alan H. 1982. "Rational Expectations, Risk, Uncertainty, and Market Responses." In P. Wachtel, ed., *Crisis in the Economic and Financial Structure*. Salomon Brothers Series on Financial Institutions and Markets. Lexington, Massachusetts: Lexington Books.

Minsky, Hyman. 1977. "A Theory of Systemic Fragility." In E. A. Altman and A. W. Sametz, eds., *Financial Crises*. New York: Wiley Interscience.

Ogawa, Alicia. 1995. "Testimony before the House Committee on Banking and Financial Services." United States House of Representatives, Washington, D. C., October 16.

Pratt, Richard T. 1988. "Testimony before the Committee on Banking, Housing, and Urban Affairs." United States Senate, Washington, D. C., August 3.

Scott, Kenneth E. 1991. "The Moral Hazard Hypothesis." In R. J. Herring and A. C. Shah, eds., *Reforming the American Banking System*, Philadelphia: The Wharton Financial Institutions Center.

Simon, Herbert A. 1978. "Rationality as Process and as Product of Thought." *American Economic Review* 68(May): 1–16.

Tversky, Amos, and Daniel Kahneman. 1982. "Availability: A Heuristic for Judging Frequency and Probability." In D. Kahneman, P. Slovic, and A. Tversky, eds., *Judgment under Uncertainty: Heuristics and Biases*, New York: Cambridge University Press.

Yoshitomi, Masaru. 1996. "The 'Jusen' Debacle and Japanese Economy." Speech delivered at the Weiss Center International Lecture Series, April 17, Philadelphia.

13

The Case for International
Banking Standards

Morris Goldstein

Based on a discussion of several key themes or lessons that emerge from chapters 9–11 of this volume, this chapter makes the case for a voluntary international banking standard as a way to reduce the frequency of banking crises in the future, particularly in developing countries.

Themes and Lessons from the Case Studies

The three case studies on the forces driving banking crises in Japan, Scandinavia, and the United States and a burgeoning recent literature on banking crisis reveal six major themes or lessons.

Liberalization Can Induce Major Banking Crises

Despite the significant potential benefits of financial liberalization, implementing such liberalization in the wrong way can bring about a major banking crisis. By the wrong way, I mean introducing financial liberalization in a context where explicit and implicit government guarantees underwrite the downside risks of new investment opportunities, where bank owners do not have enough of their own money at stake, where bank regulation and supervision is not strengthened to take account of the newly liberalized environment, and where both a pent-up demand for the liberalized activity and easy financing to accommodate that demand are present.

Under these conditions, bank balance sheets typically expand rapidly and the concentration of bank lending to the newly liberalized activities grows. In the end a sharp shift in economic conditions—be it a tightening of monetary policy, a sharp drop in private capital inflows, a depreciation of the exchange rate, or the onset of prolonged slowing of economic activity— exposes banks' vulnerability (see Goldstein and others 1993).

In the Japanese, Scandinavian, and U.S. cases, elements of this common adverse scenario are present, and if the sample is widened to consider emerging economies as well as industrial countries, the link between financial liberalization and banking crises becomes even more apparent. For example, Kaminsky and Reinhart (1996) found that in their sample of 20 emerging economies and smaller industrial countries, in 18 of 25 cases, financial liberalization had preceded banking crises some time during the previous five years. In a similar vein, Goldstein and Reinhart (forthcoming) found that proxies for financial liberalization, such as increases in the money multiplier and in real interest rates, are among the better early warning indicators of banking crises in emerging economies during the past 25 years.

Being clear about the identity of the real villain is important here. It is not financial liberalization. After all, liberalization usually lowers the cost of capital, increases the return to savers, provides improved opportunities for risk diversification, and increases market discipline on errant borrowers. Also, as chapter 9 in this volume emphasizes, an outmoded regulatory structure can both prevent banks from responding to changes in market realities and expose them to high levels of interest rate risk. The real villain is a piecemeal approach that alters only one side of the risk-taking equation, namely, the potential gains to risk taking, without altering the other side, namely, the costs of bringing a bank closer to insolvency. In short, if uninsured and insured bank creditors view liberalized activities as falling under the safety net, if banks are undercapitalized relative to the riskiness of their operating environment, if liberalization is not preceded by a strengthening of the regulatory and supervisory framework, and if the real exchange rate is allowed to become seriously overvalued, then financial liberalization is not going to generate a happy outcome for banks.

Accounting, Disclosure, and Legal Frameworks Are Important

Accounting, disclosure, and legal frameworks matter. Where such frameworks are weak, vulnerability to a banking crisis will be higher. If the asset classification system is one where loan classification depends only on the payment status of the loan and not on a forward-looking evaluation of the borrower's creditworthiness and on the market value of the loan's collateral, the likely outcome is a high incidence of the "evergreening" of bad loans, an understatement of the true size of nonperforming loans, and an overstatement of the real cushion provided by bank capital (see de Juan 1996; Goldstein 1997). All this in turn will cloud the financial condition of banks. Similarly, if public disclosure of banks' financial condition is poor, then it will be harder for bank creditors to monitor and to discipline weak banks. Likewise, if the legal system makes it difficult for banks to seize and dispose of collateral on delinquent loans, the market for these impaired assets is going to be less liquid and bank profitability is apt to be lower.

As illustrated in chapter 10 of this volume and in other studies, the Japanese banking crisis has been replete with these kinds of accounting and disclosure problems. For example, in September 1992 the Japanese Ministry of Finance was reporting nonperforming loans in the major banks as just over ¥ 12 trillion, when any reasonable estimate of banks' exposure to the property sector together with a ballpark estimate of the decline in real estate prices would have produced a much larger figure, probably double or triple that cited (see Goldstein and others 1993). Along the same lines, the official definition of nonperforming loans has long excluded loans restructured at more than the official discount rate. In addition, until recently public disclosure of nonperforming loans covered only the 21 major banks as a group, which made it harder for the market to distinguish weak banks from stronger ones.

The Japanese case is not an isolated example. Studies have documented that accounting procedures consistently produced an underestimate of the extent of the asset deterioration at savings and loan institutions (S&Ls) during the U.S. saving and loan crisis (see, for example, Kane 1989). Chapter 11 notes that mark-to-market accounting rules in Denmark left Danish bankers with fewer opportunities for hiding their problems than their Finnish, Swedish, and Norwegian counterparts; thus it seems more than coincidental that Denmark alone among the Scandinavian countries was in the end able to avoid providing any government capital injection to its large banks.

On the legal side, problems in seizing collateral and disposing of it along with high land transaction taxes have made it harder for Japanese banks to unload their bad property loans. In contrast, asset sales in both the Swedish banking crisis and the U.S. S&L crisis were huge, without anywhere near the impediments seen in the Japanese case.

Excessive Credit Creation and Unsound Financing Are Dangerous

Fisher (1932), Minsky (1972), and Kindleberger (1978) were correct when they warned about excessive credit creation and unsound financing during the expansion phase of the business cycle. This then comes crashing down when the bubble inevitably bursts.

The Goldstein and Reinhart (forthcoming) study of early warning indicators of banking crises consistently finds that recession and a decline in equity prices are among the top five indicators. Data limitations prevented parallel tests on property prices, but if appropriate (monthly) data had been available, they too would probably send good early warning signals. Lending booms are often part of the same story and feature prominently in the three case studies, as well as in some Latin American banking crises (see Gavin and Hausman 1996).

Some authors have argued that it is more difficult for banks to discriminate between good and bad credit risks when the economy is expanding rapidly, because many bank borrowers will (temporarily) be profitable and liquid (see Gavin and Hausman 1996). Sharp swings in equity and real estate prices take on particular importance in these bubble scenarios, because loans are frequently concentrated in these sectors, because equity price declines reduce the net worth of firms, and because real estate and equities often serve as the collateral for bank loans (see Goldstein and Turner 1996). When economic activity slows markedly, the same shock that reduces the borrower's ability to pay simultaneously reduces the value of the collateral for bank loans.

One might think that over time these excesses during the expansionary phase of the business cycle would become less pronounced. Apparently this is not the case.

Regulatory Forbearance Adds to the Costs of a Crisis

Bank supervisors' failure to take prompt corrective action against undercapitalized banks almost always adds considerably to the ultimate costs of a banking crisis. Ironically, a common justification for not taking prompt corrective action is that the government budget does not have the funds to absorb such costs. In the end, gambling for resurrection by liquid, but insolvent, banks typically increases the budgetary tab. Chapters 9 and 10 provide dramatic testimony about the costs of delayed action, as does a voluminous earlier literature.

Because of the substantial costs associated with supervisory inaction, I favor the structured early intervention approach to bank supervision pioneered by Benston and Kaufman (1988) and included in modified form in the Federal Deposit Insurance Corporation Improvement Act (FDICIA) of 1991. An effective counterweight to strong pressures for regulatory forbearance will not occur without a more rule-based supervisory regime. Because of greater government ownership and involvement in the banking system and high levels of connected lending, such pressures for regulatory forbearance tend to be stronger in developing than in industrial countries (see Goldstein 1997; Honohan 1996). Put in other words, where we really need FDICIA is in developing countries.

Admittedly, not enough time has passed to get a definitive reading on the impact of FDICIA. Nevertheless, as Benston and Kaufman (1997) show, the preliminary signs are encouraging, including the finding that a higher share of uninsured creditors has gone unprotected during Federal Deposit Insurance Corporation bank resolutions since FDICIA came on stream.

Seen in this light, Japan's announced plan to introduce prompt corrective action procedures into its bank supervisory regime in 1998 is welcome, although whether the Ministry of Finance will retain enough influence in bank closure decisions under the new regime to blunt its impact remains to be seen. Taking a wider view, it is disappointing that prompt corrective action and least-cost resolution have not so far found their way into the supervisory regimes of more Group of Ten countries.

Financial Institutions That Have Lost Market Share and Franchise Value Are a Threat

Governments should beware of financial institutions that because of technological advances or changes in monetary or regulatory policy have lost market share and franchise value. These are the institutions most likely to abandon the principles of sound finance to avoid downsizing.

Years ago, some small shops in the United States used to display a small sign near the cash register that said: "Don't go away mad. Just go away." Unfortunately, financial firms threatened with extinction frequently do not go gently into the night. In this connection, chapter 10 notes that the *jusen* companies turned to real estate lending in the second half of the 1980s to substitute for lost consumer business, business they lost to banks who had turned to it themselves after seeing much of their corporate lending decline. Similarly, agricultural cooperatives provided funds to the *jusen* when the demand for agricultural credit slackened. Echoes of the same theme can be seen in Norway's experience, where banks increased the riskiness of their portfolios after losing market share to less regulated finance companies. In analyzing the changing fortunes of U.S. banks during the past few decades, Weisbrod, Lee, and Rojas-Suarez (1992) have likewise argued that increases in the riskiness of bank portfolios accompany declines in franchise value.

Heavy Dependence on Foreign Currency Denominated Borrowing Is Risky

Heavy dependence on foreign currency denominated borrowing by banks and their customers calls for considerable caution. Chapter 11 notes that in both Finland and Sweden banks resorted heavily to foreign currency denominated borrowing, and that these loans became much harder to service as the national currencies depreciated during the crisis. This is a common experience, especially as one moves beyond the industrial countries. In Mexico, for example, when the peso depreciated from 3.1 to 5.3 to the U.S. dollar between December 1993 and December 1994, the foreign currency liabilities of Mexican banks almost doubled (see Mishkin 1996). As another indicator of such vulnerability, at the time of the peso crisis almost 60 percent of the liabilities of large and medium-size Mexican companies were denominated in foreign currencies, as compared to 10 percent of their assets (see Bank for International Settlements 1996). Thailand is an even more recent dramatic example of large currency and maturity mismatches by banks and their customers. Goldstein and Reinhart (forthcoming) found that large appreciations of the real exchange rate from trend, that is, a highly overvalued real exchange rate, are at the top of the heap in terms of signaling ability for banking crises. Furthermore, as Mishkin (1996) emphasized, a heavy burden of foreign currency denominated debt makes it harder for a country to escape from a banking crisis, because depreciation of the nominal exchange rate will, by definition, not lower the banking system's liabilities in real terms.

The Need for an International Banking Standard

The lessons outlined in this chapter are by no means new ones, yet we have nevertheless witnessed a worldwide epidemic of banking crises since 1980 (see Caprio and Klingebiel 1996; Honohan 1996; Goldstein 1997; Lindgren, Garcia, and Saal 1996). This in turn raises the question of how can we best motivate the kind of reforms that would make banking crises less frequent and severe in the future.

A promising approach to reform would be agreement on a voluntary international banking standard (see Goldstein 1997). Such an international banking standard would set out minimum standards, applicable to industrial and developing countries alike, with regard to

- Transparency for government involvement and ownership in the banking system
- Limits on connected lending
- Accounting and provisioning practices

- Public disclosure of banks' financial condition
- Banks' internal controls
- Capital adequacy (in relation to the riskiness of banks' operating environment)
- Safeguards against regulatory forbearance, modeled along the lines of the prompt corrective action and least-resolution provisions of the FDICIA
- Cooperation among home and host-country banking supervisors.

Although subscription to an international banking standard would be voluntary, public disclosure of which countries were and were not participating would establish market penalties for slow movers. Experience with other voluntary international standards in the financial area, including the Group of Thirty's guidelines on clearance and settlement of securities and on risk management of derivatives and the International Monetary Fund's Special Data Dissemination Standard, suggests that such standards can induce countries to make improvements that they would not be willing to make on their own. This lack of willingness could be either because they may see unilateral action as impairing their competitiveness with other firms or countries, or because a country's unilateral reforms are less credible to markets than adherence to an internationally agreed standard monitored by an impartial international agency. To be sure, an international banking standard would not end banking crises. That is an unreasonable objective, especially given that avoiding such crises also depends on reforms in macroeconomic and exchange rate policies that clearly lie outside the field of banking supervision. A more realistic objective is for an international banking standard to contribute to a lower frequency of serious banking crises, especially among developing countries. That by itself would be a valuable accomplishment.

In April 1997, the official sector endorsed and supported the case for an international banking standard with the publication of two key reports (Basle Committee on Banking Supervision 1997; Working Party on Financial Stability 1997). Both these reports contain minimum international guidelines or checklists on good banking and supervisory regimes and practices, against which countries can evaluate their national systems. These reports are a welcome and significant step forward in motivating banking reform. However, how could these reports, especially the "core principles," be strengthened? Four revisions should top the priority list as follows.

- To begin with, the core principles should take a tougher line on greater transparency for government involvement in the banking system. One reason governments often prefer to channel assistance to ailing industries through the banking system rather than the government budget is that the former is less visible, and therefore less subject to public scrutiny. Minimum transparency guidelines would alter that incentive. This is not a minor technical quibble. The lending practices of state owned banks and other banks subject to government pressure are a huge source of past, present, and future credit losses, and something needs to be done about it (see Goldstein and Turner 1996).

- A second worthwhile revision would be to alter present international capital adequacy guidelines. Simply urging countries with volatile operating environments to consider holding higher levels of bank capital is not enough. As Goldstein and Turner (1996) show, many emerging economies have neither set national standards much above the Basle 8 percent risk-weighted standard nor do their banks hold capital much above that in countries with much more stable operating environments, for example, the Group of Three countries. Probably the best option would be to make regulatory capital requirements for credit risk closer to the value at risk approach used for market risk. This would generate higher capital requirements for banks operating in more volatile countries. A second-best option would be to specify say, a minimum 12 percent risk-weighted standard for countries (developing or industrial) that satisfy certain risk criteria, while retaining the existing 8 percent standard for countries with less risky banks.

- Revision number three should address the thorny problem of incentive incompatibilities in the safety net and strong pressures for regulatory forbearance. Some type of FDICIA-like prompt corrective action and least-cost resolution provisions should find their way into the core principles.

- Last but not least, the International Monetary Fund and the World Bank should be given a larger role in whistle-blowing and in monitoring country compliance with the core principles. These organizations need to be a backstop against the danger of weak monitoring and enforcement by national bank supervisors and private credit rating agencies, at least during the first several years of implementation. If monitoring of the principles is not closely watched and if cases of serious and persistent noncompliance are not brought to the attention of markets, then the market premium for being a member in good standing of the club will not be sufficient to motivate reform.

An international banking standard is not world government. It is sensible rules of the road for the international financial superhighway.

References

Basle Committee on Banking Supervision. 1997. "Core Principles for Effective Banking Supervision." Basle, Switzerland.

Bank for International Settlements. 1996. *Sixty-Sixth Annual Report*. Basle, Switzerland.

Benston, George, and George Kaufman. 1988. *Risk and Solvency Regulations of Depository Institutions: Past Policies and Current Options*. Monograph Series in Finance and Economics. New York: New York University Press.

_____. 1997. "FDICIA after Five Years: A Review and Evaluation." *Journal of Economic Perspectives*.

Caprio, Gerard, and Daniela Klingebiel. 1996. "Bank Insolvencies: Cross-Country Experience." World Bank, Washington, D. C.

de Juan, Aristobulo. 1996. "The Roots of Banking Crises: Microeconomic Issues and Regulation and Supervision." In Ricardo Hausman and Liliana Rojas-Suarez, eds., *Banking Crises in Latin America*. Washington, D. C.: Inter-American Development Bank and The Johns Hopkins University Press.

Fisher, Irving. 1932. *Booms and Depressions*. New York: Adelphi.

Gavin, Michael, and Ricardo Hausman. 1996. "The Roots of Banking Crises: The Macroeconomic Context." In Ricardo Hausman and Liliana Rojas-Suarez, eds., *Banking Crises in Latin America*. Washington, D. C.: Inter-American Development Bank and The Johns Hopkins University Press.

Goldstein, Morris. 1997. *The Case for an International Banking Standard*. Policy Analyses in International Economics no. 47. Washington, D. C.: Institute for International Economics.

Goldstein, Morris, and Carmen Reinhard. Forthcoming. *Forecasting Financial Crises: Early Warning Signals for Emerging Economies*. Washington, D. C.: Institute for International Economics.

Goldstein, Morris, and Philip Turner. 1996. *Banking Crises in Emerging Economies: Origins and Policy Options*. Economic Papers no. 46. Basle, Switzerland: Bank for International Settlements.

Goldstein, Morris, David Folkerts-Landau, and others. 1993. *International Capital Markets Report*, part II, *Systemic Issues in International Finance*. Washington, D. C.: World Economic and Financial Surveys, International Monetary Fund.

Honohan, Patrick. 1996. "Financial System Failures in Developing Countries: Diagnosis and Prediction." International Monetary Fund, Washington, D. C.

Kaminsky, Graciela, and Carmen Reinhart. 1996. "The Twin Crises: The Causes of Banking and Balance of Payments Problems." Board of Governors of the Federal Reserve System and the International Monetary Fund, Washington, D. C.

Kane, Edward. 1989. *The S&L Insurance Mess: How Did It Happen?* Washington, D. C.: The Urban Institute Press.

Kindleberger, Charles. 1978. *Manics, Panics, and Crashes.* New York: Basic Books.

Lindgren, Carl-Johan, Gillian Garcia, and Mathew Saal. 1996. *Bank Soundness and Macroeconomic Policy.* Washington, D. C.: International Monetary Fund.

Minsky, Hyman. 1972. "Financial Instability Revisited: The Economics of Disaster." In *Reappraisal of the Federal Reserve Discount Mechanism.* Washington, D. C.: Board of Governors of the Federal Reserve System.

Mishkin, Frederick. 1996. "Asymmetric Information and Financial Crisis: A Developing Country Perspective." Paper prepared for the World Bank Annual Conference on Development Economics, April 25–26, Washington, D. C.

Weisbrod, Steven, Howard Lee, and Liliana Rojas-Suarez. 1992. "Bank Risk and the Declining Franchise Value of the Banking Systems in the United States and Japan." Working Paper no. 92/45. International Monetary Fund, Washington, D. C.

Working Party on Financial Stability in Emerging Market Economies. 1997. "Financial Stability in Emerging Market Economies." Washington, D. C.

Part V. Commonalities, Mistakes, and Lessons

14

Global Banking Crises: Commonalities, Mistakes, and Lessons

Douglas D. Evanoff

This chapter and the others in this part of the volume evaluate factors common to banking crises and extract the lessons that can be drawn to avoid repetition of past mistakes. Although some country-specific factors are obviously involved, a number of similarities tie banking crises in different countries together. What are those similarities and, most important, what regulatory structures will best address the problems they raise?

Probably the single most important cause of financial crises is macroeconomic instability. Significant swings in asset prices, most recently exemplified in real estate and equity price bubbles in a number of countries, can lead to solvency problems across much of the banking industry. A second common factor in financial crises is the inability to access the true value of bank portfolios accurately. This may not necessarily result from the standard opaqueness of bank assets, but from the regulatory failure to convey available information to those capable of disciplining bank behavior and encouraging closure before losses mount. This includes inadequate disclosure rules, inadequate provisioning rules, and divergence between accounting and market values of assets. A third similarity in financial crises is a mispriced and poorly structured safety net. This chapter will focus on the last item.

Given the importance of the financial sector, the hope is that governments can take advantage of historical lessons and minimize the likelihood of future crises. This chapter offers one way to correct a

250 Global Banking Crises: Commonalities, Mistakes, and Lessons

potential problem with existing regulatory structures that should lead to a more stable financial systems.

Safety Net Reform

Chapter 15 in this volume sets out a framework and principles for a well-structured financial safety net. Probably the single most important aspect of this framework is that the safety net should be incentive compatible. Structuring it so that on an ex ante basis behavior is influenced in a manner consistent with the social good is imperative. All too often regulators concentrate on resolving problems ex post. By having a well-structured, incentive-compatible regulatory structure in place, banks operating in their own self-interest will behave prudently and many of the all-too-common moral hazard problems can be avoided.

The major problems seem to lie with the implementation process. Policymakers must realize that often they are dealing with the political economy, not just economics. Although they are related, constraints on the political economy are much less binding. For example, many would argue that an element common to well-structured safety nets is a requirement for prompt corrective action by regulators.[1] Frequently, however, there is significant subjectivity and potential for "gaming" of the prompt corrective action guidelines. In the United States, because of the relatively stable banking environment since the enactment of prompt corrective action, it is probably too early to determine whether such action has been successful and whether it was implemented effectively, although some will argue that the industry's stability may partly have been the result of the introduction of requirements for prompt corrective action. If the industry runs into difficulties, whether regulators will adhere to the spirit of the law or whether they will seek ways to avoid implementing prompt corrective action remains to be seen.

Another desirable feature of a well-structured financial safety net that has potential implementation problems is the need for an independent regulatory agency. The agency should have long-term objectives and should address problems quickly to avoid additional losses. This is seldom the case in developing countries, because significant political pressure is frequently brought to bear on supervisors and regulators. A well-functioning

---

1. In the United States, prompt corrective action was introduced in the 1991 Federal Deposit Insurance Corporation Improvement Act. For a discussion of the act and the effectiveness of prompt corrective action, see Benston and Kaufman (1997).

financial system must be developed over time as market discipline is imposed and economic agents see the consequences of their actions. Politicians, however, seem to have a much shorter time horizon that is frequently determined by the timing of the next election. This often conflicts with the need for an independent regulatory agency with a long-term horizon.

The importance of having incentive-compatible regulation with means to force regulators to abide by the ex ante policy cannot be overemphasized. Ideally, regulators' objectives would somehow be aligned with society's objectives; however, the means to accomplish this are not obvious, because the short-run attractiveness of forbearance is so great (see, for example, Kane 1996 on optimal contracting).

If the regulatory and safety net structure is so important in creating a healthy financial sector, what is the best way to structure the regulatory framework to create the desired environment? One alternative is the narrow bank concept. By separating the safety net from the riskier aspects of banking, this proposal would essentially make the safety net redundant for the narrow bank and would use marketplace forces to regulate all other financial activities. Other alternatives include private deposit insurance, coinsurance, and risk-based insurance premiums.

Subordinated Debt Proposal

An alternative proposal combines incentive-compatible regulation with limited subjectivity for regulators. For countries with mature capital markets, it would require relatively minor changes to existing capital requirements. The essence of this proposal is to alter existing requirements for bank capital adequacy to reassign the disciplinary role that uninsured depositors are currently expected to assume to subordinated debt holders. (For alternative perspectives on subordinated debt proposals see Horvitz 1984; Litan 1997; Wall 1989. For a comprehensive discussion of a subordinated debt proposal see Evanoff 1993, 1994). That is, change capital requirements to give subordinated debt holders a larger role. Under this structure banks would not only be allowed to count a certain amount of subordinated debt as capital, they would be required to. For example, an 8 percent capital requirement could be restructured to require a minimum of 4 percent equity and 4 percent subordinated debt. This relatively minor change could have significant benefits.

Why is this a preferred regulatory structure? Typically, equity alone serves the role of capital; however, for banks subordinated debt serves as a buffer against income variations for both uninsured depositors and the bank insurance fund. Equity holders stand to share in all the up-side gains from bank investments, but their down-side liability is limited only to the extent of their investment. Equity holders, therefore, have a tendency to allow the bank to hold a riskier portfolio than they would without limited liability. This tendency is inversely related to the level of capitalization. At lower capital levels equity holders may strongly encourage the bank to take on risky assets in an attempt to achieve a large, albeit low probability, payoff that could restore the bank to solvency. Debt holders (either uninsured depositors or subordinated debt holders) do not stand to realize the up-side gains and suffer more from having the bank fall further into insolvency. This places them in a position to scrutinize bank investment behavior more rigorously.

Why not simply let uninsured depositors discipline bank risk taking? Many argue that depositors are not ideal disciplinarians because they do not have sufficient information to monitor the bank adequately. Although they are not explicitly insured, because of regulators' general reluctance to impose losses on deposits, a perception that all depositors may be implicitly insured is common. As a result, they may act as if they were insured, thereby failing to discipline the bank adequately. This partially results from the significant concern about systemic risk associated with depositor discipline. The fear is that bank runs may occur as depositors unable to distinguish between solvent and insolvent banks will exit all banks, leading to significant liquidity crises and possibly driving "good" banks into insolvency. Although the evidence on the potential for systemic bank runs is relatively sketchy, regulators operate as if the potential for runs were significant. As a result, pressures for regulator forbearance increase and resolution procedures may not be implemented. The use of subordinated debt holders to discipline banks essentially eliminates these concerns. By the nature of their role as investors, debt holders will demand information on banks' viability, because they realize they will be one of the first groups on which losses will be imposed. In addition, because the debt would have a fixed term, the debt holders cannot run. They can only "walk" as the debt matures. Thus regulators should not hesitate to impose losses on this group, and they could handle any failure resolution in an orderly fashion (see Evanoff 1993 for more discussion of the advantages of the subordinated debt proposal and a critique of cited disadvantages).

How does the proposal to increase reliance on subordinated debt compare to other reform proposals? The most common alternatives include the narrow bank, private deposit insurance, co-insurance, or risk-based insurance premiums. Most of these alternatives attempt to increase the use of market forces to encourage prudent behavior.[2] Increasing the role of subordinated debt would similarly increase reliance on market forces, but without increasing the potential for deposit runs. The subordinated debt proposal may also be more politically palatable than the alternatives and more easily implemented than either risk-based premiums or co-insurance. Finally, and perhaps most important, the subordinated debt proposal permits a more orderly failure resolution process. As a bank approached insolvency, market discipline would be applied via a slow methodical process in which maturing debt would become progressively more difficult to roll over. When combined with the prompt corrective action process introduced in the 1991 Federal Deposit Insurance Corporation Improvement Act, the troubled bank is disciplined and, if necessary, resolved by a combination of market and regulatory forces.

As stated earlier, this type of regulatory proposal is more applicable for countries with developed capital markets. Recently Argentina has implemented a regulatory program with somewhat similar characteristics that requires the inclusion of long-term debt in bank capital (see Calomiris 1997). The debt is expected to increase market discipline. The Bankers' Roundtable (1997) has recently recommend a similar approach for the United States.

In summary, while there may be country-specific factors leading to financial crises, there do appear to be some commonalities. Given the important role of the financial sector, hopefully we can take advantage of historical lessons and minimize the potential for future crises. Here we have offered one means of correcting a potential problem with existing regulatory structures, which should lead to a more stable financial system.

References

The Bankers' Roundtable. 1997. "Deposit Insurance Reform in the Public Interest." Report of the Subcommittee and Working Group on Deposit Insurance Reform Retail Issues and Deposit Insurance Committee. Washington, D. C.

Benston, George, and George Kaufman. 1997. "FDICIA after Five Years." *The Journal of Economic Perspectives* 11 (3): 139–58.

Calomiris, Charles. 1997. "Designing the Post-Modern Bank Safety Net: Lessons from Developed and Developing Economies." Paper presented at the Bankers' Roundtable Program for Reforming Federal Deposit Insurance, May 2–3, American Enterprise Institute, Washington, D. C.

---

2. For the narrow bank proposal, this discipline would occur in the new nonbanks toward which most of the traditional banking activities would shift as banks' activities were restricted.

Evanoff, Douglas. 1993. "Preferred Sources of Market Discipline." *Yale Journal on Regulation* 10 (Summer): 347–67.

_____. 1994. "Capital Requirements and Bank Regulatory Reform." In Charles Stone and Anne Zissu, eds., *Global Risk Based Capital Regulations* vol. 1. Burr Ridge, Illinois: Irwin Professional Publishing.

Horvitz, Paul. 1984. "Subordinated Debt Is Key to New Bank Capital Requirements." *American Banker* (December 31).

Kane, Edward. 1996. "Foundations of Financial Regulation." In *Proceedings of a Conference on Bank Structure and Competition*. Chicago: Federal Reserve Bank of Chicago.

Litan, Robert. 1997. "Regulation: Disciplining Large Banks after FDICIA." *Journal of Retail Banking Service* 19 (Summer): 57–61.

Wall, Larry. 1989. "A Plan for Reducing Future Deposit Insurance Losses: Puttable Subordinated Debt." *Economic Review* (Federal Reserve Bank of Atlanta) 74 (4): 2–17.

15

Deposit Insurance

Gillian G. Holway Garcia

This chapter proposes a set of best practices for deposit insurance systems (DISs) in normal times and during emergencies. These best practices draw on recent experience in dealing with financial crises around the world, but are also influenced by the emphasis that modern finance theory places on good incentive structures for financial soundness. The chapter also examines departures from best practices as revealed by an International Monetary Fund survey of 50 different DISs.

Best Practices for the Deposit Insurer in Normal Times and during Crises

In most countries, banks are the most important financial institutions for intermediating between savers and borrowers, for executing monetary policy, and for providing payment services. At the same time, the configuration of their portfolios makes them particularly vulnerable to illiquidity and insolvency. In particular, they are highly leveraged and maintain liquid assets that are intended principally to be sufficient to meet withdrawals in normal times. The concern is that the demise of one bank, if handled poorly, can spill over to others, thereby creating negative externalities and causing a more general problem for other banks in the system. For these reasons, many governments consider interceding in the functioning of the free market to provide a safety net for banks that generally includes a lender of last resort and a system of deposit protection (the DIS), in addition to a system of bank regulation and supervision.

Countries often have several objectives when they establish a DIS (see Garcia 1996 for a discussion of the tradeoff between short-term assurances and long-term stability and a more in-depth examination of issues relating to deposit insurance). Some of these objectives are achievable, while others are not. One of the most common, but regrettably unrealistic, goals is to avoid a potential crisis or to resolve an existing one. The incompatibility arises because doing so will, most probably, require a full guarantee, which conflicts with the incentives needed to keep the banking system sound in the long run. In addition, while a well-constructed DIS has its advantages, poorly designed systems have their pitfalls.

Mistakes in Designing a DIS

The pitfalls of a poorly designed DIS are numerous, but agency problems, moral hazard, and adverse selection can be particularly serious if a DIS is not incentive compatible. Deposit insurance is unlike most other forms of insurance (life, health, property, and casualty) in several respects. Regular insurance involves just two parties: the guarantor and the entity protected. However, a deposit insurance contract involves three parties: the DIS, the depositor, and the depositor's bank (see Kane 1995). Both the latter benefit from the guarantee, because the small depositor's accounts are protected, while the bank receives a credit enhancement that both enables it to raise funds at a lower rate and shields it from widespread withdrawals by retail depositors. Furthermore, while regular insurance usually protects against the adverse effects of independent events, particularly acts of God, bank failures are often not independent events, but occur in waves and frequently result from mistakes made by one of the beneficiaries, that is, the bank itself.

The deposit protection contract affects many different groups, directly or indirectly, and they may become subject to moral hazard. The most evident danger is that the protection extended to depositors will make them less careful initially in selecting their bank, and later will deter them from moving their funds to a safer haven. Furthermore, in the knowledge that runs are unlikely, bank owners and managers will take on additional risk in their asset portfolios, reduce the amount of capital and liquid reserves they hold to enable them to weather shocks, or both. In addition, the reduced fear of runs enables other entities that are not formally part of the insurance contract to change their behavior, sometimes in regrettable ways. For example, regulators may be reluctant to require unsound banks to take remedial action, because a threat of market discipline to force the regulators to act does not exist, and the guarantee may provide "cover" for politicians to enable them to demand such forbearance.

Adverse selection can occur when a voluntary DIS charges premiums that are not adjusted for the risk that the bank places on the guarantee fund. In this situation the strongest banks are likely to remain outside the DIS or to withdraw from it if they have already become members. When strong banks withdraw, the premiums charged to remaining members have to be raised to cover the costs of paying the depositors of failed banks. The increase may induce the next layer of stronger banks to withdraw until only the weakest banks remain in the system. Such a system is unlikely to remain solvent. In short, a poorly designed DIS can cause deterioration in the condition of the banking system.

Best Practices in Normal Times

First and foremost, the DIS should be clearly, explicitly defined in law and regulation to reduce moral hazard (table 15.1). It should also be highly transparent so that all members of society know the rules under which the DIS operates, otherwise they cannot protect their interests. Such transparency is reinforced when the authorities move to discipline problem banks promptly to restore them to health. If deterioration continues despite remedial actions, the authorities need to close or merge troubled banks expeditiously when (or preferably just before) they become insolvent. Prompt action also reduces the likelihood that a failing bank will engage in risky and potentially expensive gambles for redemption if it is allowed to continue in business. The supervisor needs good information on the bank's condition to take appropriate action. Nonproprietary information should also be released to the public to support market discipline.

The DIS needs to be well-funded, preferably by the member banks. Sometimes the government shares the initial cost of capitalizing the fund with the banking system. To reduce the problem of adverse selection, ideally the DIS should charge premiums that adequately reflect the risk that each bank places on the insurance guarantee fund. While measuring their risk accurately is difficult, several countries, including Argentina, Bulgaria, Portugal, Sweden, and the United States, currently risk-adjust their insurance premiums (but note that each of these systems is compulsory despite the risk-adjusted premiums). As noted earlier, in the absence of such risk adjustment, the DIS must be compulsory.

Coverage should be low enough to encourage large depositors and sophisticated creditors to discipline their banks by demanding higher risk premiums from weaker banks or refusing to provide funds to these banks

Table 15.1. *Best Practices for the Deposit Insurance System in Normal Times and Departures from Them*

Best practice	Departures from best practice	Issues
Avoid incentive problems.	Create additional agency problems, moral hazard, and adverse selection.	A poorly designed DIS can weaken the banking system.
Lay out system explicitly in law and regulation.	The system is implicit and ambiguous.	Transparency.
Provide supervisor with a system of prompt remedial actions.	Remedial actions do not exist or are late.	Should these remedial powers be mandatory or discretionary?
Resolve failed depository institutions promptly.	Keeping open banks that should be closed.	The importance of closure policies.
Keep coverage low.	Providing high, even full, coverage.	The appropriate level and the use of co-insurance.
Make membership compulsory.	The scheme is voluntary.	How to avoid adverse selection.
Pay out covered deposits quickly.	There are delays in payment.	How to effect prompt payment.
Make adequate sources of funding available to avoid insolvency.	The DIS is underfunded or insolvent.	Underfunding can prevent the DIS from closing banks and protecting deposits.
Charge risk-adjusted premiums.	Premiums are flat rate.	How to set premiums according to risk.
Make sure supervisors have good information.	Information is bad.	Which data are needed for supervisory discipline.
Disclose reliable and comprehensive information.	There is little or misleading disclosure.	Accurate disclosure is needed for market discipline.
Ensure that the DIS agency is independent.	There is political interference.	How to prevent political interference while promoting accountability.
Have bankers on the advisory, but not the main, board.	Bankers are in control.	Conflict of interests.

Table 15.1. (Continued)

Best practice	Departures from best practice	Issues
Ensure close relations with the lender of last resort and supervisor.	Relationships are weak.	Poor lender-of-last-resort policies that raise costs to the DIS. Sharing of information.

outright.[1] To this end, some countries use a system of co-insurance (preferably above a fully covered, low minimum level) to reduce the incentive to run while maintaining market discipline. Whatever the degree of coverage, small depositors at failed banks typically need access to their funds rapidly, thus it behooves the DIS to compensate insured depositors immediately, but certainly within 30 days, otherwise the DIS's credibility may be undermined and its effectiveness correspondingly compromised.

The DIS will need funding sufficient to meet the demands being placed on it. An underfunded scheme will prove to be an obstacle to closing failed banks, and so may lead to costly forbearance.[2] A scheme that relies on an accumulated fund will need to charge premiums that are adequate to build a fund large enough to meet these demands in both normal and adverse circumstances, although in adverse circumstances it should also be able to borrow temporarily to cover any shortfalls. The government should either provide these funds for the DIS itself or guarantee their repayment. The DIS can then make a special levy on banks or raise premiums until the debt is repaid.

The DIS should be independent from political interference, but accountable for its mistakes. Accountability can be achieved by having the DIS's financial statements independently audited, and by requiring it to report periodically to the government and to the public. Achieving a balance between independence and accountability will require careful consideration of the particular political and institutional arrangements in the country designing the scheme. The deposit insurer may be a separate department of the central bank, which may also be the supervisory agency, especially in small countries with limited financial expertise. Elsewhere,

1. One or two times per capita GDP is a rough rule of thumb for appropriately limited coverage.
2. The best known example of an insolvent insurance scheme is perhaps the Federal Savings and Loan Insurance Corporation in the United States, which practiced forbearance for a number of years, with costly consequences for U.S. taxpayers.

it may constitute a separate agency. This agency will not have the power to grant or withdraw bank licenses or to provide lender-of-last-resort credit to failing banks. Therefore, it will need to have close and cooperative working relationships with the bank supervisor and with the lender of last resort. The DIS's board of directors should not comprise bankers, who may suffer conflicts of interest with the taxpayer. Bankers can form a consultative committee to advise the board, however.

The role and objectives of the DIS agency can either be broadly or narrowly construed. Under a narrow interpretation, the DIS would merely manage the fund and pay out funds due to depositors. With a broader mandate, it would also act as the receiver of banks whose licenses have been withdrawn, determine the method of their resolution, undertake their sale or liquidation, and dispose of the remaining failed bank assets.

Departures from Best Practices

Regrettably, departures from best practices are common, and a poor incentive structure gives rise to moral hazard and adverse selection. Systems are frequently implicit and ambiguous, rather than being clearly and transparently defined (Kyei 1995 lists systems of implicit deposit insurance). Coverage is frequently high, leading to moral hazard (see Lindgren and Garcia 1996 for coverage limits in 50 countries). Membership is sometimes voluntary and flat-rate premiums disregard the risk a bank places on the system. When the premium level is set too low, the fund itself may become bankrupt, leading to a lack of prompt corrective action and a reluctance to close failed banks. Political interference may impede supervisory action, and the DIS's relationships with the supervisor and the lender of last resort may be impaired so that nonviable banks continue in business. Allowing weak banks to continue to deteriorate and insolvent banks to continue to operate places burdens on sound banks, and typically results in deterioration of the banking system.

Departures from best practices can also occur in other areas. Insured depositors may receive their funds only after an extended delay, so that retail payments systems are disrupted. Depositors who find themselves without their transactions and savings balances may curtail their expenditure, which can cause or exacerbate a recession. The information on which the supervisors rely when considering disciplining or closing a bank may be misleading, so that appropriate actions are not taken. The information that is released to the public may be inadequate or misleading, so that market discipline is absent. A DIS with such problems is unlikely to strengthen the financial system and can contribute to weakening it.

Adjustments to Best Practices during a Systemic Crisis

A DIS cannot be expected to handle the costs of a systemic crisis that involves pervasive failures. In such a situation, the government will need to provide financial assistance. Such support is appropriate when widespread failures are the result of errors in macroeconomic policy or natural or political disasters of various sorts, because the private sector cannot adequately protect itself against such events.

Once a widespread crisis is in progress, the government may deem it necessary to institute a full guarantee, either from scratch or to override an existing scheme with limited coverage. However, it should do so only for a limited period. Lindgren and Garcia (1996) discuss comprehensive coverage during a crisis and methods for removing it in due course (see table 15.2).

The best practice for crisis coverage is to make it clear that comprehensive coverage is a temporary measure that is distinct from the regular DIS. The government should provide the funding for this additional coverage. However, these best practices are sometimes violated by having comprehensive coverage that is extended too readily and for an unnecessarily long time. In addition, the government may fail to provide crisis backing for the fund, which then becomes insolvent or illiquid. As noted,

Table 15.2. Best Practices if Extending Full Coverage during a Crisis

Best practice	Departures from best practice	Issues
Replace any DIS temporarily.	Replace the limited DIS too readily.	When does an override become necessary?
Extend full coverage.	Full coverage is offered too readily.	When does full coverage become necessary?
Let it be known that full coverage is only temporary.	High or full coverage is available for too long, even continuously.	How to remove a full guarantee?
Have government backing for the fund.	The fund becomes insolvent and/or illiquid.	Reconciling interests of bankers and taxpayers.

Source: Lindgren and Garcia (1996).

when the DIS is insolvent or illiquid, the authorities may be reluctant to close failed banks.

Deposit Insurance Practices Around the World

International Monetary Fund staff recently conducted a survey of 50 different systems of explicit deposit insurance in selected countries (for details of this survey see Lindgren and Garcia 1996). Of these 50 countries 4 are in Africa, 12 in the Americas, 7 in Asia, 23 in Europe, and 4 in the Middle East (table 15.3). The survey throws some light on the extent to which countries have adopted best practices.

While two of the three systems in the United States were started in the 1930s, other countries did not begin to adopt systems of deposit protection until the 1960s and later. As figure 15.1 shows, 9 schemes were initiated in the 1960s and 6 in the 1970s. As the incidence of banking crises escalated in the 1980s, 17 were initiated during the decade, and 15 new DISs commenced in the first 7 years of the 1990s as banking problems continue to spring up on all continents.

To avoid the problem of adverse selection, 41 of the schemes surveyed were compulsory (figure 15.2). Nevertheless, 7 were voluntary and none of these imposed risk-adjusted premiums as an alternative way to combat adverse selection.

As concerns types of deposits covered, 8 systems covered deposits of all types and 14 covered most kinds (figure 15.3). By contrast, 12 DISs excluded foreign currency deposits, 36 did not cover interbank deposits, and 8 guaranteed only household deposits. Schemes that discriminate between types of deposit face an additional administrative burden.

Thirty-eight of the DISs maintained a deposit insurance fund, while 9 imposed ex post levies on surviving banks when failure occurred, and 39 charged premiums (figure 15.4). Nineteen assessed premiums on deposits of all types, while 14 assessed only insured deposits. While the latter procedure is fairer in that it avoids the cross-subsidization of insured depositors by uninsured depositors, it is more complex to administer.

To reduce moral hazard, 43 systems limited the coverage they offered (figure 15.5); however, coverage was often high and considerably exceeded the one to two times per capita GDP rule of thumb to assess coverage (see Kyei 1995; Lindgren and Garcia 1996) Four DISs covered each deposit individually, even if a depositor held several accounts at the failed bank. Most countries (45) applied the coverage limit to the sum of the deposits that a depositor held at a failed bank. Five systems offered full coverage. Some of

Table 15.3. *Countries with Explicit Deposit Insurance Systems*

Africa	Americas	Asia	Europe	Middle East
Kenya	Argentina	Bangladesh	Austria	Bahrain
Nigeria	Brazil	India	Belgium	Kuwait
Tanzania	Canada	Japan	Bulgaria	Lebanon
Uganda	Chile	Marshall Islands	Czech Republic	Oman
	Colombia	Micronesia	Denmark	
	Dominican Republic	Philippines	Finland	
	El Salvador	Taiwan (China)	France	
	Mexico		Germany	
	Peru		Greece	
	Trinidad and Tobago		Hungary	
	United States		Iceland	
	Venezuela		Ireland	
			Italy	
			Luxembourg	
			Netherlands	
			Norway	
			Poland	
			Portugal	
			Spain	
			Sweden	
			Switzerland	
			Turkey	
			United Kingdom	

Source: Lindgren and Garcia (1996).

Figure 15.1. *The Decade the DIS First Began*

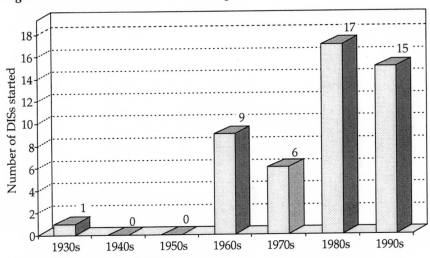

Source: Lindgren and Garcia (1996).

Figure 15.2. *Legal Status of DIS Schemes*

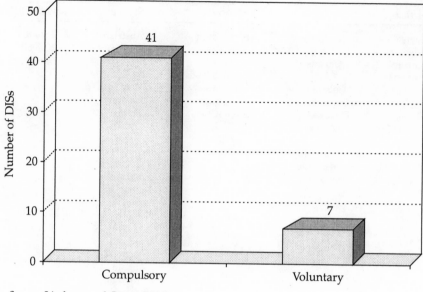

Source: Lindgren and Garcia (1996).

Figure 15.3. *Types of Deposits Covered*

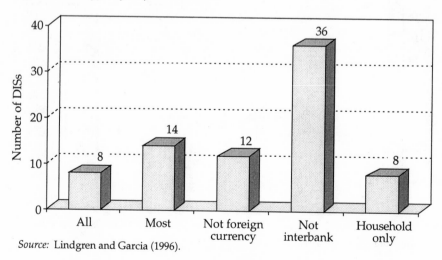

Source: Lindgren and Garcia (1996).

Figure 15.4. *Types of Funding*

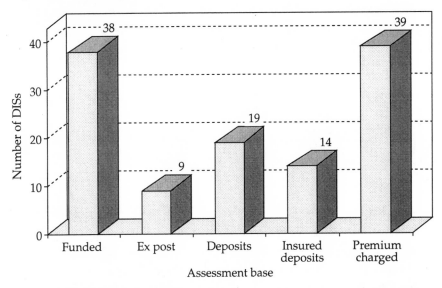

Source: Lindgren and Garcia (1996).

Figure 15.5. *Deposit Coverage*

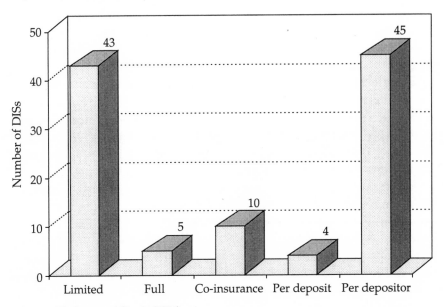

Source: Lindgren and Garcia (1996).

the countries that offered full coverage had done so when declaring a financial emergency, with the intention of replacing full emergency coverage with a limited system when the banking system became sound. Sweden has already followed this course and Finland plans to do so. Ten systems used co-insurance to combat moral hazard.

Of the 50 systems surveyed, 46 were privately funded, although 33 have received financial help from official sources either to get the system started or when it faced a systemic crisis (figure 15.6).

DIS administration varied widely from country to country: 11 of the schemes were privately administered, the government ran 23 of the schemes, and 14 were jointly operated (figure 15.7).

Conclusions

While banks are important to the economy, they are vulnerable to illiquidity and insolvency. For these reasons, most governments have chosen to implement a financial safety net to deal with these contingencies. A system of depositor protection that guards the holders of small deposits when their bank fails has, in recent years, become part of this safety net in a growing number of countries. A well-designed DIS can strengthen incentives for good governance for banks through internal governance from owners and managers, discipline from the markets, and oversight from bank regulation and supervision, but a poorly designed system will impair all three strands of discipline and lead to a deterioration in the soundness of the banking system. Consequently, an important lesson to be learned from country experiences is that good design is essential.

Experience has also taught that a DIS faces problems of incentive compatibility for owners, managers, depositors, borrowers, regulators, and politicians. A well-designed DIS needs to build good incentives for all these groups. It can, for instance, promote good internal governance by forcing the closure of critically undercapitalized institutions, making membership compulsory, and charging risk-adjusted premiums. It can encourage sophisticated creditors to exert market discipline by providing only low coverage and disclosing good information about the condition of individual banks. The DIS and the supervisory authority should both be able to rely on political independence to limit politicians' encouragement for forbearance. Nevertheless, both authorities need to be held accountable to avoid regulatory capture and to ensure that their actions serve the public interest. Unfortunately, these best practices are all too frequently violated.

Figure 15.6. *Funding Sources*

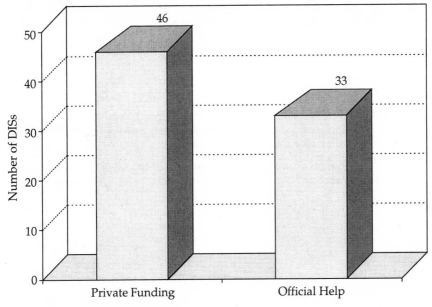

Source: Lindgren and Garcia (1996).

Figure 15.7. *Administration*

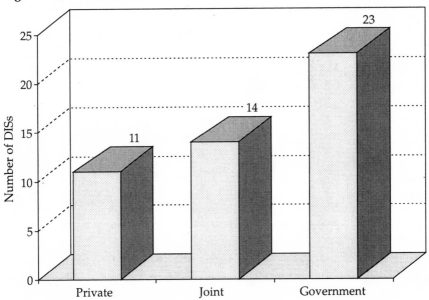

Source: Lindgren and Garcia (1996).

References

Garcia, Gillian. 1996. "Deposit Insurance: Obtaining the Benefits and Avoiding the Pitfalls." Working Paper no. 96/83. International Monetary Fund, Washington, D. C.

Kane, Edward J. 1995. "Three Paradigms for the Role of Capitalization Requirements in Insured Financial Institutions." *Journal of Banking and Finance* 19 (June): 431–59.

Kyei, Alexander. 1995. "Deposit Protection Arrangements: A Survey." Working Paper no. 95/134. International Monetary Fund, Washington, D. C.

Lindgren, Carl-Johan, and Gillian Garcia. 1996. "Deposit Insurance and Crisis Management." Monetary and Exchange Affairs Department Operational Paper no. 96/3. International Monetary Fund, Washington, D. C.

Lindgren, Carl-Johan, Gillian Garcia, and Matthew I. Saal. 1996. "Bank Soundness and Macroeconomic Policy." International Monetary Fund, Washington, D. C.

16

Understanding and Preventing Bank Crises

Edward J. Kane

What the public perceives as a banking crisis is best understood as an open, and typically prolonged, struggle between economic sectors. The struggle is about how to allocate across society an unpaid bill for losses that have accumulated or are still accumulating at banks. Two categories of policy tools exist for managing a banking crisis, namely, (a) remedies to be used once a crisis surfaces, and (b) preventive measures whose socially advantageous use is restrained by political pressure for adopting weak supervisory systems. As in so many other human endeavors, an ounce of well-placed prevention is worth many ounces of cure.

Life Cycle of a Banking Crisis

Banking crises typically pass through five distinct stages as follows:

1. *Embryonic stage.* A subsurface festering of hidden bank losses emerges repeatedly during the expansionary phase of every nation's business cycle. Incentives exist for banks to take on unacknowledged risks and surreptitiously to accrue unbooked losses that exceed the absorptive capacity of banking capital and explicit insurance funds. The precise causes of bank losses vary somewhat from cycle to cycle and from country to country, but six major components that cause loss may be discerned, namely:
   - Overly aggressive bank underwriting. Bad loans may look attractive even to strong banks for one of the three following principal reasons:

- — Rapid entry of new institutions, because entry squeezes profit margins and creates pressure for existing banks to fight for market share
- — Weaknesses in the information borrowers supply to bank lending officers
- — Political pressure that favors well-connected people and specific economic sectors.
- Insufficient diversification of well-understood, but concentrated, risks.
- Poor provisioning in accounting statements for anticipatable loan losses.
- Occurrence of unfavorable macroeconomic and balance of payment shocks.
- Inefficiencies in bureaucratic decisionmaking that are inherent in state ownership of banks. Inefficiencies tend to convert loans, at least partly, into outright gifts. Resistance to booking the implied gifts as accounting losses has proven to be a nasty problem for transition economies, one that makes enlisting local and foreign private capital on easy terms hard for banks in these countries.
- Bank managers' ability to hide risks and financial weaknesses from depositors and other outsiders. This ability is enhanced by
  - — Uninformative accounting systems for reporting bank income and net worth
  - — Weaknesses in the domestic system of bank supervision
  - — Conditions that create strong implicit and explicit deposit insurance protection for depositors and other bank creditors.

2. *Accelerating risk-shifting stage.* Distortion in risk-taking incentives is intensified as loan losses absorb more and more of a bank's economic capital. Managers begin to recognize that they will lose their jobs unless their bank scores some outlandish profits. In this stage, bank managers intensify their risk-taking and loss-causing activities. They slide into patterns of looting and go-for-broke risk taking. This stage is also marked by the beginning of silent runs and an increasing collateralization of deposits owned by informed customers. When the first diagnosis of impending crisis occurs, information that triggers aggressive loss shifting begins to move across a universe of differentially well-informed stakeholders. The supervisory authorities gamble that they can finesse the pain of expressly allocating losses to taxpayers by adopting strategies that combine cheerful public statements with ineffective disciplinary action that buys them some time.

3. *Emergency room hospitalization stage.* As more depositors become informed about the insolvencies, the silent run generates more and more noise. Evidence of loss shifting becomes palpable and leads to a spreading loss of public confidence in the banking system. Customer access to bank accounts is reduced and conflict about loss distribution moves overtly into the political arena. Two symptoms characterize the transition from the second stage to the third stage:
   - The nation's news media begin to feature stories about sky-high deposit rates, and even about depositor runs.
   - Authorities begin openly to debate plans for assigning losses via bailouts, mergers, or closures. This phase may drag on for years, as it has in Japan, or it may last only a few weeks.

4. *Recapitalization stage.* Recapitalization occurs when a combination of cures absorbs or softens losses. The easiest cure occurs when good luck unfolding in the nation's macroeconomic and balance of payments environments restores troubled bank assets to health. The cumulative exit of a substantial number of ruined banks during the hospitalization stage further enhances the health of surviving banks. The resulting reduction in competitive pressure dramatically improves expected future profit margins for industry survivors. The capitalized value of improved future profit projections constitutes an inflow of intangible private capital. The further injection of free (or nearly free) implicit and explicit bailout capital from the government, that is, from taxpayers, usually plays an important part in rebuilding the value of equity shares.

5. *Incentive reform and blame distribution stage.* Highly selective prosecution of dishonest bankers for civil or criminal transgressions helps taxpayers to put the process behind them. Typically, the government selects whom to prosecute for what types of behaviors to reinforce its preferred characterization of the causes of the crisis. This characterization is almost always a propagandistic effort to shift blame to designated scapegoats. Court cases generate a flow of news that the government can and does manage to whitewash well-connected parties who deserve to be held to account. Bankers' incentives to renew the cycle of loss shifting are often wished away. Even when the authorities adopt genuine reforms, risk-shifting opportunities are eventually renewed. This is because the learning experience fades rapidly from taxpayers' memory as the crisis recedes into the past. As time passes, bank lobbyists can successfully lobby to eliminate supervisory rules whose burden would make sense if the lessons of previous crises remained current.

Unintended Perversity of Deposit Insurance

Explicit deposit insurance prevents either aggressive bank risk-shifting or the ebb and flow of economywide events from harming covered deposits. Precisely for this reason, deposit insurance reduces incentives for insured depositors to take the trouble to inform themselves about expanding bank loss exposures or to respond to bad news about their bank when evidence of its distress first surfaces. In this way, deposit insurance can permit small problems to fester and to cumulate into massive problems whenever a country's regulators choose to delay confronting losses and risk taking at the banks under their jurisdiction.

A recent World Bank-International Monetary Fund study (Demirgüç-Kunt and Detragiache 1997) confirms this perversity based on a careful econometric examination of banking crises in 65 countries during 1981–94. The study finds robust evidence that, controlling for the effects of macroeconomic and balance of payments influences, the probability that a country will undergo a financial crisis is higher if a country has an explicit deposit insurance scheme than if it does not.

To appreciate the policy implications of this finding, one can use finance theory to benchmark the optimal postloan response of creditors who encounter evidence of trouble at their bank. In the absence of either explicit or implicit government guarantees, a bank's creditors will discipline any bank that expands its leveraged risk taking or that seems to be experiencing opportunity cost losses. This discipline forces a troubled bank either to shrink, to raise more capital, or to pay higher interest rates for borrowed funds.

As guarantors of bank debt, deposit insurers may be seen as stepping into the shoes of the depositors whose positions they insure (Black, Miller, and Posner 1978). The policy scandal is that deposit insurance, as administered in contemporary times, is rarely accompanied by market-mimicking patterns of monitoring and regulatory response to evidence of bank weakness or aggressiveness. Demirgüç-Kunt and Detragiache's (1997) evidence implies that disciplinary forbearance is higher when an explicit deposit insurance scheme exists than when it does not. It also implies that the crucial and unsolved problem in deposit insurance is how to make it in regulators' self-interest to exercise market-mimicking discipline when and as an institution weakens or lends aggressively.

This is a stubborn problem, because in tough economic times, strong counterincentives against market-mimicking regulatory behavior support regulatory forbearance. Counterincentives may be portrayed as "carrots" and "sticks." On the one hand, sticks of disinformational public criticism that well-placed spokespersons for banking institutions routinely issue against stern disciplinary action support forbearance. Bankers can easily accuse regulators of creating a credit crunch and kicking the nation's banks when they are down. This kind of criticism threatens to damage the professional reputation of any regulators who dutifully transmit market-mimicking pressures to distressed banks. On the other hand, carrots of subtle, incentive-based compensation make forbearance attractive. Incentive payments come in two forms: an immediate flow of "campaign contributions" to elected officials and an implicit promise of postgovernment job opportunities to any top regulators who manage to complete their term in office without stepping on the toes of the regulated industry.

In stressful times, direct and indirect industry pressure on regulators is intense. For top regulators, the path of least resistance is to use accounting leeway to cover up evidence of developing banking weakness. Following this path means that in tough economic times officials deliberately communicate to taxpayers an inaccurate picture of the true opportunity costs of their regulatory policy decisions. To remove this temptation, taxpayers and what we may call "safe-driver banks" must wake up to the risks that deposit insurance conveys to them. They must demand changes in regulators' information and reporting systems and in the employment contracts that society writes with regulatory managers. To overcome regulators' incentives to mismeasure banking losses and taxpayer loss exposures, taxpayers must subject top regulators to personal penalties and tie these penalties carefully to reproducible estimates of the monetary damages that taxpayers suffer when they are asked to rely on disinformation.

Reworking Regulatory Incentives

Repeated occurrences around the world of regulatory forbearance that is damaging to taxpayers indicate that something is wrong with regulatory incentives. Looking at government deposit insurance systems as taxpayer owned corporations, the fundamental problem with government deposit insurance can be described as an agency cost that is supported by inadequate creditor and stockholder discipline on the managers of the deposit insurance system. What lessens and delays taxpayers' ability to discipline regulators is their need to test and decode disinformation. By disinformation I mean half-truths that industry lobbyists or public officials introduce to lead the media and taxpayers to draw erroneous conclusions about the wisdom and beneficiaries of poorly conceived policies. Authorities must be given incentives to characterize the quality of their supervisory performance truthfully to enable the press and other outside experts to help taxpayers to monitor the performance of bank regulators more effectively.

Kane (1987) likens the problem of deposit insurance reform to the problem of readying police cars and their drivers to succeed in the task of chasing getaway cars operated by bank robbers and risk shifters. In every country in the world, unexploited opportunities exist to improve deposit insurance vehicles and to enhance the skills and incentives of these vehicles' drivers to assure better policing.

To engineer the best possible fleet of police cars, regulatory system engineers should repeatedly examine the complete catalogue of feasible upgrades for their deposit insurance automobiles. Upgrades may be envisioned as relating to the four interdependent automotive subsystems on which a real-world police driver relies, namely:

- The information subsystem (windshield, wipers, windows)
- The monitoring subsystem (angles of the driver's seat and rear-view mirrors)
- The regulatory response subsystem (power controls, brakes, and steering)
- The incentive subsystem (how recoverable funds are divided between the robbers, police, and rightful owners).

The Information Subsystem

Improving the information subsystem is the most important area of reform. The goal is to give drivers an optimal degree of vision. The commonsense of this is simple enough. A police car's windshield, side windows, and rear window should not be permitted to become blemished or highly tinted. Keeping each surface clean at all times should also be possible. In particular, it is important to assure that the car's windows do not routinely fog up at critical times in the chase.

In deposit insurance, the accounting principles used to report bank and regulator performance govern the information subsystem. Good vision requires meaningful information about bank performance and portfolio values. The criterion for meaningfulness is what a private guarantor with good incentives would want to know about the bank. Such a guarantor would examine the bank's expanded balance sheet. This balance sheet would incorporate all sources of value to the bank, including the capitalized value of intangible assets and liabilities, such as guarantees, commitments, customer relationships, and fee-for-service business. On this balance sheet managers would be required to enter their best estimates of the market value (that is, the opportunity cost) of all items. A private guarantor would also require each institution to account in a reproducible way for the overall loss exposure that the institution transmits to the deposit insurer. Finally, a private guarantor would enforce these reporting requirements by establishing strongly nonlinear penalties for banks and managers that can be proved after the fact to have filed fraudulent or negligent reports.

The Monitoring Subsystem

In police car chases monitoring relates to how frequently and where an automobile's design features encourage the driver to look at the road. The analogue for deposit insurance is how bank examinations are targeted in frequency and in scope. The experience reviewed by Demirgüç-Kunt and Detragiache (1997) indicates that supervisory monitoring can be improved in three ways as follows:

- By placing greater focus on fraud detection, risk exposures, and risk management policies
- By requiring frequent electronic reporting of critical information
- By increasing the skills and reducing the turnover of bank examiners.

The Regulatory Response Subsystem

Group of Ten (G-10) countries have made measures of a bank's risk-based capital position the centerpiece of modern banking supervision. Some observers believe that the G-10 system can, with only a few minor adjustments, be adapted for effective use by other countries as well. I hold this view to be simplistic.

The police car analogy is intended to clarify that the G-10 risk-based system is inefficient because it mismeasures and mismonitors its central elements of bank risk and bank capital. The system seeks to control accounting numbers rather than economic values and seeks to use balance sheet restrictions to overcome weaknesses that could be more cheaply addressed by adjustments in regulators' information, monitoring, and incentive systems. These restrictions restrain accounting capital, restrict what activities a bank may undertake, and limit acceptable degrees of balance sheet mismatch. Overworking these restrictions imposes costly burdens on safe-driver banks, burdens that do not protect strong banks and taxpayers from exploitation by aggressive banks at macroeconomically stressful times.

The Incentive Subsystem

Authorities have a strong interest in protecting their professional reputations. This gives officials an incentive to cover up increases in the accumulating losses and loss exposures that banks shift onto government deposit insurance funds during their particular term in office. To be able to counteract this incentive in troubled times, public service contracts must offer top regulatory officials a strongly nonlinear counterincentive. Public service contracts must encourage officials to recognize increases in losses and loss exposures in a timely fashion and to remedy emerging problems promptly. The first step is to reduce the power regulatory officials now enjoy to suppress information about bank performance that is also relevant for assessing regulatory performance. At a minimum, this implies that the examination ratings that regulators assign to individual banks should be available for inspection by academics and the press. It also implies that the pricing and loss control systems any government deposit insurer employs should—as a matter of statute—be tested regularly in global markets for private reinsurance or subordinated debt. Whenever these systems prove uneconomic in private markets for reinsurance or subordinated debt, officials and taxpayers should treat this finding not as evidence of a failure of private insurance or securities markets, but as a signal that the authorities need to reprice and rework their coverage schemes until their loss exposures can be economically reinsured.

The second step in incentive reform is to introduce incentive compensation into the public service contracts written between society and top financial regulators. Incentives to remedy problems promptly could be enhanced if ex post monetary penalties were visited on top regulators not merely if deposit insurance losses happen to surface during their watch, but also if what can be proved to have been anticipatable losses accrue within, say, 18 months of a responsible official's departure from office. A workable way to bond this penalty scheme would be to set up a fund of deferred compensation (or pension payments) for top regulators. The size of the fund would be an addition to current wages. Its value would be set both to compensate officials for their increased human capital risk and to bond the truthfulness of the regulatory performance measurements they report during their time in office.

Summary

Technological advances in managing financial risk can be seen as parallel to those that have been built into modern automobiles. Today, experts can design much more comfortable and reliable automobiles and deposit insurance systems than they could in the past. The object of financial reform should be to strengthen every link in the four-part chain of regulatory subsystems in a balanced fashion.

Authorities in most countries are eager to establish a safety net for banks and to operate a system of legal controls on fraudulent behavior in financial transactions. What they have not proved eager to do is to operate the safety net and fraud controls at minimum cost to taxpayers and safe-driver banks.

Three kinds of agency costs exist in bank regulation: (a) the costs taxpayers incur in monitoring and constraining regulators, (b) the costs regulators incur in submitting to taxpayer monitoring and discipline and in voluntarily bonding their performance, and (c) the residual waste and damage taxpayers suffer when the financial system is stressed because of the defects they tolerate in monitoring and enforcing regulators' contractual duties and in bonding regulatory performance. Whenever the marginal costs of the first two categories of agency cost are held at inordinately low levels, taxpayer damage is bound to prove inefficiently high.

References

Black, Fisher, Merton Miller, and Richard Posner. 1978. "An Approach to the Regulation of Bank Holding Companies." *Journal of Business* 51 (July): 379–411.

Demirgüç-Kunt, A., and Enrica Detragiache. 1997. "The Determinants of Banking Crises: Evidence from Developed and Developing Countries." World Bank and International Monetary Fund, Washington, D.C.

Kane, Edward J. 1987. "No Room for Weak Links in the Chain of Deposit Insurance Reform." *Journal of Financial Services Research* 1 (September): 77–111.

17

Banking Crises in Perspective: Two Causes and One Cure

Geoffrey P. Miller

To paraphrase Tolstoy, every banking crisis is a crisis in a different way; every period of good fortune in banking is fortunate alike. So it might appear from reading the many well-informed and thoughtful accounts of banking disasters in widely different economic systems, some of them contained in this volume. Yet the apparent divergence of crises and convergence of periods of stability may be illusory. We are interested in the causes of crises because we want to avoid their recurrence, and we investigate in detail the particular features of individual episodes. We pay less attention to the distinguishing features of periods of banking stability.

The Two Main Causes of Banking Crises

Banking crises in different countries do not vary as much as might appear to be the case. When one reads the accounts of banking crises in various countries at an abstract level, only two avoidable causes of banking crises are apparent: bad macroeconomic policy and bad regulation.

Bad macroeconomic policy can be in the form of inappropriate monetary policy, for example, the Fed's failure to inject sufficient liquidity into the system during the Depression, or the Bank of Japan's excessively loose policy during 1987–89, the period of the bubble economy (Miller 1996c). It can also take the form of an ill-advised exchange rate policy, as in the case of a devaluation that destabilizes a nation's banking system (and possibly other nations' systems as well). An example is the Mexican peso devaluation of December 1994, which affected not only Mexico, but also Argentina and other countries (Miller 1996b).

Bad regulation typically takes the form of government policies that enhance moral hazard, coupled with poor supervision (see Kaufman 1997). Often the effects are felt during periods of liberalization in which the regulatory structure fails to keep pace with rapid changes either in markets or in laws. The U.S. savings and loan crisis falls in this category. The deregulation of deposit interest rates during the early 1980s, which was itself a response to the Fed's macroeconomic policies of the late 1970s, radically changed the character of the depository institution business by allowing banks and savings and loan institutions to compete for deposits on a nationwide basis. Such competition in itself may not have been destabilizing, and clearly served important goals, but the government's failure to reform the deposit insurance safety net led to a situation not unlike the "O" rings in the space shuttle Challenger: flat-rate, effectively infinite deposit insurance, coupled with interest rate competition for deposits, reversed the role of the price system by directing investor funds to the poorest and most risky depository institutions that were willing to pay the highest interest rates. The disaster in the U.S. banking industry of the 1980s was just as inevitable, in retrospect, as the explosion of the space shuttle (Barth 1991; Macey and Miller 1997). Banking crises in other countries have often followed the pattern of rapid liberalization along with inadequate supervision, followed by widespread failures.

These two causes—poor macroeconomic policy and bad regulation—are preventable causes of banking crises. Some crises may simply be unavoidable, for example, severe external shocks to a nation's economy may destabilize its banking system even if the authorities handle macroeconomic policy and banking regulation relatively well. However, examples of a purely exogenous crisis are hard to find. Nearly always, macroeconomic failures, regulatory failures, or both can be identified as proximate causes. Yet we cannot rule out the possibility that a sufficiently large and unexpected external shock may be enough, in itself, to trigger a banking crisis in a particular country, particularly if that country has a small, open economy that is not insulated either by size or by barriers to capital flows against the effect of sudden and unexpected changes in world economic conditions.

If macroeconomic policy and regulation are the only two causes of banking crises, one might think that avoiding banking crises would be relatively easy. Unfortunately, this is not the case, for a number of reasons. One of the most important reasons is that bad macroeconomic policies and misguided regulation may be easy to spot ex post, but difficult to identify before the fact: foresight in identifying the causes of banking crises is as rare as hindsight is ubiquitous. Take the interest rate deregulation of the U.S. banking industry. Virtually no one fully appreciated the relationship between deposit interest rates and deposit insurance that would precipitate the savings and loan crisis. After the fact, the flaw in the regulatory design was obvious, but at the time, only a few prescient analysts pointed out the problem.

For another example consider the case of Japan's monetary policy blunders around the period of the bubble economy. In the light of hindsight, it appears obvious that the Japanese economy during 1987–89 was in the midst of a speculative boom unjustified by the economic fundamentals, but at the time it was far from clear that the good times were a transitory boom rather than a permanent enhancement in Japan's wealth. Price-earnings ratios on the Tokyo stock exchange appeared excessive, but plenty of financial analysts concluded that these numbers were justified by the underlying economic fundamentals. There was no inflation on the horizon. At the time, many believed that Japan really was in the midst of an economic miracle.

The case of Japan should be a sobering lesson for U.S. policymakers today. Like Japan of the bubble period, since 1995 the United States has experienced the rosiest of economic conditions: share market prices have been increasing rapidly for three years, with the stock market regularly reaching new records; unemployment, as in Japan during the bubble period, is at exceptionally low levels; and despite the push on wages that might be expected from a full employment economy, there is little or no sign of inflation. Until recently, asset price increases in the United States were limited to the equities market, and real estate had been fairly quiet, but mid-1996 through mid-1997 witnessed upward pressure on rents and sales prices in urban areas, both in the commercial and residential real estate markets. Unlike Japan, an enormous flow of credit to real estate development has not occurred, but the United States is awash in credit at the consumer level, with close to $2 trillion in outstanding credit card lines and rapidly increasing levels of home equity borrowing. Is the U.S. in the midst of a bubble economy? A few doomsayers have suggested as much, but their voice has been drowned in the general euphoria. Although Alan Greenspan attempted to douse the fires with dour comments about "irrational exuberance" in the stock market, the market shrugged off his warnings and continued to hit record highs. Only time will tell whether these good economic conditions represent economic fundamentals or an unjustified period of financial speculation.

The problems of identifying bad macroeconomic policy and inappropriate regulations are exacerbated by the political obstacles that policymakers often face in responding to problems even when they are apparent. In the case of Japan's bubble economy, for example, the Bank of Japan faced a daunting set of impediments to tightening policy. The United States was putting pressure on Japan to maintain loose monetary conditions to stimulate Japan's domestic economy, and thereby increase the demand for U.S. imports. The Bank of Japan faced pressure not to take actions that might have adversely affected share market prices in the wake of the stock market crash of October 1987. Perhaps most important, the bank faced political opposition from powerful interest groups, including politicians who were getting rich from the share and real estate market price increases of the bubble era. Any action by the bank against the bubble economy could have encountered severe political and diplomatic opposition. Given that Japan's economy seemed to be roaring along and the virtual absence of any signs of inflation, the bank's delayed intervention against the bubble until it was well developed is not surprising. Although the bank subsequently admitted error in not acting sooner, whether it could have done otherwise is not clear.

The Narrow Bank Concept

Thus relatively severe epistemological and political factors inhibit policymakers' ability to devise appropriate responses to the danger of banking crises. Even though we can often understand what happened in retrospect, taking the necessary concrete actions to prevent a crisis from occurring ex ante is much more difficult. However, we have some reason for optimism that constructive reforms may yet be implemented. One of the most promising such reforms has been well known in policy circles since the 1930s, although it is known by a variety of different names: the narrow or mutual fund bank. A narrow bank is simply a bank that offers transaction accounts and fully backs deposits by investing in a well-diversified pool of highly secure, short-term securities. The intellectual origin of the narrow bank was a proposal by Henry Simons and others at the University of Chicago for 100 percent reserve banks—proposals that themselves originated in the American banking crisis of 1933 (see Simons 1948). More recently, the concept was dubbed a narrow bank and espoused by a number of policy analysts as a secure alternative to commercial banks or thrift institutions that offer payment services by means of demand deposits (see Litan 1987, for example). More recently, narrow banking has been advocated as a useful way for traditionally vulnerable economies in Latin America to cope with moral hazard and banking crises (Fernandez and Schumacher 1996; Miller 1996a).

The advantages of a narrow bank are obvious. Because its assets are fully collateralized by short-term money market instruments, the chances of a run on such an institution are virtually none. With full disclosure depositors know that their funds are backed by adequate collateral, and therefore have no reason to lose confidence in their banks. Even a liquidity run is virtually impossible. With assets fully invested in money market instruments, a narrow bank can cash out its investments in a matter of hours to meet even unanticipated demands by depositors. Even greater security can be achieved if the narrow bank promises to pay its depositors their share of the net asset value of the institution at any particular time—as in the case of money market mutual funds—because the claim of depositors in such an institution is in the form of demand equity rather than demand debt. There is little or no premium to withdrawing funds early from a money market mutual fund, as all investors receive only their pro rata share of net asset value. Given the extremely low probability of catastrophic failure, the narrow bank could be insured, either by the federal government or by a private sector insurer, at a fairly low insurance premium.

A regime of narrow banking is perfectly consistent with the existence of "broad banks," which would continue to operate as banks do now. However, if narrow banking is to play a role in preventing banking crises, broad banks should preferably not be funded with demand debt. Broad banks could continue to provide credit to the full range of borrowers commercial banks currently serve, including individuals and small and medium-size businesses. Such broad banks could issue term debt in financial markets— including very short-term debt such as commercial paper—but would be prohibited by law from offering demand deposit accounts. Broad banks already exist, for example, many consumer finance companies fund their operations in securities markets and advance loans to customers. "Monoline" credit card companies, although chartered as ordinary commercial banks and appropriately treated as banks for many regulatory purposes, in reality operate like broad banks to the extent that they depend for their financing on issues of securitized credit card receivables rather than on-demand deposits. These institutions could fail, but they are not subject to destabilizing runs because their debt is in the form of term securities rather than accounts withdrawable on demand.

Such a regime of narrow banking, which to a great extent matches the duration of assets and liabilities on the balance sheet and substantially eliminates

284 Banking Crises in Perspective: Two Causes and One Cure

the run risk that plagues the commercial bank structure, might appear obviously preferable to the traditional form of the banking firm as a way to facilitate a payments system. However, if a narrow bank enjoys so many advantages, why does it not already dominate the banking industry? I believe that the answer to this puzzle is not that the narrow bank suffers from any type of intrinsic flaw. Rather, conditions for the growth of a substantial number of narrow banks were, until recently, not present in the U.S. economy, and are still not present in the economies of many developing countries. A narrow bank requires a large and well-developed market in short-term financial assets in which to invest depositors' funds. Today, the United States is well supplied with short-term money market instruments, and narrow banks, that is, money market mutual funds, have no difficulty in investing all their assets, but short-term money markets were not nearly as well developed in the past. Narrow banks cannot exist in the absence of well-developed money markets because they lack the markets in which to purchase assets. Today, however, there is no market impediment to the development of narrow banks in the United States—and we observe them. As already noted, the money market mutual fund with checking privileges is nothing more than a narrow bank by another name.

Could narrow banking provide a cure for banking crises? This would be overly optimistic: banking crises can occur for a variety of reasons other than runs on the payments system. Nevertheless, narrow banking could clearly add stability and mitigate the effects of crises when they occur. If the public has confidence that the assets of a narrow bank are, as promised, invested in liquid and safe money market instruments, such narrow banks are not likely to experience the hemorrhage of withdrawals that typically occurs to commercial banks during a banking crisis. The payments system would be more secure, and the costs of ensuring it lower. In short, narrow banking, while not a panacea, offers great promise as a method for reducing instability in banking markets, particularly in developing countries.

Why, then, are countries with traditionally vulnerable banking markets not adopting narrow banking? Two principal reasons appear to account for this. First, while money markets in the United States have evolved to the point where the liquidity and volume to support a large narrow banking sector are plentiful, the same is not true for many developing countries, which are just beginning to foster the development of money markets in their domestic economies. Of course, narrow banks in developing countries could invest their assets in international markets, including the United States, where short-term money markets are better developed, but issues of exchange risk would have to be dealt with, and developing country governments may not want to allow so much domestic capital to go abroad for political reasons. Thus until short-term money markets become better developed, narrow banking is unlikely to play as large a role as might otherwise be the case.

A second impediment to the development of narrow banking in developing economies is legal. Most countries do not support a legal structure in which mutual funds can offer checking privileges, and so a change in the law would be required. However, at present, a sufficiently well-developed domestic constituency to support such changes does not exist in many countries. Mutual funds are not well established, and when they are they are often affiliated with commercial banks that would naturally oppose a reform that relegated them to the status of pure financial intermediaries and removed their role as payments system agents. Banks and other interest groups are likely to fight any attempt to change the law to facilitate mutual fund banking.

Thus while mutual fund banking makes considerable theoretical sense as a device to control instability in the payments system, a number of practical and political constraints will probably prevent this device from achieving its promise in the near and intermediate future.

References

Barth, James R. 1991. *The Great Savings and Loan Debacle.* Washington, D. C.: The American Enterprise Institute.

Fernandez, Roque, and Liliana Schumacher. 1996. "Does Argentina Provide a Case for Narrow Banking?" In Suman K. Bery and Valeriano F. Garcia, eds., *Preventing Banking Sector Distress and Crises in Latin America.* Washington, D. C.: World Bank.

Kaufman, George G. 1997. "Preventing Banking Crises in the Future: Lessons from Past Mistakes." *The Independent Review* 2 (1): 55–78.

Litan, Robert. 1987. *What Should Banks Do?* Washington, D. C.: The Brookings Institution.

Macey, Jonathan R., and Geoffrey P. Miller. 1997. *Banking Law and Regulation,* 2nd ed. New York: Aspen Law and Business.

Miller, Geoffrey P. 1996a. "Banca de fondos mutuos para America Latina?" In Ernesto Aguirre, Roberto Junguito, and Geoffrey Miller, eds., *La Banca Central en America Latina.* Bogota, Colombia: Tercer Mundo S.A.

_____. 1996b. "Is Deposit Insurance Inevitable? Lessons from Argentina." *International Review of Law and Economics* 16 (2): 211–32.

_____. 1996c. "The Role of a Central Bank in a Bubble Economy." *Cardozo Law Review* 18 (2): 1053–82.

Simons, Henry. 1948. *Economic Policy for a Free Society.* Chicago: University of Chicago Press.

18

Bank Crises: Commonalities, Mistakes, and Lessons Viewed from a South Asian Standpoint

John Williamson

Like other countries, the nations of South Asia are seeking ways to overcome the severe banking difficulties they currently face. In India, for example, nonperforming loans amount to some 15 percent of the portfolio (though the proportion is declining); the figure stands at around 25 percent in Pakistan, where the new government has, with great determination, launched a program designed to stem the flow of new bad loans and to recover what is recoverable of the loans not being serviced; and is more than 35 percent in Bangladesh, where the government is also beginning to contemplate actions to address the situation.

Despite the level of nonperforming loans, the region has not experienced any bank runs. Anyone with experience in Latin America tends to be surprised at the way that bad news fails to provoke open crises in South Asia. I presume that this is because South Asia has little history of expropriating those who are too slow to get themselves at the front of the line, but instead tends to bail out all and sundry. This is both a blessing and a curse: a blessing because it means that policymakers who act promptly will have time for their corrective measures to take effect without being interrupted by a crisis, but a curse inasmuch as it gives policymakers who do not act promptly lots of rope with which to hang their long-suffering citizens.

Commonalities

The stylized description of a banking crisis that I have found most compelling is that of Gavin and Hausmann (1996). They see the origin of a bank crisis as lying in a credit boom (a theme often echoed during our conference), which leads to an erosion of asset quality, partly (most importantly, according to them) because bankers find it difficult to evaluate the quality of borrowers when lenders are competing to push money, and so virtually all borrowers can find the money to service their existing debts by borrowing from some source or other. If a macroeconomic crisis develops, perhaps for reasons quite unrelated to the credit boom, the flow of new loans will be interrupted and many of these marginal borrowers will find servicing their debts difficult. At that point the banks will find their bad debts multiplying, and if the public recognizes this and is not convinced that the process will end in a bailout, the possibility of a bank run emerges.

In seeking commonalities among bank crises, the natural question to ask is whether both elements in this story, careless lending during a prior credit boom and a macroeconomic crisis, are essential conditions for a bank crisis to occur. In theory the answer is surely no. One can envisage enough bad lending decisions to undermine a bank's financial integrity without the need for a macroeconomic crisis to change relative prices, cut demand, or otherwise jeopardize the ability of many existing borrowers to service their debts. Similarly, one can envisage a macroeconomic crisis so severe that changes in relative prices or a cut in demand prevent a multitude of borrowers from continuing to service their debts, even though these loans appeared perfectly prudent before the macroeconomic crisis developed. Not only are these circumstances imaginable, but we have heard of instances where they have actually occurred during the course of the conference. We heard yesterday from Paul Bydalek about the Brazilian state banks that became insolvent without any macroeconomic crisis (see chapter 6 in this volume). To that example I would add the public sector banks in Bangladesh and Pakistan, which have become insolvent primarily as a result of providing directed credit as ordered by the government to nonviable state enterprises. We also heard yesterday from Michael Mussa one very clear example of a banking crisis that was derivative to a macroeconomic crisis without any particularly bad prior lending, namely, in the United States during the Great Depression, while we heard from Javier Gonzalez Fraga a more recent, though slightly less clear case, namely, that of Argentina in 1991–94. Hence I conclude that there are no factors common to all bank crises.

Mistakes

Despite the lack of similarities, Honohan (1997) argues that all banking crises have originated from macroeconomic shocks, from careless lending, from government direction of credit, or from a combination (as in the Gavin Hausmann story). There is sufficient regularity to provide some guidance as to what should be avoided.

A first mistake is to acquiesce in a credit boom. No tried and trusted policy instruments are available with which to curb a credit boom comparable to open-market operations as a mechanism for curbing a monetary expansion, especially if macroeconomic policy is demanding low interest rates to keep demand up or the exchange rate from becoming overvalued. Nevertheless, when a capital inflow is feeding a credit boom, one possibility (as Chile and Colombia have demonstrated) is to impose reserve requirements on foreign loans to mitigate the inflow. Another is to raise reserve requirements in general if fungibility is too great to get leverage from a measure targeted against foreign capital. If an asset bubble is accompanying a credit boom, then one might hope also for measures like higher margin requirements.

A second mistake is to fail to precede or accompany financial liberalization by creating an effective system of prudential supervision. This is a textbook instance of the proposition that liberalization requires changing the state's role rather than eliminating its role: when the state gets out of the business of directing credit to particular enterprises, but lets the banks decide which loans offer the most attractive combination of return and risk, it needs to have in place a mechanism for ensuring that banks will not be tempted to select excessively risky loans in the hope that losses will ultimately be socialized while profits will remain private. A lot have been said on this topic during the conference, so I shall not elaborate further.

A third mistake is to indulge in macroeconomic policies of a character calculated to produce shocks, such as high fiscal deficits, overvalued real exchange rates (see Kaminsky, Lizondo, and Reinhart [1997], who suggest that an overvalued exchange rate is the best single leading indicator of a financial crisis), excessive current account deficits, or procyclical rather than Keynesian responses to changes in commodity prices.

Much of the discussion at this conference would lead one to add forbearance as a fourth mistake. I believe this needs qualification. Certainly one wants prompt corrective action as soon as it becomes apparent that a bank is in difficulty, rather than allowing it to hang on in the hope that events will take a turn for the better, otherwise costs usually explode. However, once banks have reformed their lending practices, there may be circumstances in which it makes sense to allow them to strengthen their balance sheets by maintaining high margins, even if this requires some delay in the timetable for financial liberalization. For example, given India's fiscal problems, requiring existing bank borrowers to pay for recapitalizing the banks may be more prudent than imposing this burden on the taxpayers.

Lessons

The World Bank is hoping that making sizable loans to both Bangladesh and Pakistan to support banking reform may be possible in the not too distant future. As a way to describe the lessons I have learned from banking crises, I will discuss the sorts of actions the Bank will need to see taken before it is prepared to sanction such loans.

In the first place, the Bank is not prepared to contemplate recapitalizing the banking systems until they have undergone fundamental reforms adequate to terminate bad lending. In Bangladesh they speak of the default culture, meaning that business people who borrow from the commercial banks feel no obligation to service their debts. (And this in the land of the Grameen Bank, whose poor women borrowers have a repayment rate of more than 98 percent!) The willful defaulters will either have to start repaying or be going to jail before the Bank lends for recapitalization. Note that this conflicts with Michael Borish's dictum yesterday that recapitalization should be up-front and one-time. The reason is that there seems to be a conflict between the two criteria, inasmuch as an up-front recapitalization would invite the perpetuation of bad lending, and the Bank gives priority to the need to make it a one-time event.

The fundamental reforms the Bank seeks encompass legal reforms to facilitate the recovery of collateral and to prohibit connected lending; governance reforms so that banks will be run by bankers (and not civil servants) who will spend enough time in office to have an impact, are appointed through a process that minimizes the chance of corruption, have the right to hire their own staff rather than having staff imposed on them by a central ministry or a trade union, and are allowed to establish the salaries they pay to enable them to attract good staff and to motivate them to work conscientiously; and a requirement for banks to upgrade their credit appraisal systems so they can decide for themselves which borrowers are good credit risks. In the longer term, the way to consolidate such changes is to privatize the banks. The Bank also hopes to see implementation of most of the reforms proposed by Goldstein, namely, transparency, disclosure, international accounting standards, capital adequacy, and so on (see chapter 13 in this volume). The Bank would certainly expect to see a prohibition of directed lending and the continuing pursuit of defaulters, and, of course, the introduction of a functioning system of supervision.

This conference has made me wonder whether there may not be a case for adding to the reforms that we urge. An attractive suggestion that the Bank might consider adding to its reform stipulations is that banks should be required to have part of their capital in the form of long-term, subordinated debt, so that the market has an incentive to ponder the creditworthiness of the banks, thereby providing a market measure of their risk exposure as a form of early warning of impending trouble. Another interesting idea is for bank shareholders to accept double liability.

References

Gavin, Michael, and Ricardo Hausmann. 1996. "The Roots of Banking Crises: The Macroeconomic Context." In R. Hausmann and L. Rojas-Suarez, eds., *Banking Crises in Latin America*. Washington, D. C.: Inter-American Development Bank.

Honohan, Patrick. 1997. "Banking System Failures in Developing and Transitional Countries: Diagnosis and Prediction." Working Paper no. 39. Bank for International Settlements, Basle, Switzerland.

Kaminsky, Graciela L., Saul Lizondo, and Carmen M. Reinhart. 1997. "Leading Indicators of Currency Crises." Working Paper no. 97/79. International Monetary Fund, Washington, D. C.

Part VI. Preventing Future Banking Crises: What Can and Should Be Done?

19

Suggestions for Improvements

Joseph Bisignano

The history of banking is a history of bank failures. Many of the reasons banks failed in the past are similar to reasons that cause them to fail today, that is, insufficient and inefficient internal and external regulation, or in other words, deficient risk management both from inside the institution and by outside market forces (shareholders and creditors) and official supervisory and regulatory bodies. The bankruptcies of the Bardi and Peruzzi Florentine merchant banking companies in the 14th century were the result of excessive sovereign lending: Edward III of England failed to pay back a total of 1.5 million gold florin. Insufficient diversification and capital was their undoing (Hunt 1990). Their decline was also related to political and economic instability in Florence during the 1340s. The next major Florentine banking failure was that of the Medici bank in the late 15th century, primarily because of the lack of serious banking training and only modest interest on the part of Lorenzo the Magnificent. Another cause was Lorenzo's insufficient corporate governance of Francesco Sassetti, to whom he had transferred all major banking powers (de Roover 1963). Poor internal controls led to major problems at the bank's branches in London and Lyon. Lorenzo, who had little in the way of banking acumen, was also deceived by false banking reports submitted by his agents. These same agents were also inadequately supervised by Lorenzo's chief operating officer, Sassetti. On top of that the Medici bank had political problems. A conspiracy in which Giuliano de Medici was killed and Lorenzo was injured was organized by the second largest Florentine banking family, the Pazzi. Thus risky sovereign lending, principal-agent problems, and shifting political and economic conditions brought down the major Florentine banks in the 14th and 15th centuries. As for irresponsible financial behavior on the part of government and its crippling influence on the financial system, we have only to look at 17th century France and the trial of Nicolas Fouquet (Dent 1973). Little wonder that the Netherlands succeeded Italy as a financial powerhouse and not France.

We might think that we have come a long way from the banking crises of the 15th, 16th, and 17th centuries, and in many ways we have. On the whole, major banking crises are fewer and governments are more capable of both preventing crises and limiting their impact when they occur. Yet while we may believe that we have a better understanding of the factors that have contributed to recent financial crises and are more confident in suggesting possible remedies, nonetheless, we do not appear confident. Part of this lack of confidence results from the size of some of the recent banking crises and their unexpected frequency.

Let me illustrate this lack of confidence by noting that recognizing the origins of recent banking problems is much easier than implementing feasible solutions or preventing their reoccurrence. Berg (chapter 11 in this volume) states that looking back on the Scandinavian banking crises, the modes of behavior are in most cases easily understood when one considers the environments in which decisions were taken, and that clearly bankers, lenders, and politicians would behave much differently if placed in similar positions in the future. Thus, he argues, this may mean that the financial system is inherently unstable when it becomes subject to extremely large disturbances. Cargill, Hutchison, and Ito (chapter 10 in this volume) also give us cause for concern when they argue that the real change needed to promote stability in the Japanese financial system is in policy attitude. Their concern centered on the lack of willingness to depart from the extensive system of deposit guarantees in Japan. And Corrigan (chapter 20 in this volume) notes that the most difficult thing to promote is a deeper credit culture, defined as the unspoken understanding among debtors and creditors that each has duties and responsibilities toward the other. He characterizes such a culture as grounded in a coherent and consistent set of laws, regulations, and judicial practices.

While governments, regulators, and financial market participants are now a bit wiser as a result of several recent banking crises, potential instability may remain, and may be part of the evolution of many financial systems. This evolution is in part a competition between organized markets and financial intermediaries, consistent with Coase's classic question of why a "firm" exists at all in a market economy. This competition has been a source of the weakness of some intermediaries who have lost their privileged position because of a relaxation of the constraints on financial intermediation, the development of new intermediaries and international capital markets, and the changes in the stock of financial intellectual capital. As Kindleberger (1992) notes, when the information advantage of any intermediary, either in commerce or finance, is lost, direct trading replaces intermediation.

The relaxation of constraints on intermediation, together with technological innovations and the removal of restrictions on capital flows, have made decisionmaking at many financial intermediaries more difficult, particularly for those unaccustomed to rapid technological change, disintermediation, and competition. The problem of financial stability is compounded when supervision is weak and inexperienced. Decisionmaking becomes increasingly subject to what Ellsberg (1961) once described as "ambiguity"; new environments create uncertainty about the causal process that is generating alternative outcomes. This is related to what Herring (chapter 12 in this volume) refers to as disaster myopia.

The ability to adjust to a new environment is made more difficult when information systems and corporate control mechanisms are inadequate, and when equilibrium asset prices are subject to uncertainty or ambiguity. The initial optimism about financial deregulation, both in industrial and in developing economies, is followed by surprise and shock when major financial institutions are brought to their knees, followed by further surprise when weakened governments are later seen kneeling beside them.

We can learn something about banking crises from economic historians who have studied the evolution of institutions. They have argued that when major changes occur in the economic environment, such as those brought about by rapid economic growth and financial deregulation, and in the absence of identifiable criteria for decisionmaking, modes of behavior rather than equilibrium conditions are what guide economic behavior (see, for example, Alchian 1950; North 1990). This behavior can be described as a search for institutional survival. Prudent behavior in a protected, if inefficient, financial institutional environment is sometimes replaced by aggressive, opportunistic behavior in a deregulated environment (for several good examples see Rotberg 1992). The instances here are many: the aggressive property and portfolio lending behavior of U.S. saving and loan associations, the rapid growth and speculative lending of Swedish finance companies, and the speculative French and Japanese property investments by a variety of financial intermediaries, all of which are examples of a major decline in concern with credit quality. Developing countries also provide us with plenty of examples of excessive lending, asset price explosions, and financial collapse.

Some financial institutions' inability to adjust to a new structural environment, their assumed privileged political position, the lack of efficient information and governance systems that would permit private markets to discipline them—or worse, government ownership or control—all help to "kick in" any and all explicit and implicit government support programs. In this environment of released constraints on intermediation and competition and rapid change in technical knowledge there is the potential problem of "opposite momentums," that is, excessive inertia on the part of the public sector, which is reluctant to intervene in a new economic environment even in the face of considerable speculative activity, as in real estate, and "excessive momentum" on the part of the private sector, where financial institutions are fighting for survival by expanding rapidly into new areas and lending aggressively. Official impediments that limit the ability of financial intermediaries to fail explicitly (the exit problem), such as government forbearance, ownership, or financial assistance, or to be taken over by other intermediaries, aggravate the problem and expand the financial hole to be later filled by the taxpayers.[1] In the recent past, both the public and the private sectors have misperceived risks related to major changes in the financial environment because of the existence of ambiguous risks or latent hazard problems; low-probability, high social cost events like the collapse of the exchange rate; or an asset price bubble. The difficulty of identifying equilibrium asset prices has made asset price bubble forbearance a nontrivial problem for public authorities.

One way to improve financial stability is through greater financial disclosure and improved accounting systems, but we should remember that differences in corporate financial disclosure systems among the major economies rest partly on the Anglo-Saxon preference for promoting equity markets, a preference all countries do not share. Limited financial disclosure in some countries is a protective devise against takeover. In many countries the survival motive causes firms to restrict shareholding, limit information disclosure, and seek close relationships with financial intermediaries and the government to protect them against takeover. Financial systems reflect much more than just alternative means of finance. They also represent protective mechanisms that managements use both in their

---

1. France provides an interesting example of the problem of excessive government protection and the use of banks as an instrument of economic policy, both resulting in their weakening (see Mauro and Robert 1997).

own interests and those of their owners. Financial information barriers are being broken down, but in many countries this is occurring slowly (for a comparison of different financial disclosure systems see Lowenstein 1996).

Because of the characteristic mismatch in the balance sheets of deposit-taking banks, in the past they have universally been heavily regulated, the most common form of regulation being the suppression of competition. Innovations in technology and finance in a few countries are driving banks in a direction that might be considered natural for an institution with liquid liabilities. This direction is to reduce the balance sheet mismatch by converting previously illiquid assets into more liquid ones and to transfer (sell) these assets to intermediaries with longer-term liabilities, that is, to institutional investors (namely, asset-backed securitization). This suggests that competition between intermediated and market-sourced finance, together with technological innovations, are to some extent pushing traditional banking intermediation in the direction of a more narrow bank and turning several banks into something resembling security firms.

Banks can originate loans, after screening loan applicants, and then securitize loan pools, providing contingent credit insurance. Promoted by innovations in information and financial technology, securitization can be looked upon as a market solution to a traditional imperfection in intermediation that previously required significant regulation and insurance to avoid instability. Advances in technology now permit the formation, servicing, and trading of securitized assets. This solution is not readily available, however, in financial systems with serious constraints on information availability or strong relational banking contracts.

An example of the search for survival behavior in banking is the current wave of mergers and acquisitions. While little empirical evidence confirms the existence of significant economies of scale in banking, we continue to see numerous mergers and acquisitions, often of large, healthy institutions. Although observers have suggested a variety of possible reasons for this acquisition activity, including economies of scale in back-office operations, greater interests of shareholders in increasing the market value of banks, and the impact of technology, research has not uncovered the reason for such a major change in bank acquisition behavior (see, for example, Amel 1996; Boyd and Graham 1991). The evidence continues to suggest relatively modest returns to scale in banking. Large bank acquisitions and mergers might, however, reflect the preferences of bank managers more than those of shareholders. These mergers may be banks' attempts to come under the umbrella of the too big to fail doctrine or under the regulatory protection larger banks obtain from threats of hostile takeover.

The best thing that ever happened to the American automobile industry was the importation of Japanese cars. Similarly, the banking industry
in some countries may be improved by competition from institutions that
are more transparent, more diversified, and with better asset pooling technologies (mutual funds). The response of some banks, as in the United
States, has been to offer mutual fund services in addition to their existing
money market mutual funds. The search for survival has recently seen
some banks aggressively bidding for asset management firms (see *American Banker* 1997a). Equities now make up a third of all assets invested in
mutual funds managed by U.S. banks (see *American Banker* 1997b). The
pressure from capital markets is also causing some U.S. banks to move
aggressively into the securities industry. In the last 10 years 44 American
banks have established securities units, permitted by the Fed under section 20 of the Glass-Steagall Act, and the Fed has recently raised the rev-
enue bank securities affiliates can earn from their new securities powers
to 25 percent (see *American Banker* 1997c). In Europe, German and Swiss
banks have purchased merchant banks in London.

The Basle Committee on Banking Supervision's proposal for improving banking systems (Bank for International Settlements 1997) contains a
number of suggestions, but greater stability in banking will require more
than common standards for banking supervision. In some countries it
will require a major change in the way governments perceive their proper
role in the financial system and the institutions they create to implement
their objectives. Unfortunately, major institutional changes do not often
come about simply as a result of public debate. Often it takes a crisis to
effect real, long-lasting institutional change.

References

Alchian, Armen. 1950. "Uncertainty, Evolution, and Economic Theory." *Journal of
Political Economy* (June): 211–21.

American Banker. 1997a. "Fleet Poised to Pay $600 Million for Oregon Money Man-
ager." August 14, pp. 1, 13.

_____. 1997b. "Stock Portfolio Now a Third of Bank Funds' Assets." August 13, pp.
1, 7–10.

_____. 1997c. "With Rules Eased, Banks Flock to Securities Underwriting." August
18, pp. 1, 7.

Amel, Dean F. 1996. "Trends in the Structure of Federally Insured Depository Institutions: 1984–94." *Federal Reserve Bulletin* 82 (1): 1–15.

Bank for International Settlements. 1997. "Core Principles for Effective Banking
Supervision." Basle Committee on Banking Supervision, Basle, Switzerland.

Boyd, John, and Stanley L. Graham. 1991. "Investigating the Banking Consolidation Trend." *Quarterly Review* (Federal Reserve Bank of Minneapolis) (Spring): 3–15.

Dent, Julian. 1973. *Crisis in Finance: Crown, Financiers, and Society in Seventeenth-Century France.* London: David and Charles Newton Abbot.

de Roover, Raymond. 1963. *The Rise and Decline of the Medici Bank.* Cambridge, Massachusetts: Harvard University Press.

Ellsberg, Daniel. 1961. "Risks, Ambiguity, and the Savage Axioms." *The Quarterly Journal of Economics* (November): 643–69.

Hunt, Edwin S. 1990. "A New Look at the Dealings of the Bardi and Peruzzi with Edward III." *The Journal of Economic History* L (1): 149–62.

Kindleberger, Charles P. 1992. "Intermediation, Disintermediation, and Direct Trading." In S. Fazzari and D. P. Papadimitriou, eds., *Financial Conditions and Macroeconomic Performance: Essays in Honor of Hyman P. Minsky.* Armonk, New York: M. E. Sharpe.

Lowenstein, Louis. 1996. "Financial Transparency and Corporate Governance: You Manage What You Measure." *Columbia Law Review* 96 (June): 1335–62.

Mauro, Frederic, and Fabrice Robert. 1997. "Banques: votre santé nous intéresse: synthèse du rapport du groupe de travail de la commission des finances du Sénat." *Revue de l'Economie FinancièPre* (39).

North, Douglass C. 1990. *Institutions, Institutional Change, and Economic Performance.* Cambridge, U.K.: Cambridge University Press.

Rotberg, Eugene H. 1992. "Risk-Taking in the Financial Services Industry." In *Risk Management in Financial Services.* Paris: Organisation for Economic Co-operation and Development.

20

Building a Better and Safer Banking System in Latin America and the Caribbean

E. Gerald Corrigan

During the past 10 years, many countries at all stages of economic development have experienced major problems with individual banking institutions or entire banking systems. While many reasons account for these developments, and while those reasons vary from country to country, several common denominators have been present in virtually all such episodes. These common denominators include the following:

- Rapid changes in the macroeconomic and macrofinancial environment
- Inadequate internal controls and procedures, together with lapses in official supervision or poorly developed official supervisory policies and practices
- Concentrated patterns of credit or market risk exposure.

In almost all cases, the proximate cause of banking sector problems can be traced to large credit losses. This has been true in industrial countries with mature systems of banking supervision and regulation, such as Japan and the United States, as well as in developing countries with relatively untested systems of banking supervision, such as, Argentina, Brazil, and Mexico. This clearly suggests that even well-developed and

---

This chapter was initially prepared as a paper for the conference on Building Effective Banking Systems in Latin America and the Caribbean, sponsored by the Inter-American Development Bank.

mature systems of banking supervision alone do not provide assurances that countries can avoid severe banking problems.

In every country that has experienced severe banking sector crises, the direct and indirect costs of such episodes have been astonishingly high. Such costs are reflected in several ways, including the following:

- Direct fiscal costs ranging from 5 to 10 percent of GDP have not been uncommon, even though countries have used a variety of devices to spread such costs over an extended time frame.
- Tens, if not hundreds, of billions of dollars of precious domestic savings have been poured into the black hole of bad credits in a setting in which such savings are in short supply. This is especially troubling in Latin America, where low domestic savings rates are perhaps the largest single barrier to sustained high rates of economic growth to begin with.
- GDP growth has been severely restrained by the paralyzing effects of banking crises on both lenders and borrowers.
- Considerable moral hazard problems have grown out of governments' decisions to protect depositors and other creditors.
- Public and political confidence in banking systems has been impaired in ways that can stand in the way of precisely the kinds of reforms that are needed to remedy the prevailing problems and build the progressive banking and financial systems that are so vital to countries' long-run success.

In many emerging market countries, including Argentina, Brazil, and Mexico, banking sector problems have been especially acute despite the presence of wide net interest margins. On the surface, these wide margins should provide ample cash flow to absorb credit losses, but in reality, not only have such interest margins not been remotely adequate to cushion credit losses, they have also imposed extraordinarily heavy interest cost burdens on many borrowers.

While the symptoms and costs of banking sector problems are widely recognized, the magnitude of the remedial task is often significantly underestimated. To put that task in some perspective, the following three observations should be kept in mind:

- First, the acute and costly nature of the problem in most developing countries primarily reflects a host of historical institutional weaknesses that severely complicate the relationships between creditors and debtors. The resulting absence of a credit culture almost ensures a high incidence of credit problems, especially in the face of volatile economic and financial conditions.

- Second, under the best of circumstances, including solid economic performance, remedying these institutional problems will take a number of years, despite the implementation of largely successful stopgap and damage control programs.
- Third, the building of progressive and profitable banking systems in these countries will entail a mix of short-term and longer term initiatives on the part of the banks, the authorities, and the governments at large, as well as enlightened support and leadership from the international community, including the International Monetary Fund, the World Bank, and regional development banks.

The Banking System's Role and Characteristics of National Banking Systems

For all countries, but especially for countries that require relatively high rates of GDP growth in the face of massive infrastructure needs, high levels of poverty, and young and rapidly growing populations, an effective domestic banking system is one of the most basic prerequisites for robust economic performance over time.

In a globally integrated market economy, national banking systems—and the individual banks that make up such systems—must be able to attract the capital necessary to support the risk-taking activities inherent in the conduct of the banking business. Such capital resources will only be forthcoming in a setting in which investors—domestic or foreign—can reasonably project returns on that capital that are sufficiently attractive relative to alternative investments to justify the deployment of capital to this purpose. This probably implies that rates of return on equity capital at viable banks in emerging market countries will have to average at least 15 percent over time.

In turn, achieving rates of return sufficient to attract the large amounts of capital needed to support healthy banking systems will require a regulatory and political environment that accepts the central proposition that prudential standards associated with safety and soundness can and must be framed in a manner that promotes efficiency, flexibility, and profitability in the banking sector. In other words, the imperative of profitability in the banking sector cannot be ignored, especially in a setting in which there is a danger that naïve political considerations could result in a business environment that is fundamentally incompatible with the high rates of profitability that are essential for success.

Given this general background, let us begin with a brief review of the three core functions of national banking systems, namely:

- *To mobilize domestic savings in a safe and efficient manner.* This, of course, is the deposit gathering function, which must be rooted in the conviction on the part of the public that deposit balances—especially current account balances—will be paid at par and on demand.
- *To channel those savings, through the credit decisionmaking process, to their most efficient uses.* The credit decisionmaking process must be rigorous, objective, and impartial, because only then will national savings be channeled into the most productive investments, which in turn will promote growth and permit borrowers to service their debts in a timely fashion, thereby ensuring the safety of depositors' funds.
- *To provide efficient, low cost, safe, and widely available means of making and receiving payments.* Public trust in the banking system will only flourish in a setting in which bank clients—small and large—have virtually complete confidence that they can make and receive payments on a safe and timely basis. Achieving absolute payment finality in the shortest time possible is essential. Interbank and large value payments, in particular, should be final and irrevocable on the same day they are initiated.

While these core functions of the banking system are conceptually simple and straightforward, they are often overlooked, or even worse, confused with social or political objectives that seek to encourage or direct banking activities—especially credit extensions—toward particular industries or classes of activity. More generally, there is often a tendency to view any one of these core banking system functions in isolation from the others. Any such tendency is both misguided and counterproductive, because these core functions are a mutually dependent package deal. In other words, a failure to achieve any one of them will ultimately produce failure in the other two.

These essential functions of a progressive and profitable banking system imply certain key characteristics or traits that should be associated with the structure and workings of a national banking system. Those characteristics or traits include the following:

- The broadly based availability of cost-efficient and safe banking services to all segments of society. This implies the presence of smaller, more specialized banking institutions that can serve narrow segments of the market, such as the agricultural, small business, and rural communities.
- The presence of market-driven interest rates for virtually all financial instruments, which in turn presuppose the absence of internal

and external credit controls and the conduct of monetary policy through indirect policy instruments, that is, open market operations.

- The private ownership of all banking institutions, widely distributed across owners. As an extension of this, government owned banks should be discouraged, and where present should be phased out. This trait is critical for achieving the highest degree of impartiality in the credit decisionmaking process and for creating a competitive, level playing field.

- The presence of a competitive, level playing field for all banking institutions, domestic and foreign. This implies that all regulations, taxes, and other governmentally imposed mandates that affect the cost or ease of doing business should not discriminate against or in favor of individual institutions or classes of institutions, except where necessary for prudential reasons.

- The presence of efficient, safe, and liquid money, debt, and equity capital markets with particular emphasis on state-of-the-art interbank and national government securities markets. The short-run priority is interbank and government securities markets, which are the bedrock upon which all other money and capital markets will ultimately rest. The development of these markets presupposes a major operational and regulatory role for the central bank.

- The wide availability of efficient and trusted payment, delivery, and settlement systems that ensure the absolute finality of all financial transactions in the shortest time frame possible. Achieving this will entail a high degree of coordination and cooperation between the public and private sectors.

- A suitable regulatory, legal, and judicial framework that establishes, with the highest degree of certainty possible, the rights and obligations of parties to financial transactions and provides appropriate disclosure and other requirements, with particular emphasis on the need to protect small and unsophisticated depositors and investors. As part of this, the legal and institutional framework for resolving problem credit situations must be emphasized, because a relatively high incidence of problem loans is likely to remain a characteristic of emerging economies' banking systems for some time to come.

- A firm but flexible system of prudential supervision whose goal is to ensure the banking system's safety and stability. The system of prudential supervision must cover eight closely interrelated tasks as follows:
  — Granting charters for all banking institutions and approving major changes in activities, ownership, and so on

— Establishing essential prudential norms in such areas as capital, liquidity, and lending limits
— Establishing rules for the regular reporting and disclosure of key statistical information
— Analyzing such statistical information on a regular and systematic basis using the in-house experts of the central bank or other supervisory authorities
— Carrying out annual on-site examination or inspection of all banking institutions, with particular emphasis on the credit quality of loans, the adequacy of internal controls, and the adequacy of internal and external audits, which is the most difficult and most important feature of an effective system of banking supervision
— Communicating the results of examinations and other supervisory initiatives to the top management and boards of directors of all banking institutions in a regular, systematic, and timely fashion
— Having a well-defined framework for initiating timely remedial actions against banks that have or are developing problems that might threaten their viability
— Establishing clear rules and procedures for dealing with insolvent banks.

- The presence of a suitable system of deposit insurance administered by a body other than the central bank or prime supervisory authority and a well-defined emergency liquidity or lender of last resort facility at the central bank. The central bank's liquidity facility should be used only for short-term credit extensions against high quality collateral.

- A strong and independent central bank that is engaged in all aspects of the central banking trilogy, namely, the conduct of monetary policy, the supervision of banking institutions, and the oversight and operation of the payments system. As an extension of this, clear rules must be in place as to which institutions have direct access to the central bank's account, payment, and credit facilities.

As with the three core functions of a banking system, these key characteristics of an effective banking system are another interdependent package deal, though practicalities clearly require the establishment of national priorities in deciding the order in which countries plan and execute efforts to achieve these characteristics. Setting such priorities requires, in the first instance, a rigorously objective analysis as to where each country's banking system currently stands relative to each characteristic. This analysis should be performed jointly by representatives of the banking industry, the supervisory authorities, and an independent third party. With that analysis in hand, the priorities and initiatives set for the future must be viewed in the context of a clear vision of the desired structure of the banking system over the long run. Such a vision is necessary to ensure that short-run initiatives are consistent with a coherent, longer term view of the desired future structure of the banking and financial system.

The Structure of the Banking System

Decisions about the desired structure of a national banking system entail careful analysis of a host of complex, and often competing, issues, including, but not limited to, the following:

- The characteristics of the persons or legal entities that should be permitted to own and control banks
- The scope and range of activities the banks should be empowered to conduct
- The competitive environment within which banks must function
- The class of institutions that should have direct access to the central bank's account, payment, and credit facilities
- The design and reach of the official safety net, including deposit insurance, the lender of last resort, and the *de facto* protections provided by official supervision
- The approach taken by the government with respect to how it provides financial support for policy-based lending activities.

To rationalize these issues in a coherent manner, there must, in the first instance, be a clear and workable definition of a bank. This seemingly straightforward issue of defining a bank is not an easy task, especially in a highly competitive environment in which close substitutes for specific bank functions, such as taking deposits or making loans, are widespread. The most practical—but hardly perfect—definition of a bank is one that is built around the dual criteria of taking deposits from the public and extending credit. The term deposit is given meaning by applying it to any obligation that is payable at par on demand or at maturity durations that fall within some specified threshold, and/or applying it to any obligation that is covered in whole or in part by deposit insurance. If the term deposit is properly specified, the terms loan and credit can be more loosely specified, so long as both terms are incorporated into the definition of a bank.

With that in mind, individual countries can choose between several banking structure models while recognizing that no "right" banking structure exists for all countries at all times. Broadly speaking, however, countries can choose from the following models:

- The so-called universal bank model, in which banks can engage in a wide range of financial activities, including the full range of traditional banking and securities activities. This model is typical of the arrangements most European countries follow and is widespread in most emerging market countries.
- The specialized bank model, as was the case in Japan and the United States, which prohibits the coexistence of banking and securities activities within the same institution. In practice, in the United States, and to a lesser extent in Japan, market and competitive forces have largely displaced the narrowly defined specialized bank models.
- The holding company model, in which particular classes of financial activity must be conducted in a separate subsidiary of a holding company rather than directly in the bank or the bank's subsidiary.
- A mixed system in which stand-alone banks performing traditional banking activities coexist with more diversified universal banks and/or bank holding companies.

Given an acceptable and workable definition of a bank, individual countries can choose which model they believe best suits their own situation, recognizing that, for all practical purposes, the specialized bank model is largely a thing of the past. While the exact model chosen may not be of overriding consequence, the manner in which the model is applied can matter a great deal. In this regard, the following key points should receive particular attention:

- First, under any approach, the scope of activities for the institutions in question should be restricted to lines of business that are distinctly financial in nature. Even with this proviso, the blending of insurance with banking and securities activities raises a host of difficult managerial and regulatory issues.
- Second, industrial groups should not be allowed to own and control banks or banking groups and vice versa. Where such arrangements already exist, they should be phased out over time, and, in the interim, the authorities should adopt extremely restrictive regulations to limit or prevent the direct or indirect extension of credit from a bank, its holding company, or its affiliates to the industrial concerns in question.

- Third, government ownership of banks should be phased out over time.
- Fourth, all banks and banking groups should be subject to full-scale, consolidated supervision in which the central bank plays a prominent role.
- Fifth, only banks or banks within bank groups should have direct access to the central bank's account, credit, and payment facilities.
- Sixth, nonbank financial institutions should not be permitted to (a) take deposits; (b) represent themselves as banks; and (c) have direct access to the central bank's account, payment, and credit facilities, even though they may extend credit. An entity that is clearly separate from the central bank and other bank regulators should regulate such nonbank financial institutions. The scope of regulation for such institutions may be less intense than that of the banks, but the regulators should be politically independent along the lines of the Securities and Exchange Commission in the United States or the Securities and Investment Board in the United Kingdom.
- Seventh, exchanges, clearinghouses, net settlement systems, and securities depositories should all be regulated. To the extent that they have direct access to the central bank for final settlement services, the regulator should be the central bank.
- Finally, the deposit insurance fund and the entity responsible for liquidating insolvent banks should be independent public entities removed and separate from the central bank and banking supervisors.

This eight-point list of banking structure "do's" and "don'ts" is not intended to be exhaustive, nor is it to deny that a great deal of fine-tuning will be associated with their application in a given country. However, when taken in the context of a clear and workable definition of a bank, it does provide a broad framework within which an individual country can develop its vision of a desired future structure and seek to ensure that actions in the short run are compatible with that long-run vision.

The list has one glaring omission, namely, how to address the difficult issue of policy-based lending. Starting in the 1930s and continuing throughout the postwar period, virtually every government created special vehicles or modalities to help foster politically or socially desirable forms of credit extension. In the United States, for example, government owned or sponsored policy-based credit institutions have played a major role for many years in such areas as housing, agriculture, and small business finance. In most countries, and in most areas of policy-based lending, the government provides substantial subsidies for such activities, either directly or indirectly.

Given the pressing economic needs of specific sectors of emerging market economies, and given the experience of all the major industrial countries, suggesting that developing countries refrain from programs that encourage policy-based lending would be completely unreasonable. However, government owned or sponsored financial institutions that are engaged in policy-based lending could usefully follow certain guidelines. Such guidelines should include the following:

- The government's fiscal accounts should clearly show all startup and net ongoing costs, including interest subsidies.
- The management of such institutions should be independent, private sector practitioners who should be compensated accordingly. A majority of boards of directors should also come from the private sector.
- The institutions should be subject to all relevant accounting and disclosure standards and should be subject to rigorous and regular audits by private, independent auditors. Summary audit reports should be made public.
- A fraction—however small—of the initial capital should come from private investors if at all possible.
- The institutions should be specialized, that is, if a country decides to sponsor policy-based lending institutions in, for example, housing and agriculture, these functions should not be commingled in a single institution, but rather should be housed in two specialized institutions.
- A date should be set for beginning the gradual privatization of such institutions.
- The funding of such institutions should take the form of capital market debt, even if such debt must carry partial or full government guarantees. They should not be permitted to take deposits from the public.
- The government should have no influence, direct or indirect, on the day-to-day management of the institutions, especially in relation to the credit decisionmaking process.

Obviously, there is no easy way to design a banking structure that provides for government owned or sponsored policy-based lending financial institutions. By the same token, almost all governments have relied on such institutions, especially at critical stages of economic development or in the early stages of recovery from major economic catastrophes or wars. That being the case, expecting governments in emerging market economies not to rely on such institutions would be wholly unrealistic. Looked at in that light, the suggestions outlined are an attempt to provide room for such institutions in a manner that does not materially compromise the objectives of a banking structure that is dominated by market-based principles aimed at the emergence of a progressive, profitable, and stable banking and financial system over time.

The Nature and Causes of Banking Sector Problems

The problems associated with weak and unstable banking systems in many emerging market economies fall into two major categories. The first is the widely recognized problem associated with massive losses and resulting weak or insolvent banks, which can generally be traced to asset quality and related problems. The second major problem, which receives little attention, is the extent to which banking systems in such countries fail to measure up to the key characteristics of effective banking systems discussed earlier. To provide some perspective on the nature and depth of these shortcomings, table 20.1 "grades" the current status of banking systems in the major Latin American countries that are experiencing serious problems relative to the 10 characteristics discussed earlier.

In looking at the grades and recognizing their subjective nature, several things stand out as follows:

- First, the countries in question have made progress in a number of areas despite major obstacles.
- Second, individual countries are lagging significantly behind their peers in several key areas.
- Third, the low grades in the areas of banking services, the legal framework, and bank examinations are especially troubling, because all three areas are so basic, and all three are so difficult to improve significantly, even in the long term. For example, unless national banking systems make progress in their ability and willingness to provide cost-effective and safe banking services to all segments of society, the political support for other necessary reforms will be difficult to muster. Even worse, the tendency to rely on government owned banks will persist, and might even grow.

Thus while much attention has been paid to the destabilizing and costly problems associated with failing and insolvent banks in the countries in question, such problems are only part of the story. Indeed, any permanent solution to the banking sector's problems is unlikely unless efforts to deal with the insolvent bank issue are coupled with efforts to develop banking systems along the broader lines suggested by the preceding analysis.

The above analysis notwithstanding, the core problem associated with the banking crises in Argentina, Brazil, and Mexico is—plain and simple— a credit problem. As in other countries, some of the credit problems are

Table 20.1. *Latin American Banking Systems "Graded" against 10 Characteristics of Effective Banking Systems*

Characteristic	Grade	Observations
Banking services	Low	To greater or lesser degree, major problem in all countries
Financial markets	Medium	While problems exist, all countries have made major progress
Wide ownership	Low	Problems in all countries, even where government owned banks are not a major problem
Level playing field	Mixed	Varies considerably from country to country
Money and capital markets	Medium	Progress being made, but major efforts still needed
Payments system	Mixed	Taking account of current status and programs under development, progress reasonably good, but Argentina lags behind considerably
Legal framework	Low	Major problems in all countries that add considerably to credit costs
Banking supervision	Medium	Considering the starting point, significant progress has been made, but major problems remain, especially with bank examinations which, by itself, would be rated low in all countries
Deposit insurance	Incomplete	Cannot be judged at this time, because crisis environment has forced the hand of authorities
Independent central banks	Medium	Major progress has been made, but appreciation of the central banking trilogy is mixed at best

firm-specific, growing out of blatantly poor management and/or fraud or other forms of misconduct by bank officials. More generally, the problems in Latin America have been aggravated by such factors as (a) the increase in macroeconomic instability, (b) the large-scale presence of government controlled banks, and (c) a high incidence of connected lending and investing to industrial or commercial groups. While these and other factors are relevant to an understanding of the anatomy of the Latin American banking crises, the problem, in a nutshell, is the pervasive and systematic presence of bad loans.

This said, a number of myths about credit problems in the Latin American banking systems need to be shattered, including the following:

- It is a myth to suggest that the banking crisis in Mexico and, indirectly, the crisis in Argentina, were caused by the Mexican peso crisis of early 1995. To be sure, the peso crisis made things much worse, but the evidence that the core problem was building rapidly even before the peso crisis is overwhelming. The same can be said of Brazil, where the advent of relatively low inflation simply brought to the surface problems that were being papered over by inflation.
- It is a myth to suggest that the widespread credit problems are simply the result of Latin American bankers' lack of experience or expertise in extending credit. The incidence of serious credit problems at foreign banks in the region supports this view.
- It is a myth to suggest that the seemingly high interest rates and interest spreads are a symptom of a lack of competition or other structural imperfections in banking markets. High rates and spreads reflect the need to cover high credit costs as an integral part of the cost of doing business. Indeed, it is high credit costs that explain the apparent anomaly of high spreads and low profits.
- It is a total myth to suggest that the banking problems in Latin America will be solved by improved banking supervision, even if improved supervision is clearly needed. The asset quality problem in most Latin American banks reflects a complex interaction of a series of deeply rooted institutional problems. Unless these problems are addressed, improved supervision will either (a) reveal a continued high incidence of bad loans, or (b) result in a broadly based stoppage of credit flows to large segments of the economy, the result of which can only be slower growth or recession, together with heightened economic and political instability.

To put the Latin American credit problems in perspective, let us consider the dynamics of the cradle-to-grave life cycle of bank credits and the interplay of that cycle with the critical elements of the bank supervisory process (see figure 20.1).

The first page of figure 20.1 starts with a list of the supervisory policy overlay, which should guide the credit cycle for both the bank and the supervisor.

Figure 20.1. Life Cycle of Bank Credits

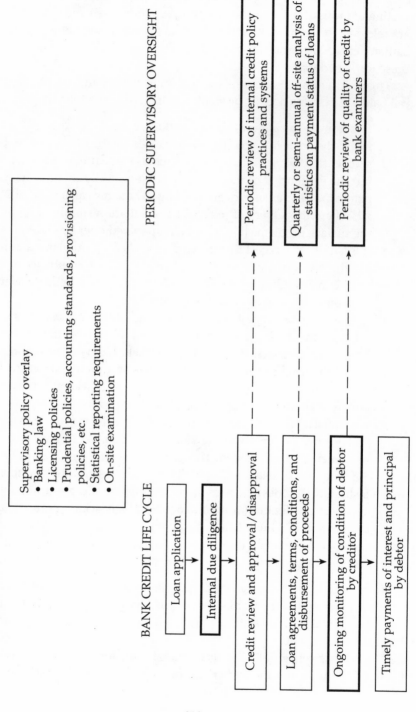

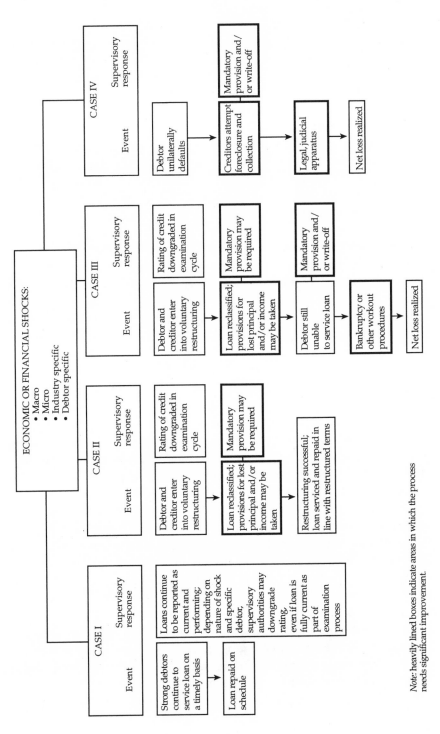

ECONOMIC OR FINANCIAL SHOCKS:
- Macro
- Micro
- Industry specific
- Debtor specific

CASE I

Event	Supervisory response
Strong debtors continue to service loan on a timely basis	Loans continue to be reported as current and performing; depending on nature of shock and specific debtor, supervisory authorities may downgrade rating, even if loan is fully current as part of examination process
Loan repaid on schedule	

CASE II

Event	Supervisory response
Debtor and creditor enter into voluntary restructuring	Rating of credit downgraded in examination cycle
Loan reclassified; provisions for lost principal and/or income may be taken	Mandatory provision may be required
Restructuring successful; loan serviced and repaid in line with restructured terms	

CASE III

Event	Supervisory response
Debtor and creditor enter into voluntary restructuring	Rating of credit downgraded in examination cycle
Loan reclassified; provisions for lost principal and/or income may be taken	Mandatory provision may be required
Debtor still unable to service loan	Mandatory provision and/or write-off
Bankruptcy or other workout procedures	
Net loss realized	

CASE IV

Event	Supervisory response
Debtor unilaterally defaults	
Creditors attempt foreclosure and collection	Mandatory provision and/or write-off
Legal, judicial apparatus	
Net loss realized	

Note: heavily lined boxes indicate areas in which the process needs significant improvement.

Note that for the most part, the Latin American authorities have made great progress in developing such policies. The problem, therefore, is not so much a matter of policy as a matter of practice and execution.

The left side of the first page of figure 20.1 traces a simple case of a typical loan, which in this instance is serviced and repaid on schedule. However, the two heavily lined boxes on the right side of the page identify the first two areas in which institutional considerations impinge on the effectiveness of the credit cycle. First, except for large corporate borrowers, major impediments stand in the way of even the most elementary forms of credit due diligence on the part of the banks. Independent information of credit histories is either limited or nonexistent, financials are often not available or have little value, and even tax returns may be hard to come by. In such circumstances, effective—much less timely—due diligence is not easy to achieve. Obviously, where major institutional impediments hinder the credit due diligence process, the incidence of bad loans will be high and/or creditworthy borrowers will be denied access to credit. Second, credit due diligence should occur not only when a loan is made, but also during the period in which the loan is outstanding. In the countries in question, the same institutional barriers that stand in the way of effective initial due diligence also limit after-the-fact due diligence, with the result that the creditor bank is limited in its ability to anticipate problems and take steps to cope with problems before they become serious.

On the side of supervisory practices, there are also two major problems. First, one of the most basic tasks of the bank examination process is a detailed review of an individual bank's internal credit systems, policies, and procedures. Such a review requires a high level of sophistication on the part of bank examiners, in a setting in which the reviews can only be conducted on site at the bank. For perfectly understandable reasons, in many banks the frequency and quality of such reviews fall short. Second, the key to the bank supervisory process is the on-site examination of a sample of individual loans to determine their current and future status with regard to prospects for timely servicing and repayment. The loan-by-loan review of individual credit files is an extraordinarily difficult task that requires an enormous amount of experience and judgment on the part of the examiner. This task is, unquestionably, the weakest link in the supervisory process in all emerging market countries, because without some credible insights into the future status of loans, having meaningful insight into the condition of a bank is impossible. Similarly, while both the banks and the banking supervisors need new and forward-looking loan classification schemes, the only way the supervisors can implement such loan classification schemes is through the loan-by-loan review that occurs as part of the on-site examination process. Recruiting, training, and retaining examinations personnel who will perform this task rigorously and objectively is probably the greatest challenge facing central banks and other supervisory bodies in virtually all emerging market countries.

The second page of figure 20.1 introduces economic or financial shocks and then traces four hypothetical cases of the manner in which such shocks can affect the quality of credit and the behavior of both the bank and its supervisor. In brief, the case studies are as follows:

- *Case I:* the borrower is strong enough to continue to service and repay the loan on schedule. The key point in this case is that even with the loan current and performing, the bank examiner (or the bank) might still downgrade the loan, because of the greater risk that the loan may not be serviced in a timely manner. This is clearly an example of a situation in which the examiner's experience and judgment are critical.
- *Case II:* the bank and the borrower enter into a voluntary restructuring, perhaps even before the debtor stops paying interest on the loan. In this case the assumption is that the restructuring works, and that under the new terms the loan is serviced and repaid on a timely basis. In many instances in Latin America, the restructuring vehicle of choice is interest capitalization, which can create the illusion that all is well with the loan in question, when in reality the loan should be downgraded and provisions taken for lost principal and/or interest. In all such cases, however, the identification and proper classification and accounting treatment of such restructured loans—especially those that involve interest capitalization—is a demanding task for both the bank and the bank examiner. A particularly difficult judgment is when, and under what circumstances, a restructured loan should be classified as performing.
- *Case III:* the situation becomes much more complex in that even after restructuring, the debtor cannot service the loan and the bank must resort to extraordinary measures in an effort to minimize its loss on the loan. In this case, major questions first arise with regard to the timeliness with which both the bank and the supervisor recognize the need to reclassify the loan and to establish the necessary reserves to cover the likely loss. Unfortunately, in most Latin American countries the loss rate on such loans tends to be quite high, because the

institutional, legal, and judicial framework for resolving such situations is uncertain and makes the process extremely time consuming.

- *Case IV:* this is the worst case in that the borrower simply walks away from the debt obligation. Regrettably, this is not an unusual phenomenon, especially in the face of a major economic shock and in circumstances in which debtors believe—rightly or wrongly—that their unilateral action will not result in any sanction or penalty. Needless to say, in these cases the potential for loss is high, especially given the problems associated with the institutional, legal, and judicial setting in which the bank must seek relief.

The specifics of the four cases aside, in all cases there are major points of vulnerability with regard to the effectiveness with which both the bank and the supervisor are able to anticipate, recognize, and properly respond to problem loans. On the supervisory side, only effective, on-site examination can provide reasonable assurance that the loan classification process and the system of reserves and provisions are working satisfactorily. In turn, this implies the presence of a large and skillful team of examination personnel—something that is difficult to achieve even over the long run. And, as we have seen in the United States, even the presence of a large and well-trained examination staff does not provide remotely fail-safe protection against major banking problems.

In Latin America (and elsewhere) the historic lack of a credit culture that firmly establishes—in law, tradition, and custom—the relationship between creditors and debtors and their duties and responsibilities within the relationship severely complicates the problems associated with the credit life cycle. One particular and costly aspect of this lack of a well-established credit culture is the enormously complex set of issues that arises with regard to the collection process for bad loans. These problems ensure that the ultimate losses on such bad loans will be high, if for no other reason than because the passage of time usually means larger eventual losses.

The main purpose of figure 20.1 is to illustrate that finding permanent solutions to the credit problems in Latin American banking systems is a complex, multifaceted task that will take time and will not be solved simply by improved supervisory policies and practices. Indeed, what is needed are basic reforms that will, over time, help build a true credit culture.

The Building Blocks for Comprehensive Reform

This section outlines the major components of a comprehensive, multiyear reform program that could bring the performance standards of the major

Latin American banking systems up to industrial country or Organisation for Economic Co-operation and Development standards in five to seven years. Obviously, the needs will vary from country to country, such that some of the building blocks may not be relevant for one country while being critically important for another. The individual building blocks are described only in the most general terms, and thus do not begin to do justice to the enormous complexities associated with the various initiatives implied by each building block.

Reform Architecture: Vision and Goals

A necessary first step of an overall reform strategy is the rigorous review of the current state of the banking system relative to the key characteristics of an effective banking system as outlined earlier. Obviously, that list of criteria can be amended to suit the needs of individual countries. Ideally, the group performing the review should consist of representatives of (a) private sector banks, (b) the central bank and the ministry of finance, and (c) an independent third party. Such a review will help to set priorities and to shape a vision of what the desired banking structure should be.

The second step is to develop a coherent statement that outlines the desired legal and operational characteristics of the future banking system, including the design of the official safety net. This statement should cover (a) the supervisory framework; (b) the access to the central bank's account, payment, and credit facilities; and (c) the system of deposit insurance. In some countries, few or no major structural changes will be needed, while in others, major changes may be necessary. In some countries, consideration of banking structure issues may entail the need for sweeping legislative changes and the always difficult task of building political support for such changes.

The third step in building the architecture for reform consists of developing specific goals to be achieved during the next five to seven years. While some such goals will be qualitative, some can and should be quantitative and easily measurable.

Short-Term Priorities

With the reform architecture in place, the next set of tasks involves establishing short-term priorities. While these priorities will obviously differ from one country to another, the following items will probably be common to most countries:

- Redouble efforts to ensure that the full scope of the insolvent bank situation is completely understood and that the likelihood of further bank failures is low. The authorities should leave no stone unturned in their efforts to satisfy themselves that the risks of further adverse surprises are well understood.
- Accelerate the final resolution of banks in which the government or central bank has intervened through liquidation, mergers, or other means, including developing a plan or an approach to begin the privatization of insolvent government owned banks.
- Commence a vigorous program to monitor the condition of restructured banks, including newly merged banks, to ensure that financial recovery is occurring as contemplated.
- Develop and make public a comprehensive plan whereby the banking system will be brought into full compliance with all internationally accepted accounting, disclosure, and supervisory standards by a specific date.
- Develop comprehensive estimates—using base case, best case, and worst case scenarios—of the total fiscal and public sector borrowing impacts of bank resolutions, and put in place a quarterly system to track and monitor actual costs relative to estimated costs.
- Take immediate regulatory or legislative steps to curtail, if not eliminate, interconnected lending or investing by banks to affiliated companies or entities.
- Take the necessary steps to accelerate the development and effectiveness of private credit bureaus, including providing a regulatory or legal framework to protect the rights of individuals and legal entities.
- Take the necessary steps to accelerate the training of bank supervisory personnel, especially bank examiners, while at the same time augmenting the size and professional qualifications of bank supervisory personnel.

Longer Term Programs

The initial step in establishing longer term programs is to develop a comprehensive program for the liquidation, sale, or other resolution of the vast quantity of bad loans that the government and/or central bank own. While such a program will probably have to rely on a vehicle of the Resolution Trust Corporation type for its execution, private sector experts—including experts drawn from the international community—must play a major role in the disposition of the bad assets. The task of seeking to maximize recovery rates on bad bank loans is difficult under the best of circumstances, and in the institutional setting of the countries in question will be even more difficult. Qualified and experienced institutions and individuals (who probably work for the government in an agent capacity) are essential to achieve even modest recovery rates on the loans in question.

The program for disposing of bad assets must be organized and managed according to the highest standards of management, controls, and audits. While high standards are always desirable, in this area they are especially critical because the potential for manipulation or abuse is high. Needless to say, mismanagement or scandal in connection with the asset disposition programs would be extremely embarrassing for the government in question. Even worse, it could contaminate the environment within which the overall reform effort must proceed.

While conditions vary greatly from country to country, the accelerated development of financial infrastructure, including wholesale and retail payments systems, net settlement systems for various classes of financial instruments, exchanges, and clearing houses, is needed in all the countries, but especially in Argentina. While the development of financial infrastructure is critical to the development of liquid money and capital markets, it is also essential in terms of the banking system's ability to deliver low cost and high quality banking services to all segments of society nationwide.

The privatization of the large government owned banks (or the conversion of such institutions into policy lending institutions that do not take deposits structured along the lines described earlier) is clearly not something that will occur in the near term. However, the planning for such major privatizations should begin in the not too distant future, even as efforts to privatize some of the smaller provincial banks proceed in the near term.

The last and most difficult item on the list of longer term programs is to promote the emergence of a deeper credit culture. This is so difficult because for both lenders and borrowers, a credit culture is partly more a state of mind than a collection of practices, regulations, and laws. The essence of a credit culture lies in the unspoken understanding among debtors and creditors that each has duties and responsibilities in relation to the other and is based on a foundation of a coherent and consistent set of laws, regulations, and judicial practices. Thus a number of countries need to review their commercial codes, bankruptcy laws, and other administrative rules and procedures that establish the rights and obligations of both sides of the credit process, with the aim of revising the laws, regulations, and administrative rulings governing these critical relationships as necessary.

International Coordination and Cooperation

Given the complex and costly efforts that will be required on the part of so many countries to bring their domestic banking systems up to contemporary standards, clearly most will need outside help. Some of that help is taking the form of enhanced technical and financial assistance from the International Monetary Fund, the World Bank, and the regional development banks. In addition, individual central banks from the industrial countries and institutions such as the Bank for International Settlements can be of great assistance in such areas as improving banking supervision and building financial infrastructure in payments, clearance, and settlement systems and the like. Finally, at the level of the Group of Seven or the Group of Ten, and in collaboration with the International Monetary Fund, further consideration should be given to (a) the kinds of bilateral or multilateral assistance that might be mustered to support these efforts; and (b) the further steps that might be taken to help reduce the vulnerability of relatively small, open emerging market economies from highly destabilizing external shocks, while recognizing that the primary responsibility in that regard lies with the countries themselves.

21

Bank Restructuring Revisited

Andrew Sheng

For about a decade I worked almost exclusively on bank distress and bank restructuring issues, but for the last four years I have been working in Hong Kong, one of the world's most dynamic market economies. With capital adequacy ratios of more than 18 percent and one of the most profitable bank margins in Asia, if not the world, bank restructuring has not been the highest priority. However, revisiting the subject and reflecting on its lessons with a little more distance and objectivity would be a useful exercise.

At the end of 1980s I estimated that 33 countries had banking fragility problems. Of the International Monetary Fund's 180 members, in the last 15 years 130 suffered from varying degrees of bank distress or fragility. This is not a cold; it is an epidemic that is symptomatic of our times. What has gone wrong, what can we do to prevent it, and what should we do to cure it? I recently concluded (Sheng 1996a) that the reasons for bank failure were so complex and so country-specific that generalizing a solution was impossible. The recent International Monetary Fund Central Banking Seminar (IMF 1997) arrived at roughly the same conclusion.

When bank problems arise, someone always seems to expect a silver bullet—the quick fix. But no quick fixes, no easy solutions, are available. Bank problems do not happen overnight; they have extremely complex roots. Many of the factors are country-specific. Accordingly, bank fragility is a symptom of a deeper malaise in an economy. Some of the problems are structural, others cyclical; they are political and sectoral, involving legal, social, institutional, and incentive dimensions. The only common factor is that sooner or later these problems manifest themselves in the banking system.

The 1980s gave us many memorable slogans. The Norwegians came up with: "Bad banking, bad policies, and bad luck." The Malaysian experience was: "Never let monkeys look after bananas." And Aristobulo de Juan came up with the classic: "How good bankers became bad bankers through evergreening." In trying to encapsulate the essence of the lessons of bank restructuring, I agreed with Jerry Caprio that a banking crisis is an event, but that bank restructuring is a process. It covers four steps, sometimes sequential, sometimes parallel: diagnosis, damage control, loss allocation, and restoration of the right incentive structure. This generalization did not capture wide acceptance, and Lindgren, Garcia, and Saal (1996) have a much better mantra: private governance, market discipline, and official oversight. To which I would add: robust infrastructure.

Lessons from the 1990s

The chapters in this volume all point to the complexity and multidimensional aspect of bank distress, with long, painful, and messy solutions. Even in the Group of Ten (G-10) countries, everything from re-nationalization, carve-outs, mergers, resolution trusts, lifeboats, and wait and see have been tried. Some worked, others are still in the throes of messy resolution. Bad banks are not the monopoly of developing countries. Even bank supervisors of Organisation for Economic Co-operation and Development quality cannot prevent bank failures. These governments are now beginning to carve the supervisory function out of their central banks.

I believe that the growth of derivative markets, globalization, and financial deregulation and innovation have shed new light on the question of bank distress. Finance is a derivative of the real sector. This is, of course, a two-way relationship at the heart of the binary nature of property rights. A right is normally an obligation of another party. Such contractual obligations form the networks between contractual parties in financial markets, and it is these contractual networks that transmit contagion when participants in that network fail.

The benefits of derivatives are threefold: first, they allocate risks more efficiently; second, they generate useful information on market behavior; and third, they lower the transaction costs of trading in the underlying asset. However, derivatives are considered dangerous because they add volatility to financial markets, they are not well understood (risks are opaque), and they are highly leveraged.

This describes banks perfectly. They are not transparent in their operations, they assume risk transformation functions, and they are highly leveraged. It is perhaps no coincidence that widespread bank distress has been closely associated with globalization, deregulation, the rise of derivatives, speculative behavior, and asset bubbles. What the market is saying is that banks fail because they have not, for many reasons, adjusted to a more volatile, risky environment, with greater competition and changing markets. Internal governance did not manage risks well, market discipline was unable to check such behavior, and official oversight failed to prevent losses being socialized. In transition economies we can say that the financial infrastructure, especially payment systems, was unreliable, inefficient, and added to the inflation tax on payments.

A bank run is a natural market response to a bank failure. If we suppress the symptoms of failure through deposit insurance and we do nothing through forbearance, we are exactly like the doctor that treats cancer with painkillers.

Banking in the 21st Century

I believe it was Bill Gates who said that in the 21st century banking will be important, but not necessarily banks. In the industrial economies banks are rapidly shedding their old structures, forming financial conglomerates to invest in highly sophisticated skills and deliver a global product range, and managing their risks more smartly. By contrast, in emerging markets, where risks are considerably higher, the banking supervision rules still suggest Glass-Steagall types of compartmentalization.

In a world of much higher risks, consumers essentially have three choices about where to put their money: a no-leverage mutual fund that invests in high risk, high return assets, a hedge fund that leverages into even higher risks, and a no-leverage deposit in a highly leveraged bank that yields low returns with a cap on the lending rate. Which investment is likely to fail unless the government steps in to bail the consumers out?

In essence, the old style, highly franchised, highly protected bank cannot survive unchanged in a rapidly changing global market. This is the vivid lesson not only of transition economies, but also of many advanced economies where some banks have been sheltered against global competition and domestic policy mistakes.

If a derivative malfunctions, do you fix the derivative or the underlying asset? We know that the delta between the derivative and the underlying asset is nonlinear and quite complex, with feedback effects. Not fixing the derivative can worsen the underlying asset, but it remains a truism that if the underlying asset is broke, the derivative will continue to malfunction. Recapitalizing old banks into new banks without fixing the real economy, where the deficits are either in the budget or in the enterprise sector, is doomed to failure. In other words, take care of the fundamentals, and the derivatives will take care of themselves.

The Four Asymmetries

Bank failures reflect large losses in the domestic economy. Bank failure is only the symptom of real sector loss distribution. Somebody must bear the pain. If you accept this basic premise, you can fix the problem by looking at the four asymmetries of all derivatives.

The first asymmetry is *risk asymmetry*: banks fail because they did not manage their risks well, sometimes because of outdated regulations, sometimes because of a bad macroeconomic environment, sometimes because of bad incentives. We all know that banks run a fundamental maturity mismatch, especially in the property sector, where they borrow short to lend long. Other banks fail when they run a currency mismatch, by borrowing excessively in foreign exchange under the illusion that they can always obtain the foreign exchange from the central bank. Policymakers must identify what the risks are and examine how the banks are addressing these risks. Hong Kong has established the Mortgage Corporation, equivalent to Fannie Mae in the United States, to reduce concentration risks and to enable banks to manage their maturity risks in mortgage lending.

The second asymmetry is *information asymmetry*, which leads to adverse selection and moral hazard problems, and which Mishkin (1996) uses to explain bank failures. Current accounting and disclosure standards are highly inadequate for dealing with the complex risks we face. In Hong Kong we believe strongly that disclosure is vital for competition and market forces to work. In the last few years, we have moved bank disclosure standards to world-class levels.

The third asymmetry is *leverage asymmetry*, which I consider to be the real Achilles heel of financial systems. In a society with high savings and basically disciplined behavior, leverage will tend to be low. However, in an economy with low savings rates, certain sectors of the economy will be much more highly leveraged than others, resulting in greater degrees of risk and increased volatility in prices. The greater the degree of leverage, the greater the volatility in asset prices and the greater the volatility in duration.

Leverage is at the heart of the financial sector, because banks themselves are highly leveraged institutions. The value of an asset is highly correlated to its duration and the level of interest rates. The longer the duration, the larger the decline in asset value because of an increase in interest rates. Recent experience with financial fragility suggests the existence of the law of changing duration as follows: "Under conditions of uncertainty, the duration of a financial institution's liabilities shortens and the duration of assets lengthens" (Sheng 1996b).

By the very nature of banking, banks borrow short to lend long. However, as an economy runs into greater political or economic uncertainty, a flight to quality would result in debtors defaulting or slowing down payments, resulting in the duration of loan assets increasing, while the duration of liabilities contracted, causing massive liquidity problems. The need to liquidate assets forces down asset prices further in a classic deflation cycle.

Leverage is also at the heart of contagion or systemic risks. By definition, asset bubbles are only dangerous if they are financed by leverage. As Goldstein pointed out (see chapter 13 in this volume), rapid credit growth is one of the best explanations for bank failure. Bill Taylor, the late Fed director of banking supervision and one of the wisest bank regulators I have had the privilege to know, told me that if a bank doubled its loans in the last three years, it was a sure sign that the bank would have problems within the next three years. Markets behave "normally" as long as private participants are solvent. However, as finance theory tells us, private agents maximize their returns by using leverage. The higher the leverage, the higher the risks and the returns. At certain levels of leverage, the market participant crosses the risk-return frontier, and its losses are socialized. Market uncertainties are worsened by poor disclosure, so that neither the regulators nor market participants know when insolvent players begin to double up losses.

In Hong Kong, we deal with this problem through variations in the loan-to-value ratio. Banks are free to lend to a booming property market, as long as they comply with prudent loan-to-value ratios, currently at 70 percent. However, when property prices rise, under moral suasion the banks reduce the loan-to-value ratio to 60 percent, and have even lowered it to 50 percent. This prevents the banks from being hurt. In the 1994/95 cycle, when property prices declined as much as 45 percent, the banks were not affected at all.

In the context of transition economies, the fundamental problem is that under the legacy of state planning, the state is overleveraged, the enterprise is overleveraged, and the banks are overleveraged. This is why I believe that capital market development is complementary to bank restructuring issues. Capital market development must have priority to deleverage enterprises and to restore the capital-debt ratios to more manageable levels.

This leaves the fourth asymmetry, which is the *adjustment asymmetry*. As we all realize, financial markets adjust faster than the real sector. In the past, highly regulated financial markets could not adjust to distortions in the real economy, thereby hiding a multitude of sins. However, globalization, deregulation, and financial innovation have resulted in the financial markets detecting and by-passing real sector distortions. If domestic regulations prevent a transaction onshore, it simply moves offshore.

The recent lessons from Mexico and Thailand suggest that the market is quick to punish even the slightest policy mistakes. However, real sector adjustments take time to effect. Saying that we should not fall into such problems is easy; however, it is also a fact of life that we can all make mistakes. Worse, because we live in an interdependent world, and an increasingly integrated world, domestic economic problems are compounded by international policy mistakes. We are affected by externalities whether we like it or not. Small economies that thought they were prepared for reasonable size external shocks today discover that international prices, such as the exchange rates of G-10 economies, can fluctuate 10 to 20 percent in a few days. Being lowly leveraged is not enough. Not relying on short-term borrowing or running a foreign currency mismatch is more important.

Toward National and Sectoral Risk Management

To summarize, from a derivative market perspective, I believe we cannot generalize a solution for bank failures, because the real sector failures are multidimensional. Derivative markets are supposed to help manage risks, but are themselves the sources of new risks. Thus a review of the risks of the economy as a whole requires an understanding of the way growth has been financed in each sector and of the relationships between the sectors. If domestic financial systems are inefficient, the private sector, or even the public sector, may resort to external financing, thereby exposing the economy to the volatility of capital flows. Such flows are not in themselves the causes of economic or financial problems, but are the effects of distortive incentives in the market, possibly a combination of policy mistakes and weaknesses in economic fundamentals.

Given the larger risks in open financial markets that can feed back into shocks on the real sector and vice versa, central banks must focus on national risk management. To withstand greater shocks and to allow the market to work better, an economy requires a combination of credible policies, sound fundamentals, good supervision, robust infrastructure, and a nondistortive incentive structure (see Glaessner and Mas 1991; Yam 1995).

The following preconditions appear to be necessary for a stable financial system:

- Credible policies demand monetary and fiscal policies that are consistent with each other and are applied consistently.
- Sound fundamentals include a high domestic savings rate, a sustainable balance of payments position, high foreign exchange reserves, and prudent debt management.
- Good supervision involves good disclosure standards, good understanding of the risks that the financial sector is absorbing, awareness of the degree of leverage in the economy, and the detection of imbalances that are appearing in the economy. For example, the banking system must have the capacity to avoid excessive credit concentrations and risks and to manage market risks well.
- A robust financial infrastructure encompasses an efficient payments and settlements system for domestic and international transactions.
- A nondistortive incentive structure that removes taxation or regulatory restrictions that encourage risk concentrations or excessive leverage in any economic sectors. Avoidance of moral hazard in an economy is essential.

In sum, prevention is better than cure.

References

Glaessner, Thomas, and Ignacio Mas. 1991. "Incentive Structure and Resolution of Financial Institution Crises: Latin American Experience." Technical Paper. World Bank, Latin American Technical Department, Washington, D. C.

IMF (International Monetary Fund). 1997. "Banking Soundness and Monetary Policy in a World of Global Capital Flows," Proceedings of the Seventh Central Banking Seminar, January 27–31, Washington, D. C.

Lindgren, Carl-Johan, Gillian Garcia, and Mathew Saal. 1996. *Bank Soundness and Macroeconomic Policy*. Washington, D. C.: International Monetary Fund.

Mishkin, Frederic S. 1996. "Understanding Financial Crises: A Developing Country Perspective." Working Paper no. 5600. National Bureau for Economic Research, Washington, D. C.

Sheng, Andrew, ed., 1996a. *Bank Restructuring: Lessons from the 1980s*. Washington, D. C.: World Bank.

_____. 1996b. *Managing the Risks of Growth: Hard Money and Resilient Financial Systems*. Basle, Switzerland: Bank for International Settlements.

Yam, Joseph. 1995. *International Capital Flows: Opportunity or Threat? View from Hong Kong*. Basle, Switzerland: Bank for International Settlements.

22

What Can and Should Be Done to Prevent Future Financial Crises?

Edwin M. Truman

Banking experts generally agree about objectives with respect to preventing future financial crises and about the features of a robust financial system and a sound supervisory regime. A review of chapters 13 and 20 in this volume, of the publication of the Working Party on Financial Stability in Emerging Market Economies (1997) sponsored by the Group of Ten (G-10), and of the Basle Committee on Banking Supervision's (1997) "Core Principles of Effective Banking Supervision" reveals a high level of congruence.

Despite the high level of congruence, this is not to say that disagreements on substance or of emphasis do not arise. Disagreements exist with respect to the state's role in banking, the appropriateness and appropriate design of deposit insurance systems, the structure of the financial system (including the mix, if any, between banking and commerce), the whistle-blower with respect to unsound practices (the market, national supervisors, or international financial institutions such as the International Monetary Fund), and the exit policies for banking and financial institutions. One reason for the disagreements is that no author or group has a corner on truth in this area; there are no magic pills or instant solutions to the problems. If there were, we would have taken the pills and adopted the solutions decades ago.

How Do We Get Where We Want to Go with the Banking and Financial System?

There is somewhat more disagreement about how to establish a financial system that is robust for the following reasons:

- Views about objectives such as those cited above differ.
- Different interests are involved in the structure and functioning of a financial system: customers, borrowers, depositors, shareholders and managers of institutions, and taxpayers and the public sector. Thus we have a set of problems in political economy.
- Problems associated with financial systems are multifaceted (see, for example, chapter 20 in this volume).
- Problems to be addressed are not just the problems of the banking system, but of the financial system as a whole. For some (see chapter 21) the nonbanking sector of the financial system represents an area where scope for reform exists. For others (see chapter 5) it represents a potential threat to stability. For still others an incomplete banking system is a bar to a fully functioning financial system.
- No country starts with a blank sheet of paper. The financial system is and should be in a constant state of change. In this sense all countries are in transition, not just the so-called transition economies of Eastern Europe and the former Soviet Union. One advantage we all have is that we can learn from each other.

A major aspect of our common problem is the establishment of a credit culture, a set of generally accepted business practices in which, for example, debts are normally honored and the value of assets can be and is consistently evaluated. The establishment of a properly functioning credit culture often requires profound social change and a dynamic, forward-looking process of change. This is not simple. Change must be seen to be in the common interests of creditors, debtors, politicians, and supervisors, to name just four groups.

Where Does This Leave Us with Respect to Preventing Banking Crises?

As concerns designing the banking and financial system, being comprehensive is important, for example, having clear rules on both the entry and exit of firms. Moreover, the various features of the overall design must be mutually compatible. Mutual compatibility leads to the issue of incentives.

Here one can say that war is too important to leave to generals, economic policy is too important to leave to economists, and banking supervision is too important to leave to either economists or accountants.

Economists tend to stress the role of proper incentives. Market discipline provides one set of incentives, but as in the case of Japan, market discipline requires the underpinnings of a market culture, which may not be present. Remsik entreats us to support the truth in the area of disclosure (see chapter 8) and Sheng questions whether we know the truth (see chapter 21). Again as in the case of Japan, as well as, apparently, in the Czech Republic, we have differences between the tax and accounting systems that tend to distort or obscure the truth.

Kane reminds us to focus on incentives (see chapter 16), but in my view this advice is easy to articulate and less easy to put into effective operation. One reason is that we return to the issue of political economy, where the objectives of different agents need to be reconciled. As a consequence, views about proper incentives differ too. For example, stakeholders have an incentive to be bailed out, not to be closed out. Saying that the public interest lies in closing out stakeholders of insolvent institutions is easy, but the political process may not cooperate.

Thus in addition to thinking about incentives, we must also seek to strike the proper balance between differing objectives. This is clearly the case with regard to deposit insurance systems. It is arguably also the case with respect to accounting systems and to standards for closing institutions.

Finally, we must remember that our goal is not to maximize the prevention of crises or to minimize the number of banking failures. As Leipziger illustrated in the case of Argentina (see chapter 4), letting some institutions fail is often constructive. We are dealing with a two-by-two matrix of stringent and less stringent supervisory regimes on the one hand, and favorable and unfavorable macroeconomic outcomes on the other hand. Examining the cells where the macroeconomic outcomes were favorable to see what kinds of supervisory regimes were associated with that success might be useful, as might looking at the cells where the overall performance was negative.

We also need to be mindful of the role of the private sector. In the end, the objective of a robust financial system is not to allow supervisors, finance ministers, and central bankers to sleep more soundly at night, but to provide an environment in which all agents can prosper and function efficiently. Thus the private sector must see it as in their interests to have a strong financial system and a sound supervisory regime.

Where Is the International Interest?

Building a robust financial system is principally a national responsibility. Doing so must be seen to be in the self-interest of the country involved. Moreover, moral hazard considerations arise if international bodies take over the responsibility for national supervisory regimes. If the regimes break down or institutions within them fail, will the international bodies be liable for the bailouts? While international financial institutions can and do have leverage, care must be taken that they do more than install another layer of weak regulation.

Nevertheless, there is an international interest in effective national banking supervision. As Lissakers pointed out (see chapter 3), many banking supervision and regulation issues no longer stop at the water's edge. National failures can have direct and indirect spillovers. The direct spillovers will involve financial institutions in other countries to the extent that they are counterparties to failed institutions; the indirect spillovers may involve such things as the tequila effect flowing from the weak banking system in Mexico to the weak banking system in Argentina or financial crises that lead to extraordinary international financial support. We all have an interest in financial stability. We often jointly share the costs of mistakes, and the consequences of accidents are spread across national boundaries, as illustrated by the role of foreign creditors in Sweden's banking crisis (see chapter 11).

One area with a clear international interest that is often underappreciated involves the establishment of overseas operations. Domestic financial institutions often have subsidiaries and branches in foreign markets. If the domestic financial system is weak or comes under stress, the operations of financial institutions abroad may be affected. By the same token, if host authorities act precipitously with respect to foreign institutions operating in their jurisdiction, this can have implications for the stability of the financial institution as a whole and the home country's financial system.

A related dimension is the potential for foreign financial markets to substitute for domestic financial markets if domestic institutions and supervisory regimes are weak. If national authorities do not want this to happen, then they need to strengthen their own regimes. A connected issue involves foreign institutions as a source of strength for domestic financial markets. New Zealand, partly by accident, may have carried this approach to an extreme. Another case involves Poland, where for a time foreign institutions' access to the domestic financial market was limited to the purchase in whole or in part of a domestic institution. One might question the wisdom of this policy.

A further complication arises if national authorities follow Goldstein's advice (see chapter 13) and place limits on the foreign borrowing of nationally chartered institutions. Should such regulations apply to foreign institutions as well? If they do not, what happens to the level playing field? If they do, is the host country cutting itself off from a reliable source of capital inflow?

These are not easy questions to answer. One response, emphasized by Marshall (see chapter 5) is international cooperation. We have some recent examples of such cooperation in the drafting of the Basle Committee on Banking Supervision's (1997) banking supervision principles by a group of G-10 and non-G-10 supervisors. Similarly, the Working Party on Financial Stability in Emerging Market Economies (1997) involved representatives of G-10 and non-G-10 economies. Cooperation also is important in day-to-day operations and can be manifested in conferences like the one from which these proceedings are drawn.

Where Does Macroeconomic Stability Fit In?

Clearly macroeconomic stability is relevant to the success or failure of a supervisory regime. However, this is sometimes easier said than done. Miller reminded us of the case of Japan (see chapter 17). There the challenge for the Japanese authorities was to distinguish secular growth trends from asset market bubbles. In retrospect, all is crystal clear, but at the time it was more opaque.

A subtopic often found under the heading of macroeconomic stability is financial market liberalization. For some the answer is to slow down the pace of liberalization or never to start. Some say that this is what went wrong in Thailand. I would instead emphasize the need to get it right the first time, which may require a deliberate process of reform, and to make sure that the supervisory regime is equipped to monitor institutions in a more liberal environment and that the managements of the institutions are also equipped to operate responsibly as well—the culture issue again. Liberalization is the other side of the coin from financial modernization.

Conclusion

In all of this we must remember that we are dealing with human beings and human behavior, behavior that is inherently incomplete, flawed, and fallible. We cannot risk-proof the financial system and we do not want to put it on automatic pilot. Perhaps this is what Berg (see chapter 11) means when he suggests that we should accept some inherent instability in the financial system. However, we also should recall that humans can learn and can derive benefits from the mistakes of others. Thus while we may not achieve perfection with respect to future banking crises, we can hope that we will do better.

References

Basle Committee on Banking Supervision. 1997. "Core Principles of Effective Banking Supervision." Basle, Switzerland.

G-Ten-Sponsored Working Party on Financial Stability in Emerging Market Economies. 1997. "Financial Stability in Emerging Market Economies: A Strategy for the Formulation, Adoption, and Implementation of Sound Principles and Practices to Strengthen Financial Systems." Basle, Switzerland.

Part VII. Conference Overview

23

Summary

George G. Kaufman

This conference was important because it pulled together the experiences of a broad range of countries that differ from each other in their economic, social, and legal structures and include industrial, emerging, and transition economies. It therefore permitted us to identify similarities and differences in the causes, resolution, and prevention of banking crises. Not surprisingly, the similarities dominated the discussions. Indeed, for many of us, particularly those in the United States, which had the "honor" of staging the first major banking crisis, it was *dèja vu* over again, and again, and again. Basically, the same causes were reported across the board, with some adjustment for timing and banking structures in individual countries, particularly in transition economies, where insolvent state owned banks masqueraded as banks rather than as the extensions of the central government that they are, and in emerging economies, where exchange rate and balance of payments risks are important.

Equally important, the solutions and cures recommended for the crises were also basically the same:

- Emphasize market discipline to supplement regulatory discipline.
- Increase the stress on accuracy and truth in accounting and reporting of what Corrigan calls "intelligence" to make private markets work better and enhance the responsiveness and accountability of bankers and regulators.
- Increase transparency and the disclosure of bankers' and regulatory agencies' activities.

- Make bank regulators more independent from political influence and subject to greater accountability to the public.
- Provide sufficient private capital to absorb bank losses and adverse exogenous shocks.
- Privatize state owned banks fully and completely.
- Permit foreign ownership of banks to augment domestic private capital and intensify competition.
- Improve the legal system, particularly bankruptcy laws.
- Improve bank infrastructure, including the training and sophistication of both bankers and bank regulators.

Conference participants suggested that proper sequencing of corrective actions is important for lasting favorable results. The insolvencies need to be resolved first. Then and only then should any new, incentive-compatible prudential regulatory structure be added. Otherwise, the structure would be primarily a facade and would not last long. However, each component should be part of an overall comprehensive plan and improvements should not be piecemeal. Many participants also noted that the crises did not occur overnight. Substantial warnings were given, but not acted on. Why?

The American philosopher George Santayana speculated that "those who cannot remember the past are condemned to repeat it." I find it more interesting to discover what those who do remember the past do. My limited observations indicate that they are as likely not to agonize first and then repeat it.

The general consensus appears to be that we know how to resolve most ongoing bank problems economically, but that there are serious political problems in implementing the necessary solutions, particularly in getting public agreement to use public (taxpayer) funds to resolve insolvencies and validate the explicit and implicit government guarantees to protect depositors from loss. Governments and regulators are under political pressure to delay taking actions that they know are correct, but would likely be painful and unpopular. By reducing the threat of runs on banks, the safety net permits regulators to forbear taking these actions.

This scenario is again one many of us have seen before. We have observed such regulatory response, or lack of response, over and over again. The worldwide evidence clearly demonstrates that many regulators have become poor and unfaithful agents for their healthy bank and taxpayer principals, and have, albeit unintentionally, exacerbated the frequency of banking crises. The regulators' poor agent problem has been much more costly than the banks' moral hazard problem. After all, private insurers have learned to control and live with moral hazard behavior throughout their existence. Likewise highway departments have learned that putting guardrails on mountain passes only encourages some drivers to increase their speed and increases rather than decreases the likelihood and severity of accidents.

But many of us are regulators or advisors to regulators. We are the ones that have not acted in a timely manner. Can we change ourselves? Shakespeare reminded us that "the fault, dear Brutus, is not in our stars." Indeed, many regulators have actively been fighting a number of the generally agreed upon components of a solution package, namely, higher capital requirements, market value accounting, and greater disclosure and transparency for both banks and regulatory agencies.

Participants agreed that financial liberalization and deregulation are important, but should be undertaken only after the appropriate market and regulatory infrastructure has been put in place to avoid misuse. They recognized that liberalization is not an exogenous event out of the blue, but a response to pending or ongoing problems. However, it must be done right.

State owned banks had few supporters. They are a cancer that needs to be removed to cure the patient. Indeed, as already noted, state owned banks are banks in name only. They are institutions that allocate credit to favored sectors and bestow political favors as part of government policy. Thus their bottom line differs from that for private banks in that it is not economic profit. Some participants argued that many governments are too weak to control their state owned banks, but I disagree. These governments are sufficiently strong to use their state owned banks to further their own agendas, which happen to differ from ours. To correct this, the state owned banks need to be fully privatized and recapitalized. This requires sufficient public funds to fill in their negative net worth hole, as was difficult for many governments to do. The public sees their funds being used to bail out rich, if not crooked, bankers. At most, only depositors should be protected, not shareholders or managers. After this is done, a banking and credit culture must be built, often almost from scratch. Making collectable loans and actually collecting them on a timely basis is not a strong point with many state owned banks. Some participants also argued that privatizing state owned nonbank enterprises was equally important because they do not have a good loan repayment record. Indeed, governments may have to privatize them first to avoid having recapitalized banks quickly return to insolvency by lending to them.

Participants also made the point that many emerging and transition countries have successfully managed to enact correct sounding laws and regulations. However, this has not been matched by their enforcement, which is frequently lax or nonexistent. Again, this is a principal-agent problem.

Banking problems in emerging and transition countries have recently become a more urgent concern for industrial countries as they have recognized that any negative net worths are effectively deficits on the governments' budgets and could accelerate requests for assistance from international agencies or the industrial countries directly. This explains the sudden interest in banking standards, best practice guidelines, and so on by the International Monetary Fund, World Bank, Group of Ten, and Group of Thirty.

One issue was not raised. What are the implications of the proposed designs for failsafe banking structures for virtual or Internet banking if and when it comes, which it surely will in time? Where are these banks and their customers located? Who can affect them and how? How quickly can the banks or customers move to avoid restrictive regulation? How can one impose sanctions or closure if the banks' whereabouts are unknown or subject to change? Are we focusing too much attention on the last war and not enough on the next? But this would be a good topic for another conference.

24

Concluding Thoughts

Gerard Caprio, Jr.

As chapter 23 has captured the highlights of the conference, this chapter will dwell briefly on what we did not say or on what we emphasized insufficiently. Regarding the causes of banking crises, we were reminded of the role of disaster myopia: humans' apparent tendency to assign unrealistically low probabilities to remote events. As Charles Kindleberger suggested, each generation is entitled, perhaps doomed, to its own financial follies. Undoubtedly, disaster myopia was a factor in the wave of banking failures seen in virtually every country since around 1980. Widespread bank failure had not been common since the 1930s, so perhaps the puzzle that needs to be explained is why it took so long for another wave.

Notwithstanding the likely role disaster myopia played, consideration of the relationship between probability formation and penalties would be useful, especially in crafting solutions to banking crises. If the penalty for loan losses were death by torture, bank failure would be rare, but naturally risk taking likely would be so minimal that economic growth would be much less too. Herein lies the dilemma: we all want to encourage "sensible" risk taking, "prudent" or "safe and sound" banking, but we also want financial intermediaries that will not be averse to taking those prudent risks. Some bad loans, and indeed some bank failures, surely must be optimal, but the rub is how to define excessive risk taking, other than to know it when we see it. The boom in bank failures suggests that the recent wave of failures, with often double-digit fiscal costs (as a percentage of GDP), is excessive. How should this experience determine the policy response?

Many cures for unsafe banking aim to improve government supervision—in effect, to supervise better the risks bankers can take. Thus one popular solution is to take best practice on bank supervision and merely replicate it in all countries. As noted elsewhere (Caprio 1997), the problem here is the dearth of demonstrably good practice; systemic bank insolvency has occurred in industrial countries, where one might have expected less of a problem because of their markedly more diversified economies. Moreover, institutions in emerging market countries differ noticeably from those in many of their Organisation for Economic Co-operation and Development counterparts, so that even when good practice can be found, the transplanting process will be difficult. For example, how can governments commit to closing banks promptly when they do not have adequate fiscal revenues? Or if countries' legal and accounting systems were such that they could both know the true net worth position of banks and close them when this position shrank to unacceptable low levels, would we still call those countries developing? Although trying to learn lessons from other countries is clearly useful, the authorities also need to try to ascertain both what will work and what is feasible given their institutions.

Strategy is relatively easy, while tactics have to be tailored to each country's situation. I believe that bank failure occurs not only because of macroeconomic disturbances, but also because of microeconomics, that is, incentive failures. Not only are many financial systems incapable of withstanding relatively unforeseen events—the first, if not the second, oil price shock, or the first, but not the second, peso problem—but they cannot even tolerate the recent fluctuations of commodity prices or interest and exchange rates. Indeed, in many countries, remarkably little pain was associated with failure, and indeed, in some cases bust bankers continued controlling financial institutions. Thus I would focus on providing bigger carrots and larger sticks for sound banking.

Here, taking what might be called the coward's way out—or what I prefer to call the honest researcher's position—would seem to be appropriate. Given that owners, the market, and supervisors all are possible sources of sound corporate governance for banks and that risk taking appears to be excessive, then trying to improve each group's ability and incentives to monitor banks seems to be the sensible approach. If owners are allowing management to get away with inadequate risk assessment or monitoring, then owners need more at risk, and this can be accomplished in a variety of ways, for example, higher capital, greater franchise value, increased liability limits, or mutual liability (see Caprio 1997; Hellmann, Murdoch, and Stiglitz 1997). The market in most countries needs both a greater ability to monitor banks, such as better developed accounting, auditing, and disclosure systems (and the auditors likely need more at risk as well), but it also needs the incentive to do so. If all bank liabilities are insured, there will be no market monitoring, so compelling banks to issue some uninsured (subordinated) debt is attractive (Calomiris 1997). Demirgüç-Kunt and Detragiache (1997) showed that the presence of an explicit deposit insurance system increases the likelihood of a banking crisis, so some caution in extending these systems appears sensible.

Recommendations to improve supervisors' ability and incentives to monitor banks is a growth industry: supervisors need political independence, but also need either incentives that will induce them to act appropriately or a compulsory system. The United States has opted for the latter in the form of prompt, corrective action and structured early intervention, and this may work. Kane's proposal of a bonded regulator also is attractive in principle (see chapter 16 in this volume). I would argue that ability matters: in markets where supervisors earn 10 percent or less of the compensation of bankers, establishing greater independence or compelling various actions will prove fruitless, as supervisors who show any modicum of skill will be lured into banking. Furthermore, in response to derivatives, some experts in industrial economies are urging that supervisors merely pass judgment on the risk models banks are using, and mete out penalties if owners and managers fail to apply them properly. This approach is attractive in emerging markets, not only because derivatives are spreading there, but also because it may be a better way to leverage scarce supervisory talent. Moreover, fans of higher liability limits for bankers will recognize these penalties as a way of raising those limits, even as postclosure assessments, in effect similar to the double liability in force for some U.S. national banks in the late 19th and early 20th centuries.

Lastly, at a simplistic level, banks must fail because they concentrate their risks excessively, making too many loans that have the common characteristic of failing. Although in some countries bankers have concentrated their risk because it was in their perceived interest to do so, making loans to related companies, for example, or because they had no incentive to plan, such as examining the sensitivity of their portfolios to various possible shocks, in other instances they did not diversify because of the small size and concentrated nature of the home economy. In other words, one reason for widespread bank failure is that the end of the colonial period saw the emergence of a plethora of banking systems with an insufficient economic base to allow reasonable portfolio diversification, and capital controls made overseas expansion difficult or prohibited it. Allowing foreign or regional banks in and domestic banks out would seem necessary as part of the solution, on the understanding, of course, that bankers can lose money far from home at least as easily as they can do so at home.

Another reason for caution in deciding on one recommended approach to reduce the occurrence of systemic bank insolvencies is that relatively little research has been done to analyze how governments have responded. We know what has not worked, but relatively little time has passed—in many cases not yet a full business cycle—since many solutions have been adopted. So I would end by an appeal both for more research and another conference. The research should look into how various approaches are working, such as Argentina's recent adoption of subordinated debt coupled with increased information disclosure, New Zealand's virtual surrender of supervision to market forces, the promulgation of international banking standards, and, of course, the Federal Deposit Insurance Corporation Improvement Act in the United States. Conferences should review these lessons, but also address the more basic issue, namely, how countries' financial systems, in and out of crises, are performing their key functions of mobilizing and allocating resources, providing payments systems and corporate governance, and delivering risk management tools.

References

Calomiris, Charles W. 1997. *The Postmodern Bank Safety Net: Lessons from Developed and Developing Economies.* Washington, D. C.: The AEI Press.

Caprio, Gerard. 1997. "Safe and Sound Banking in Developing Countries: We're Not in Kansas Anymore." Policy Research Working Paper no. 1739. World Bank, Washington, D. C. Also in George G. Kaufman, eds., *Research in Financial Services: Private and Public Policy.* Greenwich, Connecticut: JAI Press.

Demirgüç-Kunt, Asli, and Enrica Detragiache. 1997. "The Determinants of Banking Crises: Evidence from Developed and Developing Countries." World Bank, Development Research Group, Washington, D. C.

Hellmann, Thomas, Kevin Murdoch, and Joseph Stiglitz. 1997. "Financial Restraint and the Market Enhancing View." Stanford University, Graduate School of Business, Palo Alto, California.

Contributors

James R. Barth is the Lowder Eminent Scholar in Finance at Auburn University. Until November 1989, he was the chief economist of the Office of Thrift Supervision, and before that the chief economist of the Federal Home Loan Bank. Professor Barth has also been a professor of economics at George Washington University,; visiting scholar at the U.S. Congressional Budget Office, the Federal Reserve Bank of Atlanta, and the Office of the Comptroller of the Currency; and associate director of the economics program at the National Science Foundation. Professor Barth has published more than 100 articles in professional journals and books, is the author of *The Great Savings and Loan Debacle* (American Enterprise Institute, 1991), coeditor of *The Reform of Federal Deposit Insurance: Disciplining the Government and Protecting Taxpayers* (Harper Business, 1992), coeditor of *Emerging Challenges for the International Financial Services Industry* (JAI Press, 1992), and co-author of *The Future of American Banking* (M. E. Sharpe, 1992). He has also given numerous speeches and lectures on the thrift and banking industries, is a member of the Advisory Council of Purdue University's Credit Research Center, and is associated with Cornerstone Research. Professor Barth serves on the editorial boards of the *Journal of Financial Services Research, Review of Pacific Basin Financial Markets and Policies,* and *Financial Services Review.* Professor Barth received his Ph.D. in economics from Ohio State University, with his dissertation supported by a Federal Reserve Bank of Cleveland fellowship.

Sigbjørn Atle Berg is an assistant director with the governor's staff at Norges Bank, the central bank of Norway, and professor in banking at the Department of Economics, University of Oslo. He has published research papers on the efficiency and productivity growth of banking industries and on the oligopolistic interactions between institutions in banking markets. In addition, Professor Berg has worked on government white papers on the Norwegian banking crisis and on the reform of the Norwegian system of government banks. Mr. Berg graduated from the University of Oslo, and held teaching positions there before joining the Research Department of the Central Bank in 1986.

Joseph Bisignano is the deputy manager of the Monetary and Economic Department of the Bank for International Settlements, which he joined in 1985. From 1972 to 1985, he held a number of positions at the Federal Reserve Bank of San Francisco, attaining the rank of senior vice president and director of research. He was also a visiting assistant professor at Stanford University from 1975 to 1976 and a consultant at the Bank for International Settlements from 1978 to 1979. Before beginning his career at the Federal Reserve Bank of San Francisco, Mr. Bisignano was an assistant professor of economics at Rutgers University.

Michael Stephen Borish is president and founder of Michael Borish & Company, a management consulting company founded in 1996 that specializes in financial analysis, business management, and strategic planning. Prior to starting his own company, Mr. Borish was a financial analyst with the World Bank for three years, where he managed the financial sector reform component of a US$110 million credit to Bosnia and Herzegovina, designed a private regional investment fund project for Poland, and advised officials on banking sector reform in Albania and Croatia. Mr. Borish was also the chief financial officer for J. E. Austin Associates, where he directed private sector assessments in nine African countries and supervised advisory services to agribusiness enterprises in Eastern Europe. He began his professional career as a banker with Continental Illinois Bank and Bank of America.

Paul L. Bydalek is president of Atlantic Rating and Atlantic Capital in Brazil. Atlantic Rating gathers, analyzes, and publishes data on the Brazilian financial system. In 1996, Atlantic Rating and Fitch Investor Service of New York agreed to work together to rate Brazilian corporate issuers. Mr. Bydalek founded Atlantic Capital in 1981 to house intermediation between Brazilian and U.S. capital markets. From 1991–95, Atlantic Capital was one of the leading advisors to the BNDES, the national development bank. It successfully helped the government to privatize companies and generated US$1 billion in sales proceeds. Mr. Bydalek is a trained U.S. banker with many years of experience, both in the United States and in Brazil. He was at Citicorp from 1960–70 and Security Pacific Bank from 1970–80.

Gerard Caprio, Jr., has been with the World Bank since 1988, and is currently research manager in the Development Economics and Chief Economist Vice

Presidency. He was formerly lead economist for the Finance and Private Sector Development Division, Policy Research Department. Prior to joining the World Bank, Mr. Caprio was with Morgan Guaranty Trust Company, where he was vice president and head of the Global Economics Unit. He directed global forecasting for Europe, Japan, and the United States, focusing on interest and exchange rates. Mr. Caprio also served on the Board of Governors of the Federal Reserve System, providing macroeconomic analysis and forecasting of major foreign countries. He has written numerous books and articles on financial reform, monetary policy, and international finance.

Thomas F. Cargill is professor of economics at the University of Nevada, Reno. He has written extensively on financial and monetary topics in Japan and the United States and has been a visiting scholar at the Bank of Japan, the Japanese Ministry of Finance, the Ministry of Posts and Telecommunications, the Federal Deposit Insurance Corporation, and the Federal Reserve Bank of San Francisco. Selected publications include "Political Business Cycles with Endogenous Election Timing: Evidence from Japan" (with M. Hutchison) (*Review of Economics and Statistics,* November 1991); "The Bank of Japan and the Federal Reserve: Liberalization, Independence, and Regulatory Responsibilities" (in *Studies in the Contemporary Japanese Economy,* 1995); "Bank Credit Cards: Consumer Irrationality Versus Market Forces" (with J. Wendel) (*Journal of Consumer Affairs,* Winter 1996); and *The Political Economy of Japanese Monetary Policy* (MIT Press, 1997). He is currently working on Japan's postal savings system, central bank independence, and a comparative study of the political economy of financial liberalization in Japan and the United States. He received his Ph.D. in economics from the University of California at Davis in 1968.

E. Gerald Corrigan was named managing director at Goldman Sachs & Co. in 1996. He serves as cochair of both the Risk Committee and the Global Compliance and Controls Committee, and is a member of the firm's Commitments Committee. Mr. Corrigan joined Goldman Sachs in 1994 as chairman, international advisors and senior advisor to the Executive Committee. Mr. Corrigan ended a 25-year career with the Federal Reserve System when he stepped down from his position as president and chief executive officer of the Federal Reserve Bank of New York in 1993, a position he had held since 1985. In that capacity, he became a permanent voting member of the Federal Open Market Committee and he was also named vice chairman of the committee, a position traditionally held by the president of the New York Fed. Mr. Corrigan's career at the New York Fed began in 1968, when he joined the Domestic Research Division as an economist and served in a variety of staff and official positions. In 1976 he was named vice president of the Bank, and in 1979, Mr. Corrigan became special assistant to Federal Reserve Board Chairman Paul A. Volcker.

Douglas D. Evanoff is a senior economist and assistant vice president responsible for the Financial Studies Section of the Economic Research Department of the Federal Reserve Bank of Chicago. He is also a faculty member of the Graduate School of Business at DePaul University, Chicago, and chairman of the Federal Reserve Bank of Chicago's annual Conference on Bank Structure and Competition. Mr. Evanoff's current research interests include bank cost analysis, merger analysis, the effect of regulatory barriers in banking, and payment system mechanisms. He has published studies on banking structure, bank regulation, bank efficiency, the U.S. payments system, and correspondent banking. Mr. Evanoff holds a Ph.D. in economics from Southern Illinois University.

Jeffrey A. Frankel was appointed a member of the Council of Economic Advisers by President Clinton in April 1997. He is also a professor of economics at the University of California, Berkeley. In addition, until September 1996, he was a research associate of the National Bureau of Economic Research in Cambridge, Massachusetts, where he directed the International Finance and Macroeconomics program, and Senior Fellow, Institute for International Economics, Washington, D. C. Mr. Frankel served on the Council of Economic Advisers from 1983 to 1984 as senior staff economist, with responsibility for international economic policy. In 1988 and 1989 he was a visiting professor of public policy at Harvard University. He has also been a visiting scholar at the International Monetary Fund and the Federal Reserve Board and has held appointments at the University of Michigan, Yale University, the World Bank, and the Federal Reserve Bank of San Francisco. Mr. Frankel is a specialist in international economics, finance, and macroeconomics. His research interests include the globalization of financial markets, the workings of the foreign exchange market, targets and indicators for monetary policy, the term structure of interest rates, the monetary determinants of agricultural prices, international macroeconomic policy coordination, regional trading blocs, financial issues in Japan and the Pacific, emerging markets, and trade and growth in East Asia. Recent books by Mr. Frankel include *The Internationalization of Equity Markets* (University of Chicago Press 1994), *Financial Markets and Monetary Policy* (Massachusetts Institute of Technology Press 1995), *The Microstructure of Foreign Exchange*

Markets (University of Chicago Press 1996), and *Regional Trading Blocs* (International Institute of Economics 1997). He has also published a number of journal articles and co-authored several books.

Gillian G. Holway Garcia joined the International Monetary Fund in 1993. She works in the Monetary and Exchange Affairs Department on bank soundness, financial liberalization in developing and transition economies, financial safety nets, restructuring of failed banking systems, and best practices for regulating and supervising banks in countries at all stages of development. She co-authored a major study of the Fund's executive board, *Bank Soundness and Macroeconomic Policy,* that examines the causes and consequences of bank unsoundness in the Fund's 181 member countries. Before joining the Fund, Ms. Garcia spent nine years working for the U.S. Congress, some three years at the General Accounting Office working to reform the U.S. financial system, and five years on the staff of the Senate Banking Committee. At the committee she worked on the Financial Institutions Reform, Recovery, and Enforcement Act of 1989; the Federal Deposit Insurance Corporation Improvement Act of 1991; interstate banking; and Glass-Steagall reform.

Morris Goldstein is the Dennis Weatherstone Senior Fellow in International Finance at the Institute for International Economics in Washington, D. C. Dr. Goldstein's recent institute publications include *The Case for an International Banking Standard* (Policy Analyses in International Economics, no. 47, April 1997), *Private Capital Flows to Emerging Markets after the Mexican Crisis* (with Guillermo Calvo and Eduard Hochreiter, September 1996), and *The Exchange Rate System and IMF: A Modest Agenda* (Policy Analyses in International Economics, no. 39, June 1995). His current projects include books on *Forecasting Financial Crises: Early Warning Signals for Emerging Markets* with Carmen Reinhart, and *The Dollar, the Euro, and the Yen* with C. Fred Bergsten. Other recent publications include *From Halifax to Lyons: What Has Been Done about Crisis Management?* (Princeton Essays in International Finance, December 1996), and "Banking Crises in Emerging Economies: Origins and Policy Options" (with Philip Turner, Bank for International Settlements Economic Papers, no. 46, October 1996). Dr. Goldstein served as a staff member of the International Monetary Fund for 25 years, during the last 8 of which he was deputy director of the Fund's Research Department. Dr. Goldstein has also served as senior technical advisor at the U.S. Treasury, as a visiting research associate at the London School of Economics, and as a Baker-Weeks Research Fellow at The Brookings Institution. He has published widely in the field of international economics and has been a frequent speaker at public policy conferences dealing with international monetary issues. Dr. Goldstein holds an A.B. degree in economics from Rutgers College, and a Ph.D. in economics from New York University.

Richard J. Herring is the Julian Aresty Professor of Finance and vice dean and director of the Undergraduate Division of the Wharton School at the University of Pennsylvania. Previously he was director of the Financial Institutions Center at the University of Pennsylvania. He has been an International Affairs Fellow at the Council on Foreign Relations, an IBM Postdoctoral Fellow, a Harold Stonier Fellow, and a Charles Grosvenor Osgood Fellow. Dr. Herring has taught international finance and international banking at the Wharton School since 1972, where he received the Hauck award for distinguished undergraduate teaching. In addition he has taught in a variety of executive education programs at Wharton and at several other institutions. Dr. Herring's publications include articles on international banking, balance of payments problems, and the foreign exchange and eurocurrency markets and a number of books and monographs. He also serves on the editorial board of six scholarly journals. Dr. Herring is a member of the Board of Directors of the International Trade and Finance Association and a Trustee of BT Institutional Funds. He is a member of the Shadow Financial Regulatory Committee, the International Faculty on Corporate and Capital Market Law, and the Biennial Multinational Banking Seminar, and has been a Fellow of the World Economic Forum. Dr. Herring has served as a consultant for several agencies, including the U.S. Department of the Treasury, the Federal Reserve Board, the Council of Economic Advisers, the International Monetary Fund, and the World Bank, as well as a number of commercial banks and nonfinancial corporations. Dr. Herring received his A.B. in economics from Oberlin College and his M.A. and Ph.D. degrees from Princeton University.

William C. Hunter is senior vice president and director of research at the Federal Reserve Bank of Chicago. Prior to joining the Chicago Fed in 1995, he was vice president at the Federal Reserve Bank of Atlanta. Mr. Hunter has taught at many universities and has worked as a consultant to the Small Business Administration, the Chicago Mercantile Exchange, numerous private corporations, and foreign banking organizations. He is an associate editor of the *Journal of Financial Services Research* and the *Financial Review,* and a past associate editor of the *Journal of Financial Research.* He has published more than 40 articles in a variety of financial and economics journals.

Michael M. Hutchison is professor of economics at the University of California, Santa Cruz; research associate at the Center for Pacific Basin Monetary and Economic Studies at the Federal Reserve Bank of San Francisco; and research associate of the Economic Policy Research Unit at the Copenhagen Business School. Prior to joining the Santa Cruz faculty in 1985, Professor Hutchison was an economist at the Federal Reserve Bank of San Francisco. He has published numerous academic journal articles and written and edited several books, including *Exchange Rate Policy and Interdependence: Lessons from the Pacific Basin* and *The Political Economy of Japanese Monetary Policy*. Dr. Hutchison received his Ph.D. in economics from the University of Oregon in 1983.

Takatoshi Ito is professor of economics at the Institute of Economic Research at Hitotshubasi University and a research associate at the National Bureau of Economic Research. He has taught macroeconomics, Japanese economy, and international finance and central banking at Hitotshubashi University, the University of Tokyo, Harvard University, and the University of Minnesota. From 1994–97 Dr. Ito was senior advisor in the Research Department of the International Monetary Fund. He has written extensively on Japanese financial and monetary policy issues and is the author of *The Japanese Economy* and a co-author of *The Political Economy of Japanese Monetary Policy*. Dr. Ito received his Ph.D. in economics from Harvard University.

Edward J. Kane is the James F. Cleary Professor in Finance at Boston College. From 1972 to 1992 Professor Kane was the Everett D. Reese Chair of Banking and Monetary Economics at Ohio State University. Before that he taught at Boston College, Princeton University, and Iowa State University. He has held visiting positions at Istanbul University, Simon Fraser University, Arizona State University, the University of Arizona, and Deakin University (Australia). Professor Kane has consulted for numerous organizations, including the Federal Deposit Insurance Corporation, the Office of the Comptroller of the Currency, the World Bank, the American Bankers Association, three foreign central banks, various components of the Federal Reserve System, the Congressional Budget Office, the Joint Economic Committee, and the Office of Technology Assessment of the U.S. Congress. He is a past president of the American Finance Association and a former Guggenheim Fellow. In addition to writing three books, he has published widely in professional journals and currently serves on seven editorial boards. He served for 11 years as a charter member of the Shadow Financial Regulatory Committee and for 12 years as a trustee and member of the Finance Committee of Teachers Insurance. Professor Kane received a B.S. degree from Georgetown University in 1957 and a Ph.D. from Massachusetts Institute of Technology in 1960.

George G. Kaufman is the John F. Smith, Jr., Professor of Economics and Finance at Loyola University, Chicago. From 1959 to 1970 he was at the Federal Reserve Bank of Chicago, and after teaching for 10 years at the University of Oregon, he returned as a consultant to the bank in 1981. Professor Kaufman's teaching and research interests are in financial economics, institutions, and markets. He is cochair of the Shadow Financial Regulatory Committee. Professor Kaufman received a B.A. from Oberlin College, an M.A. from the University of Michigan, and a Ph.D. in economics from the University of Iowa.

Danny M. Leipziger is division chief of the Regulatory Reform and Private Enterprise Division of the World Bank, where he has been employed for 15 years. Mr. Leipziger has worked extensively on East Asia and Latin America, and was most recently the Bank's lead economist for Argentina and Chile. Before joining the World Bank Mr. Leipziger worked for the U.S. Department of State and the U.S. Agency for International Development. He has extensive research, policy, and development experience and is a recognized expert on the Republic of Korea. His publications include *Korea: Transition to Maturity* (Praeger 1988), *Korea: Distribution of Income and Wealth* (World Bank 1992), *Lessons of East Asia* (University of Michigan Press 1997), and *The Lender of Last Resort Function Under a Currency Board: The Case of Argentina* (1997). He has published widely in the field of development economics, especially in the area of industrial policy. Mr. Leipziger received his doctorate in economics from Brown University in 1972.

Karin Lissakers was appointed as the executive director for the United States at the International Monetary Fund in 1993. Prior to assuming this role, from 1985 to 1993 she was a lecturer at and director of the International Business and Banking Program at Columbia University. Before joining Columbia, Ms. Lissakers was a senior associate at the Carnegie Endowment for two years and deputy director of the Economic Policy Planning Staff at the United States Department of State for two years. She has also served as a staff member on several committees of the United States Senate. She has published numerous articles and papers on international banking and finance. Her most recent book, *Banks, Borrowers, and the Establishment*, examines the international debt crisis.

Robert E. Litan is director of economic studies at The Brookings Institution. Dr. Litan served in the United States government as associate director of the Office of Management and Budget, deputy assistant attorney general, regulatory and legal staff specialist with the President's Council of Economic Advisors, and a member of the Commission on the Causes of the Savings and Loan Crisis. From 1979–90 Dr. Litan practiced law in Washington, specializing in regulatory litigation, banking, and international trade matters. He has published more than a dozen books and 100 articles. His most recent books include *Globalphobia: Confronting Fears about Open Trade; Going Digital; American Finance for the 21st Century; Financial Regulation in a Global Economy; Footing the Bill for Superfund Cleanups;* and *Growth with Equity.* Dr. Litan is both an economist and an attorney. He received his J.D. from Yale Law School and his Ph.D. in economics from Yale University.

Jorge Marshall has been vice president of the Board of Governors of the *Banco Central de Chile* since December 1993. Prior to this assignment, Mr. Marshall was minister of the economy and undersecretary of the economy. During his tenure at the Ministry of the Economy, he promoted significant reforms to the intellectual property law, the foreign investment statute, the administration of fisheries, and the competition regime in the telecommunications system. He also played a key role in several trade agreements between Chile and other Latin American countries. Between 1984 and 1990, Mr. Marshall worked as a fellow at the University of Santiago and in the masters program of Georgetown University in Santiago. He has also been a consultant for the United Nations, World Bank, United Nations Development Programme-International Labour Organisation, and the *Corporación de Investigaciones Económicas para Latinoamérica.*

Geoffrey P. Miller is professor of law at New York University Law School and director of the Law School's Center for the Study of Central Banks. Previously Professor Miller served as a judicial clerk to Judge Carl McGowan of the U.S. Court of Appeals for the District of Columbia Circuit and to Justice Byron White of the United States Supreme Court, and worked as an attorney in the United States Department of Justice Office of Legal Counsel and at a private law firm. Prior to joining New York University in 1995, Professor Miller was the Kirkland and Ellis Professor at the University of Chicago Law School, where he served as associate dean, director of the Program in Law and Economics, and editor of the *Journal of Legal Studies.* He is the author of more than 60 scholarly articles in the fields of corporate law, banking law, legal ethics, separation of powers, civil procedure, and law and economics, and has published *Banking Law and Regulation* (2d ed., Aspen Law and Business 1997) with Jonathan R. Macey. He attended Columbia University Law School, where he was editor-in-chief of the *Law Review.*

Fernando Montes-Negret has worked at the World Bank since 1984 in various capacities. He is currently a principal financial economist in the Financial Sector Development Department, where he is responsible for work in a number of policy areas, including enterprise and bank restructuring, bank twinning, and analysis of interest rates and bank spreads. Prior to this assignment, Mr. Montes-Negret was a senior financial economist for the former Soviet Union, particularly Belarus and the Ukraine (1992–93) and senior country economist for China, East Asia, and the Pacific Region (1989–92). Mr. Montes-Negret has also had a long career with the government of Colombia, serving as deputy governor of Colombia's central bank, advisor to the minister of economic development of Colombia (1980–81), and undersecretary to the minister of finance (1977).

Michael H. Moskow is president of the Federal Reserve Bank of Chicago. He serves as the Chicago Federal Reserve System's chief executive officer and is a voting member of the Federal Open Market Committee, the Federal Reserve System's most important policymaking body. Mr. Moskow began his career teaching economics and management at Temple University, Lafayette College, and Drexel University. From 1969–77 he held a number of senior positions with the U.S. government, including senior staff economist, Council of Economic Advisors; assistant secretary for policy development and research, U.S. Department of Housing and Urban Development; director, Council on Wage and Price Stability; and undersecretary of labor, U.S. Department of Labor. Mr. Moskow has also held senior positions at Esmark, Inc., Estronics, Inc., Velsicol Chemical Corporation, Dart and Kraft, Inc., and Premark International, Inc. (a spinoff of Dart and Kraft). In 1991 President Bush appointed Mr. Moskow as deputy United States trade representative with the rank of ambassador. In 1993 Mr. Moskow was named professor of strategy and international management at the Kellogg Graduate School of Management, Northwestern University. Mr. Moskow is a member of the board of directors of the National Bureau of Economic Research, where he also serves on the executive committee. He is the author of 7 books and more than 20 articles. Mr. Moskow received a B.A. in economics from Lafayette College, Easton, Pennsylvania, and an M.A. in economics and a Ph.D. in business and applied economics from the University of Pennsylvania.

Ivan Remsik is a senior vice president at Visa International in London, responsible for business development in central and southeastern Europe. Prior to joining Visa, Mr. Remsik was the executive director of Zivnostenska Bank in Prague for six years, where he was responsible for overseeing the finance, personal and private banking, and information technology departments. He managed the financial restructuring of the bank's balance sheet related to its privatization and transformation of its accounting systems to international accounting standards. Before his position as executive director, Mr. Remsik was general manager in charge of managing application software development and implementing and supervising mid-size computer operations.

Andrew Sheng Len Tao joined the Hong Kong Monetary Authority, which is responsible for the core central bank functions of regulating and promoting financial markets in Hong Kong, as deputy chief executive (monetary) in 1993. Prior to joining the Hong Kong Monetary Authority, Mr. Sheng held various positions at the World Bank from 1983 through 1993: senior financial specialist, chief of the Financial Policy and Systems Division, and senior manager, Financial Markets and Payments System. Mr. Sheng also worked for the Central Bank of Malaysia for 13 years, where his responsibilities included economic research, accounting and branches, and bank and insurance regulation. He is the author and editor of numerous articles and books on money and banking, and has lectured at numerous seminars.

Edwin M. Truman is staff director of the Division of International Finance, Board of Governors of the Federal Reserve System, which he joined in 1977. He is one of three economists on the staff of the Federal Open Market Committee and is an alternate member of the Board of Directors of the Bank for International Settlements. Mr. Truman is a member of the Euro-Currency Standing Committee of the Group of Ten central bank governors and attends meetings of Working Party Three of the Economic Policy Committee of the Organisation for Economic Co-operation and Development. He has participated in a number of Group of Ten groups preparing reports on various topics, including most recently the Working Party on Financial Stability in Emerging Markets' Economies and the Working Group on the Resolution of Sovereign Liquidity Crises. He was a member of the Working Group on Exchange Market Intervention formed after the economic summit in 1982. He served on the staff of the Committee on the Reform of the International Monetary System and Related Issues and was a member of the several Committee of Twenty working groups. Mr. Truman is a former associate professor of economics at Yale University, where he also received his Ph.D. in economics in 1967. He received his B.A. from Amherst College in 1963 and an L.L.D. from Amherst College in 1988. His publications include works on European economic integration, international monetary economics, economic development, and international debt problems.

John Williamson has been on leave from the Institute for International Economics since 1996 to serve as chief economist for South Asia at the World Bank. At the institute, he was a senior fellow since its founding in 1981. Prior to this, Mr. Williamson was an advisor to the International Monetary

Fund, where he worked mainly on questions of international monetary reform related to the work of the Committee of Twenty. He was also an economic consultant to the U.K. Treasury from 1968–70 and taught at several universities, including the University of York, the Pontificia Universidade Catolica do Rio de Janeiro, the Massachusetts Institute of Technology, the London School of Economics, and Princeton University. He has published numerous books on international monetary issues.

Conference Agenda

June 11–13, 1997

Harrison Conference Center
Chicago, Illinois

Sponsored by
The Federal Reserve Bank of Chicago
and the Economic Development Institute of the World Bank

Wednesday, June 11
7:00 p.m.   Reception and Dinner
                         Welcome:
                         Michael Moskow, Federal Reserve Bank of Chicago
                         Danny M. Leipziger, World Bank
                         William C. Hunter, Federal Reserve Bank of Chicago

                         Keynote Speaker:
                         Jeffrey Frankel, Council of Economic Advisers

Thursday, June 12
8:30 a.m.–12:00 p.m.   Bank Failures in Developing Countries and Transition
                         Economies

8:30 a.m.–9:45 a.m.   Session 1: Panel on Latin America
                         Chair:
                         Danny M Leipziger, World Bank

                         Panelists:
                         Thomas Glaessner, World Bank
                         Paul Bydalek, Atlantic Rating, Brazil
                         Danny M. Leipziger, World Bank
                         Jorge Marshall, Central Bank of Chile

9:45 a.m.–10:15 a.m.   Audience Discussion

10:15 a.m.–10:30 a.m.   Break

10:30 a.m.–11:45 a.m.   Session II: Transition Economies
Chair: Jonathan Fiechter, World Bank

Speaker: Michael Borish, Borish & Company

Discussants:
Donald Billings, U.S. Treasury
Lajos Bokros, World Bank
Ivan Remsik, Visa International

11:45 a.m.–12:30 p.m.   Audience Discussion

12:30 p.m.–2:00 p.m.   Lunch
Keynote Speaker:
Michael Moskow, Federal Reserve Bank of Chicago

2:15 p.m.–3:45 p.m.   Bank Failures in Developed Countries
Chair:
William C.Hunter, Federal Reserve Bank of Chicago

Speakers:
United States: James Barth, Auburn University and
Robert Litan, Brookings Institution
Japan: Thomas Cargill, University of Nevada at Reno
Michael Hutchison, University of California at Santa Cruz
Scandinavia: Sigbjørn A. Berg, Norges Bank

3:45 p.m.–4:00 p.m.   Break

4:00 p.m.–5:30 p.m.   *Discussants:*
Richard Herring, University of Pennsylvania
Morris Goldstein, Institute for International Economics

Audience Discussion

6:30 p.m.   Cocktails

7:00 p.m.   Dinner
Keynote Speaker:
Karin Lissakers, International Monetary Fund

Friday, June 13

8:30 a.m.–10:00 a.m.	Panel of Researchers: Commonalities, Mistakes, and Lessons

Chair:
Douglas Evanoff, Federal Reserve Bank of Chicago

Panelists:
Nicolas Eyzaguirre Guzman, International Monetary Fund and Central Bank of Chile
Gillian Garcia, International Monetary Fund
Edward Kane, Boston College
Geoffrey Miller, New York University
John Williamson, World Bank

Audience Discussion

10:00 a.m.–10:15 a.m.	Break

10:15 a.m.–12:00 p.m.	Panel of Regulators: What Can and Should Be Done to Prevent Future Banking Crises

Chair:
Anil Kashyap, University of Chicago

Panelists:
Joseph Bisignano, Bank for International Settlements
E. Gerald Corrigan, Goldman Sachs
Jonathan Fiechter, World Bank
Andrew Sheng, Hong Kong Monetary Authority
Edwin Truman, Board of Governors of the Federal Reserve System

Audience Discussion

12:30 p.m.–2:00 p.m.	Lun ch

Conference Overview
Gerard Caprio, Jr., World Bank
George G. Kaufman, Loyola University and Federal Reserve Bank of Chicago

Conference Participants

Vichan Amorojanavong
Bank of Thailand
Bangkok, Thailand

Myrtha A. Badio
Banque de la Republique d'Haiti
Port-au-Prince, Haiti

James Barth
Auburn University
Auburn, AL

Philip F. Bartholomew
*Office of the Comptroller
of the Currency*
Washington, D. C.

Piotr Bednarski
National Bank of Poland
Warsaw, Poland

Sigbjørn Berg
Norges Bank
Oslo, Norway

John M. Berry
Washington Post
Washington, D. C.

Donald Billings
U.S. Treasury
London, England

Joseph Bisignano
Bank for International Settlements
Basle, Switzerland

William C. Blethen
Bank of America
Los Angeles, CA

Lajos Bokros
The World Bank
Washington, D. C.

Guillermo Bolanos
Banco Central de Costa Rica
San Jose, Costa Rica

Rodrigo Bolanos
Banco Central de Costa Rica
San Jose, Costa Rica

Javier Bolzico
*Banco Central
de la Republica Argentina*
Buenos Aires, Argentina

Michael Borish
Borish & Company
Silver Spring, MD

James L. Bothwell
U.S. General Accounting Office
Washington, D. C.

Paul Bydalek
Atlantic Rating
São Paulo, Brazil

Gerard Caprio, Jr.
The World Bank
Washington, D. C.

Thomas Cargill
University of Nevada
Reno, NV

Georgette Carisma
Banque de la Republique d'Haiti
Port-au-Prince, Haiti

Sergei Chernov
The World Bank
Washington, D. C.

E. Gerald Corrigan
Goldman Sachs
New York, NY

Teresa Curran
Federal Reserve Bank
San Francisco, CA

Francisco V. Debera
*Superintendencia de Bancos
y otras Instituciones Financieras*
Caracas, Venezuela

Leonid Demtchuk
Prudential Banking Supervision
Moscow, Russia

Douglas Evanoff
Federal Reserve Bank of Chicago
Chicago, IL

Jonathan Fiechter
The World Bank
Washington, D. C.

Robert M. Fitzgerald
Chicago Clearing House Association
Chicago, IL

Alex Fleming
The World Bank
Washington, D. C.

Jeffrey A. Frankel
Council of Economic Advisers
Washington, D. C.

Fred Furlong
Federal Reserve Bank
San Francisco, CA

Rosario Garat Percovich
*Superintendencia de Instituciones
de Intermediacion Financiera*
Montevideo, Uruguay

Gillian Garcia
International Monetary Fund
Washington, D. C.

Sergio Ghigliazza
*Centro de Estudios Monetarios
Latino Americanos*
Mexico City, Mexico

Alton Gilbert
Federal Reserve Bank
St. Louis, MO

Luis Giorgio
*Centro de Estudios Monetarios
Latino Americanos*
Mexico City, Mexico

Thomas C. Glaessner
The World Bank
Washington, D. C.

Odette Marie Go
The World Bank
Washington, D. C.

Morris Goldstein
Institute for International Economics
Washington, D. C.

Clifford Griep
Standard & Poor's
New York, NY

Nicolas Eyzaguirre Guzman
International Monetary Fund/
Bank of Chile
Washington, D. C.

Elizabeth Hart
The Northern Trust Company
Chicago, IL

Werner Herman
Swiss National Bank
Zurich, Switzerland

Richard Herring
University of Pennsylvania
Philadelphia, PA

Soon-Woo Hong
Bank of Korea
Seoul, Korea

William C. Hunter
Federal Reserve Bank
Chicago, IL

Henry Jeffers
Central Bank of Trinidad and Tobago
Port-of-Spain, Trinidad

Edward Kane
Boston College
Boston, MA

Anil Kashyap
University of Chicago
Chicago, IL

George Kaufman
Loyola University
Chicago, IL

Mark Kawa
Federal Reserve Bank
Chicago,IL

Michio Kitahara
Bank of Japan
Tokyo, Japan

Daniela Klingebiel
The World Bank
Washington, D. C.

Masaharu Kuhara
The Long-Term Credit Bank
of Japan, Ltd.
Chicago, IL

Leonard Lapidus
U.S. Treasury
Washington, D. C.

Danny M. Leipziger
The World Bank
Washington, D. C.

Cathy Lemieux
Federal Reserve Bank
Chicago, IL

Karin Lissakers
International Monetary Fund
Washington, D. C.

Ernesto Livacic
Superintendencia de Bancos de Chile
Santiago, Chile

Ouk Maly
National Bank of Cambodia
Phnom Penh, Cambodia

Jorge Marshall
Banco de Chile
Santiago, Chile

Geoffrey Miller
New York University
New York, NY

Michael Moskow
Federal Reserve Bank of Chicago
Chicago, IL

Syed Amirul Mulk
Ministry of Finance
Dhaka, Bangladesh

Michael Mussa
International Monetary Fund
Washington, D. C.

Radu Musteata
National Bank of Moldova
Chisinau, Moldova

Rezso Nyers
*Hungarian Banking
and Capital Market Supervision*
Budapest, Hungary

B.L. Patwardhan
State Bank of India
Chicago, IL

Eugenio Pendas
*Ministerio de Economia
y Obras y Servicios Publicos*
Buenos Aires, Argentina

Michael E. Plaskett
Federal Reserve Bank
Chicago, IL

Paolo Marullo Reedtz
Banca d'Italia
Rome, Italy

Ivan Remsik
Visa International
London, England

Alberto Reyes
Bangko Sentral ng Pilipinas
Manila, Philippines

Budi Rochadi
Bank Indonesia
Jakarta, Indonesia

Mary S. Rosenbaum
Federal Reserve Bank
Atlanta, GA

Eric Rosengren
Federal Reserve Bank
Boston, MA

Jakob Rotte
De Nederlandsche Bank
Amsterdam, The Netherlands

Rasmus Ruffer
Indiana University
Bloomington, IN

Terry Schwakopf
Federal Reserve Bank
San Francisco, CA

Andrew Sheng
Hong Kong Monetary Authority
Hong Kong

Ewa Sleszynska-Charewicz
National Bank of Poland
Warsaw, Poland

Anatoly Stepanenko
The National Bank of Ukraine
Kiev, Ukraine

Tatiana Stoujouk
The National Bank of Ukraine
Kiev, Ukraine

Jack Sustman
University of Illinois
Wilmette, IL

Alan Thompson
Banco Central de Costa Rica
San Jose, Costa Rica

Jacques Trigo Loubiere
*Superintendencia de Bancos
    y Entidades Financieras de Bolivia*
La Paz, Bolivia

Edwin Truman
Federal Reserve Bank
Washington, D. C.

Larisa Tsyplakova
*The National Bank
    of the Kyrgyz Republic*
Bishkek, Kyrgyz Republic

C.M. Vasudeve
Ministry of Finance
New Delhi, India

Andres Vernon
*National Banking & Securities
    Commission of Mexico*
Mexico City, Mexico

Mary Elizabeth Ward
The World Bank
Washington, D. C.

John Williamson
The World Bank
Washington, D. C.

Haitao Zhai
People's Bank of China
New York, NY

Index

(Page numbers in italics indicate material in figures or tables.)